LUTHER'S WORKS

American Edition

VOLUME 36

Published by Concordia Publishing House

and Fortress Press in 55 volumes.

General Editors are Jaroslav Pelikan (for vols. 1-30)

and Helmut T. Lehmann (for vols. 31-55).

LUTHER'S WORKS

VOLUME 36

Word and Sacrament

II

EDITED BY

ABDEL ROSS WENTZ

GENERAL EDITOR

HELMUT T. LEHMANN

FORTRESS PRESS / PHILADELPHIA

Library of Congress Catalog Card Number 55-9893

ISBN 0-8006-0336-2

Printed in the United States of America

Printed in 2025

GENERAL EDITORS' PREFACE

The first editions of Luther's collected works appeared in the sixteenth century, and so did the first efforts to make him "speak English." In America serious attempts in these directions were made for the first time in the nineteenth century. The Saint Louis edition of Luther was the first endeavor on American soil to publish a collected edition of his works, and the Henkel Press in New Market, Virginia, was the first to publish some of Luther's writings in an English translation. During the first decade of the twentieth century, J. N. Lenker produced translations of Luther's sermons and commentaries in thirteen volumes. A few years later the first of the six volumes in the Philadelphia (or Holman) edition of the *Works of Martin Luther* appeared. But a growing recognition of the need for more of Luther's works in English has resulted in this American edition of Luther's works.

The edition is intended primarily for the reader whose knowledge of late medieval Latin and sixteenth-century German is too small to permit him to work with Luther in the original languages. Those who can will continue to read Luther in his original words as these have been assembled in the monumental Weimar edition (*D. Martin Luthers Werke.* Kritische Gesamtausgabe; Weimar, 1883-). Its texts and helps have formed a basis for this edition, though in certain places we have felt constrained to depart from its readings and findings. We have tried throughout to translate Luther as he thought translating should be done. That is, we have striven for faithfulness on the basis of the best lexicographical materials available. But where literal accuracy and clarity have conflicted, it is clarity that we have preferred, so that sometimes paraphrase seemed more faithful than literal fidelity. We have proceeded in a similar way in the matter of Bible versions, translating Luther's translations. Where this could be done by the use of an existing English version—King James, Douay, or Revised

Standard—we have done so. Where it could not, we have supplied our own. To indicate this in each specific instance would have been pedantic; to adopt a uniform procedure would have been artificial—especially in view of Luther's own inconsistency in this regard. In each volume the translator will be responsible primarily for matters of text and language, while the responsibility of the editor will extend principally to the historical and theological matters reflected in the introduction and notes.

Although the edition as planned will include fifty-five volumes, Luther's writings are not being translated in their entirety. Nor should they be. As he was the first to insist, much of what he wrote and said was not that important. Thus the edition is a selection of works that have proved their importance for the faith, life, and history of the Christian church. The first thirty volumes contain Luther's expositions of various biblical books, while the remaining volumes include what are usually called his "Reformation writings" and other occasional pieces. The final volume of the set will be an index volume; in addition to an index of quotations, proper names, and topics, and a list of corrections and changes, it will contain a glossary of many of the technical terms that recur in Luther's works and that cannot be defined each time they appear. Obviously Luther cannot be forced into any neat set of rubrics. He can provide his reader with bits of autobiography or with political observations as he expounds a psalm, and he can speak tenderly about the meaning of the faith in the midst of polemics against his opponents. It is the hope of publishers, editors, and translators that through this edition the message of Luther's faith will speak more clearly to the modern church.

J. P.
H. T. L.

CONTENTS

ABBREVIATIONS

C. R. – *Corpus Reformatorum*, edited by C. G. Bretschneider and H. E. Bindseil (Halle, 1834-1860).

CL – *Luthers Werke in Auswahl*, edited by Otto Clemen *et al.* (Bonn, 1912-1933; Berlin, 1955-1956).

EA – *D. Martin Luthers sämmtliche Werke* (Frankfurt and Erlangen, 1826-1857).

LW – American edition of *Luther's Works* (Philadelphia and St. Louis, 1955-).

MA[3] – *Martin Luther*. Ausgewählte Werke (München, 1948-).

Migne – *Patrologiae, Series Latina*, 221 vols. in 222 (Paris, 1844-1904), J. P. Migne, editor.

PE – *Works of Martin Luther* (Philadelphia, 1915-1943).

St. L. – *D. Martin Luthers sämmtliche Schriften*, edited by Johann Georg Walch. Edited and published in modern German, 23 vols. in 25 (St. Louis, 1880-1910).

WA – *D. Martin Luthers Werke*. Kritische Gesamtausgabe (Weimar, 1883-).

WA, Br – *D. Martin Luthers Werke*. Briefwechsel (Weimar, 1930-1948).

WA, TR – *D. Martin Luthers Werke*. Tischreden (Weimar, 1912-1921).

WA, DB – *D. Martin Luthers Werke*. Deutsche Bibel (Weimar, 1906-).

INTRODUCTION TO VOLUME 36

The writings translated in this volume center about Luther's teaching concerning the Lord's Supper. While he still adhered to the doctrine of transubstantiation in 1519[1] and in 1520 moderately objected to the mass as a sacrifice,[2] it was his opponents who compelled him to state his views concerning the Lord's Supper more clearly and firmly.

In the very first sentence of *The Babylonian Captivity* (1520) here translated Luther informs us that his Roman opponents are driving him along the road to greater clarity and more determined opposition to the Roman view of the sacrament. The attacks of the Roman ecclesiastics and theologians only goad him to more vigorous and detailed expression of his convictions. In *The Babylonian Captivity* he levels his aim at the entire sacramental system of the Roman church because it has now become clear to him this is the fundamental cause and the chief implement of the corrupt practices of the church. He deals with the sacraments in general and with each one individually, but his chief concern is with the sacrament of the Lord's Supper. He clarifies the new principles that have developed in his thinking since his earlier writings on the subject, and for the first time he sets them down in orderly form. And when he titles this document on the "Babylonian Captivity" a "prelude," it is implied that more will follow.

The next four treatises in this volume may be regarded as selections from the symphony to which *The Babylonian Captivity* was the "prelude." The occasions that called them forth from Luther's pen and the circumstances under which they were written are described in the several introductions to the treatises. These documents have been selected out of a large body of Luther's writings on this subject because they will introduce the English reader to some of Luther's main ideas about the Lord's Supper.

---

[1] *A Treatise Concerning the Blessed Sacrament of the Holy and True Body of Christ and Concerning the Brotherhoods* [hereinafter cited as *A Treatise Concerning the Blessed Sacrament*]. *PE* 2, 9-31.

[2] *A Treatise on the New Testament that is the Holy Mass. PE* 1, 294-326.

After writing *The Babylonian Captivity,* Luther was thoroughly committed to a new conception of the sacraments. As a parish priest he now began to draw the practical implications of his newly won position. Since his ideas were clearly in conflict with those of the official church, he realized that they would involve serious changes in the practices of the church in celebrating the Lord's Supper. The exaltation of the Word in the sacrament and the concept of the priesthood of every believer would necessarily eliminate the Roman idea of sacrifice in the mass. The saying of private masses would have to stop; and the cup could no longer be withheld from the laity. In the course of time false practices and abuses, or "misuses" as he called them, would have to be removed from the services of evangelical congregations.

After his experience at the Diet at Worms Luther abandoned all hope that such changes would be effected by the church authorities. So he felt that, wherever he had responsibility for human souls, he must now himself undertake such practical changes as would be necessary to conform with the teaching of the Scriptures. From his seclusion on the Wartburg he began to mention these matters in letters that he wrote to Melanchthon and Spalatin. In a letter to Melanchthon on August 1, 1521, he wrote: "I will no more celebrate a private mass forever." [8] In the celebration of the public mass he suggested that the priest remove every word that suggested the idea of sacrifice. This practical idea he then proceeds to develop in the second of the treatises in this volume, *The Misuse of the Mass* (1521). Here the burden of his thought is to emphasize and interpret the Words of Institution as against the human devices that have been imposed on the celebration of the sacrament.

The next change that Luther sought to bring about in the practice of the church was to restore the cup to the laity. Already in 1519 he had suggested that a general council of the church might well restore the two elements to all Christians, but at that time he attached little importance to the matter. The next year, in *A Treatise on the New Testament that is the Holy Mass,* he began to question the authority of the church to withhold the cup. Then in *The Babylonian Captivity* and especially in *The Misuse of the Mass* he strongly condemned the practice as contrary to the Scriptures. The idea continued to grow in importance with him and in 1522 he

---

[8] *WA,* Br 2, 372.

devoted a whole book to the subject, *Receiving Both Kinds in the Sacrament*, the third treatise in this volume. Here he discussed the scriptural and the various practical aspects of using one or both of the elements in the sacrament. While vigorously condemning the pope's "spoliation of the sacraments," Luther also insisted that in instituting these practical reforms regard must be had for the timid conscience of the ordinary man. He called this treatise "a little work concerning the evangelical form of the communion."

The next treatise, *The Adoration of the Sacrament* (1523), seeks to answer a practical question. What should be the attitude of the worshiper to the elements in the sacrament? Is it to be respect and reverence or adoration or worship? Is the host to be elevated and reserved, or is it not? Though the answer involved profound theological implications and careful exegesis of Scripture, to the rank and file of worshipers it was a practical question. Luther's discussion of the matter was occasioned by his correspondence and personal contacts with the Bohemian Brethren. In his treatise Luther advances to new ground in his understanding and interpretation of the sacrament. Four years earlier in *A Treatise Concerning the Blessed Sacrament* he had held that the essence of the sacrament lies in the fact that it incorporates the participant in the spiritual body of Christ while the elements are merely signs of that incorporation. Now, after a more careful interpretation of I Cor. 10:16, 17, he distinguished clearly between the spiritual body of Christ, which includes all believers, and the body which is distributed in the sacrament with the bread and wine. In this connection Luther stressed the Pauline idea to which he afterwards clung with great tenacity, that unworthy guests at the communion also receive the Lord's body. This became one of the points of distinction between Luther's view of the real presence of Christ in the sacrament and the view of other leading reformers.

In this document Luther also emphasized the importance of the Words of Institution, their meaning, their promise, and their power. He says it is far more important to reverence the Word than to reverence the host in the sacrament. He concludes that the practice of bowing the head and bending the knee before the sacrament may be left to the free choice of the communicant. There is both a proper and an improper adoration. It is improper if it is regarded as necessary or as a work of righteousness, or if there is not the right faith in the Word. It is entirely proper and suitable if it is an unconscious accompaniment of genuine faith in the Word and genuine reverence for Christ's real body.

The Abomination of the Secret Mass (1525) was part of Luther's effort to rid the congregations of the abuses growing out of the sacrifice of the mass. Already in 1521 he had vowed to Melanchthon that he would never again celebrate a private mass and then had written his book on *The Misuse of the Mass.* He had thought that a practical reform in this matter might well begin by reducing, at least in Wittenberg, the number of private masses. These were the masses, sometimes called hedge masses, in which only one person read and heard the Gospel and only one partook of the sacrament. He also advised a reduction in the number of masses for the dead. With the elimination of the idea of sacrifice all such masses lost their significance and became a burden to the conscience of an evangelical Christian. After several years of occasional preaching on the subject and writing letters about it, Luther proceeded to write a little book on it.

The treatise of 1525 on *The Abomination* is no major advance in thought beyond that of 1521 on *The Misuse.* Indeed, the Latin title for the treatise of 1521 was *The Abrogation of the Mass,* and *The Abomination* is in essence a more vigorous and more detailed statement of one aspect of the "abrogation" Luther had advocated four years earlier.

The last of the writings in this volume, *The Sacrament of the Body and Blood of Christ—Against the Fanatics* (1526), is one of several documents that Luther wrote that year to define more fully the views that he had now reached concerning the Lord's Supper. The deviations of the Swiss and South German reformers from his own position had come to his attention several years earlier but he seemed reluctant to engage them in controversy. But when the advocates of the Swiss view became aggressive or represented their view as that of Luther, the reformer's followers in Wittenberg pressed for an answer and got one in a series of sermons. These were published several months later under the above title.

The editor is indebted to Professor Frederick C. Ahrens of Gettysburg College, Gettysburg, Pennsylvania, who translated two selections and assisted in the revision of another.

A. R. W.

LUTHER'S WORKS

VOLUME 36

THE BABYLONIAN CAPTIVITY OF THE CHURCH

1520

Translated by A. T. W. Steinhäuser and revised by Frederick C. Ahrens and Abdel Ross Wentz

INTRODUCTION

The primary importance of this treatise for the present-day reader of Luther lies in its courageous interpretation of the sacraments. But it is important also for its place in Luther's progressive assault upon the total position of the Romans. In *An Open Letter to the Christian Nobility*[1] Luther demolished the three walls behind which Rome sat entrenched in her spiritual-temporal power. Now in *The Babylonian Captivity of the Church* he enters and takes her central stronghold and sanctuary—the sacramental system by which she accompanied and controlled her members from the cradle to the grave. Only then could he set forth, in language of almost lyrical rapture, *The Freedom of a Christian.*[2]

Luther was thinking of such a treatise long before it was written. In the first of the reformatory treatises of 1520, as they have been called, we read at the close: "I know another little song about Rome, and if their ears itch to hear it, I will sing it for them and I will pitch it in a high key. Dost thou take my meaning, beloved Rome?"[3] In this book on the "Babylonian Captivity," later that year, he fulfils his promise and the "little song" becomes a veritable "prelude."

Luther intends his book to be only an introduction to his major engagement on this theme of the sacraments. He expects that after this "Prelude" the Romans will gird themselves for battle and attack him in force, but he intends to keep one step ahead of them and lead them on. In fact, he fully expects a papal bull against him threatening him with the most dire consequences if he does not recant, and in the closing paragraphs of this treatise he explains in bitter irony that he intends this document to be the beginning or prelude of his "recantation." If he is to recant or rechant or unsing what he has been singing hitherto, he will not really "change his tune," but will only "pitch it in a higher key."

This book is therefore only a skirmish preliminary to the main engagement, or, as a musician might say, a mere prelude introducing

[1] *PE* 2, 55-164.
[2] *LW* 31, 327-377.
[3] *PE* 2, 164.

the main theme of the suite. It is a promise of more complete and more positive treatises on the sacraments in the future. And this promise was fulfilled. For that reason this "Prelude" is presented first among the treatises in this volume on the sacraments.

The theme that is presented by the Prelude Luther calls "The Babylonian Captivity of the Church." The reference is clear from the contents of the document: just as the Jews were carried away from Jerusalem into captivity under the tyranny of the Babylonian Empire, so in Europe the Christians have been carried away from the Scriptures and made subject to the tyranny of the papacy. This tyranny has been exercised by the misuse of the sacraments, chiefly the sacrament of the Lord's Supper.

After Luther had promised in his first reformatory treatise of 1520 that he would "sing another little song about Rome if their ears itch to hear it," he found that some ears were itching to hear the new song. This was brought home to him especially by two writings. One of these appeared in the summer of 1520; the other had been published the previous autumn but had not reached Wittenberg until some months later. The first came from the pen of Augustinus Alveld, that "celebrated Romanist of Leipzig," against whom Luther had fulminated in *The Papacy at Rome*, promising further disclosures if "Alveld came again." He did come again, this time with a *Tractatus de communione sub utraque specie* [*Treatise Concerning Communion in Both Kinds*]. It was dedicated June 23, 1520. "The Leipzig ass has set up a fresh braying against me, full of blasphemies"; thus Luther describes it in a letter to Spalatin, July 22, 1520.

The other work was the anonymous tract of a "certain Italian friar of Cremona," who has only recently been identified as Isidoro Isolani, a Dominican hailing from Milan, who taught theology in various Italian cities, wrote a number of controversial works, and died in 1528. The title of the tract is *Revocatio Martini Lutheri Augustiniani ad sanctam sedem* [*The Recantation of the Augustinian Martin Luther before the Holy See*]. Its date is November 22, 1519, at Cremona. It begins and ends with a letter, and one paragraph from each of these is translated in Preserved Smith, *Luther's Correspondence* (Philadelphia, 1913), Vol. I, No. 199.

These two writings may be regarded as the immediate occasion for the writing of *The Babylonian Captivity*, but the *Captivity* is in no sense a direct reply to either of them. "I will not reply to Alveld," Luther writes on August 5 to Spalatin, "but he will be the occasion of my publishing something by which the vipers will be more irritated than ever." [4] Indeed, he had promised some such work more than half a year before, in a letter to Spalatin of December 18, 1519: "There is no reason why you or anyone else should expect from me a treatise on the sacraments [besides baptism, the Lord's Supper, and penance] until I am taught by what text I can prove that they are sacraments. I regard none of the others as a sacrament, for there is no sacrament except where there is a direct divine promise, exercising our faith. We can have no intercourse with God except by the word of Him promising, and by the faith of man receiving. At another time you shall hear more about their fables of the seven sacraments." [5]

Thus the Prelude grows under his hand and assumes the form of an elaborate examination of the whole sacramental system of the church. He makes short work of his two opponents, and after a few pages of delicious irony, of which Erasmus was suspected in some quarters of being the author, he turns his back on them and addresses himself to a positive and constructive treatment of the larger theme, lenient toward all nonessentials, but inexorable toward everything truly essential, that is, scriptural.

Luther discusses each one of the seven sacraments of the Roman church, but devotes nearly half of the book to the Lord's Supper and Baptism. The worst tyranny of the papacy he finds in the sacrament of the Lord's Supper and to this he gives his chief attention. The first captivity is the withholding of the cup from the laity; the second is found in the doctrine of transubstantiation; and the third is the sacrifice of the mass. The Sacrament of the Altar is not a magical device by which the priest brings God down from heaven but God's own revelation of himself where he is. In his discussion of Baptism Luther repudiates monasticism and insists that no vow should ever be taken beyond the baptismal vow.

The other five ceremonies he rejects as sacraments. Penance he would retain in purified form, but not as a sacrament, because

[4] Smith, *op. cit.*, No. 283.
[5] *Ibid.*, No. 206.

it lacks a visible sign appointed by God; however, he strongly rejects priestly absolution. Everywhere he repudiates the authority of the church to institute new means of grace or new promises of mercy, and everywhere he bases upon the Holy Scriptures his general conception of a sacrament and his understanding of the individual sacraments.

Passage after passage, often whole pages, from the *Explanations of the Ninety-five Theses,*[6] *A Treatise on Baptism,*[7] *A Discussion of Confession,*[8] *A Treatise on the New Testament that is the Holy Mass*[9] and *A Treatise Concerning the Blessed Sacrament*[10] are transferred bodily to this new and definitive work, and find in it the goal toward which they had been unconsciously tending.

The *Captivity* was written in Latin because it is a theological treatise and was not intended for the rank and file of the Christian congregation. In this respect the treatise stands in contrast with the other five treatises in this volume on the sacraments, all of which were written in German and were intended for the individual Christian, whether layman or theologian.

All in all, the Prelude was a deadly dagger aimed at the very heart of sacramentalism and clericalism and monasticism. It was the most devastating assault Luther had yet undertaken against Roman teaching and practice. It marked Luther's final and irrevocable break with the church of Rome. There is special significance in the fact that in the same letter to Spalatin (October 3) in which he mentions the arrival of Eck in Leipzig armed with the papal bull, he also announces the publication of his book on the captivity of the church for the following Saturday (October 6).[11]

Both sides of the controversy took the book very seriously. In ducal Saxony it was rigorously suppressed. Before the imperial council at Worms, the middle of December, 1520, and again at the imperial diet the following February, the papal nuncio Aleander bitterly assailed the *Captivity* as completely blasphemous because it questioned the authority of the pope. John Glapion, the father

[6] *LW* 31, 83-252.
[7] *PE* 1, 56-71.
[8] *Ibid.*, 81-101.
[9] *Ibid.*, 294-326.
[10] *PE* 2, 9-31.
[11] Smith, *op. cit.*, No. 303.

confessor of Charles V, declared that it shocked him from head to foot. Erasmus now saw that his efforts to restore peace in the church would be futile: "The breach is irreparable." The University of Paris promptly condemned the document. One of Luther's most bitter enemies, Thomas Murner, translated it into German, confident that it would expose Luther to the rank and file of the people as a radical heretic and dangerous foe of the church. Of special significance was the action of Henry VIII of England. Not content with ordering Luther's writings to be publicly burned in London, he also turned theologian and wrote a book of 78 quarto pages dedicated to the pope, denouncing Luther and defending the Catholic positions on the sacraments. Henry's book so pleased the pope that he issued a special bull declaring that it was written with the help of the Holy Spirit, granting an indulgence of ten years to everyone who would read it, and bestowing upon Henry and his successors the title "Defender of the Faith."

On the other hand, the *Captivity* cleared the atmosphere for many thoughtful people and brought Luther not a few new friends. The most outstanding example of this was John Bugenhagen, who had previously regarded Luther as a reckless heretic, but on reading through the *Captivity* was completely converted to the cause of the Reformation and became one of Luther's ablest co-workers in the movement.

Julius Köstlin, probably the most thorough among modern analysts of Luther's theological development, says of the treatise: "The whole treatment of the subject is earnest and dignified. It is based upon biblical principles and shows thorough insight into the meaning of the Bible. At the same time it shows thorough acquaintance with the positions of the opponents and uses a dialectic that is a match for all the arts of the scholastics. Among all the scientific works of Luther this one stands at the top, but it also presents with clarity and warmth the simple religious interest of the Christian soul. It is sharp in its attitude toward the errors and tyranny of Rome but conservative toward the past and considerate toward such external practices as cannot be abrogated at once without injury to human consciences."

This is the fourth published translation of this treatise into English. The first was made by Wace and Buchheim (London,

1896). The second was by A. T. W. Steinhäuser and is included in the second volume of the Philadelphia edition of Luther's works (1915). The third came from the facile pen of Bertram Lee Woolf (*Reformation Writings of Martin Luther:* Vol. I, The Basis of the Protestant Reformation) and was published by the Lutterworth Press of London in 1952.

This revision is based on Steinhäuser's translation, but in every word there has been careful comparison with the original text and with the other English translations. The result is in some measure a new translation. The English of the Steinhäuser text has been revised in order to bring it into accord with present-day usage. Effort has been made also to conform a bit more closely to Luther's words. Some changes have been made in the interest of greater readability. We have sought to limit the use of intolerably long sentences. Also, there is more frequent paragraphing. The quotations from the Bible have been changed to the Revised Standard Version, except in the few instances where the context requires the King James Version or the Vulgate. Several paragraphs in the original that were omitted by Steinhäuser have been included here. The footnotes in Steinhäuser have, for the most part, been reproduced here, and they have been supplemented a bit.

The original Latin text of the treatise is in *WA* 6, 497-573.

THE BABYLONIAN CAPTIVITY OF THE CHURCH

A Prelude of Martin Luther On the Babylonian Captivity of the Church

Jesus

Martin Luther, Augustinian, to his friend, Hermann Tulich,[1] greeting.

Whether I wish it or not, I am compelled to become more learned every day, with so many and such able masters eagerly driving me on and making me work. Some two years ago I wrote on indulgences, but in such a way that I now deeply regret having published that little book.[2] At that time I still clung with a mighty superstition to the tyranny of Rome, and so I held that indulgences should not be altogether rejected, seeing that they were approved by the common consent of so many. No wonder, for at the time I was still engaged singlehanded in this Sisyphean task. Afterwards, thanks to Sylvester,[3] and aided by those friars who so strenuously defended indulgences, I saw that they were nothing but impostures of the Roman flatterers, by which they rob men of their money and their faith in God. Would that I could prevail upon the booksellers and

[1] Tulich was born at Steinheim, near Paderborn, in Westphalia; graduated from Wittenberg (A.B., 1511); was a proofreader in Melchior Lotter's printing-house at Leipzig. He returned to Wittenberg in 1519 and received the doctorate in 1520; became professor of poetry at the university; rector of the same, 1525. He was a staunch supporter of Luther; rector of the school at Lüneberg from 1532 until his death in 1540.

[2] Probably the *Explanations of the Ninety-five Theses* (1518). *LW* 31, 83-252.

[3] Sylvester Prierias (more properly called Mazzolini), from Prierio in Piedmont (1456-1523), was a prior of the Dominicans. He became Grand Inquisitor and Censor of Books in 1515. He and others of the order (e.g., Tetzel and Hochstraten) had written against Luther.

persuade all who have read them to burn the whole of my booklets on indulgences, and instead of all that I have written on this subject adopt this proposition: INDULGENCES ARE WICKED DEVICES OF THE FLATTERERS OF ROME.

Next, Eck and Emser[4] and their fellow-conspirators undertook to instruct me concerning the primacy of the pope. Here too, not to prove ungrateful to such learned men, I acknowledge that I have profited much from their labors. For while I denied the divine authority of the papacy, I still admitted its human authority.[5] But after hearing and reading the super-subtle subtleties of these coxcombs,[6] with which they so adroitly prop up their idol (for my mind is not altogether unteachable in these matters), I now know for certain that the papacy is the kingdom of Babylon and the power of Nimrod, the mighty hunter [Gen. 10:8-9]. Once more, therefore, that all may turn out to my friends' advantage, I beg both the booksellers and my readers that after burning what I have published on this subject they hold to this proposition: THE PAPACY IS THE GRAND HUNTING OF THE BISHOP OF ROME. This is proved by the arguments of Eck, Emser, and the Leipzig lecturer on the Scriptures.[7]

Now they are making a game of schooling me concerning communion in both kinds and other weighty subjects: here I must take pains lest I listen in vain to these "eminent teachers" [8] of mine. A certain Italian friar of Cremona has written a "Recantation of

---

[4] Johann Eck (properly Maier) from Eck in the Allgäu (1486-1543), had become professor at Ingolstadt in 1510. His criticism of the Ninety-five Theses in his *Obelisci*, to which Luther replied with the *Asterisci* (*WA* 1, 281-314; *St.L.* 18, 536-589), culminated in their Leipzig disputation in 1519. Jerome Emser (1477-1527) had been a humanist professor at Erfurt during Luther's student days, and was later secretary to Duke George of Saxony in Dresden. Luther is referring to the treatises both men published against him as a consequence of the disputation.

[5] *Resolutio Lutheriana super propositione sua decima tertia de potestate papae (per autorem locupletata)* (1519). *WA* 2, 180-240.

[6] *Trossulorum*, originally a designation for Roman knights who had conquered the city Trossulum, later came to have the derogatory sense of a fop, someone who pretends to rank and authority. *St.L.* 19, 6 n. 1.

[7] Augustinus Alveld, a Franciscan. This reference by Luther is his chief claim to fame. Cf. the Introduction.

[8] *Cratippos*. Cratippus, a peripatetic philosopher of Mytilene, had taught Cicero's son at Athens and received the rights of Roman citizenship through the orator's efforts. In addition to instructing the youth of Athens, he wrote on divination and the interpretation of dreams.

Martin Luther before the Holy See,"[9] which is not that I revoke anything, as the words declare, but that he revokes me. This is the kind of Latin the Italians are beginning to write nowadays. Another friar, a German of Leipzig, that same lecturer, as you know, on the whole canon of Scripture [Alveld] has written against me concerning the sacrament in both kinds and is about to perform, as I understand, still greater and more marvelous things. The Italian [Isolani] was canny enough to conceal his name, fearing perhaps the fate of Cajetan[10] and Sylvester. The man of Leipzig, on the other hand, as becomes a fierce and vigorous German, boasts on his ample title page of his name, his life, his sanctity, his learning, his office, his fame, his honor, almost his very clogs.[11] From him I shall doubtless learn a great deal, since he writes his dedicatory epistle to the Son of God himself: so familiar are these saints with Christ who reigns in heaven! Here it seems three magpies are addressing me, the first in good Latin, the second in better Greek, the third in purest Hebrew. What do you think, my dear Hermann, I should do, but prick up my ears? The matter is being dealt with at Leipzig by the "Observance" of the Holy Cross.[12]

Fool that I was, I had hitherto thought that it would be well if a general council were to decide that the sacrament should be administered to the laity in both kinds.[13] This view our more than learned friar would correct, declaring that neither Christ nor the apostles had either commanded or advised that both kinds be administered to the laity; it was therefore left to the judgment of the church what to do or not to do in this matter, and the church must be obeyed. These are his words.

---

[9] *Revocatio Martini Lutheri Augustiniani ad sanctam sedem* by Isidoro Isolani. Cf. the Introduction. Cf. *WA* 6, 486-487.

[10] Thomas Cajetan (1469-1534), Italian cardinal, general of the Dominican order and foremost authority on Thomistic theology, found himself unequal to the task of testing and refuting Luther at Augsburg. Cf. *Proceedings at Augsburg* (1518). *LW* 31, 253-292.

[11] The title page of Alveld's treatise contained twenty-six lines. Luther's *Calopodia* (perhaps originally intended as *calcipodium*) may have been a reference to the wooden-soled sandals worn by Alveld's order.

[12] Concerning Alveld's lengthy title and his peculiar spelling, IHSVH, for Jesus, which he tried to justify by arguments involving an admixture of the three languages, cf. *WA* 6, 485. He was a member of the stricter Observantine Franciscans, at that time separate from the Conventuals.

[13] *A Treatise Concerning the Blessed Sacrament* (1519). *PE* 2, 9-10.

You will perhaps ask, what madness has entered into the man, or against whom is he writing? For I have not condemned the use of one kind, but have left the decision about the use of both kinds to the judgment of the church. This is the very thing he attempts to assert, in order to attack me with this same argument. My answer is that this sort of argument is common to all who write against Luther: either they assert the very things they assail, or they set up a man of straw whom they may attack. This is the way of Sylvester and Eck and Emser, and of the men of Cologne and Louvain,[14] and if this friar had not been one of their kind, he would never have written against Luther.

This man turned out to be more fortunate than his fellows, however, for in his effort to prove that the use of both kinds was neither commanded nor advised, but left to the judgment of the church, he brings forward the Scriptures to prove that the use of one kind for the laity was ordained by the command of Christ. So it is true, according to this new interpreter of the Scriptures, that the use of one kind was not commanded and at the same time was commanded by Christ! This novel kind of argument is, as you know, the one which these dialecticians of Leipzig are especially fond of using. Does not Emser profess to speak fairly of me in his earlier book,[15] and then, after I had convicted him of the foulest envy and shameful lies, confess, when about to confute me in his later book,[16] that both were true, and that he has written in both a friendly and an unfriendly spirit? A fine fellow, indeed, as you know!

But listen to our distinguished distinguisher of "kinds,"[17] to whom the decision of the church and the command of Christ are the same thing, and again the command of Christ and no command of Christ are the same thing. With such dexterity he proves that only one kind should be given to the laity, by the command of

[14] The universities of Cologne and Louvain had ratified Eck's "victory" over Luther at Leipzig.

[15] *De disputatione Lipsicensi* (1519).

[16] *A venatione Luteriana Aegocerotis Assertio* (1519).

[17] *speciosum speciatorem*. In this play on words, Luther coined the second word to hint at the *species* or elements in the sacrament, while at the same time connoting ironically someone who tries to make his case appear plausible and favorable. *St.L.* 19, 9 n. 1.

Christ, that is, by the decision of the church. He puts it in capital letters, thus: THE INFALLIBLE FOUNDATION. Then he treats John 6 [:35, 41] with incredible wisdom, where Christ speaks of the bread of heaven and the bread of life, which is He Himself. The most learned fellow not only refers these words to the Sacrament of the Altar, but because Christ says: "I am the living bread" [John 6:51] and not "I am the living cup," he actually concludes that we have in this passage the institution of the sacrament in only one kind for the laity. But here follow the words: "For my flesh is food indeed, and my blood is drink indeed" [John 6:55] and, "Unless you eat the flesh of the Son of man and drink his blood" [John 6:53]. When it dawned upon the good friar that these words speak undeniably for both kinds and against one kind—presto! how happily and learnedly he slips out of the quandary by asserting that in these words Christ means to say only that whoever receives the sacrament in one kind receives therein both flesh and blood. This he lays down as his "infallible foundation" of a structure so worthy of the holy and heavenly "Observance."

I pray you now to learn along with me from this that in John 6 Christ commands the administration of the sacrament in one kind, yet in such a way that his commanding means leaving it to the decision of the church; and further that Christ is speaking in this same chapter only of the laity and not of the priests. For to the latter the living bread of heaven, that is the sacrament in one kind, does not belong, but perhaps the bread of death from hell! But what is to be done with the deacons and subdeacons,[18] who are neither laymen nor priests? According to this distinguished writer they ought to use neither the one kind nor both kinds! You see, my dear Tulich, what a novel and "Observant" method of treating Scripture this is.

But learn this too: In John 6 Christ is speaking of the Sacrament of the Altar, although he himself teaches us that he is speaking of faith in the incarnate Word, for he says: "This is the work of God, that you believe in him whom he has sent" [John 6:29]. But we'll

[18] These are the sixth and fifth of the seven grades through which clergy advanced to the priesthood. Some then-contemporary Catholic theologians (e.g., Cajetan and Durandus) doubted whether the Sacrament of Order was actually received by deacons. They were later overruled by the Council of Trent which decided that it was. *The Catholic Encyclopedia* (15 vols.), IV, 650.

have to give him credit: this Leipzig professor of the Bible can prove anything he pleases from any passage of Scripture he pleases. For he is an Anaxagorian,[19] or rather an Aristotelian,[20] theologian for whom nouns and verbs when interchanged mean the same thing and any thing. Throughout the whole of his book he so fits together the testimony of the Scriptures that if he set out to prove that Christ is in the sacrament he would not hesitate to begin thus: "The lesson is from the book of the Revelation of St. John the Apostle." All his quotations are as apt as this one would be, and the wiseacre imagines he is adorning his drivel with the multitude of his quotations. The rest I will pass over, lest I smother you with the filth of this vile-smelling cloaca.

In conclusion, he brings forward I Cor. 11 [:23], where Paul says that he received from the Lord and delivered to the Corinthians the use of both the bread and the cup. Here again our distinguisher of kinds, treating the Scriptures with his usual brilliance, teaches that Paul permitted, but did not deliver, the use of both kinds. Do you ask where he gets his proof? Out of his own head, as he did in the case of John 6. For it does not behoove this lecturer to give a reason for his assertions; he belongs to that order whose members prove and teach everything by their visions.[21] Accordingly we are here taught that in this passage the apostle did not write to the whole Corinthian congregation, but to the laity alone—and therefore gave no "permission" at all to the clergy, but deprived them of the sacrament altogether! Further, according to a new kind of grammar, "I have received from the Lord" means the same as "it is permitted by the Lord," and "I have delivered to you" is the same as "I have permitted to you." I pray you, mark this well. For by this method not only the church, but any worthless fellow, will be at liberty, according to this master, to turn all the universal commands, institutions, and ordinances of Christ and the apostles into mere "permission."

I perceive therefore that this man is driven by a messenger of

---

[19] Anaxagoras (*circa* 500-428 B.C.), a Greek philosopher, was accused of atheism by his contemporaries because of his new interpretation of the myths of the gods.

[20] For Luther's opinion of Aristotle, cf. *An Open Letter to the Christian Nobility. PE* 2, 146-147.

[21] The Franciscans. Perhaps an allusion to the seraphic vision of St. Francis.

Satan [II Cor. 12:7] and that he and his partners are seeking to make a name for themselves in the world through me, as men who are worthy to cross swords with Luther. But their hopes shall be dashed. In my contempt for them I shall never even mention their names, but content myself with this one reply to all their books. If they are worthy of it, I pray that Christ in his mercy may bring them back to a sound mind. If they are not worthy, I pray that they may never leave off writing such books, and that the enemies of truth may never deserve to read any others. There is a true and popular saying:

"This I know for certain—whenever I fight with filth,
Victor or vanquished, I am sure to be defiled."[22]

And since I see that they have an abundance of leisure and writing paper, I shall furnish them with ample matter to write about. For I shall keep ahead of them, so that while they are triumphantly celebrating a glorious victory over one of my heresies (as it seems to them), I shall meanwhile be devising a new one. I too am desirous of seeing these illustrious leaders in battle decorated with many honors. Therefore, while they murmur that I approve of communion in both kinds, and are most happily engrossed with this important and worthy subject, I shall go one step further and undertake to show that all who deny communion in both kinds to the laity are wicked men. To do this more conveniently I shall compose *a prelude on the captivity of the Roman church.*[23] In due time, when the most learned papists have disposed of this book, I shall offer more.

I take this course, lest any pious reader who may chance upon this book, should be offended by the filthy matter with which I deal and should justly complain that he finds nothing in it which cultivates or instructs his mind or which furnishes any food for learned reflection. For you know how impatient my friends are that I waste my time on the sordid fictions of these men. They say that

---

[22] The saying was also used later (1530) in the explanation to the fable about the ass and the lion in Luther's little book on Aesop's Fables, which included his translation of 14 of the fables. *Luthers Werke*, ed. Arnold E. Berger, III, 113. Cf. *MA*[3] 2, 405-406.

[23] We have retained the italics of the original for the most part where they serve the purpose of emphasis, or of pointing up the organizational structure of the treatise, or both.

the mere reading of them is ample confutation; they look for better things from me, which Satan seeks to hinder through these men. I have finally resolved to follow the advice of my friends and to leave to those hornets the business of wrangling and hurling invectives.

Of that Italian friar of Cremona [Isolani] I shall say nothing. He is an unlearned man and a simpleton, who attempts with a few rhetorical passages to recall me to the Holy See, from which I am not as yet aware of having departed, nor has anyone proved that I have. His chief argument in those silly passages[24] is that I ought to be moved by my monastic vows and by the fact that the empire has been transferred to the Germans.[25] Thus he does not seem to have wanted to write my "recantation" so much as the praise of the French people and the Roman pontiff. Let him attest his allegiance in this little book, such as it is. He does not deserve to be harshly treated, for he seems to have been prompted by no malice; nor does he deserve to be learnedly refuted, since all his chatter is sheer ignorance and inexperience.

To begin with, I must deny that there are seven sacraments, and for the present[26] *maintain that there are but three: baptism, penance, and the bread.*[27] *All three have been subjected to a miserable captivity by the Roman curia, and the church has been robbed of all her liberty.* Yet, if I were to speak according to the usage of the Scriptures, I should have only one single sacrament,[28] but with three sacramental signs, of which I shall treat more fully at the proper time.

---

[24] Cf. p. 13 n. 9.

[25] Cf. *An Open Letter to the Christian Nobility, PE* 2, 153 n. 2, and 153-158. Luther is probably referring to the fact that German kings, since Charles the Great in 800 A.D., had been called Roman Emperors after receiving papal coronation. Perhaps, though, he is referring to the election of the half-German Charles V on May 28, 1519, despite the papal agitation in favor of a French king. *Luther's Werke für das christliche Haus*, ed. Buchwald, *et al.* (Braunschweig, 1890) [hereinafter cited as Buchwald], II, 386 n. 1. Cf. *LW* 35, 406, n. 88.

[26] The "present" did not last very long as far as penance was concerned. Cf. p. 124.

[27] Luther uses the commonly accepted designation for the Lord's Supper, a name derived from the fact that the wine was being withheld from the laity.

[28] In I Tim. 3:16 Christ himself is called the *sacramentum* (Vulgate). Cf. *PE* 2, 177 n. 5; Julius Köstlin, *The Theology of Luther,* trans. Charles E. Hay (Philadelphia, 1897), I, 403; and below, pp. 93-94.

Now concerning the sacrament of the bread first of all.[29]

I shall tell you now what progress I have made as a result of my studies on the administration of this sacrament. For at the time when I was publishing my treatise on the Eucharist,[30] I adhered to the common custom and did not concern myself at all with the question of whether the pope was right or wrong. But now that I have been challenged and attacked, nay, forcibly thrust into this arena, I shall freely speak my mind, whether all the papists laugh or weep together.

In the first place the sixth chapter of John must be entirely excluded from this discussion, since it does not refer to the sacrament in a single syllable. Not only because the sacrament was not yet instituted, but even more because the passage itself and the sentences following plainly show, as I have already stated,[31] that Christ is speaking of faith in the incarnate Word. For he says: "My words are spirit and life" [John 6:63], which shows that he was speaking of a spiritual eating, by which he who eats has life; whereas the Jews understood him to mean a bodily eating and therefore disputed with him. But no eating can give life except that which is by faith, for that is truly a spiritual and living eating. As Augustine[32] also says: "Why do you make ready your teeth and your stomach? Believe, and you have eaten." [33] For the sacramental eating does not give life, since many eat unworthily. Hence Christ cannot be understood in this passage to be speaking about the sacrament.

Some persons, to be sure, have misapplied these words in their teaching concerning the sacrament, as in the decretal *Dudum*[34] and many others. But it is one thing to misapply the Scriptures and another to understand them in their proper sense. Otherwise, if in this passage Christ were enjoining a sacramental eating, when he

[29] Luther inserted this sentence instead of a subtitle as in the case of the other sacraments to follow.
[30] *A Treatise Concerning the Blessed Sacrament* (1519). *PE* 2, 9-31.
[31] Cf. p. 15.
[32] St. Augustine (354-430), bishop of Hippo in North Africa.
[33] *Sermo* 112, cap. 5. Migne 38, 645.
[34] Luther's reference to the Decretals is correct. His citation of *Dudum* is wrong. It should have been *Quum Marthae, Decretalium Gregorii IX*, lib. iii, tit. XLI: *de celebratione missarum, et sacramento eucharistiae et divinis officiis*, cap. 6. Cf. the text in *Corpus Iuris Canonici*, ed. Aemilius Friedberg (Graz, 1955), II, col. 638.

says: "Unless you eat my flesh and drink my blood, you have no life in you" [John 6:53], he would be condemning all infants, all the sick, and all those absent or in any way hindered from the sacramental eating, however strong their faith might be. Thus Augustine, in his *Contra Julianum,*[35] Book II, proves from Innocent[36] that even infants eat the flesh and drink the blood of Christ without the sacrament; that is, they partake of them through the faith of the church. Let this then be accepted as proved: John 6 does not belong here. For this reason I have written elsewhere[37] that the Bohemians[38] cannot properly rely on this passage in support of the sacrament in both kinds.

Now there are two passages that do bear very clearly upon this matter: the Gospel narratives of the Lord's Supper and Paul in I Cor. 11. Let us examine these. Matthew [26], Mark [14], and Luke [22] agree that Christ gave the whole sacrament to all his disciples. That Paul delivered both kinds is so certain that no one has ever had the temerity to say otherwise. Add to this that Matt. [26:27] reports that Christ did not say of the bread, "eat of it, all of you," but of the cup, "drink of it, all of you." Mark [14:23] likewise does not say, "they all ate of it," but "they all drank of it." Both attach the note of universality to the cup, not to the bread, as though the Spirit foresaw this schism, by which some would be forbidden to partake of the cup, which Christ desired should be common to all. How furiously, do you suppose, would they rave against us, if they had found the word "all" attached to the bread instead of to the cup? They would certainly leave us no loophole to escape. They would cry out and brand us as heretics and damn us as schismatics. But now, when the Scripture is on our side and against them, they will not allow themselves to be bound by any force of logic. Men of the most free will[39] they are,

[35] *Contra Julianum* ii, cap. 36. Migne 44, 699-700.

[36] Innocent I, bishop of Rome 402-417, energetic opponent of Pelagius and other heretics.

[37] *Verklärung etlicher Artikel in einem Sermon vom heiligen Sakrament* (1520). *WA* 6, 80.

[38] Followers of the martyred John Huss (1369-1415); permitted by compromise agreements with Rome to administer Communion in both kinds.

[39] For Luther's denial of his opponents' doctrine of the complete freedom of the will, cf. his *De servo arbitrio* (1525), *WA* 18, 600-787, *St.L.* 18, 1668-1969; *The Bondage of the Will,* trans. J. I. Packer and O. R. Johnston (Westwood, New Jersey, 1957).

even in the things that are God's; they change and change again, and throw everything into confusion.

But imagine me standing over against them and interrogating my lords, the papists. In the Lord's Supper, the whole sacrament, or communion in both kinds, is given either to the priests alone or else it is at the same time given to the laity. If it is given only to the priests (as they would have it), then it is not right to give it to the laity in either kind. For it must not be given rashly to any to whom Christ did not give it when he instituted the sacrament. Otherwise, if we permit one institution of Christ to be changed, we make all of his laws invalid, and any man may make bold to say that he is not bound by any other law or institution of Christ. For a single exception, especially in the Scriptures, invalidates the whole. But if it is given also to the laity, it inevitably follows that it ought not to be withheld from them in either form. And if any do withhold it from them when they ask for it they are acting impiously and contrary to the act, example, and institution of Christ.

I acknowledge that I am conquered by this argument, which to me is irrefutable. I have neither read nor heard nor found anything to say against it. For here the word and example of Christ stand unshaken when he says, not by way of permission, but of command: "Drink of it, all of you" [Matt. 26:27]. For if all are to drink of it, and the words cannot be understood as addressed to the priests alone, then it is certainly an impious act to withhold the cup from the laymen when they desire it, even though an angel from heaven [Gal. 1:8] were to do it. For when they say that the distribution of both kinds is left to the decision of the church, they make this assertion without reason and put it forth without authority. It can be ignored just as readily as it can be proved. It is of no avail against an opponent who confronts us with the word and work of Christ; he must be refuted with the word of Christ, but this we[40] do not possess.

If, however, either kind may be withheld from the laity, then with equal right and reason a part of baptism or penance might also be taken away from them by this same authority of the church. Therefore, just as baptism and absolution must be administered in

---

[40] Here Luther identifies himself with the erring priesthood.

their entirety, so the sacrament of the bread must be given in its entirety to all laymen, if they desire it. I am much amazed, however, by their assertion that the priests may never receive only one kind in the mass under pain of mortal sin; and that for no other reason except (as they unanimously say) that the two kinds constitute one complete sacrament, which may not be divided. I ask them, therefore, to tell me why it is lawful to divide it in the case of the laity, and why they are the only ones to whom the entire sacrament is not given? Do they not acknowledge, by their own testimony, either that both kinds are to be given to the laity or that the sacrament is not valid when only one kind is given to them? How can it be that the sacrament in one kind is not complete in the case of the priests, yet in the case of the laity it is complete? Why do they flaunt the authority of the church and the power of the pope in my face? These do not annul the words of God and the testimony of the truth.

It follows, further, that if the church can withhold from the laity one kind, the wine, it can also withhold from them the other, the bread. It could therefore withhold the entire Sacrament of the Altar from the laity and completely annul Christ's institution as far as they are concerned. By what authority, I ask. If the church cannot withhold the bread, or both kinds, neither can it withhold the wine. This cannot possibly be gainsaid; for the church's power must be the same over either kind as it is over both kinds, and if it has no power over both kinds, it has none over either kind. I am curious to hear what the flatterers of Rome will have to say to this.

But what carries most weight with me, however, and is quite decisive for me is that Christ says: "This is my blood, which is poured out for you and for many for the forgiveness of sins." [41] Here you see very clearly that the blood is given to all those for whose sins it was poured out. But who will dare to say that it was not poured out for the laity? And do you not see whom he addresses when he gives the cup? Does he not give it to all? Does he not say that it is poured out for all? "For you" [Luke 22:20], he says—let this refer to the priests. "And for many" [Matt. 26:28],

[41] A harmony of Matt. 26:28 and Luke 22:20 in the Vulgate, whereby "for you" and "for many" are conjoined in the traditional manner of the canon of the mass. Cf. p. 37 n. 84, and p. 319.

however, cannot possibly refer to the priests. Yet he says: "Drink of it, all of you" [Matt. 26:27]. I too could easily trifle here and with my words make a mockery of Christ's words, as my dear trifler[42] does. But those who rely on the Scriptures in opposing us must be refuted by the Scriptures.

This is what has prevented me from condemning the Bohemians,[43] who, whether they are wicked men or good, certainly have the word and act of Christ on their side, while we[44] have neither, but only that inane remark of men: "The church has so ordained." It was not the church which ordained these things, but the tyrants of the churches, without the consent of the church, which is the people of God.

But now I ask, where is the necessity, where is the religious duty, where is the practical use of denying both kinds, that is, the visible sign, to the laity, when everyone concedes to them the grace of the sacrament[45] without the sign? If they concede the grace, which is the greater, why not the sign, which is the lesser? For in every sacrament the sign as such is incomparably less than the thing signified. What then, I ask, is to prevent them from conceding the lesser, when they concede the greater? Unless indeed, as it seems to me, it has come about by the permission of an angry God in order to give occasion for a schism in the church, to bring home to us how, having long ago lost the grace of the sacrament, we contend for the sign, which is the lesser, against that which is the most important and the chief thing; just as some men for the sake of ceremonies contend against love. This monstrous perversion seems to date from the time when we began to rage against Christian love for the sake of the riches of this world. Thus God would show us, by this terrible sign, how we esteem signs more than the things they signify. How preposterous it would be to admit that the faith of baptism is granted to the candidate for baptism, and yet to deny him the sign of this very faith, namely, the water!

---

[42] Alveld, cf. above, p. 12 n. 7.

[43] Cf. p. 20 n. 38.

[44] Cf. p. 21 n. 41.

[45] The *res sacramenti*. The sacrament consisted of two parts—the *sacramentum*, or external sign, and the *res sacramenti*, or the thing signified, the sacramental grace.

Finally, Paul stands invincible and stops the mouth of everyone when he says in I Cor. 11 [:23]: "For I received from the Lord what I also delivered to you." He does not say: "I permitted to you," as this friar of ours lyingly asserts out of his own head.[46] Nor is it true that Paul delivered both kinds on account of the contention among the Corinthians. In the first place, the text shows that their contention was not about the reception of both kinds, but about the contempt and envy between rich and poor. The text clearly states: "One is hungry and another is drunk, and you humiliate those who have nothing" [I Cor. 11:21-22]. Moreover, Paul is not speaking of the time when he first delivered the sacrament to them, for he does not say "I receive from the Lord" and "I give to you," but "I received" and "I delivered"—namely, when he first began to preach among them, a long while before this contention. This shows that he delivered both kinds to them, for "delivered" means the same as "commanded," for elsewhere he uses the word in this sense. Consequently there is nothing in the friar's fuming about permission; he has raked it together without Scripture, without reason, without sense. His opponents do not ask what he has dreamed, but what the Scriptures decree in the matter, and out of the Scriptures he cannot adduce one jot or tittle in support of his dreams, while they can produce mighty thunderbolts in support of their faith.

Rise up then, you popish flatterers, one and all! Get busy and defend yourselves against the charges of impiety, tyranny, and lèse-majesté against the gospel, and of the crime of slandering your brethren. You decry as heretics those who refuse to contravene such plain and powerful words of Scripture in order to acknowledge the mere dreams of your brains! If any are to be called heretics and schismatics, it is not the Bohemians or the Greeks,[47] for they take their stand upon the Gospels. It is you Romans who are the heretics and godless schismatics, for you presume upon your figments alone against the clear Scriptures of God. Wash yourself of that, men!

But what could be more ridiculous and more worthy of this

[46] The passage from Alveld is quoted in *WA* 6, 505 n. 1.

[47] Greek Church is a common designation for that entire branch of Christendom known as Eastern Orthodoxy, which was split from Western or Latin Christianity in the year 1054. Its theologies and liturgies are written mostly in the Greek language.

friar's brains than his saying that the Apostle wrote these words and gave this permission, not to the church universal, but to a particular church, that is, the Corinthian? Where does he get his proof? Out of one storehouse, his own impious head. If the church universal receives, reads, and follows this epistle as written for itself in all other respects, why should it not do the same with this portion also? If we admit that any epistle, or any part of any epistle, of Paul does not apply to the church universal, then the whole authority of Paul falls to the ground. Then the Corinthians will say that what he teaches about faith in the Epistle to the Romans does not apply to them. What greater blasphemy and madness can be imagined than this! God forbid that there should be one jot or tittle in all of Paul which the whole church universal is not bound to follow and keep! The Fathers never held an opinion like this, not even down to these perilous times of which Paul was speaking [II Tim. 3:1-9] when he foretold that there would be blasphemers and blind, insensate men. This friar is one of them, perhaps even the chief.

However, suppose we grant the truth of this intolerable madness. If Paul gave his permission to a particular church, then, even from your own point of view, the Greeks and Bohemians are in the right, for they are particular churches. Hence it is sufficient that they do not act contrary to Paul, who at least gave permission. Moreover, Paul could not permit anything contrary to Christ's institution. Therefore, O Rome, I cast in your teeth, and in the teeth of all your flatterers, these sayings of Christ and Paul, on behalf of the Greeks and the Bohemians. I defy you to prove that you have been given any authority to change these things by as much as one hair, much less to accuse others of heresy because they disregard your arrogance. It is rather you who deserve to be charged with the crime of godlessness and despotism.

Concerning this point we may read Cyprian,[48] who alone is strong enough to refute all the Romanists. In the fifth book of his treatise, *On the Lapsed,* he testifies that it was the widespread custom in that church [at Carthage] to administer both kinds to the laity, even to children, indeed, to give the body of the Lord

[48] Bishop of Carthage, (249-258), who was beheaded as a martyr for the faith. The treatise was written about 251-252.

into their hands. And of this he gives many examples. Among other things, he reproves some of the people as follows: "The sacrilegious man is angered at the priests because he does not immediately receive the body of the Lord with unclean hands, or drink the blood of the Lord with unclean lips." [49] He is speaking here, you see, of irreverent laymen who desired to receive the body and the blood from the priests. Do you find anything to snarl at here, wretched flatterer? Will you say that this holy martyr, a doctor of the church endowed with the apostolic spirit, was a heretic, and that he used this permission in a particular church?

In the same place Cyprian narrates an incident that came under his own observation. He describes at length how a deacon was administering the cup to a little[50] girl, and when she drew away from him he poured the blood of the Lord into her mouth.[51] We read the same of St. Donatus, and how trivially does this wretched flatterer dispose of his broken chalice! [52] "I read of a broken chalice," he says, "but I do not read that the blood was administered." [53] No wonder! He that finds what he pleases in the Holy Scriptures will also read what he pleases in the histories. But can the authority of the church be established, or the heretics be refuted, in this way?

But enough on this subject! I did not undertake this work for the purpose of answering one who is not worthy of a reply, but to bring the truth of the matter to light.

---

[49] St. Cyprian, "The Lapsed," trans. Maurice Bévenot, S. J. (Westminster, Maryland, 1957), p. 31. (Vol. 25 of *Ancient Christian Writers.*)

[50] *infanti*, a child under the age of seven years. *St.L.* 19, 21 n. 2.

[51] St. Cyprian, *op. cit.*, pp. 32-33.

[52] Donatus, bishop of Arezzo, whither he had fled during the persecution of Diocletian (303-305); martyred under Julian the Apostate, August 7, 362. In a collection of legendary lives of the saints, compiled by Jacobus de Voragine (*circa* 1230-1298), it is related: "And one day, as Gregory relates in his *Dialogue*, the people were receiving the holy Communion in the Mass, and the deacon was distributing the Blood of Christ, when the pagans pushed him so rudely that he fell, and the holy chalice was shattered. As he and the people were sorely grieved thereat, Donatus gathered the fragments of the chalice, and having prayed, restored it to its former shape." *The Golden Legend of Jacobus de Voragine*, trans. Granger Ryan and Helmut Ripperger (New York, 1941), Part Two, 433-434.

[53] Alveld quotes the story of the broken cup in order to refute the practice in administration of the sacrament which it implies. He says: "I read of the repairing of the chalice in Gregory, but do not find there the administration of the blood." Cf. *WA* 6, 506 n. 2.

I conclude, then, that it is wicked and despotic to deny both kinds to the laity, and that this is not within the power of any angel, much less of any pope or council. Nor does the Council of Constance[54] give me pause, for if its authority is valid, why not that of the Council of Basel as well, which decreed to the contrary that the Bohemians should be permitted to receive the sacrament in both kinds? That decision was reached only after considerable discussion, as the extant records and documents of the Council show. And to this Council the ignorant flatterer refers[55] in support of his dream; with such wisdom does he handle the whole matter.

The first captivity of this sacrament, therefore, concerns its substance or completeness, which the tyranny of Rome has wrested from us. Not that those who use only one kind sin against Christ, for Christ did not command the use of either kind, but left it to the choice of each individual, when he said: "As often as you do this, do it in remembrance of me" [I Cor. 11:25]. But they are the sinners, who forbid the giving of both kinds to those who wish to exercise this choice. The fault lies not with the laity, but with the priests. The sacrament does not belong to the priests, but to all men. The priests are not lords, but servants in duty bound to administer both kinds to those who desire them, as often as they desire them. If they wrest this right from the laity and deny it to them by force, they are tyrants; but the laity are without fault, whether they lack one kind or both kinds. In the meantime they must be preserved by their faith and by their desire for the complete sacrament. These same servants are likewise bound to administer baptism and absolution to everyone who seeks them, because he has a right to them; but if they do not administer them, the seeker has the full merit of his faith, while they will be accused before Christ as wicked servants. Thus the holy fathers of old in the desert did

[54] Alveld had cited the *Decretum Constantiense,* which approved the withholding of the cup from the laity. Cf. *WA* 6, 507 n. 1.

[55] The Council of Constance did sanction withholding of the cup from the laity, and burned John Huss at the stake for disputing it (July 6, 1415). Alveld, however, was wrong, as Luther says, in citing also the Council of Basel. That Council concluded the *Compactata* of Prague (November 30, 1433), granting to the followers of Huss (the "Bohemians") the privilege of administering the sacrament in both kinds.

not receive the sacrament in any form for many years at a time.[56]

Therefore I do not urge that both kinds be seized upon by force, as if we were bound to this form by a rigorous command, but I instruct men's consciences so that they may endure the Roman tyranny, knowing well that they have been forcibly deprived of their rightful share in the sacrament because of their own sin. This only do I desire—that no one should justify the tyranny of Rome, as if it were doing right in forbidding one kind to the laity. We ought rather to abhor it, withhold our consent, and endure it just as we should do if we were held captive by the Turk and not permitted to use either kind. This is what I meant by saying that it would be a good thing, in my opinion, if this captivity were ended by the decree of a general council,[57] our Christian liberty restored to us out of the hands of the Roman tyrant, and every one left free to seek and receive this sacrament, just as he is free to receive baptism and penance. But now we are compelled by the same tyranny to receive the one kind year after year, so utterly lost is the liberty which Christ has given us. This is the due reward of our godless ingratitude.

The second captivity of this sacrament is less grievous as far as the conscience is concerned, yet the gravest of dangers threatens the man who would attack it, to say nothing of condemning it. Here I shall be called a Wycliffite[58] and a heretic by six hundred names. But what of it? Since the Roman bishop has ceased to be a bishop and has become a tyrant, I fear none of his decrees; for I know that it is not within his power, nor that of any general council, to make new articles of faith.

Some time ago, when I was drinking in scholastic theology, the learned Cardinal of Cambrai[59] gave me food for thought in his

[56] Cf. *A Treatise Concerning the Ban, PE* 2, 40.

[57] Cf. above, p. 13 n. 13.

[58] John Wycliffe (d. 1384), the most prominent English reformer before the Reformation and keenest of medieval critics of the doctrine of transubstantiation, was posthumously condemned as a heretic by the Council of Constance on May 4, 1415. Cf. p. 287 n. 17.

[59] Pierre d'Ailly (1350-1420), a pupil of Ockham, influenced Luther greatly. He was chairman of that session of the Council of Constance which examined and condemned John Huss in 1415. Luther is referring to d' Ailly's *Questiones quarti libri sententiarum*, quest. 6, E; folio cclxiv a.

comments on the fourth book of the *Sentences*.[60] He argues with great acumen that to hold that real bread and real wine, and not merely their accidents,[61] are present on the altar, would be much more probable and require fewer superfluous miracles—if only the church had not decreed otherwise. When I learned later what church it was that had decreed this, namely the Thomistic[62]—that is, the Aristotelian church—I grew bolder, and after floating in a sea of doubt,[63] I at last found rest for my conscience in the above view, namely, that it is real bread and real wine, in which Christ's real flesh and real blood are present in no other way and to no less a degree than the others assert them to be under their accidents. I reached this conclusion because I saw that the opinions of the Thomists, whether approved by pope or by council, remain only opinions, and would not become articles of faith even if an angel from heaven were to decree otherwise [Gal. 1:8]. For what is asserted without the Scriptures or proven revelation may be held as an opinion, but need not be believed. But this opinion of Thomas hangs so completely in the air without support of Scripture or reason that it seems to me he knows neither his philosophy nor his logic. For Aristotle speaks of subject and accidents so very differently[64] from St. Thomas that it seems to me this great man is to be pitied not only for attempting to draw his opinions in matters of faith from Aristotle, but also for attempting to base them upon a man whom he did not understand, thus building an unfortunate superstructure upon an unfortunate foundation.

---

[60] Famous medieval textbook of theology, compiled *circa* 1150 by Peter Lombard (d. 1160), and containing brief statements or "sentences" of the main arguments pro and con with respect to the principal themes in Christian doctrine. The fourth book treats of the sacraments in general.

[61] The qualities which, in medieval thought, were held to adhere to the invisible "substance," and together with it, form the object. In transubstantiation the "substance" of the bread and wine was changed into the "substance" of Christ's body and blood, while only the "accidents" or "form" of the bread and wine (such as shape, color, and taste) remained.

[62] The name refers to Thomas Aquinas (1225-1274), a Dominican, greatest of the scholastic theologians, still regarded as the foremost doctrinal authority in the Roman Catholic church.

[63] *inter sacrum et saxum.* In his *Adagia*, Erasmus says the phrase is used of those who in their perplexity are carried to the point of grave danger. *CL* 1, 438 n. 29.

[64] Aristotle held that a subject and its accidents are inseparable; neither can exist apart from the other. Cf. *MA*[3] 2, 406.

Therefore I permit every man to hold either of these opinions, as he chooses. My one concern at present is to remove all scruples of conscience, so that no one may fear being called a heretic if he believes that real bread and real wine are present on the altar, and that every one may feel at liberty to ponder, hold, and believe either one view or the other without endangering his salvation. However, I shall now set forth my own view.

In the first place, I do not intend to listen or attach the least importance to those who will cry out that this teaching of mine is Wycliffite, Hussite, heretical, and contrary to the decree of the church. No one will do this except those very persons whom I have convicted of manifold heresies in the matter of indulgences, freedom of the will and the grace of God, good works and sins, etc. If Wycliffe was once a heretic, they are heretics ten times over; and it is a pleasure to be blamed and accused by heretics and perverse sophists, since to please them would be the height of impiety. Besides, the only way in which they can prove their opinions and disprove contrary ones is by saying: "That is Wycliffite, Hussite, heretical!" They carry this feeble argument always on the tip of their tongues, and they have nothing else. If you ask for scriptural proof, they say: "This is our opinion, and the church (that is, we ourselves) has decided thus." To such an extent these men, who are reprobate concerning the faith [II Tim. 3:8] and untrustworthy, have the effrontery to set their own fancies before us in the name of the church as articles of faith.

But there are good grounds for my view, and this above all—no violence is to be done to the words of God, whether by man or angel. They are to be retained in their simplest meaning as far as possible. Unless the context manifestly compels it, they are not to be understood apart from their grammatical and proper sense, lest we give our adversaries occasion to make a mockery of all the Scriptures. Thus Origen[65] was rightly repudiated long ago because, ignoring the grammatical sense, he turned the trees and everything else written concerning Paradise into allegories, from which one could have inferred that trees were not created by God. Even so

[65] Origen of Alexandria (*circa* 184-253) whose principles of allegorical exegesis were the source of many lengthy controversies, beginning as early as the fourth century.

here, when the Evangelists plainly write that Christ took bread [Matt. 26:26; Mark 14:22; Luke 22:19] and blessed it, and when the Book of Acts and the Apostle Paul in turn call it bread [Acts 2:46; I Cor. 10:16; 11:23, 26-28], we have to think of real bread and real wine, just as we do of a real cup (for even they do not say that the cup was transubstantiated). Since it is not necessary, therefore, to assume a transubstantiation effected by divine power, it must be regarded as a figment of the human mind, for it rests neither on the Scriptures nor on reason, as we shall see.

Therefore it is an absurd and unheard-of juggling with words to understand "bread" to mean "the form or accidents[66] of bread," and "wine" to mean "the form or accidents of wine." Why do they not also understand all other things to mean their "forms or accidents"? And even if this might be done with all other things, it would still not be right to enfeeble the words of God in this way, and by depriving them of their meaning to cause so much harm.

Moreover, the church kept the true faith for more than twelve hundred years, during which time the holy fathers never, at any time or place, mentioned this transubstantiation (a monstrous word and a monstrous idea), until the pseudo philosophy of Aristotle began to make its inroads into the church in these last three hundred years.[67] During this time many things have been wrongly defined, as for example, that the divine essence is neither begotten nor begets; that the soul is the substantial form of the human body. These and like assertions are made without any reason or cause, as the Cardinal of Cambrai[68] himself admits.

Perhaps they will say that the danger of idolatry demands that the bread and wine should not be really present. How ridiculous! The laymen have never become familiar with their fine-spun philosophy of substance and accidents, and could not grasp it if it were taught to them. Besides, there is the same danger in the

---

[66] Cf. p. 29 n. 61.

[67] Luther is referring to the official establishment of transubstantiation as a fixed dogma by the Fourth Lateran Council of 1215 under Innocent III. The concept was perhaps several centuries in developing prior to that time, though the earliest documentable use of the term in its technical sense was probably in a treatise by Stephen of Autun (d. 1139). *The New Schaff-Herzog Encyclopedia of Religious Knowledge* (12 volumes) [hereinafter cited as Schaff-Herzog], XI, 494.

[68] Cf. p. 28 n. 59.

accidents which remain and which they see, as in the case of the substance which they do not see. If they do not worship the accidents, but the Christ hidden under them, why should they worship the [substance of the] bread, which they do not see?

And why could not Christ include his body in the substance of the bread just as well as in the accidents? In red-hot iron, for instance, the two substances, fire and iron, are so mingled that every part is both iron and fire. Why is it not even more possible that the body of Christ be contained in every part of the substance of the bread?

What will they reply? Christ is believed to have been born from the inviolate womb of his mother. Let them say here too that the flesh of the Virgin was meanwhile annihilated, or as they would more aptly say, transubstantiated, so that Christ, after being enfolded in its accidents, finally came forth through the accidents! The same thing will have to be said of the shut door [John 20:19, 26] and of the closed mouth of the sepulchre,[69] through which he went in and out without disturbing them.

Out of this has arisen that Babel of a philosophy of a constant quantity distinct from the substance,[70] until it has come to such a pass that they themselves no longer know what are accidents and what is substance. For who has ever proved beyond the shadow of a doubt that heat, color, cold, light, weight, or shape are mere accidents? Finally, they have been driven to pretend that a new substance is created by God for those accidents on the altar, all on account of Aristotle, who says: "It is the nature of an accident to be in something," and endless other monstrosities. They would be rid of all these if they simply permitted real bread to be present. I rejoice greatly that the simple faith of this sacrament is still to be found, at least among the common people. For as they do not understand, neither do they dispute whether accidents are present without substance, but believe with a simple faith that Christ's body and blood are truly contained there, and leave to those who have nothing else to do the argument about what contains them.

[69] Matt. 28:2; Mark 16:4; Luke 24:2; John 20:1.

[70] According to scholastic teaching the substance of the bread ceases to exist. Its quantity, however, together with the other accidents, remains the same. Cf. p. 29 n. 61.

But perhaps they will say: "Aristotle teaches that in an affirmative proposition subject and predicate must be identical," or (to quote the monster's own words in the sixth book of his *Metaphysics*)[71]: "An affirmative proposition requires the agreement of the subject and the predicate." They interpret argreement to mean identity. Hence, when I say: "This is my body," the subject cannot be identical with the bread, but must be identical with the body of Christ.

What shall we say when Aristotle and the doctrines of men are made to be the arbiters of such lofty and divine matters? Why do we not put aside such curiosity and cling simply to the words of Christ, willing to remain in ignorance of what takes place here and content that the real body of Christ is present by virtue of the words?[72] Or is it necessary to comprehend the manner of the divine working in every detail?

But what do they say when Aristotle admits that all of the categories[73] of accidents are themselves a subject—although he grants that substance is the chief subject? Hence for him "this white," "this large," "this something," are all subjects, of which something is predicated. If that is correct, I ask: If a "transubstantiation" must be assumed in order that Christ's body may not be identified with the bread, why not also a "transaccidentation," in order that the body of Christ may not be identified with the accidents? For the same danger remains if one understands the subject to be "this white or this round[74] is my body." And for the same reason that a "transubstantiation" must be assumed, a "transaccidentation" must also be assumed, because of this identity of subject and predicate.

If however, merely by an act of the intellect, you can do away with the accident, so that it will not be regarded as the subject

[71] Luther should be referred not to the *Metaphysics* but to the *Organon*, where in chapter 6 on *De Interpretatione*, Aristotle indicates that for affirmative and negative propositions having the same subject and predicate to be truly contradictory, subject and predicate must be unequivocally (univocally) identical. In chapter 10 he holds that "the subject and predicate in an affirmation must each denote a single thing." Richard McKeon (ed.), *The Basic Works of Aristotle* (New York, 1941), pp. 43, 49.

[72] Cf. *A Treatise Concerning the Blessed Sacrament* (1519). *PE* 2, 20.

[73] Namely: substance, quantity, quality, relation, place, time, position, state, action, and affection. McKeon, p. 8.

[74] i.e., the host, or wafer.

when you say, "this is my body," why not with equal ease transcend the substance of the bread, if you do not want it to be regarded either as the subject, so that "this my body" is no less in the substance than in the accident? After all, this is a divine work performed by God's almighty power, which can operate just as much and just as well in the accident as it can in the substance.

Let us not dabble too much in philosophy, however. Does not Christ appear to have anticipated this curiosity admirably by saying of the wine, not *Hoc est sanguis meus*, but *Hic est sanguis meus*? [Mark 14:24]. He speaks even more clearly when he brings in the word "cup" and says: "This cup [*Hic calix*] is the new testament in my blood" [Luke 22:20; I Cor. 11:25]. Does it not seem as though he desired to keep us in a simple faith, sufficient for us to believe that his blood was in the cup? For my part, if I cannot fathom how the bread is the body of Christ, yet I will take my reason captive to the obedience of Christ [II Cor. 10:5], and clinging simply to his words, firmly believe not only that the body of Christ is in the bread, but that the bread is the body of Christ. My warrant for this is the words which say: "He took bread, and when he had given thanks, he broke it and said, 'Take, eat, this (that is, this bread, which he had taken and broken) is my body'" [I Cor. 11:23-24]. And Paul says: "The bread which we break, is it not a participation in the body of Christ?" [I Cor. 10:16]. He does not say "in the bread there is," but "the bread itself is[75] the participation in the body of Christ." What does it matter if philosophy cannot fathom this? The Holy Spirit is greater than Aristotle. Does philosophy fathom their transubstantiation? Why, they themselves admit that here all philosophy breaks down. That the pronoun "this," in both Greek and Latin, is referred to "body," is due to the fact that in both of these languages the two words are of the same gender. In Hebrew, however, which has no neuter gender, "this" is referred to "bread," so that it would be proper to say *Hic* [bread] *est corpus meum*. Actually, the idiom of the language[76] and common sense both prove that the subject ["this"] obviously points to the bread and not to the body, when he says:

---

[75] Not *in pane est* but *ipse panis est*.

[76] Luther assumes that the language Jesus spoke on that occasion was certainly not Greek, but probably Hebrew.

Hoc est corpus meum, das ist meyn leyp, that is, "This very bread here [*iste panis*] is my body."

Thus, what is true in regard to Christ is also true in regard to the sacrament. In order for the divine nature to dwell in him bodily [Col. 2:9], it is not necessary for the human nature to be transubstantiated and the divine nature contained under the accidents of the human nature. Both natures are simply there in their entirety, and it is truly said: "This man is God; this God is man." Even though philosophy cannot grasp this, faith grasps it nonetheless. And the authority of God's Word is greater than the capacity of our intellect to grasp it. In like manner, it is not necessary in the sacrament that the bread and wine be transubstantiated and that Christ be contained under their accidents in order that the real body and real blood may be present. But both remain there at the same time, and it is truly said: "This bread is my body; this wine is my blood," and vice versa. Thus I will understand it for the time being to the honor of the holy words of God, to which I will allow no violence to be done by petty human arguments, nor will I allow them to be twisted into meanings which are foreign to them. At the same time, I permit other men to follow the other opinion, which is laid down in the decree, *Firmiter,*[77] only let them not press us to accept their opinions as articles of faith (as I have said above).[78]

The third captivity of this sacrament is by far the most wicked abuse of all, in consequence of which there is no opinion more generally held or more firmly believed in the church today than this, that the mass is a good work and a sacrifice. And this abuse has brought an endless host of other abuses in its train, so that the faith of this sacrament has become utterly extinct and the holy sacrament has been turned into mere merchandise, a market, and a profit-making business. Hence participations,[79] brotherhoods,[80]

---

[77] *Firmiter, Decretalium Gregorii IX,* lib. i, tit I: *de summa trinitate et fide catholica,* cap. 1, sec. 3. *Corpus Iuris Canonici, op. cit.,* II col. 5.

[78] Cf. p. 28.

[79] Though not actually present, one could obtain spiritual "participation" in masses which, for example, were read in a monastery.

[80] These confraternities and sodalities paid to have masses said for them, and engaged in devotional exercises for gaining merit. Membership in such an association provided each person the benefits accruing from the "good works" (prayers and attendance at masses) of all the other members.

intercessions, merits, anniversaries,[81] memorial days[82] and the like wares are bought and sold, traded and bartered, in the church. On these the priests and monks depend for their entire livelihood.

I am attacking a difficult matter, an abuse perhaps impossible to uproot, since through century-long custom and the common consent of men it has become so firmly entrenched that it would be necessary to abolish most of the books now in vogue, and to alter almost the entire external form of the churches and introduce, or rather re-introduce, a totally different kind of ceremonies. But my Christ lives, and we must be careful to give more heed to the Word of God than to all the thoughts of men and of angels. I will perform the duties of my office and bring to light the facts in the case. As I have received the truth freely [Matt. 10:8], I will impart it without malice. For the rest let every man look to his own salvation; I will do my part faithfully so that no one may be able to cast on me the blame for his lack of faith and his ignorance of the truth when we appear before the judgment seat of Christ [2 Cor. 5:10].

In the first place, in order that we might safely and happily attain to a true and free knowledge of this sacrament, we must be particularly careful to put aside whatever has been added to its original simple institution by the zeal and devotion of men: such things as vestments, ornaments, chants, prayers, organs, candles, and the whole pageantry of outward things.[83] We must turn our eyes and hearts simply to the institution of Christ and this alone, and set nothing before us but the very word of Christ by which he instituted the sacrament, made it perfect, and committed it to us. For in that word, and in that word alone, reside the power, the nature, and the whole substance of the mass. All the rest is the work of man, added to the word of Christ, and the mass can be held and remain a mass just as well without them. Now the words of Christ, in which he instituted this sacrament, are these:

"Now as they were eating, Jesus took bread, and blessed, and broke it, and gave it to his disciples and said, 'Take, eat; this is my body, which is given for you.' And he took a cup, and when he had

---

[81] Masses said on behalf of the soul of a deceased person daily for a year or annually on the anniversary of his death.

[82] Masses for the dead were read on memorial days.

[83] Cf. *A Treatise on the New Testament that is the Holy Mass.* *PE* 1, 296-297.

given thanks he gave it to them, saying, 'Drink of it, all of you; for this cup is the new testament in my blood, which is poured out for you and for many for the forgiveness of sins. Do this in remembrance of me.'" [84]

These words the Apostle also delivers and more fully expounds in I Cor. 11 [:23-26]. On them we must rest; on them we must build as on a firm rock, if we would not be carried about with every wind of doctrine [Eph. 4:14], as we have till now been carried about by the wicked doctrines of men who reject the truth [Titus 1:14]. For in these words nothing is omitted that pertains to the completeness, the use, and the blessing of this sacrament; and nothing is included that is superfluous and not necessary for us to know. Whoever sets aside these words and meditates or teaches concerning the mass will teach monstrous and wicked doctrines, as they have done who have made of the sacrament an *opus operatum*[85] and a sacrifice.

Let this stand, therefore, as our first and infallible proposition—the mass or Sacrament of the Altar is Christ's testament, which he left behind him at his death to be distributed among his believers. For that is the meaning of his words, "This cup is the new testament in my blood" [Luke 22:20; I Cor. 11:25]. Let this truth stand, I say, as the immovable foundation on which we shall base all that we have to say. For, as you will see, we are going to overthrow all the godless opinions of men which have been imported into this most precious sacrament. Christ, who is the truth, truly says that this is the new testament in his blood, poured out for us [Luke 22:20]. Not without reason do I dwell on this sentence; the matter is of no small moment, and must be most deeply impressed on our minds.

Thus, if we enquire what a testament is, we shall learn at the

---

[84] Luther's rendering of the Words of Institution is similar to that of the canon of the mass in that it represents a harmony of the several scriptural accounts, incorporating features from all of them—Matt. 26:26-28; Mark 14:22-24; Luke 22:19-20; I Cor. 11:23-25. It differs from the canon of the mass in that it excludes all phrases not explicitly found in the scriptural accounts themselves, Vulgate version. Cf. the canon of the mass text on p. 319. Cf. also *PE* 6, 74, 107-108, 126, 160.

[85] A work accomplished or finished, which is supposed to impart grace simply by virtue of its having been properly performed, without reference to any faith or lack of faith on the part of the person for whom it is performed. Cf. *A Treatise Concerning the Blessed Sacrament* (1519), *PE* 2, 22-23, where Luther discusses this term.

same time what the mass is, what its right use and blessing, and what its wrong use.

A testament, as everyone knows, is a promise made by one about to die, in which he designates his bequest and appoints his heirs. A testament, therefore, involves first, the death of the testator, and second, the promise of an inheritance and the naming of the heir. Thus Paul discusses at length the nature of a testament in Rom. 4, Gal. 3 and 4, and Heb. 9. We see the same thing clearly also in these words of Christ. Christ testifies concerning his death when he says: "This is my body, which is given, this is my blood, which is poured out" [Luke 22:19-20]. He names and designates the bequest when he says "for the forgiveness of sins" [Matt. 26:28]. But he appoints the heirs when he says "For you [Luke 22:19-20; I Cor. 11:24] and for many" [Matt. 26:28; Mark 14:24], that is, for those who accept and believe the promise of the testator. For here it is faith that makes men heirs, as we shall see.

You see, therefore, that what we call the mass is a promise of the forgiveness of sins made to us by God, and such a promise as has been confirmed by the death of the Son of God. For the only difference between a promise and a testament is that the testament involves the death of the one who makes it. A testator is a promiser who is about to die, while a promiser (if I may put it thus) is a testator who is not about to die. This testament of Christ is foreshadowed in all the promises of God from the beginning of the world; indeed, whatever value those ancient promises possessed was altogether derived from this new promise that was to come in Christ. Hence the words "compact," "covenant," and "testament of the Lord" occur so frequently in the Scriptures. These words signified that God would one day die. "For where there is a testament, the death of the testator must of necessity occur" (Heb. 9 [:16]). Now God made a testament; therefore, it was necessary that he should die. But God could not die unless he became man. Thus the incarnation and the death of Christ are both comprehended most concisely in this one word, "testament."

From the above it will at once be seen what is the right and what is the wrong use of the mass, and what is the worthy and what the unworthy preparation for it. If the mass is a promise, as has been said, then access to it is to be gained, not with any works, or powers, or merits of one's own, but by faith alone. For where there is the Word of the promising God, there must necessarily be the faith of the accepting man. It is plain therefore, that the beginning of our salvation is a faith which clings to the Word of the promising God, who, without any effort on our part, in free and unmerited mercy takes the initiative and offers us the word of his promise. "He sent forth his word, and thus [*sic*] healed them," [86] not: "He accepted our work, and thus healed us." First of all there is God's Word. After it follows faith; after faith, love; then love does every good work, for it does no wrong, indeed, it is the fulfilling of the law [Rom. 13:10]. In no other way can man come to God or deal with him than through faith. That is to say, that the author of salvation is not man, by any works of his own, but God, through his promise; and that all things depend on, and are upheld and preserved by, the word of his power [Heb. 1:3], through which he brought us forth, to be a kind of first fruits of his creatures [Jas. 1:18].

Thus, in order to raise up Adam after the fall, God gave him this promise when he said to the serpent: "I will put enmity between you and the woman, and between your seed and her seed; he shall bruise your head, and you shall bruise his heel" [Gen. 3:15]. In this word of promise Adam, together with his descendants, was carried as it were in God's bosom, and by faith in it he was preserved, waiting patiently for the woman who should bruise the serpent's head, as God had promised. And in that faith and expectation he died, not knowing when or who she would be, yet never doubting that she would come. For such a promise, being the truth of God, preserves even in hell those who believe it and wait for it. After this came another promise, made to Noah—to last until the time of Abraham—when a bow was set in the clouds as a sign of the covenant [Gen. 9:12-17], by faith in which Noah and his descendants found God gracious. After that, he promised Abraham that all the nations should be blessed in his seed [Gen. 22:18]. And this is Abraham's bosom [Luke 16:22], into which his descendants have been received. Then to Moses and the children of Israel [Deut. 18:18], especially to David [II Sam. 7:12-16], he gave the plainest promise of Christ, and thereby at last made clear what the promise to the men of old really was.

[86] Ps. 107:20. *Sic* is Luther's own interpolation into the Vulgate text.

And so it finally came to the most perfect promise of all, that of the new testament, in which, with plain words, life and salvation are freely promised, and actually granted to those who believe the promise. And he distinguishes this testament from the old one by a particular mark when he calls it the "new testament" [Luke 22:20; I Cor. 11:25]. For the old testament given through Moses was not a promise of forgiveness of sins or of eternal things, but of temporal things, namely, of the land of Canaan, by which no man was renewed in spirit to lay hold on the heavenly inheritance. Wherefore also it was necessary that, as a figure of Christ, a dumb beast should be slain, in whose blood the same testament might be confirmed, as the blood corresponded to the testament and the sacrifice corresponded to the promise. But here Christ says "the new testament in my blood" [Luke 22:20; I Cor. 11:25], not somebody else's, but his own, by which grace is promised through the Spirit for the forgiveness of sins, that we may obtain the inheritance.

According to its substance, therefore, the mass is nothing but the aforesaid words of Christ: "Take and eat, etc." [Matt. 26:26], as if he were saying: "Behold, O sinful and condemned man, out of the pure and unmerited love with which I love you, and by the will of the Father of mercies [II Cor. 1:3], apart from any merit or desire of yours, I promise you in these words the forgiveness of all your sins and life everlasting. And that you may be absolutely certain of this irrevocable promise of mine, I shall give my body and pour out my blood, confirming this promise by my very death, and leaving you my body and blood as a sign and memorial of this same promise. As often as you partake of them, remember me, proclaim and praise my love and bounty toward you, and give thanks."

From this you will see that nothing else is needed for a worthy holding of mass than a faith that relies confidently on this promise, believes Christ to be true in these words of his, and does not doubt that these infinite blessings have been bestowed upon it. Hard on this faith there follows, of itself, a most sweet stirring of the heart, whereby the spirit of man is enlarged and enriched (that is love, given by the Holy Spirit through faith in Christ), so that he is drawn to Christ, that gracious and bounteous testator, and made a thoroughly new and different man. Who would not shed tears of gladness, indeed, almost faint for joy in Christ, if he believed with unshaken faith that this inestimable promise of Christ belonged to him? How could he help loving so great a benefactor, who of his own accord offers, promises, and grants such great riches and this eternal inheritance to one who is unworthy and deserving of something far different?

Therefore it is our one and only misfortune that we have many masses in the world, and yet none, or very few of us, recognize, consider, and receive these promises and riches that are offered to us. Actually, during the mass, we should do nothing with greater zeal (indeed, it demands all our zeal) than to set before our eyes, meditate upon, and ponder these words, these promises of Christ—for they truly constitute the mass itself—in order to exercise, nourish, increase, and strengthen our faith in them by this daily remembrance. For this is what he commands, when he says: "Do this in remembrance of me" [Luke 22:19; I Cor. 11:24]. This should be done by the preachers of the gospel in order to impress this promise faithfully upon the people, to commend it to them, and to awaken their faith in it.

But how many are there today who know that the mass is the promise of Christ? I will say nothing of those godless preachers of fables, who teach human ordinances instead of this great promise. And even if they teach these words of Christ, they do not teach them as a promise or testament, neither therefore as a means of obtaining faith.

What we deplore in this captivity is that nowadays they take every precaution that no layman should hear these words of Christ, as if they were too sacred to be delivered to the common people. So mad are we priests[87] that we arrogate to ourselves alone the so-called words of consecration, to be said secretly,[88] yet in such a way that they do not profit even us, for we too fail to regard them as promises or as a testament for the strengthening of the faith. Instead of believing them, we reverence them with I know not what superstitious and godless fancies. What else is Satan trying to do to us through this misfortune of ours but to remove every trace of the

[87] Cf. p. 21 n. 40.

[88] The words of consecration, indeed of the whole canon of the mass, were spoken very softly. Cf. *The Abomination of the Secret Mass* (1525) in this volume, pp. 310 and 314.

[true] mass out of the church, though he is meanwhile at work filling every corner of the globe with [false] masses, that is, with abuses and mockeries of God's testament—burdening the world more and more heavily with most grievous sins of idolatry, to its deeper condemnation? For what more sinful idolatry can there be than to abuse God's promises with perverse opinions and to neglect or extinguish faith in them?

For God does not deal, nor has he ever dealt, with man otherwise than through a word of promise, as I have said. We in turn cannot deal with God otherwise than through faith in the Word of his promise. He does not desire works, nor has he need of them; rather we deal with men and with ourselves on the basis of works. But God has need of this: that we consider him faithful in his promises [Heb. 10:23], and patiently persist in this belief, and thus worship him with faith, hope, and love. It is in this way that he obtains his glory among us, since it is not of ourselves who run, but of him who shows mercy [Rom. 9:16], promises, and gives, that we have and hold all good things. Behold, this is that true worship and service of God which we ought to perform in the mass. But if the words of promise are not delivered, what exercise of faith can there be? And without faith, who can have hope or love? Without faith, hope, and love, what service of God can there be? There is no doubt, therefore, that in our day all priests and monks, together with their bishops and all their superiors, are idolators, living in a most perilous state by reason of this ignorance, abuse, and mockery of the mass, or sacrament, or promise of God.

For anyone can easily see that these two, promise and faith, must necessarily go together. For without the promise there is nothing to be believed; while without faith the promise is useless, since it is established and fulfilled through faith. From this everyone will readily gather that the mass, since it is nothing but promise, can be approached and observed only in faith. Without this faith, whatever else is brought to it by way of prayers, preparations, works, signs, or gestures are incitements to impiety rather than exercises of piety. It usually happens that those who are thus prepared imagine themselves legitimately entitled to approach the altar, when in reality they are less prepared than at any other time or by any other work, by reason of the unbelief which they bring with them. How many celebrants you can see everywhere, every day, who imagine they—wretched men—have committed criminal offenses when they make some petty mistake, such as wearing the wrong vestment, or forgetting to wash their hands, or stumbling over their prayers! But the fact that they have no regard for or faith in the mass itself, namely, the divine promise, causes them not the slightest qualms of conscience. O worthless religion of this age of ours, the most godless and thankless of all ages!

Hence the only worthy preparation and proper observance is faith, the faith by which we believe in the mass, that is, in the divine promise. Whoever, therefore, desires to approach the altar or receive the sacrament, let him beware lest he appear empty-handed [Exod. 23:15; 34:20; Deut. 16:16] before the face of the Lord God. But he will be empty-handed unless he has faith in the mass, or this new testament. By what godless work could he sin more grievously against the truth of God, than by this unbelief of his? By it, as much as in him lies, he convicts God of being a liar and a maker of empty promises. The safest course, therefore, will be to go to the mass in the same spirit in which you would go to hear any other promise of God, that is, prepared not to do or contribute much yourself, but to believe and accept all that is promised you there, or proclaimed as promises through the ministry of the priest. If you do not come in this spirit, beware of attending at all, for you will surely be going to your condemnation [I Cor. 11:29].

I was right then in saying that the whole power of the mass consists in the words of Christ, in which he testifies that forgiveness of sins is bestowed on all those who believe that his body is given and his blood poured out for them. This is why nothing is more important for those who go to hear mass than to ponder these words diligently and in full faith. Unless they do this, all else that they do is in vain. This is surely true, that to every promise of his, God usually adds some sign as a memorial or remembrance of the promise, so that thereby we may serve him the more diligently and he may admonish us the more effectually. Thus, when he promised Noah that he would not again destroy the world by a flood, he added his bow in the clouds, to show that he would be mindful of his covenant [Gen. 9:8-17]. And after promising Abraham the inheritance in his seed, he gave him circumcision as a mark of his justification by faith [Gen. 17:3-11]. Thus he granted to Gideon the dry and the wet fleece to confirm his promise of victory over the Midianites [Judg. 6:36-40]. And through Isaiah he offered to Ahaz a sign that he would conquer the king of Syria and Samaria, to confirm in him his faith in the promise [Isa. 7:10-17]. And we read of many such signs of the promises of God in the Scriptures.

So in the mass also, the foremost promise of all, he adds as a memorial sign of such a great promise his own body and his own blood in the bread and wine, when he says: "Do this in remembrance of me" [Luke 22:19; I Cor. 11:24-25]. And so in baptism, to the words of promise he adds the sign of immersion in water. We may learn from this that in every promise of God two things are presented to us, the word and the sign, so that we are to understand the word to be the testament, but the sign to be the sacrament. Thus, in the mass, the word of Christ is the testament, and the bread and wine are the sacrament. And as there is greater power in the word than in the sign, so there is greater power in the testament than in the sacrament; for a man can have and use the word or testament apart from the sign or sacrament. "Believe," says Augustine, "and you have eaten." [89] But what does one believe, other than the word of the one who promises? Therefore I can hold mass every day, indeed, every hour, for I can set the words of Christ before me and with them feed and strengthen my faith as often as I choose. This is a truly spiritual eating and drinking.

Here you may see what great things our theologians of the *Sentences*[90] have produced in this matter. In the first place, not one of them treats of that which is first and foremost, namely, the testament and the word of promise. And thus they make us forget faith and the whole power of the mass. In addition, they discuss exclusively the second part of the mass, namely, the sign or sacrament; yet in such a way that here too they do not teach faith, but their preparations and *opera operata*,[91] participations[92] and fruits of the mass. They come then to the profundities, babble of transub-

[89] Cf. p. 19 n. 33.

[90] Commentators on Peter Lombard's textbook. Cf. p. 29 n. 60.

[91] Cf. p. 37 n. 85.

[92] Cf. p. 35 n. 79.

stantiation and endless other metaphysical trivialities, destroy the proper understanding and use of both sacrament and testament together with faith as such, and cause Christ's people to forget their God—as the prophet says, days without number [Jer. 2:32]. Let the others tabulate the various benefits of hearing mass; you just apply your mind to this, that you may say and believe with the prophet that God has here prepared a table before you in the presence of your enemies [Ps. 23:5], at which your faith may feed and grow fat. But your faith is fed only with the word of divine promise, for "Man shall not live by bread alone, but by every word that proceeds from the mouth of God" [Deut. 8:3; Matt. 4:4]. Hence, in the mass you must pay closest heed above all to the word of promise, as to a most lavish banquet—your utterly green pastures and sacred still waters [Ps. 23:2], in order that you might esteem this word above everything else, trust in it supremely, and cling to it most firmly, even through death and all sins. If you do this, you will obtain not merely those tiny drops and crumbs of "fruits of the mass" which some have superstitiously invented, but the very fountainhead of life, namely, that faith in the Word out of which every good thing flows, as is said in John 4:[93] "He who believes in me, 'Out of his heart shall flow rivers of living water.'" And again, "Whoever drinks of the water that I shall give him, it will become in him a spring of water welling up to eternal life" [John 4:14].

Now there are two things that are constantly assailing us, so that we fail to gather the fruits of the mass. The first is that we are sinners, and unworthy of such great things because of our utter worthlessness. The second is that, even if we were worthy, these things are so high that our fainthearted nature does not dare to aspire to them or hope for them. For who would not simply stand awe-struck before the forgiveness of sins and life everlasting rather than seeking after them, once he had weighed properly the magnitude of the blessings which come through them, namely, to have God as father, to be his son and heir of all his goods! Against this twofold faintness of ours we must lay hold on the word of Christ, and fix our gaze much more steadfastly on it than on these thoughts of our own weakness. For "great are the works of the Lord, studied

[93] John 7:38. Luther apparently had his next quotation in mind when he cited John 4.

by all who have pleasure in them" [Ps. 111:2], who is able to give "more abundantly than all that we ask or think" [Eph. 3:20]. If they did not surpass our worthiness, our grasp, and all our thoughts, they would not be divine. Thus Christ also encourages us when he says: "Fear not, little flock, for it is your Father's good pleasure to give you the kingdom" [Luke 12:32]. For it is just this incomprehensible overflowing of God's goodness, showered upon us through Christ, that moves us above all to love him most ardently in return, to be drawn to him with fullest confidence, and, despising all else, be ready to suffer all things for him. Wherefore this sacrament is rightly called "a fountain of love."

Let us take an illustration of this from human experience.[94] If a very rich lord were to bequeath a thousand gulden to a beggar or to an unworthy and wicked servant, it is certain that he would boldly claim and accept them without regard to his unworthiness and the greatness of the bequest. And if anyone should seek to oppose him on the grounds of his unworthiness and the large amount of the legacy, what do you suppose the man would say? He would likely say: "What is that to you? What I accept, I accept not on my merits or by any right that I may personally have to it. I know that I am receiving more than a worthless one like me deserves; indeed, I have deserved the very opposite. But I claim what I claim by the right of a bequest and of another's goodness. If to him it was not an unworthy thing to bequeath so great a sum to an unworthy person, why should I refuse to accept it because of my unworthiness? Indeed, it is for this very reason that I cherish all the more his unmerited gift—because I am unworthy!" With that same thought every man ought to fortify his conscience against all qualms and scruples, so that he may lay hold on the promise of Christ with unwavering faith, and take the greatest care to approach the sacrament not trusting in confession, prayer, and preparation, but rather, despairing of all these, with firm confidence in Christ who gives the promise. For, as we have said often enough, the word of promise must reign alone here in pure faith; such faith is the one and only sufficient preparation.

Hence we see how great is God's wrath with us, in that he has

[94] Repeated in a similar context in *A Treatise on the New Testament that is the Holy Mass* (1520). *PE* 1, 304-305.

permitted godless teachers to conceal the words of this testament from us, and thereby to extinguish this same faith, as far as they could. It is already easy to see what is the inevitable result of this extinguishing of the faith, namely, the most godless superstition of works. For where faith dies and the word of faith is silent, there works and the prescribing of works immediately crowd into their place. By them we have been carried away out of our own land, as into a Babylonian captivity, and despoiled of all our precious possessions. This has been the fate of the mass; it has been converted by the teaching of godless men into a good work. They themselves call it an *opus operatum*,[95] and by it they presume themselves to be all-powerful with God. Next they proceed to the very height of madness, and after inventing the lie that the mass is effective simply by virtue of the act having been performed, they add another one to the effect that the mass is none the less profitable to others even if it is harmful to some wicked priest who may be celebrating it. On such a foundation of sand they base their applications, participations,[96] brotherhoods,[97] anniversaries,[98] and numberless other lucrative and profitable schemes of that kind.

These fraudulent disguises are so powerful, so numerous, and so firmly entrenched that you can scarcely prevail against them unless you exercise unremitting care and bear well in mind what the mass is and what has been said above. You have seen that the mass is nothing else than the divine promise or testament of Christ, sealed with the sacrament of his body and blood. If that is true, you will understand that it cannot possibly be in any way a work; nobody can possibly do any thing in it, neither can it be dealt with in any other way than by faith alone. However, faith is not a work, but the lord and life of all works.[99] Who in the world is so foolish as to regard a promise received by him, or a testament given to him, as a good work, which he renders to the testator by his acceptance of it? What heir will imagine that he is doing his departed father

[95] Cf. p. 37 n. 85.
[96] Cf. p. 35 n. 79.
[97] Cf. p. 35 n. 80.
[98] Cf. p. 36 n. 81.
[99] On the relation between faith and works compare *A Treatise on Good Works* (1520), where Luther says faith is the first and highest of all good works. *PE* 1, 187. Cf. also p. 62.

a kindness by accepting the terms of the will and the inheritance it bequeaths to him? What godless audacity is it, therefore, when we who are to receive the testament of God come as those who would perform a good work for him! This ignorance of the testament, this captivity of so great a sacrament—are they not too sad for tears? When we ought to be grateful for benefits received, we come arrogantly to give that which we ought to take. With unheard-of perversity we mock the mercy of the giver by giving as a work the thing we receive as a gift, so that the testator, instead of being a dispenser of his own goods, becomes the recipient of ours. Woe to such sacrilege!

Who has ever been so mad as to regard baptism as a good work, or what candidate for baptism has believed that he was performing a work which he might offer to God on behalf of himself and communicate to others? If, then, there is no good work that can be communicated to others in this one sacrament and testament, neither will there be any in the mass, since it too is nothing else than a testament and sacrament. Hence it is a manifest and wicked error to offer or apply the mass for sins, for satisfactions, for the dead, or for any needs whatsoever of one's own or of others. You will readily see the obvious truth of this if you firmly hold that the mass is a divine promise, which can benefit no one, be applied to no one, intercede for no one, and be communicated to no one, except only to him who believes with a faith of his own. Who can receive or apply, in behalf of another, the promise of God, which demands the personal faith of each one individually? Can I give to another the promise of God, even if he does not believe? Can I believe for another, or cause another to believe? But this is what must happen if I am able to apply and communicate the mass to others; for there are but two things in the mass, the divine promise and the human faith, the latter accepting what the former promises. But if it is true that I can do this, then I can also hear and believe the gospel for another, I can be baptized for another, I can be absolved from sins for another, I can also partake of the Sacrament of the Altar for another, and—to go through the list of their sacraments also—I can marry a wife for another, get ordained for another, be confirmed for another, and receive extreme unction for another!

In short, why did not Abraham believe for all the Jews? Why

was faith in the promise made to Abraham demanded of every individual Jew?

Therefore, let this irrefutable truth stand fast: Where there is a divine promise, there every one must stand on his own feet; his own personal faith is demanded, he will give an account for himself and bear his own load [Gal. 6:5]; as it is said in the last chapter of Mark [16:16]: "He who believes and is baptized will be saved; but he who does not believe will be condemned." Even so each one can derive personal benefit from the mass only by his own personal faith. It is absolutely impossible to commune on behalf of anyone else. Just as the priest is unable to administer the sacrament to anyone on behalf of another, but administers the same sacrament to each one individually by himself. For in consecrating and administering, the priests are our servants. Through them we are not offering a good work or communicating something in an active sense. Rather, we are receiving through them the promises and the sign; we are being communicated unto in the passive sense. This is the view that has persisted with respect to the laity right up to the present day, for of them it is said not that they do something good but that they receive it. But the priests have strayed into godless ways; out of the sacrament and testament of God, which ought to be a good gift received, they have made for themselves a good deed performed, which they then give to others and offer up to God.

But you will say: What is this? Will you not overturn the practice and teaching of all the churches and monasteries, by virtue of which they have flourished all these centuries? For the mass is the foundation of their anniversaries, intercessions, applications, communications, etc., that is to say, of their fat income. I answer: This is the very thing that has constrained me to write of the captivity of the church. For it is in this manner that the sacred testament of God has been forced into the service of a most impious traffic. It has come through the opinions and ordinances of wicked men, who, passing over the Word of God, have dished up to us the thoughts of their own hearts and led the whole world astray. What do I care about the number and influence of those who are in this error? The truth is mightier than all of them. If you are able to refute Christ, who teaches that the mass is a testament and a sacrament, then I will admit that they are in the right. Or, if you can bring yourself to say that that man is doing a good work who receives the benefit of the testament, or to that end uses this sacrament of promise, then I will gladly condemn my teachings. But since you can do neither, why do you hesitate to turn your back on the multitude who go after evil? Why do you hesitate to give God the glory and to confess his truth—that all priests today are perversely mistaken who regard the mass as a work by which they may relieve their own needs and those of others, whether dead or alive? I am uttering unheard of and startling things, but if you will consider what the mass is, you will realize that I have spoken the truth. The fault lies with our false sense of security, which blinds us to the wrath of God that is raging against us.

I am ready to admit, however, that the prayers which we pour out before God when we are gathered together to partake of the mass are good works or benefits, which we impart, apply and communicate to one another, and which we offer for one another. Thus James [5:16] teaches us to pray for one another that we may be healed, and Paul in I Tim. 2 [:1-2] commands "that supplications, prayers, and intercessions be made for all men, for kings and all who are in high positions." Now these are not the mass, but works of the mass—if the prayers of heart and lips may be called works—for they flow from the faith that is kindled or increased in the sacrament. For the mass, or the promise of God, is not fulfilled by praying, but only by believing. However, as believers we pray and perform every good work. But what priest offers up the sacrifice in this sense, that he believes he is offering up only the prayers? They all imagine that they are offering up Christ himself to God the Father as an all-sufficient sacrifice, and performing a good work for all those whom they intend to benefit, for they put their trust in the work which the mass accomplishes, and they do not ascribe this work to prayer. In this way the error has gradually grown, until they have come to ascribe to the sacrament what belongs to the prayers, and to offer to God what should be received as a benefit.

We must therefore sharply distinguish the testament and sacrament itself from the prayers which we offer at the same time. Not only this, but we must also bear in mind that the prayers avail utterly nothing, either to him who offers them or to those for whom they are offered, unless the testament is first received in faith, so that it will be faith that offers the prayers; for faith alone is heard, as James teaches in his first chapter [Jas. 1:6]. There is therefore a great difference between prayer and the mass. Prayer may be extended to as many persons as one desires, while the mass is received only by the person who believes for himself, and only to the extent that he believes. It cannot be given either to God or to men. Rather it is God alone who through the ministration of the priest gives it to men, and men receive it by faith alone without any works or merits. Nor would anyone dare to be so foolish as to assert that a ragged beggar does a good work when he comes to receive a gift from a rich man. But the mass (as I have said)[100] is the gift of the divine promise, proffered to all men by the hand of the priest.

It is certain, therefore, that the mass is not a work which may be communicated to others, but the object of faith (as has been said),[101] for the strengthening and nourishing of each one's own faith.

Now there is yet a second stumbling block that must be removed, and this is much greater and the most dangerous of all. It is the common belief that the mass is a sacrifice, which is offered to God. Even the words of the canon[102] seem to imply this, when they speak of "these gifts, these presents, these holy sacrifices," and further on "this offering." Prayer is also made, in so many words, "that the sacrifice may be accepted even as the sacrifice of Abel," etc. Hence Christ is termed "the sacrifice of the altar." Added to these are the sayings of the holy fathers, the great number of examples, and the widespread practice uniformly observed throughout the world.

Over against all these things, firmly entrenched as they are, we must resolutely set the words and example of Christ. For unless we firmly hold that the mass is the promise or testament of Christ, as the words clearly say, we shall lose the whole gospel and all its comfort. Let us permit nothing to prevail against these words—

---

[100] Cf. pp. 38-43.

[101] *Ibid.*

[102] The canon of the mass is the invariable part of the liturgy of the mass in which the consecration of the bread and wine is effected. Its text was translated by Luther from the Latin in his treatise on *The Abomination of the Secret Mass* (1525), and appears on pp. 314-327 in this volume.

even though an angel from heaven should teach otherwise [Gal. 1:8]—for they contain nothing about a work or a sacrifice. Moreover, we also have the example of Christ on our side. When he instituted this sacrament and established this testament at the Last Supper, Christ did not offer himself to God the Father, nor did he perform a good work on behalf of others, but, sitting at the table, he set this same testament before each one and proffered to him the sign. Now, the more closely our mass resembles that first mass of all, which Christ performed at the Last Supper, the more Christian it will be. But Christ's mass was most simple, without any display of vestments, gestures, chants, or other ceremonies, so that if it had been necessary to offer the mass as a sacrifice, then Christ's institution of it was not complete.

Not that any one should revile the church universal for embellishing and amplifying the mass with many additional rites and ceremonies. But what we contend for is this: No one should be deceived by the glamor of the ceremonies and entangled in the multitude of pompous forms, and thus lose the simplicity of the mass itself, and indeed practice a sort of transubstantiation by losing sight of the simple "substance" of the mass and clinging to the manifold "accidents" of outward pomp. For whatever has been added to the word and example of Christ is an "accident" of the mass, and ought to be regarded just as we regard the so-called monstrances and corporal cloths in which the host itself is contained. Therefore, just as distributing a testament or accepting a promise differs diametrically from offering a sacrifice, so it is a contradiction in terms to call the mass a sacrifice, for the former is something that we receive and the latter is something that we give. The same thing cannot be received and offered at the same time, nor can it be both given and accepted by the same person, any more than our prayer can be the same thing as that which our prayer obtains, or the act of praying be the same thing as the act of receiving that for which we pray.

What shall we say then of the canon of the mass and the patristic authorities? First of all, I would answer: If there were nothing at all to be said against them, it would be safer to reject them all than admit that the mass is a work or a sacrifice, lest we deny the word of Christ and destroy faith together with the mass.

Nevertheless, in order to retain them, we shall say that we are instructed by the Apostle in I Cor. 11 [:21, 33] that it was customary for Christ's believers, when they came together for mass, to bring with them food and drink. These they called "collections," and they distributed them among all who were in want, after the example of the apostles in Acts 4 [:34-35]. From this store was taken the portion of the bread and wine that was consecrated in the sacrament. And since all this store was consecrated by the word and prayer [I Tim. 4:5], by being "lifted up" according to the Hebrew rite of which we read in Moses [Num. 18:30–32],[103] the words and rite of this lifting up or offering have come down to us, although the custom of bringing along and collecting that which was offered or lifted up has long since fallen into disuse. Thus, in Isa. 37 [:4] Hezekiah commanded Isaiah to lift up his prayer in the sight of God for the remnant. In the Psalms we read: "Lift up your hands to the holy place" [Ps. 134:2]. And again: "To thee I will lift up my hands" [Ps. 63:4]. And in I Tim. 2 [:8]: "In every place lifting holy hands." For this reason the words "sacrifice" and "offering" must be taken to refer not to the sacrament and testament, but to the collections themselves. From this source also the word "collect" has come down to us for the prayers said in the mass.

The same thing happens when the priest elevates the bread and the cup immediately after consecrating them. By this he does not show that he is offering anything to God, for he does not say a single word here about a victim or an offering. But this elevation is either a survival of that Hebrew rite of lifting up what was received with thanksgiving and returned to God, or else it is an admonition to us to provoke us to faith in this testament which the priest has set forth and exhibited in the words of Christ, so that now he also shows us the sign of the testament. Thus the oblation of the bread properly accompanies the demonstrative "this" in the words, "this is my body," and by the sign the priest addresses us gathered about him; and in a like manner the oblation of the cup properly accompanies the demonstrative "this" in the words, "this cup is the new testament, etc." For it is faith that the priest ought to awaken in us by this act of elevation. And would to God that as he elevates the sign, or sacrament, openly before our eyes, he might

[103] Cf. *LW* 35, 95, n. 24

also sound in our ears the word, or testament, in a loud, clear voice, and in the language of the people, whatever it may be, in order that faith may be the more effectively awakened. For why may mass be said in Greek and Latin and Hebrew, but not in German or any other language?

Therefore, let the priests who offer the sacrifice of the mass in these corrupt and most perilous times take heed, first, that they do not refer to the sacrament the words of the greater and lesser canon,[104] together with the collects, because they smack too strongly of sacrifice. They should refer them instead to the bread and the wine to be consecrated, or to their own prayers. For the bread and wine are offered beforehand for blessing in order that they may be sanctified by the word and by prayer [I Tim. 4:5], but after they have been blessed and consecrated they are no longer offered, but received as a gift from God. And in this rite let the priest bear in mind that the gospel is to be set above all canons and collects devised by men, and that the gospel does not sanction the idea that the mass is a sacrifice, as has been shown.

Further, when a priest celebrates public mass, he should determine to do nothing else than to commune himself and others by means of the mass. At the same time, however, he may offer prayers for himself and others, but he must beware lest he presume to offer the mass. But let him that holds private masses[105] determine to commune himself. The private mass does not differ in the least from the ordinary communion which any layman receives at the hand of the priest, and has no greater effect. The difference is in the prayers, and in the fact that the priest consecrates the elements for himself and administers them to himself. As far as the blessing[106] of the mass and sacrament is concerned we are all equals, whether we are priests or laymen.

---

[104] In printed missals prior to the Council of Trent, *canon minor* was the term used to designate collectively those offertory prayers within the canon itself which immediately preceded the consecration of the elements. These collects were of comparatively late origin, coming only gradually into use during the late middle ages. Valentin Thalhofer, *Handbuch der katholischen Liturgik* (Freiburg im Breisgau, 1890), II, 159.

[105] The private mass does not require the presence of a congregation. Besides the celebrant there need be present only a ministrant. There is no music; the mass is only read.

[106] The *res sacramenti*. Cf. p. 23 n. 45.

If a priest is requested by others to celebrate so-called "votive" masses,[107] let him beware of accepting a fee for the mass, or of presuming to offer any votive sacrifice. Rather, he should take pains to refer all this to the prayers which he offers for the dead or the living, saying to himself: "Lo, I will go and receive the sacrament for myself alone, and while doing so I will pray for this one and that one." Thus he will receive his fee for the prayers, not for the mass, and can buy food and clothing with it. Let him not be disturbed because all the world holds and practices the contrary. You have the utmost certainty of the gospel, and by relying on it, you may well disregard the belief and opinions of men. But if you disregard me and insist upon offering the mass and not the prayers alone, remember that I have faithfully warned you, and that I will be without blame on the day of judgment; you will have to bear your sin alone. I have said what I was bound to say to you as brother to brother for your salvation; yours will be the gain if you observe it, yours the loss if you neglect it. And if some should even condemn what I have said, I will reply in the words of Paul: "But evil men and impostors will go on from bad to worse, deceiving and being deceived" [II Tim 3:13].

From the above every one will readily understand the often quoted saying of Gregory[108]: "A mass celebrated by a wicked priest is not to be considered of less effect than one celebrated by a good priest. Neither would a mass of St. Peter have been better than that of Judas the traitor, if they had offered the sacrifice of the mass." This saying has served many as a cloak to cover their godless doings, and because of it they have invented the distinction between the *opus operatum* and the *opus operantis*,[109] so as to be free to lead wicked lives themselves and yet benefit other men. Gregory speaks the truth, only they misunderstand his words. For it is true beyond a question that the testament or sacrament is given and received through the ministration of wicked priests no less completely

[107] Masses celebrated on the request of congregations or individuals in connection with specific purposes or occasions, or in honor of certain mysteries (e.g., of the Holy Trinity, of the Holy Spirit, or of angels).

[108] Pope Gregory I (590-604).

[109] The former is the properly executed performance of the ritual of the mass—"the work wrought" (cf. p. 37 n. 85). The latter is the inner disposition, the faith, either of the recipient or of the celebrant—"the work of the doer."

than through the ministration of the most saintly. For who has any doubt that the gospel is preached by the ungodly? Now the mass is part of the gospel; indeed, it is the sum and substance of it. For what is the whole gospel but the good tidings of the forgiveness of sins? Whatever can be said about forgiveness of sins and the mercy of God in the broadest and richest sense is all briefly comprehended in the word of this testament. For this reason popular sermons ought to be nothing else than expositions of the mass, or explanations of the divine promise of this testament; this would be to teach the faith and truly to edify the church. But in our day the expounders of the mass make mockery and jest with allegorical explanations of human ceremonies.

Therefore, just as a wicked priest may baptize, that is, apply the word of promise and the sign of water to the candidate for baptism, so he may also set forth the promise of this sacrament and administer it to those who partake, and even partake himself, as did Judas the traitor at the supper of the Lord [Matt. 26:23-25]. It still remains the same sacrament and testament, which works its own work in the believer but an "alien work" [110] in the unbeliever. But when it comes to offering a sacrifice the case is quite different. For not the mass but the prayers are offered to God, and therefore it is as plain as day that the offerings of a wicked priest avail nothing, but, as Gregory says again: When an unworthy person is sent as the intercessor, the heart of the judge is only turned to greater disfavor. Therefore these two things—mass and prayer, sacrament and work, testament and sacrifice—must not be confused; for the one comes from God to us through the ministration of the priest and demands our faith, the other proceeds from our faith to God through the priest and demands his hearing. The former descends, the latter ascends. The former, therefore, does not necessarily require a worthy and godly minister, but the latter does indeed require such a one, for "God does not listen to sinners" [John 9:31]. He knows how to do good through evil men, but he does not accept the work of any evil man; as he showed in the case of Cain [Gen. 4:5], and as is said in Prov. 15 [:8]: "The sacrifice of the wicked is

[110] Its own work is salvation. The "alien work" is condemnation. The expression derives from Isa. 28:21.

an abomination to the Lord," and in Rom. 14 [:23]: "Whatever does not proceed from faith is sin."

But let us bring this first part to an end, though I am ready to go on with the argument if an opponent should arise. From all that has been said we conclude that the mass was provided only for those who have a sad, afflicted, disturbed, perplexed and erring conscience, and that they alone commune worthily. For, since the word of divine promise in this sacrament sets forth the forgiveness of sins, let every one draw near fearlessly, whoever he may be, who is troubled by his sins, whether by remorse or by temptation. For this testament of Christ is the one remedy against sins, past, present and future, if you but cling to it with unwavering faith and believe that what the words of the testament declare is freely granted to you. But if you do not believe this, you will never, anywhere, by any works or efforts of your own, be able to find peace of conscience. For faith alone means peace of conscience. while unbelief means only distress of conscience.

The Sacrament of Baptism

Blessed be God and the Father of our Lord Jesus Christ, who according to the riches of his mercy [Eph. 1:3, 7] has preserved in his church this sacrament at least, untouched and untainted by the ordinances of men, and has made it free to all nations and classes of mankind, and has not permitted it to be oppressed by the filthy and godless monsters of greed and superstition. For he desired that by it little children, who were incapable of greed and superstition, might be initiated and sanctified in the simple faith of his Word; even today baptism has its chief blessing for them. But if the intention had been to give this sacrament to adults and older people, I do not believe that it could possibly have retained its power and its glory against the tyranny of greed and superstition which has overthrown all things divine among us. Here too the wisdom of the flesh would doubtless have devised its preparations and dignities, its reservations, restrictions, and other like snares for catching money, until water brought as high a price as parchment[111] does now.

But Satan, though he could not quench the power of baptism in

[111] Letters of indulgence.

little children, nevertheless succeeded in quenching it in all adults, so that now there are scarcely any who call to mind their own baptism, and still fewer who glory in it; so many other ways have been discovered for remitting sins and getting to heaven. The source of these false opinions is that dangerous saying of St. Jerome[112]—either unhappily phrased or wrongly interpreted—in which he terms penance "the second plank after shipwreck," as if baptism were not penance. Hence, when men have fallen into sin, they despair of the "first plank," which is the ship, as if it had gone under, and begin to put all their trust and faith in the second plank, which is penance. This has given rise to those endless burdens of vows, religious orders, works, satisfactions, pilgrimages, indulgences, and monastic sects, and from them in turn has arisen that flood of books, questions, opinions, and man-made ordinances which the whole world cannot contain. Thus the church of God is incomparably worse off under this tyranny than the synagogue or any other nation under heaven ever was.

It was the duty of the pontiffs to remove all these evils and to put forth every effort to recall Christians to the true understanding of baptism, so that they might know what manner of men they were and how Christians ought to live. But instead of this, their only work today is to lead the people as far astray as possible from their baptism, to immerse all men in the flood of their tyranny, and to cause the people of Christ (as the prophet says) to forget him days without number [Jer. 2:32]. How unregenerate are all who bear the name of pontiff today! For they neither know nor do what is becoming to pontiffs, but they are ignorant of what they ought to know and do. They fulfil what Isa. 56 [:10, 11] says: "His watchmen are blind, they are all without knowledge; the shepherds also have no understanding; they have all turned to their own way, each to his own gain, etc."

Now, the *first* thing to be considered about baptism is the divine promise, which says: "He who believes and is baptized will be saved" [Mark 16:16]. This promise must be set far above all the

[112] St. Jerome (d. 420), ascetic, zealous exponent of the monastic life, prolific writer against the heretics, translator of an important Latin version of the Bible, was also the author of many letters—to one of which Luther is referring. *Epistola* 130, par. 9. Migne 22, 1115.

glitter of works, vows, religious orders, and whatever else man has introduced, for on it all our salvation depends. But we must so consider it as to exercise our faith in it, and have no doubt whatever that, once we have been baptized, we are saved. For unless faith is present or is conferred in baptism, baptism will profit us nothing; indeed, it will become a hindrance to us, not only at the moment when it is received, but throughout the rest of our lives. That kind of unbelief accuses God's promise of being a lie, and this is the greatest of all sins. If we set ourselves to this exercise of faith, we shall at once perceive how difficult it is to believe this promise of God. For our human weakness, conscious of its sins, finds nothing more difficult to believe than that it is saved or will be saved; and yet, unless it does believe this, it cannot be saved, because it does not believe the truth of God that promises salvation.

This message should have been impressed upon the people untiringly, and this promise should have been dinned into their ears without ceasing. Their baptism should have been called to their minds again and again, and their faith constantly awakened and nourished. For just as the truth of this divine promise, once pronounced over us, continues until death, so our faith in it ought never to cease, but to be nourished and strengthened until death by the continual remembrance of this promise made to us in baptism. Therefore, when we rise from our sins or repent, we are merely returning to the power and the faith of baptism from which we fell, and finding our way back to the promise then made to us, which we deserted when we sinned. For the truth of the promise once made remains steadfast, always ready to receive us back with open arms when we return. And this, if I mistake not, is what they mean when they say, though obscurely, that baptism is the first sacrament and the foundation of all the others, without which none of the others can be received.

It will therefore be no small gain to a penitent to remember above all his baptism, and, confidently calling to mind the divine promise which he has forsaken, acknowledge that promise before his Lord, rejoicing that he is still within the fortress of salvation because he has been baptized, and abhorring his wicked ingratitude in falling away from its faith and truth. His heart will find wonderful comfort and will be encouraged to hope for mercy when he considers that the promise which God made to him, which cannot possibly lie, is still unbroken and unchanged, and indeed, cannot be changed by sins, as Paul says (II Tim. 2 [:13]): "If we are faithless, he remains faithful—for he cannot deny himself." This truth of God, I say, will sustain him, so that if all else should fail, this truth, if he believes in it, will not fail him. In it the penitent has a shield against all assaults of the scornful enemy, an answer to the sins that disturb his conscience, an antidote for the dread of death and judgment, and a comfort in every temptation—namely, this one truth—when he says: "God is faithful in his promises [Heb. 10:23; 11:11], and I received his sign in baptism. If God is for me, who is against me?" [Rom. 8:31].

The children of Israel, whenever they turned to repentance, remembered above all their exodus from Egypt, and remembering turned back to God who had brought them out. Moses impressed this memory and this protection upon them many times, and David afterwards did the same. How much more ought we to remember our exodus from Egypt, and by this remembrance turn back to him who led us through the washing of regeneration [Titus 3:5], remembrance of which is commended to us for this very reason! This can be done most fittingly in the sacrament of bread and wine. Indeed, in former times these three sacraments—penance, baptism, and the bread—were all celebrated at the same service, and each one supplemented the other. We also read of a certain holy virgin[113] who in every time of temptation made baptism her sole defense, saying simply, "I am a Christian"; and immediately the enemy recognized the power of baptism and of her faith, which clung to the truth of a promising God, and fled from her.

Thus you see how rich a Christian is, that is, one who has been baptized! Even if he would, he could not lose his salvation, however much he sinned, unless he refused to believe. For no sin can condemn him save unbelief alone. All other sins, so long as the faith in God's promise made in baptism returns or remains, are immediately blotted out through that same faith, or rather through the truth of God, because he cannot deny himself if you confess

[113] This may be a reference to Blandina, a young slave and Christian martyr, whose courage during the persecution under the Roman emperor, Marcus Aurelius (161-180), was extolled by Eusebius. *CL* 1, 462.

him and faithfully cling to him in his promise. But as for contrition, confession of sins, and satisfaction,[114] along with all those carefully devised exercises of men: if you rely on them and neglect this truth of God, they will suddenly fail you and leave you more wretched than before. For whatever is done without faith in God's truth is vanity of vanities and vexation of spirit [Eccles. 1:2, 14].

You will likewise see how perilous, indeed, how false it is to suppose that penance is "the second plank after shipwreck,"[115] and how pernicious an error it is to believe that the power of baptism is broken, and the ship dashed to pieces, because of sin. The ship remains one, solid, and invincible; it will never be broken up into separate "planks." In it are carried all those who are brought to the harbor of salvation, for it is the truth of God giving us its promise in the sacraments. Of course, it often happens that many rashly leap overboard into the sea and perish; these are those who abandon faith in the promise and plunge into sin. But the ship itself remains intact and holds its course unimpaired. If any one is able somehow by grace to return to the ship, it is not on any plank, but in the solid ship itself that he is borne to life. Such a person is the one who returns through faith to the abiding and enduring promise of God. Therefore Peter, in II Pet. 1 [:9], rebukes those who sin, because they have forgotten that they were cleansed from their old sins, and he clearly rebukes their wicked unbelief and their ingratitude for the baptism they had received.

What is the good, then, of writing so much about baptism and yet not teaching this faith in the promise? All the sacraments were instituted to nourish faith. Yet these godless men pass over it so completely as even to assert that a man dare not be certain of the forgiveness of sins or the grace of the sacraments. With such wicked teaching they delude the world, and not only take captive, but altogether destroy, the sacrament of baptism, in which the chief glory of our conscience consists. Meanwhile they madly rage against the miserable souls of men with their contritions, anxious confessions, circumstances,[116] satisfactions, works, and endless other

[114] The three parts of the sacrament of penance.

[115] Cf. p. 58 n. 112.

[116] The penitent had to relate the conditions attendant upon his transgression to help the priest determine his state of heart and degree of guilt. Cf. Buchwald, *op. cit.*, II, 433 n. 1.

such absurdities. Therefore read with great caution the "Master of the *Sentences*" [117] in his fourth book; better yet, despise him with all his commentators, who at their best write only of the "matter" and "form" [118] of the sacraments; that is, they treat of the dead and death-dealing letter [II Cor. 3:6] of the sacraments, but leave untouched the spirit, life, and use, that is, the truth of the divine promise and our faith.

Beware, therefore, that the external pomp of works and the deceits of man-made ordinances do not deceive you, lest you wrong the divine truth and your faith. If you would be saved, you must begin with the faith of the sacraments, without any works whatever. The works will follow faith, but do not think too lightly of faith, for it is the most excellent and difficult of all works.[119] Through it alone you will be saved, even if you should be compelled to do without any other works. For faith is a work of God, not of man, as Paul teaches [Eph. 2:8]. The other works he works through us and with our help, but this one alone he works in us and without our help.

From this we can clearly see the difference in baptism between man who administers the sacrament and God who is its author. For man baptizes, and yet does not baptize. He baptizes in that he performs the work of immersing the person to be baptized; he does not baptize, because in so doing he acts not on his own authority but in God's stead. Hence we ought to receive baptism at human hands just as if Christ himself, indeed, God himself, were baptizing us with his own hands. For it is not man's baptism, but Christ's and God's baptism, which we receive by the hand of a man, just as everything else that we have through the hand of somebody else is God's alone. Therefore beware of making any distinction in baptism by ascribing the outward part to man and the inward part to God. Ascribe both to God alone, and look upon the person administering it as simply the vicarious instrument of God, by which the Lord sitting in heaven thrusts you under the water with his own hands, and promises you forgiveness of your

117 Cf. p. 29 n. 60.

118 These terms, derived from the philosophy of Aristotle, were introduced by scholastic theologians of the thirteenth century into their explanations of the sacraments. Matter was the sign, e.g., water in baptism. Form was the word, e.g., the Words of Institution.

119 Cf. p. 47 n. 99.

sins, speaking to you upon earth with a human voice by the mouth of his minister.

This the words themselves indicate, when the priest says: "I baptize you in the name of the Father, and of the Son, and of the Holy Ghost. Amen," and not: "I baptize you in my own name." It is as though he said: "What I do, I do not by my own authority, but in the name and stead of God, so that you should regard it just as if our Lord himself had done it in a visible manner. The Doer and the minister are different persons, but the work of both is the same work, or rather, it is the work of the Doer alone, through my ministry." For I hold that "in the name of" refers to the person of the Doer, so that the name of the Lord is not only to be uttered and invoked while the work is being done; but the work itself is to be done as something not one's own—in the name and stead of Another. In this sense Christ says in Matt. 24 [:5], "Many will come in my name," and Rom. 1 [:5] says, "Through whom we have received grace and apostleship to bring about obedience for the sake of his name among all the nations."

This view I heartily endorse, for there is great comfort and a mighty aid to faith in the knowledge that one has been baptized, not by man, but by the Triune God himself, through a man acting among us in His name. This will put an end to that idle dispute about the "form" of baptism, as they term the words which are used. The Greeks say: "May the servant of Christ be baptized," while the Latins say: "I baptize."[120] Others again, adhering rigidly to their pedantry, condemn the use of the words, "I baptize you in the name of Jesus Christ,"[121] although it is certain the apostles used this formula in baptizing, as we read in the Acts of the Apostles [2:38; 10:48; 19:5]; they would allow no other form to be valid than this: "I baptize you in the name of the Father, and of the Son, and of the Holy Ghost. Amen." But their contention is in vain, for they bring no proof, but merely assert their own dreams. Baptism truly saves in whatever way it is administered, if only it is administered not in the name of man, but in the name of the Lord. Indeed, I have

[120] Cf. p. 24 n. 47. The dispute had already been decided by the fifteenth-century popes: Eugene IV, Sixtus IV, and Alexander VI, who accepted the validity of the imperative or deprecatory formula of the Eastern church.

[121] Alexander of Hales (d. 1245) denied the validity of baptism "in the name of Jesus"; Peter Lombard defended it

no doubt that if anyone receives baptism in the name of the Lord, even if the wicked minister should not give it in the name of the Lord, he would yet be truly baptized in the name of the Lord. For the power of baptism depends not so much on the faith or use of the one who confers it as on the faith or use of the one who receives it. We have an example of this in the story of a certain actor who was baptized in jest.[122] These and similar perplexing disputes and questions are raised for us by those who ascribe nothing to faith and everything to works and rituals, whereas we owe everything to faith alone and nothing to rituals. Faith makes us free in spirit from all those scruples and fancies.

The *second* part of baptism is the sign, or sacrament, which is that immersion in water from which it derives its name, for the Greek *baptizo* means "I immerse," and *baptisma* means "immersion." For, as has been said, along with the divine promises signs have also been given to picture that which the words signify, or as they now say, that which the sacrament "effectively signifies." We shall see how much truth there is in this.

A great majority have supposed that there is some hidden spiritual power in the word and water, which works the grace of God in the soul of the recipient. Others deny this and hold that there is no power in the sacraments, but that grace is given by God alone, who according to his covenant is present in the sacraments which he has instituted.[123] Yet all are agreed that the sacraments are "effective signs" of grace, and they reach this conclusion by this one argument: if the sacraments of the New Law were mere signs, there would be no apparent reason why they should surpass those of the Old Law. Hence they have been driven to attribute such great

---

[122] Mentioned also in Luther's *Explanations of the Ninety-five Theses*, *LW* 31, 105, the incident is more fully described in a sermon on Matthew 18, *WA* 47, 302-303. The court jester of a certain Roman emperor, in mockery of the Christian sacrament, had himself liberally drenched in public. But while the spectators guffawed, the fool was converted through the appearance of an angel showing him a book in which were written the words of Eph. 4:5-6. He acknowledged the mock baptism to be valid, confessed Christ, and was martyred.

[123] A point at issue among the scholastics of the Middle Ages. Some held that the grace of the sacrament was contained in the sacramental sign and directly imparted through it; thus Hugo of St. Victor. Others contended that the sign was merely a symbol, but that God, according to a *pactio*, or agreement, imparted the grace of the sacrament when the sign was being used; thus Bonaventura, and especially Duns Scotus.

powers to the sacraments of the New Law that they think the sacraments benefit even those who are in mortal sin; neither faith nor grace are required—it is sufficient that no obstacle be set in the way, that is, no actual intention to sin again.

Such views, however, must be carefully avoided and shunned, because they are godless and infidel, contrary to faith and inconsistent with the nature of the sacraments. For it is an error to hold that the sacraments of the New Law differ from those of the Old Law in the effectiveness of their signs. For in this respect they are the same. The same God who now saves us by baptism and the bread, saved Abel by his sacrifice, Noah by the rainbow, Abraham by circumcision, and all the others by their respective signs. So far as the signs are concerned, there is no difference between a sacrament of the Old Law and one of the New, provided that by the Old Law you mean that which God did among the patriarchs and other fathers in the days of the Law. But those signs which were given to the patriarchs and fathers must be clearly distinguished from the legal symbols [*figurae*] which Moses instituted in his law, such as the priestly usages concerning vestments, vessels, foods, houses, and the like. For these are vastly different, not only from the sacraments of the New Law, but also from those signs which God occasionally gave to the fathers living under the law, such as the sign of Gideon's fleece [Judg. 6:36-40], Manoah's sacrifice [Judg. 13:16-23], or that which Isaiah offered to Ahaz in Isa. 7 [:10-14]. In each of these alike some promise was given which required faith in God.

The difference, then, between the legal symbols and the new and old signs is that the legal symbols do not have attached to them any word of promise requiring faith. Hence they are not signs of justification, for they are not sacraments of the faith that alone justifies, but only sacraments of works. Their whole power and nature consisted in works, not in faith. Whoever performed them fulfilled them, even if he did it without faith. But our signs or sacraments, as well as those of the fathers, have attached to them a word of promise which requires faith, and they cannot be fulfilled by any other work. Hence they are signs or sacraments of justification, for they are sacraments of justifying faith and not of works. Their whole efficacy, therefore, consists in faith itself, not in the doing of a work. Whoever believes them, fulfils them, even if he should not do a single work. This is the origin of the saying: "Not the sacrament, but the faith of the sacrament, justifies." Thus circumcision did not justify Abraham and his seed, and yet the Apostle calls it the seal of the righteousness by faith [Rom. 4:11], because faith in the promise, to which circumcision was added, justified him and fulfilled what the circumcision signified. For faith was the spiritual circumcision of the foreskin of the heart [Deut. 10:16; Jer. 4:4], which was symbolized by the literal circumcision of the flesh. In the same way it was obviously not Abel's sacrifice that justified him, but it was his faith [Heb. 11:4] by which he offered himself wholly to God, and this was symbolized by the outward sacrifice.

Thus it is not baptism that justifies or benefits anyone, but it is faith in that word of promise to which baptism is added. This faith justifies, and fulfils that which baptism signifies. For faith is the submersion of the old man and the emerging of the new [Eph. 4:22-24; Col. 3:9-10]. Therefore the new sacraments cannot differ from the old sacraments, for both alike have the divine promises and the same spirit of faith, although they do differ vastly from the old symbols—on account of the word of promise, which is the sole effective means of distinguishing them. Even so, today, the outward show of vestments, holy places, foods, and all the endless ceremonies doubtless symbolize excellent things to be fulfilled in the spirit, yet, because there is no word of divine promise attached to these things, they can in no way be compared with the signs of baptism and the bread. Neither do they justify, nor benefit one in any way, since they are fulfilled in their very observance, even in their observance apart from faith. For while they are taking place, or being performed, they are being fulfilled, as the Apostle says of them in Col. 2 [:22]: "Which all perish as they are used, according to human precepts and doctrines." The sacraments, on the contrary, are not fulfilled when they are taking place, but when they are being believed.

It cannot be true, therefore, that there is contained in the sacraments a power efficacious for justification, or that they are "effective signs" of grace. All such things are said to the detriment of faith, and out of ignorance of the divine promise. Unless you should call them "effective" in the sense that they certainly and effectively impart grace where faith is unmistakably present. But it is not in this sense that efficacy is now ascribed to them; as witness the fact that they are said to benefit all men, even the wicked and unbelieving, provided they do not set an obstacle in the way—as if such unbelief were not in itself the most obstinate and hostile of all obstacles to grace. To such an extent have they exerted themselves to turn the sacrament into a command and faith into a work. For if the sacrament confers grace on me because I receive it, then indeed I receive grace by virtue of my work, and not by faith; and I gain not the promise in the sacrament but only the sign instituted and commanded by God. Thus you see clearly how completely the sacraments have been misunderstood by the theologians of the *Sentences*. In their discussions of the sacraments they have taken no account either of faith or of promise. They cling only to the sign and the use of the sign, and draw us away from faith to the work, away from the word to the sign. Thus, as I have said,[124] they have not only taken the sacraments captive, but have completely destroyed them, as far as they were able.

Therefore let us open our eyes and learn to pay heed more to the word than to the sign, more to faith than to the work or use of the sign. We know that wherever there is a divine promise, there faith is required, and that these two are so necessary to each other that neither can be effective apart from the other. For it is not possible to believe unless there is a promise, and the promise is not established unless it is believed. But where these two meet, they give a real and most certain efficacy to the sacraments. Hence, to seek the efficacy of the sacrament apart from the promise and apart from the faith is to labor in vain and to find condemnation. Thus Christ says: "He who believes and is baptized will be saved; but he who does not believe will be condemned" [Mark 16:16]. He shows us in this word that faith is such a necessary part of the sacrament that it can save even without the sacrament, and for this reason he did not add: "He who does not believe, and is not baptized."

Baptism, then, signifies two things—death and resurrection, that is, full and complete justification. When the minister immerses

[124] Cf. p. 61.

the child in the water it signifies death, and when he draws it forth again it signifies life. Thus Paul expounds it in Rom. 6 [:4]: "We were buried therefore with Christ by baptism into death, so that as Christ was raised from the dead by the glory of the Father, we too might walk in newness of life." This death and resurrection we call the new creation, regeneration, and spiritual birth. This should not be understood only allegorically as the death of sin and the life of grace, as many understand it, but as actual death and resurrection. For baptism is not a false sign. Neither does sin completely die, nor grace completely rise, until the sinful body that we carry about in this life is destroyed, as the Apostle says in the same passage [Rom. 6:6-7]. For as long as we are in the flesh, the desires of the flesh stir and are stirred. For this reason, as soon as we begin to believe, we also begin to die to this world and live to God in the life to come; so that faith is truly a death and a resurrection, that is, it is that spiritual baptism into which we are submerged and from which we rise.

It is therefore indeed correct to say that baptism is a washing away of sins, but the expression is too mild and weak to bring out the full significance of baptism, which is rather a symbol of death and resurrection. For this reason I would have those who are to be baptized completely immersed in the water, as the word says[125] and as the mystery indicates. Not because I deem this necessary, but because it would be well to give to a thing[126] so perfect and complete a sign that is also complete and perfect. And this is doubtless the way in which it was instituted by Christ. The sinner does not so much need to be washed as he needs to die, in order to be wholly renewed and made another creature, and to be conformed to the death and resurrection of Christ, with whom he dies and rises again through baptism. Although you may say that when Christ died and rose again he was washed clean of mortality, that is a less forceful way of putting it than if you said that he was completely changed and renewed. Similarly it is far more forceful to say that baptism signifies that we die in every way and rise to eternal life, than to say that it signifies merely that we are washed clean of sins.

[125] Cf. p. 64, above, and *PE* 1, 56.
[126] *res;* cf. p. 23 n. 45, above.

Here again you see that the sacrament of baptism, even with respect to its sign, is not a matter of the moment, but something permanent. Although the ceremony itself is soon over the thing it signifies continues until we die, yes, even until we rise on the last day. For as long as we live we are continually doing that which baptism signifies, that is, we die and rise again. We die, not only mentally and spiritually by renouncing the sins and vanities of this world, but in very truth we begin to leave this bodily life and to lay hold on the life to come, so that there is, as they say, a "real" and bodily passing out of this world unto the Father.

We must therefore beware of those who have reduced the power of baptism to such small and slender dimensions that, while they say grace is indeed inpoured by it, they maintain that afterwards it is poured out again through sin, and that then one must reach heaven by another way, as if baptism had now become entirely useless. Do not hold such a view, but understand that this is the significance of baptism, that through it you die and live again. Therefore, whether by penance or by any other way, you can only return to the power of your baptism, and do again that which you were baptized to do and which your baptism signified. Baptism never becomes useless, unless you despair and refuse to return to its salvation. You may indeed wander away from the sign for a time, but the sign is not therefore useless. Thus, you have been once baptized in the sacrament, but you need continually to be baptized by faith, continually to die and continually to live. Baptism swallowed up your whole body and gave it forth again; in the same way that which baptism signifies should swallow up your whole life, body and soul, and give it forth again at the last day, clad in the robe of glory and immortality. We are therefore never without the sign of baptism nor without the thing it signifies. Indeed, we need continually to be baptized more and more, until we fulfil the sign perfectly at the last day.

You will understand, therefore, that whatever we do in this life which mortifies the flesh or quickens the spirit has to do with our baptism. The sooner we depart this life, the more speedily we fulfil our baptism; and the more cruelly we suffer, the more successfully do we conform to our baptism. Hence the church was at its best at the time when martyrs were being put to death every day and accounted as sheep for the slaughter [Ps. 44:22; Rom. 8:36], for then the power of baptism reigned supreme in the church, whereas today we have lost sight of this power amid the multitude of works and doctrines of men. For our whole life should be baptism, and the fulfilling of the sign or sacrament of baptism, since we have been set free from all else and given over to baptism alone, that is, to death and resurrection.

This glorious liberty of ours and this understanding of baptism have been taken captive in our day, and to whom can we give the blame except the Roman pontiff with his despotism? More than all others, as chief shepherd it was his first duty to proclaim this doctrine and defend this liberty, as Paul says in I Cor. 4 [:1]: "This is how one should regard us, as servants of Christ and stewards of the mysteries, or sacraments,[127] of God." Instead he seeks only to oppress us with his decrees and laws, and to ensnare us as captives to his tyrannical power. By what right, I ask you, does the pope impose his laws upon us (to say nothing of his wicked and damnable neglect to teach us these mysteries)? Who gave him power to deprive us of this liberty of ours, granted to us in baptism? One thing only, as I have said, has been enjoined upon us to do all the days of our lives—to be baptized, that is, to be put to death and to live again through faith in Christ. This and this alone, should have been taught, especially by the chief shepherd. But now faith is passed over in silence, and the church is smothered with endless laws concerning works and ceremonies; the power and understanding of baptism are set aside, and faith in Christ is obstructed.

Therefore I say: Neither pope nor bishop nor any other man has the right to impose a single syllable of law upon a Christian man without his consent; if he does, it is done in the spirit of tyranny. Therefore the prayers, fasts, donations, and whatever else the pope ordains and demands in all of his decrees, as numerous as they are iniquitous, he demands and ordains without any right whatever; and he sins against the liberty of the church whenever he attempts any such thing. Hence it has come to pass that the churchmen of our day are such vigorous guardians of "ecclesiastical liberty"—that is, of wood and stone, of lands and rents (for to such an extent has "ecclesiastical" today come to mean the same as "spiritual"!). Yet

[127] Cf. pp. 93-95.

with such verbal fictions they not only take captive the true liberty of the church; they utterly destroy it, even worse than the Turk, and in opposition to the word of the Apostle: "Do not become slaves of men" [I Cor. 7:23]. For to be subjected to their statutes and tyrannical laws is indeed to become slaves of men.

This impious and desperate tyranny is fostered by the pope's disciples, who here twist and pervert that saying of Christ: "He who hears you hears me" [Luke 10:16]. With puffed cheeks they inflate this saying to a great size in support of their own ordinances. Though Christ spoke this word to the apostles when they went forth to preach the gospel, and though it should apply only to the gospel, they pass over the gospel and apply it only to their fables. For he says in John 10 [:27, 5]: "My sheep hear my voice, but the voice of a stranger they do not hear." He left us the gospel so that the pontiffs might sound the voice of Christ. Instead they sound their own voices, and yet hope to be heard. Moreover, the Apostle says that he was not sent to baptize, but to preach the gospel [I Cor. 1:17]. Therefore, no one is obliged to obey the ordinances of the pope, or required to listen to him, except when he teaches the gospel and Christ. And the pope should teach nothing but faith without any restrictions. But since Christ says, "He who hears you [plural] hears me" [Luke 10:16], why does not the pope also hear others? Christ does not say to Peter alone, "He who hears you" [singular]. In short, where there is true faith, there the word of faith must of necessity be also. Why then does not an unbelieving pope now and then hear a believing servant of his, who has the word of faith? Blindness, sheer blindness, reigns among the pontiffs.

Others, even more shameless, arrogantly ascribe to the pope the power to make laws, on the basis of Matt. 16 [:19], "Whatever you bind, etc.," although Christ in this passage treats of binding and loosing sins, not of taking the whole church captive and oppressing it with laws. So this tyranny treats everything with its own lying words and violently twists and perverts the words of God. I admit indeed that Christians ought to bear this accursed tyranny just as they would bear any other violence of this world, according to Christ's word: "If any one strikes you on the right cheek, turn to him the other also" [Matt. 5:39]. But this is my complaint: that the godless pontiffs boastfully claim to do this by right, that they pretend to be seeking the church's welfare with this Babylon of theirs, and that they foist this fiction upon all mankind. For if they did these things and we suffered their violence, both sides being well aware that it was godlessness and tyranny, then we might easily number it among those things that contribute to the mortifying of this life and the fulfilling of our baptism, and might with a good conscience glory in the inflicted injury. But now they seek to deprive us of this consciousness of our liberty, and would have us believe that what they do is well done, and must not be censured or complained of as wrongdoing. Being wolves, they masquerade as shepherds, and being Antichrists, they wish to be honored as Christ.

I lift my voice simply on behalf of liberty and conscience, and I confidently cry: No law, whether of men or of angels, may rightfully be imposed upon Christians without their consent, for we are free of all laws. And if any laws are imposed upon us, we must bear them in such a way as to preserve that sense of freedom which knows and affirms with certainty that an injustice is being done to it, even though it glories in bearing this injustice—so taking care neither to justify the tyrant nor to murmur against his tyranny. "Now who is there to harm you," says Peter, "if you are zealous for what is right?" [I Pet. 3:13]. "All things work together for good to them that are the elect" [Rom. 8:28].

Nevertheless, since but few know this glory of baptism and the blessedness of Christian liberty, and cannot know them because of the tyranny of the pope, I for one will disengage myself, and keep my conscience free by bringing this charge against the pope and all his papists: Unless they will abolish their laws and ordinances, and restore to Christ's churches their liberty and have it taught among them, they are guilty of all the souls that perish under this miserable captivity, and the papacy is truly the kingdom of Babylon and of the very Antichrist. For who is "the man of sin" and "the son of perdition" [II Thess. 2:3] but he who with his doctrines and his laws increases the sins and perdition of souls in the church, while sitting in the church as if he were God? [II Thess. 2:4]. All this the papal tyranny has fulfilled, and more than fulfilled, these many centuries. It has extinguished faith, obscured the sacraments and oppressed the gospel; but its own laws, which are not only impious and sacrilegious, but even barbarous and foolish, it has decreed and multiplied without end.

Behold, then, our miserable captivity. "How lonely sits the city that was full of people! How like a widow has she become, she that was great among the nations! She that was a princess among the cities has become a vassal. She has none to comfort her; all her friends have dealt treacherously with her, etc." [Lam. 1:1-2]. There are so many ordinances, so many rites, so many sects,[128] so many vows, so many exertions and so many works, in which Christians are engaged today, that they lose sight of their baptism. Because of this swarm of locusts, palmerworms, and cankerworms [Joel 1:4], no one is able to remember that he is baptized, or what blessings baptism has brought him. We should be even as little children, when they are newly baptized, who engage in no efforts or works, but are free in every way, secure and saved solely through the glory of their baptism. For we are indeed little children, continually baptized anew in Christ.

In contradiction to what has been said, some might cite the *baptism of infants* who do not comprehend the promise of God and cannot have the faith of baptism; so that therefore either faith is not necessary or else infant baptism is without effect. Here I say what all[129] say: Infants are aided by the faith of others, namely, those who bring them for baptism. For the Word of God is powerful enough, when uttered, to change even a godless heart, which is no less unresponsive and helpless than any infant. So through the prayer of the believing church which presents it, a prayer to which all things are possible [Mark 9:23], the infant is changed, cleansed, and renewed by inpoured faith. Nor should I doubt that even a godless adult could be changed, in any of the sacraments, if the same church prayed for and presented him, as we read of the paralytic in the Gospel, who was healed through the faith of others [Mark 2:3-12]. I should be ready to admit that in this sense the sacraments of the New Law are efficacious in con-

[128] Luther means the divergences, rivalries, and jealousies between the various monastic orders and theological factions. E.g., cf. p. 78 n. 138.

[129] This was the position of Thomas Aquinas, going back to Augustine; it was ratified by Clement V at the Council of Vienna, 1311-12. *PE* 2, 236 n. 1.

ferring grace, not only to those who do not, but even to those who do most obstinately present an obstacle.[130] What obstacle cannot be removed by the faith of the church and the prayer of faith? Do we not believe that Stephen converted Paul the Apostle by this power? [Acts 7:58–8:1]. But then the sacraments do what they do not by their own power, but by the power of faith, without which they do nothing at all, as I have said.[131]

The question remains whether an unborn infant, with only a hand or a foot projecting from the womb, can be baptized. Here I will confess my ignorance and make no hasty decision. I am not sure whether the reason they give is sufficient—that in any part of the body whatsoever the entire soul resides. For it is not the soul but the body that is externally baptized with water. But neither do I share the view of those who insist that he who is not yet born cannot be born again (even though it has considerable force). I leave these things to the teaching of the Spirit, and meanwhile allow everyone to enjoy his own opinion [Rom. 14:5].

One thing I will add—and I wish that I could persuade everyone to do it—namely, that *all vows should be completely abolished and avoided,* whether of religious orders, or about pilgrimages or about any works whatsoever, that we may remain in that which is supremely religious and most rich in works—the freedom of baptism. It is impossible to say how much that most widespread delusion of vows detracts from baptism and obscures the knowledge of Christian liberty, to say nothing now of the unspeakable and infinite peril of souls which that mania for making vows and that ill-advised rashness daily increase. O most godless pontiffs and unregenerate pastors, who slumber on unheeding and indulge in your evil lusts, without pity for this most dreadful and perilous "ruin of Joseph"! [Amos 6:4-6].

Vows should either be abolished by a general edict, especially those taken for life, and all men recalled to the vows of baptism, or else everyone should be diligently warned not to take a vow rashly. No one should be encouraged to do so; indeed, permission should be given only with difficulty and reluctance. For we have

[130] Cf. p. 65.
[131] Cf. pp. 66-67.

vowed enough in baptism, more than we can ever fulfil; if we give ourselves to the keeping of this one vow, we shall have all we can do. But now we traverse sea and land to make many proselytes [Matt. 23:15]; we fill the world with priests, monks, and nuns, and imprison them all in lifelong vows. You will find those who argue and decree that a work done in fulfilment of a vow ranks higher than one done without a vow, and in heaven is to be rewarded above others with I know not what great rewards. Blind and godless Pharisees, who measure righteousness and holiness by the greatness, number, or other quality of the works! But God measures them by faith alone, and with him there is no difference among works, except insofar as there is a difference in faith.

With such bombast wicked men by their inventions puff up human opinion and human works, in order to lure on the unthinking masses who are almost always led by the glitter of works to make shipwreck of their faith, to forget their baptism and to injure their Christian liberty. For a vow is a kind of law or requirement. When vows are multiplied, laws and works are necessarily multiplied, and when these are multiplied, faith is extinguished and the liberty of baptism is taken captive. Others, not content with these wicked allurements, assert in addition that entrance into a religious order is like a new baptism, which may afterward be repeated as often as the purpose to live the monastic life is renewed. Thus these votaries have appropriated to themselves all righteousness, salvation, and glory, and left to those who are merely baptized nothing to compare with them. Now the Roman pontiff, that fountain and source of all superstitions, confirms, approves, and adorns this mode of life with high-sounding bulls[132] and dispensations, while no one deems baptism worthy of even a thought. And with such glittering pomp, as I have said, they drive the pliable people of Christ into a false sense of security,[133] so that in their ingratitude toward bap-

[132] *bulla*. An official mandate of the pope, which takes its name from the leaden seal with which the document was authenticated in the Middle Ages—a circular plate in form resembling an air bubble floating upon water.

[133] *in quascunque volent symplegadas*. Luther is alluding to the Symplegades rocks at the entrance to the Black Sea, through which, according to Greek legend, Jason had to lead his Argonauts in quest of the Golden Fleece. While they seemed to afford secure passage, the two cliffs actually moved on their bases and crushed whatever sought to pass.

tism they presume to achieve greater things by their works than others achieve by their faith.

Therefore, God again shows himself "perverse with the crooked" [Ps. 18:26], and to punish the makers of vows for their ingratitude and pride, he brings it about that they break their vows, or keep them only with prodigious labor, and remain sunk in them, never knowing the grace of faith and of baptism; that they continue in their hypocrisy to the end, since their spirit is not approved of God; and that at last they become a laughingstock to the whole world, ever pursuing righteousness and never attaining Righteousness, so that they fulfil the word of Isa. 2 [:8]: "Their land is filled with idols."

I am indeed far from forbidding or discouraging anyone who may desire to vow something privately and of his own free choice; for I would not altogether despise and condemn vows. But I would most strongly advise against setting up and sanctioning the making of vows as a public mode of life. It is enough that every one should have the private right to take a vow at his own peril; but to commend the vowing of vows as a public mode of life—this I hold to be most pernicious to the church and to simple souls. First, because it runs directly counter to the Christian life, for a vow is a kind of ceremonial law and a human ordinance or presumption, from which the church has been set free through baptism; for a Christian is subject to no law but the law of God. Second, because there is no instance in Scripture of such a vow, especially of lifelong chastity, obedience, or poverty.[134] But whatever is without warrant of Scripture is most hazardous and should by no means be urged upon any one, much less established as a common and public mode of life, even if it be permitted to somebody who wishes to make the venture at his own peril. For certain works are wrought by the Spirit in a few men, but they must not be made an example or a mode of life for all.

Moreover, I greatly fear that these votive modes of life of the religious orders belong to those things which the Apostle foretold: "They will be teaching lies in hypocrisy, forbidding marriage and enjoining abstinence from foods which God created to be received

[134] The threefold vow of the monastic orders involved a pledge of poverty, chastity, and obedience.

with thanksgiving" [I Tim. 4:2-3]. Let no one retort by pointing to SS. Bernard, Francis, Dominic,[135] and others, who founded or fostered monastic orders. Terrible and marvelous is God in his counsels toward the sons of men. He could keep Daniel, Hananiah, Azariah, and Mishael [Dan. 1:6-21] holy at the court of the king of Babylon (that is, in the midst of godlessness); why could he not sanctify those men also in their perilous mode of living or guide them by the special operation of his Spirit, yet without desiring it to be an example to others? Besides, it is certain that none of them was saved through his vows and his "religious"[136] life; they were saved through faith alone, by which all men are saved, and to which that showy subservience to vows is more diametrically opposed than anything else.

But every one may hold his own view on this. I will return to my argument. Speaking now in behalf of the church's liberty and the glory of baptism, I feel myself in duty bound to set forth publicly the counsel I have learned under the Spirit's guidance. I therefore counsel those in high places in the churches, first of all, to abolish all those vows and religious orders, or at least not to approve and extol them. If they will not do this, then I counsel all men who would be assured of their salvation to abstain from all vows, above all from the major and lifelong vows. I give this counsel especially to teen-agers and young people. This I do, first, because this manner of life has no witness or warrant in the Scriptures, as I have said, but is puffed up solely by the bulls (and they truly are "bulls")[137] of human popes. Second, because it greatly tends to hypocrisy, by reason of its outward show and unusual character, which engender conceit and a contempt of the common Christian life. And if there were no other reason for abolishing these vows, this one would be reason enough, namely, that through them faith and baptism are slighted and works are exalted, which cannot be

---

[135] Bernard of Clairvaux (1090-1153) founded 163 Cistercian monasteries in different parts of Europe, which by his death had increased in number to 343. Francis of Assisi (1182-1226) founded the Franciscan Order. Dominic (*circa* 1170-1221) founded the Order of Preachers, commonly known as the Dominican Order.

[136] *religio.* In medieval Latin this was a special designation for the particular piety of the monastic orders.

[137] *bulla* also means "bubble." Cf. p. 75 n. 132.

done without harmful results. For in the religious orders there is scarcely one in many thousands who is not more concerned about his works than about faith, and on the basis of this madness, they claim superiority over each other, as being "stricter" or "laxer," as they call it.[138]

Therefore I advise no one to enter any religious order or the priesthood, indeed, I advise everyone against it—unless he is forearmed with this knowledge and understands that the works of monks and priests, however holy and arduous they may be, do not differ one whit in the sight of God from the works of the rustic laborer in the field or the woman going about her household tasks, but that all works are measured before God by faith alone, as Jer. 5 [:3] says: "O Lord, do not thy eyes look for faith?" [139] and Ecclus. 32 [:23]: "In all thy works believe with faith in thy heart, for this is to keep the commandments of God." Indeed, the menial housework of a manservant or maidservant is often more acceptable to God than all the fastings and other works of a monk or priest, because the monk or priest lacks faith. Since, therefore, vows nowadays seem to tend only to the glorification of works and to pride, it is to be feared that there is nowhere less of faith and of the church than among the priests, monks, and bishops. These men are in truth heathen or hypocrites. They imagine themselves to be the church, or the heart of the church, the "spiritual" estate and the leaders of the church, when they are everything else but that. This is indeed "the people of the captivity," among whom all things freely given to us in baptism are held captive, while the few poor "people of the earth" [140] who are left behind, such as the married folk,[141] appear vile in their eyes.

[138] Divisions resulting from disputes over the interpretation of their "rules" were common among and within the religious orders. In the case of the Franciscans, for example, there were the factions known as the *zelanti* and *relaxti* in earlier times, and later on the division between the "Strict Observance" and the "Conventuals." Cf. p. 13 n. 12.

[139] Vulgate version.

[140] The reference is to the Babylonian captivity of the Jews. "The people of the captivity" is an expression taken from the Latin title to Psalm 64 (65) in the Vulgate. Nebuchadnezzar carried into captivity in Babylon only the better classes of the population. The "people of the earth," *am haarez*, the common people, were left behind (II Kings 24:14-16) and became the nucleus of the hybrid Samaritan nation.

[141] Persons under the vow of chastity held the estate of marriage to be beneath their own in terms of holiness.

From what has been said we recognize two glaring errors of the Roman pontiff.

In the first place, he grants dispensation from vows, and does it as if he alone of all Christians possessed this authority; so great is the temerity and audacity of wicked men. If it is possible to grant a dispensation from a vow, then any brother may grant one to his neighbor, or even to himself.[142] But if one's neighbor cannot grant a dispensation, neither has the pope any right to do so. For where does he get this authority? From the power of the keys? But the keys belong to all, and avail only for sins (Matt. 18 [:15-18]).[143] Now they themselves claim that vows are "of divine right." Why then does the pope deceive and destroy the poor souls of men by granting dispensations in matters of divine right, in which no dispensations can be granted? In the section, "Of vows and their redemption," [144] he babbles indeed of having the power to change vows, just as in the law the firstborn of an ass was changed for a sheep [Exod. 13:13; 34:20] as if the firstborn of an ass, and the vow he commands to be offered everywhere and always, were one and the same thing; or as if when the Lord decrees in his law that a sheep shall be changed for an ass, the pope, a mere man, may straightway claim the same power, not in his own law, but in God's! It was not a pope, but an ass changed for a pope, that made this decretal; it is so egregiously senseless and godless.

The second error is this: The pope decrees, on the other hand, that a marriage is dissolved if one party enters a monastery without the consent of the other, provided that the marriage has not yet been consummated. Now I ask you, what devil puts such monstrous things into the pope's mind? God commands men to keep faith and not break their word to one another, and again, to do good with that which is their own, for he hates "robbery with a burnt offering," as he says by the mouth of Isaiah [61:8]. But one spouse is bound by the marriage contract to keep faith with the other, and he is not his own. He cannot break his faith by any right, and whatever he does with himself is robbery, if it is done without the other's

[142] Cf. *An Open Letter to the Christian Nobility. PE* 2, 123.
[143] *Ibid.*, 75.
[144] *Magnae devotionis, Decretalium Gregorii IX*, lib iii, tit. XXXIV: ***de voto et voti redemptione,*** cap. 7. *Corpus Iuris Canonici, op. cit.*, II, col. 593.

consent. Why does not one who is burdened with debt follow this same rule and obtain admission into a religious order, so as to be released from his debts and be free to break his word? O blind, blind men! Which is greater, the fidelity commanded by God or a vow devised and chosen by men? Are you a shepherd of souls, O pope? And you who teach these things, are you doctors of sacred theology? Why then do you teach them? No doubt because you have decked out your vow as a better work than marriage; you do not exalt faith, which alone exalts all things, but works, which are nothing in the sight of God, or which are all alike as far as merit is concerned.

I am sure, therefore, that neither men nor angels can grant a dispensation from vows, if they are proper vows. But I am not fully clear in my own mind whether all the things that men vow nowadays come under the head of vows. For instance, it is simply foolish and stupid for parents to dedicate their children, before birth or in infancy, to the "religious life," or to perpetual chastity; indeed, it is certain that this can by no means be termed a vow. It seems to be a kind of mockery of God for them to vow things which are not at all in their power. As to the triple vow of the monastic orders,[145] the longer I consider it, the less I comprehend it, and I wonder where the custom of exacting this vow arose. Still less do I understand at what age vows may be taken in order to be legal and valid. I am pleased to find unanimous agreement that vows taken before the age of puberty are not valid. Nevertheless, they deceive many young children who are ignorant both of their age and of what they are vowing. They do not observe the age of puberty in receiving such children; but the children, after making their profession, are held captive and consumed by a troubled conscience as though they had afterward given their consent. As if a vow which was invalid could finally become valid with the passing of the years!

It seems absurd to me that the effective date of a legitimate vow should be predetermined for others by people who cannot predetermine it for themselves. Nor do I see why a vow taken at eighteen years of age should be valid, but not one taken at ten or twelve years. It will not do to say that at eighteen a man feels his carnal

[145] Cf. p. 76 n. 134.

desires. What if he scarcely feels them at twenty or thirty, or feels them more keenly at thirty than at twenty? Why not also set a certain age limit for the vows of poverty and obedience? But what age will you set, by which a man should feel his greed and pride, when even the most spiritual persons hardly become aware of these emotions? Therefore, no vow will ever become binding and valid until we have become spiritual, and no longer have any need of vows. You see that these are uncertain and most perilous matters, and it would therefore be a wholesome counsel to keep such lofty modes of living free of vows, and leave them to the Spirit alone as they were of old, and never in any way to change them into a mode of life which is perpetually binding.

However, let this be sufficient for the present concerning baptism and its liberty. In due time I shall perhaps discuss vows at greater length,[146] and truly there is an urgent need for this.

The Sacrament of Penance

In the third place, we are to discuss the sacrament of penance. On this subject I have already given no little offense to many people by the treatises and disputations [147] already published, in which I have amply set forth my views. These I must now briefly repeat in order to unmask the tyranny that is rampant here no less than in the sacrament of the bread. For, because these two sacraments furnish opportunity for gain and profit, the greed of the shepherds has raged in them with incredible zeal against the flock of Christ, although, as we have just seen in our discussion of vows, baptism too has sadly declined among adults and become the servant of greed.

The first and chief abuse of this sacrament is that they have completely abolished it. Not a vestige of the sacrament remains. For this sacrament, like the other two, consists in the word of divine

[146] This Luther did in November, 1521, during his sojourn at the Wartburg, in *De votis monasticis Martini Lutheri iudicium.* WA 8, 573-669.

[147] These include, among others, the *Ninety-five Theses* (1517), *LW* 31, 25-33, *WA* 1, 233-238; *A Sermon on Indulgence and Grace* (1517), Woolf, *op. cit.*, I, 50-55, *WA* 1, 239-246; *Sermo de poenitentia* (1518), *WA* 1, 319-324; *Eine Freiheit des Sermons päpstlichen Ablass und Gnade Belangend* (1518), *WA* 1, 383-393; *Explanations of the Ninety-five Theses* (1518), *LW* 31, 83-252, *WA* 1, 525-628; and *A Discussion of Confession* (1520), *PE* 1, 81-101, *WA* 6, 157-169.

promise and our faith, and they have undermined both of them. For they have adapted to their own tyranny the word of promise which Christ speaks in Matt. 16 [:19] and 18 [:18]: "Whatever you bind, etc.," and in the last chapter of John [20:23]: "If you forgive the sins of any, they are forgiven, etc." By these words the faith of penitents is aroused for obtaining the forgiveness of sins. But in all their writing, teaching, and preaching, their sole concern has been, not to teach what is promised to Christians in these words, or what they ought to believe, and what great consolation they might find in them, but only through force and violence to extend their own tyranny far, wide, and deep. It has finally come to such a pass that some of them have begun to command the very angels in heaven,[148] and to boast in incredible, mad wickedness that in these words they have obtained the right to rule in heaven and earth, and possess the power to bind even in heaven. Thus they say nothing of faith which is the salvation of the people, but babble only of the despotic power of the pontiffs, whereas Christ says nothing at all of power, but speaks only of faith.

For Christ has not ordained authorities or powers or lordships in his church, but ministries, as we learn from the Apostle, who says: "This is how one should regard us, as ministers of Christ and stewards of the mysteries of God" [I Cor. 4:1]. Just as, when he said: "He who believes and is baptized will be saved" [Mark 16:16], he was calling forth the faith of those who were to be baptized, so that by this word of promise a man might be certain of his salvation if he was baptized in faith. There was no conferring of any power there, but only the instituting of the ministry of those who baptize. Similarly, here where he says, "Whatever you bind, etc." [Matt.

---

[148] In the jubilee year of 1500, as thousands of pilgrims died of the plague on their way through war-ravaged Lombardy toward Rome, a spurious bull of Pope Clement VI from the year 1350 was widely promulgated, in which were the words: "We command the angels of paradise that their souls (the souls of pilgrims who died en route) be taken directly to the bliss of paradise, as being fully redeemed from purgatory." *WA* 30^{II}, 282; Buchwald, *op. cit.*, II, 457 n. 1. In *Defense and Explanation of All the Articles* (1521), Luther writes: "This is what happened in the days of John Huss. In those days the pope commanded the angels in heaven to lead to heaven the souls of those pilgrims who died on the way to Rome. John Huss objected to this horrible blasphemy and more than diabolic presumption. This protest cost him his life, but he at least caused the pope to change his tune and, embarrassed by this sacrilege, to refrain from such proclamation." *LW* 32, 74-75.

16:19; 18:18], he is calling forth the faith of the penitent, so that by this word of promise he might be certain that if he is absolved in faith, he is truly absolved in heaven. Here there is no mention at all of power, but only of the ministry of the one who absolves. One cannot but wonder what happened to these blind and overbearing men that they did not arrogate to themselves a despotic power from the promise of baptism; or, if they did not do it there, why they presumed to do it from the promise of penance? For in both there is a like ministry, a similar promise, and the same kind of sacrament. It cannot be denied: if baptism does not belong to Peter alone, then it is a wicked usurpation of power to claim the power of the keys for the pope alone.

Again, when Christ says: "Take, this is my body, which is given for you. This is the cup in my blood, etc." [I Cor. 11:24-25], he is calling forth the faith of those who eat, so that when their conscience has been strengthened by these words they might be certain through faith that they receive the forgiveness of sins when they have eaten. Here too, nothing is said of power, but only of the ministry.

So the promise of baptism remains to some extent, at least for infants; but the promise of the bread and the cup has been destroyed and made subservient to greed, faith has become a work and the testament has become a sacrifice. The promise of penance, however, has been transformed into the most oppressive despotism, being used to establish a sovereignty which is more than merely temporal.

Not content with these things, *this Babylon of ours has so completely extinguished faith* that it insolently *denies its necessity in this sacrament.* Indeed, with the wickedness of Antichrist it brands it as heresy for anyone to assert that faith is necessary. What more could this tyranny do than it has done? Truly, "by the waters of Babylon we sit down and weep, when we remember thee, O Zion. On the willows there we hang up our lyres" [Ps. 137:1-2]. May the Lord curse the barren willows of those streams! Amen.

Now that promise and faith have been thus blotted out and overthrown, let us see what they have put in their place. *They have divided penance into three parts—contrition, confession, and satisfaction;* but in such a way that they have removed whatever was good in each of them, and have established in each of them their caprice and tyranny.

In the first place, they teach that contrition takes precedence over, and is far superior to, faith in the promise, as if contrition were not a work of faith, but a merit; indeed, they do not mention faith at all. They stick so closely to works and to those passages of Scripture where we read of many who obtained pardon by reason of their contrition and humility of heart; but they take no account of the faith which effected this contrition and sorrow of heart, as is written of the men of Nineveh in Jon. 3 [:5]: "And the people of Nineveh believed God; they proclaimed a fast, etc." Others again, more bold and wicked, have invented a so-called "attrition,"[149] which is converted into contrition by the power of the keys, of which they know nothing. This attrition they grant to the wicked and unbelieving, and thus abolish contrition altogether. O the intolerable wrath of God, that such things should be taught in the church of Christ! Thus, with both faith and its work destroyed, we go on secure in the doctrines and opinions of men, or rather we perish in them. A contrite heart is a precious thing, but it is found only where there is an ardent faith in the promises and threats of God. Such faith, intent on the immutable truth of God, makes the conscience tremble, terrifies it and bruises it; and afterwards, when it is contrite, raises it up, consoles it, and preserves it. Thus the truth of God's threat is the cause of contrition, and the truth of his promise the cause of consolation, if it is believed. By such faith a man "merits" the forgiveness of sins. Therefore faith should be taught and aroused before all else. Once faith is obtained, contrition and consolation will follow inevitably of themselves.

Therefore, although there is some truth in their teaching that contrition is to be attained by the enumeration and contemplation (as they call it) of their sins, yet their teaching is perilous and perverse so long as they do not teach first of all the beginnings and causes of contrition—the immutable truth of God's threat and prom-

[149] Contrition involved a detestation of sin arising out of love for God and regret at having offended him. Attrition involved a hatred of sin arising out of lesser motives, such as loss of heaven, fear of hell, or the heinousness of guilt. Attrition, though imperfect, was held to be sufficient, since it predisposed the sinner to receive through the sacrament of penance that grace which transformed it into perfect contrition. Cf. *LW* 31, 21.

ise which calls forth faith—so that men may learn to pay more heed to the truth of God, by which they are cast down and lifted up, than to the multitude of their sins. If their sins are regarded apart from the truth of God, they will excite afresh and increase the desire for sin rather than lead to contrition. I will say nothing now of the insurmountable task which they have imposed upon us, namely, that we are to frame a contrition for every sin. That is impossible. We can know only the smaller part of our sins; and even our good works are found to be sins, according to Ps. 143 [:2][150]: "Enter not into judgment with thy servant; for no man living is righteous before thee." It is enough if we lament the sins which distress our conscience at the present moment, as well as those which we can readily call to mind. Whoever is in this frame of mind is without doubt ready to grieve and fear for all his sins, and will grieve and fear whenever they are brought to his knowledge in the future.

Beware then, of putting your trust in your own contrition and of ascribing the forgiveness of sins to your own remorse. God does not look on you with favor because of that, but because of the faith by which you have believed his threats and promises, and which has effected such sorrow within you. Thus we owe whatever good there may be in our penance, not to our scrupulous enumeration of sins, but to the truth of God and to our faith. All other things are the works and fruits which follow of their own accord. They do not make a man good, but are done by the man who is already made good through faith in the truth of God. Even so, "smoke goes up in his wrath; because he is angry he shakes the mountains and sets them on fire," as it is said in Ps. 18 [:8, 7]). First comes the terror of this threatening, which sets the wicked on fire; then faith, accepting this, sends up smoke-clouds of contrition, etc.

But the trouble is not so much that contrition has been exposed to tyranny and avarice, as that it has been given over completely to wickedness and pestilent teaching. It is confession and satisfaction that have become the chief workshops of greed and power.

Let us first take up *confession*.

There is no doubt that confession of sins is necessary and com-

[150] Where Luther cites correctly the Vulgate version, in which Psalms 10-146 are numbered differently than in the RSV, we have given the corresponding RSV Psalm reference.

manded of God, in Matt. 3 [:6]: "They were baptized by John in the river Jordan, confessing their sins," and in I John 1 [:9-10]: "If we confess our sins, he is faithful and just, and will forgive our sins. If we say we have not sinned, we make him a liar, and his word is not in us." If the saints may not deny their sin, how much more ought those who are guilty of great and public sins to make confession! But the institution of confession is proved most effectively of all by Matt. 18 [:15-17], where Christ teaches that a sinning brother should be told of his fault, brought before the church, accused, and if he will not hear, be excommunicated. He "hears" if he heeds the rebuke and acknowledges and confesses his sin.

As to the current practice of private confession, I am heartily in favor of it, even though it cannot be proved from the Scriptures. It is useful, even necessary, and I would not have it abolished. Indeed, I rejoice that it exists in the church of Christ, for it is a cure without equal for distressed consciences. For when we have laid bare our conscience to our brother and privately made known to him the evil that lurked within, we receive from our brother's lips the word of comfort spoken by God himself. And, if we accept this in faith, we find peace in the mercy of God speaking to us through our brother. There is just one thing about it that I abominate, and that is the fact that this kind of confession has been subjected to the despotism and extortion of the pontiffs. They reserve[151] to themselves even the secret sins, and command that they be made known to confessors named by them, only to trouble the consciences of men. They merely play the pontiff, while they utterly despise the true duties of pontiffs, which are to preach the gospel and to care for the poor. Indeed, the godless despots leave the great sins to the common priests, and reserve to themselves only those sins which are of less consequence, such as those ridiculous and fictitious things in the bull *Coena domini*.[152] To make the wickedness of their error

[151] In "reserved cases," *casus episcopales* or *casus papales*, only the bishop or pope, or one appointed by them, could absolve. Cf. *An Open Letter to the Christian Nobility*. *PE* 2, 105-106.

[152] *Coena domini* was a papal bull published annually against heretics since 1364 in the Lateran Church at Rome on Holy Thursday. But to the condemnation of their heresies were added those offenses, absolvable only by the pope or by his authorization, which might conceivably endanger or impair the papal state. Luther was named in the bull for the first time on March 28, 1521, along with Wycliffe and Huss. In 1522 Luther translated this bull into German as a New Year's present for the pope. *WA* 8, 691; cf. *PE* 2, 105-106.

even more apparent, they not only fail to reserve, but actually teach and approve things which are against the service of God, against faith and the chief commandments—such as their running about on pilgrimages, the perverse worship of the saints, the lying saints' legends, the various ways of trusting in works and ceremonies and practicing them. Yet in all of these faith in God is extinguished and idolatry fostered, as we see in our day. As a result we have the same kind of priests today as Jeroboam ordained of old in Dan and Beersheba, ministers of the golden calves [I Kings 12:26-32], men who are ignorant of the law of God, of faith, and of whatever pertains to the feeding of Christ's sheep. They inculcate in the people nothing but their own inventions with fear and violence.

Although I urge that this outrage of reserved cases should be borne patiently, even as Christ bids us bear all the tyranny of men, and teaches us that we should obey these extortioners; nevertheless, I deny that they have the right to make such reservations, and I do not believe that they can bring one jot or tittle of proof that they have it. But I am going to prove the contrary. In the first place, Christ speaks in Matt. 18 [:15-17] of public sins and says that if our brother hears us, when we tell him his fault, we have saved the soul of our brother, and that he is to be brought before the church only if he refuses to hear us, so that his sin can be corrected among brethren. How much more will it be true of secret sins, that they are forgiven if one brother freely makes confession to another? So it is not necessary to tell it to the church, that is, as these babblers interpret it, to the prelate or priest. On this matter we have further authority from Christ, where he says in the same chapter: "Whatever you bind on earth shall be bound in heaven, and whatever you loose on earth shall be loosed in heaven" [Matt. 18:18]. For this is said to each and every Christian. Again, he says in the same place: "Again I say to you, if two of you agree on earth about anything they ask, it will be done for them by my father in heaven" [Matt. 18:19]. Now, the brother who lays his secret sins before his brother and craves pardon, certainly agrees with his brother on earth, in the truth which is Christ. Of this Christ says even more clearly, confirming his preceding words: "For truly, I say to you, where two or three are gathered in my name, there am I in the midst of them" [Matt. 18:20].

Hence, I have no doubt but that every one is absolved from his secret sins when he has made confession, privately before any brother, either of his own accord or after being rebuked, and has sought pardon and amended his ways, no matter how much the violence of the pontiffs may rage against it. For Christ has given to every one of his believers the power to absolve even open sins. Add yet this little point: If any reservation of secret sins were valid, so that one could not be saved unless they were forgiven, then a man's salvation would be prevented most of all by those aforementioned good works and idolatries which are taught by the popes nowadays. But if these most grievous sins do not prevent one's salvation, how foolish it is to reserve those lighter sins! In truth, it is the foolishness and blindness of the shepherds that produce these monstrous things in the church. Therefore I would admonish those princes of Babylon and bishops of Beth-aven[153] to refrain from reserving any cases whatsoever. Let them, moreover, permit all brothers and sisters most freely to hear the confession of secret sins, so that the sinner may make his sins known to whomever he will and seek pardon and comfort, that is, the word of Christ, by the mouth of his neighbor. For with these presumptions of theirs they only ensnare the consciences of the weak without necessity, establish their wicked despotism, and fatten their avarice on the sins and ruin of their brethren. Thus they stain their hands with the blood of souls; sons are devoured by their parents. Ephraim devours Judah, and Syria Israel, with an open mouth, as Isaiah [9:20-21] says.

To these evils they have added the "circumstances,"[154] and also the mothers, daughters, sisters, sisters-in-law, branches and fruits of sins; since these most astute and idle men have worked out, if you please, a kind of family tree of relationships and affinities even among sins—so prolific is wickedness coupled with ignorance. For this conception, whatever rogue may be its author, has become a public law, like many others. Thus do the shepherds keep watch over the church of Christ: whatever new work or superstition those most stupid devotees may have dreamed of, they immediately drag

[153] Hos. 4:15, 10:5. The prophet altered the name Bethel (house of God) to Beth-aven (house of nothingness or idolatry) because of the images which had been erected there. Cf. p. 221.

[154] Cf. p. 61 n. 116.

to the light of day, deck out with indulgences, and fortify with bulls. So far are they from suppressing such things and preserving for God's people true faith and liberty. For what has our liberty to do with the tyranny of Babylon?

My advice would be to ignore all "circumstances" whatsoever. With Christians there is only one circumstance—that a brother has sinned. For there is no person to be compared with a Christian brother. And the observance of places, times, days, persons,[155] and all other rank superstition, only magnifies the things that are nothing, to the injury of the things which are everything; as if anything could be of greater weight or importance than the glory of Christian brotherhood! Thus they bind us to places, days, and persons, so that the name of "brother" loses its value, and we serve in bondage instead of being free—we, to whom all days, places, persons, and all external things are one and the same.

How unworthily they have dealt with *satisfaction*, I have abundantly shown in the controversies concerning indulgences.[156] They have grossly abused it, to the ruin of Christians in body and soul. To begin with, they have taught it in such a manner that the people have never had the slightest understanding what satisfaction really is, namely, the renewal of a man's life. Then, they so continually harp on it and emphasize its necessity, that they leave no room for faith in Christ. With these scruples they torture poor consciences to death; and one runs to Rome, one to this place, another to that; this one to Chartreuse,[157] that one to some other place; one scourges himself with rods, another mortifies his body with fasts and vigils; and all cry with the same mad zeal: "Lo, here is Christ! Lo, there!" believing that the kingdom of Christ, which is within us, will come with observation.[158]

For these monstrous things we are indebted to you, O Roman

[155] Sins were assessed differently according to whether they were committed at a holy place or not, on holy days or on ordinary days. Murder of a priest was a more grievous sin than murder of a layman. Buchwald, *op. cit.*, II, 465.

[156] Cf. p. 81 n. 147; especially in the *Explanations of the Ninety-five Theses*, *LW* 31, 85, 94-96, 152-153.

[157] This was the mother cloister and headquarters of the rigidly ascetic Carthusian order.

[158] Luke 17:20-21. A play on *observantia*, which also means "observance," a fling at the Observants. Cf. p. 78 n. 138.

See, and to your murderous laws and ceremonies, with which you have corrupted all mankind, so that they believe they can with works make satisfaction for sin to God, when he can be satisfied only by the faith of a contrite heart! Not only do you keep this faith silent with this uproar of yours, but you even oppress it, only so that your insatiable bloodsucker may have those to whom it may say, "Give, give!" [Prov. 30:15] and may traffic in sins.

Some have gone even farther and have constructed those instruments for driving souls to despair, their decrees that the penitent must rehearse all sins anew for which he neglected to make the imposed satisfaction. What would they not venture to do, these men who were born for the sole purpose of carrying all things into a tenfold captivity? Moreover, how many, I ask, are possessed with the notion that they are in a saved state and are making satisfaction for their sins, if they only mumble over, word for word, the prayers imposed by the priest, even though meanwhile they never give a thought to the amending of their way of life! They believe that their life is changed in the one moment of contrition and confession, and there remains only to make satisfaction for their past sins. How should they know better if they have not been taught otherwise? No thought is given here to the mortifying of the flesh, no value is attached to the example of Christ, who, when he absolved the woman caught in adultery, said: "Go, and do not sin again" [John 8:11], thereby laying upon her the cross, that is, the mortifying of her flesh. This perverse error is greatly encouraged by the fact that we absolve sinners before the satisfaction has been completed, so that they are more concerned about completing the satisfaction, which is a lasting thing, than they are about contrition, which they suppose to be over and done with when they have made confession. Absolution ought rather to follow on the completion of satisfaction, as it did in the early church, with the result that, after completing the work, penitents gave themselves with much greater diligence to faith and the living of a new life.

But this must suffice in repetition of what I have said more fully in connection with indulgences, and *in general this must suffice for the present concerning the three sacraments*, which have been treated, and yet not treated, in so many harmful books on the *Sentences* and on the laws. It remains to attempt some discussion of the other "sacraments"[159] also, lest I seem to have rejected them without cause.

Confirmation

It is amazing that it should have entered the minds of these men to make a sacrament of confirmation out of the laying on of hands. We read that Christ touched the little children in that way [Mark 10:16], and that by it the apostles imparted the Holy Spirit [Acts 8:17; 19:6], ordained presbyters [Acts 6:6], and cured the sick [Mark. 16:18]; as the Apostle writes to Timothy: "Do not be hasty in the laying on of hands" [I Tim. 5:22]. Why have they not also made a "confirmation" out of the sacrament of the bread? For it is written in Acts 9 [:19]: "And he took food and was strengthened,"[160] and in Ps. 104 [:15]: "And bread to strengthen man's heart." Confirmation would thus include three sacraments—the bread, ordination, and confirmation itself. But if everything the apostles did is a sacrament, why have they not rather made preaching a sacrament?

I do not say this because I condemn the seven sacraments, but because I deny that they can be proved from the Scriptures. Would that there were in the church such a laying on of hands as there was in apostolic times, whether we chose to call it confirmation or healing! But there is nothing left of it now but what we ourselves have invented to adorn the office of bishops, that they may not be entirely without work in the church. For after they relinquished to their inferiors those arduous sacraments together with the Word as being beneath their attention (since whatever the divine majesty has instituted must needs be despised of men!) it was no more than right that we should discover something easy and not too burdensome for such delicate and great heroes to do, and should by no means entrust it to the lower clergy as something common, for whatever human wisdom has decreed must be held in honor among men! Therefore, as the priests are, so let their ministry and duty be. For a bishop who does not preach the gospel or practice the cure of souls—what is he but an idol in the world [I Cor. 8:4], who has nothing but the name and appearance of a bishop?

[159] Cf. pp. 18 and 109.

[160] Luther correctly quotes *confortatus*, but thinks *confirmatus*.

But *instead of this we seek sacraments that have been divinely instituted, and among these we see no reason for numbering confirmation.* For to constitute a sacrament there must be above all things else a word of divine promise, by which faith may be exercised. But we read nowhere that Christ ever gave a promise concerning confirmation, although he laid hands on many and included the laying on of hands among the signs in the last chapter of Mark [16:18]: "They will lay their hands on the sick; and they will recover." Yet no one has applied this to a sacrament, for that is not possible.

For this reason it is sufficient to regard confirmation as a certain churchly rite or sacramental ceremony, similar to other ceremonies, such as the blessing of water and the like. For if every other creature is sanctified by the Word and by prayer [I Tim. 4:4-5], why should not man much rather be sanctified by the same means? Still, these things cannot be called sacraments of faith, because they have no divine promise connected with them, neither do they save; but the sacraments do save those who believe the divine promise.

Marriage

Not only is marriage regarded as a sacrament without the least warrant of Scripture, but the very ordinances which extol it as a sacrament have turned it into a farce. Let us look into this a little.

We have said that in every sacrament there is a word of divine promise, to be believed by whoever receives the sign, and that the sign alone cannot be a sacrament. Nowhere do we read that the man who marries a wife receives any grace of God. There is not even a divinely instituted sign in marriage, nor do we read anywhere that marriage was instituted by God to be a sign of anything. To be sure, whatever takes place in a visible manner can be understood as a figure or allegory of something invisible. But figures or allegories are not sacraments, in the sense in which we use the term.

Furthermore, since marriage has existed from the beginning of the world and is still found among unbelievers, there is no reason why it should be called a sacrament of the New Law and of the church alone. The marriages of the ancients were no less sacred than are ours, nor are those of unbelievers less true marriages than those of believers, and yet they are not regarded as sacraments.

Besides, even among believers there are married folk who are wicked and worse than any heathen; why should marriage be called a sacrament in their case and not among the heathen? Or are we going to talk the same sort of nonsense about baptism and the church and say that marriage is a sacrament only in the church, just as some make the mad claim that temporal power exists only in the church? That is childish and foolish talk, by which we expose our ignorance and foolhardiness to the ridicule of unbelievers.

But they will say, "The Apostle says in Eph. 5 [:31-32], 'The two shall become one. This is a great sacrament.'[161] Surely you are not going to contradict so plain a statement of the Apostle!" I reply: This argument like the others betrays great shallowness and a careless and thoughtless reading of Scripture. Nowhere in all of the Holy Scriptures is this word *sacramentum* employed in the sense in which we use the term; it has an entirely different meaning. For wherever it occurs it denotes not the sign of a sacred thing, but the sacred, secret, hidden thing itself. Thus Paul writes in I Cor. 4 [:1]: "This is how one should regard us, as servants of Christ and stewards of the 'mysteries' of God," that is, the sacraments. For where we have [in the Vulgate] the word *sacramentum* the Greek original has *mysterion,* which the translator sometimes translates and sometimes retains in its Greek form. Thus our verse in the Greek reads: "They two shall become one. This is a great mystery." This explains how they came to understand a sacrament of the New Law here, a thing they would never have done if they had read *mysterium,* as it is in the Greek.[162]

Thus Christ himself is called a "sacrament" in I Tim. 3 [:16]: "Great indeed, is the sacrament (that is the mystery): He was manifested in the flesh, vindicated in the Spirit, seen by angels, preached among the nations, believed on in the world, taken up in glory." Why have they not drawn out of this passage an eighth

---

[161] The quotation is from the Vulgate. Luther points to its divergence from the Greek original, which the English versions have more literally rendered with the word "mystery."

[162] Erasmus edited the first published Greek New Testament in March, 1516. Luther used Erasmus' work as soon as it came out, as may be seen in his lectures on Romans, 1515-16. In an interesting letter to Luther of February 14, 1519, Froben announces the second edition of Erasmus' New Testament, which Luther used in making his translation, 1521-22. *PE* 2, 258 n. 2.

sacrament[168] of the New Law, since they have the clear authority of Paul? But if they restrained themselves here, where they had a most excellent opportunity to invent new sacraments, why are they so unrestrained in the other passage? Plainly, it was their ignorance of both words and things that betrayed them. They clung to the mere sound of the words, indeed, to their own fancies. For, having once arbitrarily taken the word *sacramentum* to mean a sign, they immediately, without thought or scruple, made a "sign" of it every time they came upon it in the Holy Scriptures. Such new meanings of words, human customs, and other things they have dragged into the Holy Scriptures. They have transformed the Scriptures according to their own dreams, making anything out of any passage whatsoever. Thus they continually chatter nonsense about the terms: good work, evil work, sin, grace, righteousness, virtue, and almost all the fundamental words and things. For they employ them all after their own arbitrary judgment, learned from the writings of men, to the detriment of both the truth of God and of our salvation.

Therefore, sacrament, or mystery, in Paul is that wisdom of the Spirit, hidden in a mystery, as he says in I Cor. 2 [:7-8], which is Christ, who for this very reason is not known to the rulers of this world, wherefore they also crucified him, and for them he remains to this day folly [I Cor. 1:23], an offense, a stumbling stone [Rom. 9:32-33], and a sign that is spoken against [Luke 2:34]. The preachers he calls stewards [I Cor. 4:1] of these mysteries because they preach Christ, the power and the wisdom of God [I Cor. 1:24], yet in such a way that, unless you believe, you cannot understand it. Therefore, a sacrament is a mystery, or secret thing, which is set forth in words, but received by the faith of the heart. Such a sacrament is spoken of in the passage before us: "The two shall become one. This is a great sacrament" [Eph. 5:31-32], which they understand as spoken of marriage, whereas Paul himself wrote these words as applying to Christ and the church, and clearly explained them himself by saying: "I take it to mean Christ and the church" [Eph. 5:32]. See how well Paul and these men agree! Paul says he is proclaiming a great sacrament in Christ and the church, but they proclaim it in terms of man and a woman! If such

[168] Cf. pp. 18 and 109.

liberty in the interpretation of the sacred Scriptures is permitted, it is small wonder that one finds here anything he pleases, even a hundred sacraments.

Christ and the church are, therefore, a mystery, that is, a great and secret thing which can and ought to be represented in terms of marriage as a kind of outward allegory. But marriage ought not for that reason to be called a sacrament. The heavens are a type of the apostles, as Ps. 19 declares; the sun is a type of Christ; the waters, of the peoples; but that does not make those things sacraments, for in every case there are lacking both the divine institution and the divine promise, which constitute a sacrament. Hence Paul, in Eph. 5 [:29-32], following his own mind, applies to Christ these words of Gen. 2 [:24] about marriage; or else, following the general view,[164] he teaches that the spiritual marriage of Christ is also contained therein, when he says: "As Christ cherishes the church, because we are members of his body, of his flesh and his bones. 'For this reason a man shall leave his father and mother and be joined to his wife, and the two shall become one.' This is a great sacrament, and I take it to mean Christ and the church." You see, he would have the whole passage apply to Christ, and is at pains to admonish the reader to understand that the sacrament is in Christ and the church, not in marriage.[165]

Granted that marriage is a figure of Christ and the church; yet

[164] The precise meaning is not clear.

[165] The following paragraph, because it clearly breaks into the context and belongs elsewhere, is here relegated to a footnoote:

I admit, of course, that the sacrament of penance existed in the Old Law, and even from the beginning of the world. But the new promise of penance and the gift of the keys are peculiar to the New Law. Just as we now have baptism instead of circumcision, so we have the keys instead of sacrifices and other signs of penance. We said above that the same God at various times gave different promises and diverse signs for the remission of sins and the salvation of men; nevertheless, all received the same grace. Thus it is said in II Cor. 4 [:13]: "Since we have the same spirit of faith, we too believe, and so we speak." And in I Cor. 10 [:1-4]: "Our fathers all ate the same supernatural food and drank the same supernatural drink. For they drank from the supernatural Rock which followed them, and the Rock was Christ." Thus also in Heb. 11 [:13, 40]: "These all died, not having received what was promised, since God had foreseen something better for us, that apart from us they should not be made perfect." For Christ himself is, yesterday and today and forever [Heb. 13:8], the head of his church, from the beginning even to the end of the world. Therefore there are diverse signs, but the faith of all is the same. Indeed, without faith it is impossible to please God, yet by it Abel did please him (Heb. 11 [:4]).

it is not a divinely instituted sacrament, but invented by men in the church who are carried away by their ignorance of both the word and the thing. This ignorance, when it does not conflict with the faith, is to be borne in charity, just as many other human practices due to weakness and ignorance are borne in the church, so long as they do not conflict with the faith and the Holy Scriptures. But we are now arguing for the certainty and purity of faith and the Scriptures. We expose our faith to ridicule if we affirm that a certain thing is contained in the sacred Scriptures and in the articles of our faith, only to be refuted and shown that it is not contained in them; being found ignorant of our own affairs, we become a stumbling block to our opponents and to the weak. But most of all we should guard against impairing the authority of the Holy Scriptures. For those things which have been delivered to us by God in the sacred Scriptures must be sharply distinguished from those that have been invented by men in the church, no matter how eminent they may be for saintliness and scholarship.

So far concerning marriage itself.

But what shall we say *concerning the wicked laws of men by which this divinely ordained way of life has been ensnared* and tossed to and fro? Good God! It is dreadful to contemplate the audacity of the Roman despots, who both dissolve and compel marriages as they please. I ask you, has mankind been handed over to the caprice of these men for them to mock them and in every way abuse them and make of them whatever they please, for the sake of filthy lucre?

There is circulating far and wide and enjoying a great reputation a book whose contents have been confusedly poured together out of all the dregs and filth of man-made ordinances. Its title is "The Angelic *Summa*,"[166] although it ought rather to be "The More than Devilish *Summa*." Among endless other monstrosities, which

[166] The *Summa de Casibus Conscientiae*, popularly named after its author, Angelo Carletti di Chivasso (1411-1495); a favorite handbook on casuistry treating alphabetically all possible cases of conscience, for the guidance of priests hearing confession. Under the heading of "Matrimony" it listed 18 impediments to marriage. The book went through 31 editions between 1476 and 1520, and was among the papal books burned by Luther, together with the bull, December 10, 1520. (Cf. Luther's letter to Spalatin on the same day, *WA*, Br 2. 234 and 235 n. 2.)

are supposed to instruct the confessors, whereas they most mischievously confuse them, there are enumerated in this book eighteen impediments to marriage.[167] If you will examine these with the just and unprejudiced eye of faith, you will see that they belong to those things which the Apostle foretold: "There shall be those that give heed to the spirits of demons, speaking lies in hypocrisy, forbidding to marry" [I Tim. 4:1-3]. What is "forbidding to marry" if it is not this—to invent all those hindrances and set those snares, in order to prevent people from marrying, or, if they are married to annul their marriage? Who gave this power to men? Granted that they were holy men and impelled by godly zeal, why should another's holiness disturb my liberty? Why should another's zeal take me captive? Let whoever will be a saint and a zealot, and to his heart's content, only let him not bring harm upon another, and let him not rob me of my liberty!

Yet I am glad that those shameful laws have at last reached their full measure of glory, which is this: that the Romanists of our day have through them become merchants. What is it that they sell? Vulvas and genitals—merchandise indeed most worthy of such merchants, grown altogether filthy and obscene through greed and godlessness. For there is no impediment nowadays that may not be legalized through the intercession of mammon. These laws of men seem to have sprung into existence for the sole purpose of serving those greedy men and rapacious Nimrods [Gen. 10:8-9] [168] as snares for taking money and as nets for catching souls, and in order that "abomination" might stand in "the holy place" [Matt. 24:15], the church of God, and openly sell to men the pudenda of both sexes, or (as the Scriptures say) "shame and nakedness" [Lev. 18:6-18], of which they had previously robbed them by means of their laws. O worthy trade for our pontiffs to ply, instead of the ministry of the gospel, which in their greed and pride they despise, being given up to a reprobate mind [Rom. 1:28] with utter shame and infamy.

But what shall I say or do? If I enter into details, the treatise will grow beyond all bounds. Everything is in such dire confusion

---

[167] For fuller discussion of the impediments see Luther's *Vom ehelichen Leben* (1522) in *WA* 10^{II}, 280-287; also the article on "Marriage" by E. Sehling, in Schaff-Herzog, *op. cit.*, VII, 200-203.

[168] Cf. p. 12.

that one does not know where to begin, how far to go, and where to leave off. This I do know, that no state is governed successfully by means of laws. If the ruler is wise, he will govern better by a natural sense of justice than by laws. If he is not wise, he will foster nothing but evil through legislation, since he will not know what use to make of the laws nor how to adapt them to the case at hand. Therefore, in civil affairs more stress should be laid on putting good and wise men in office than on making laws; for such men will themselves be the very best of laws, and will judge every variety of case with a lively sense of equity. And if there is knowledge of the divine law combined with natural wisdom, then written laws will be entirely superfluous and harmful. Above all, love needs no laws whatever.

Nevertheless, I will say and do what I can. I ask and urge all priests and friars[169] when they encounter any impediment to marriage from which the pope can grant dispensation but which is not stated in the Scriptures, by all means to confirm[170] all marriages that may have been contracted[171] in any way contrary to the ecclesiastical or pontifical laws. But let them arm themselves with the divine law which says: "What God has joined together, let no man put asunder" [Matt. 19:6]. For the joining together of a man and a woman is of divine law and is binding, however much it may conflict with the laws of men; the laws of men must give way before it without any hesitation. For if a man leaves father and mother and cleaves to his wife [Matt. 19:5], how much more will he tread underfoot the silly and wicked laws of men, in order to cleave to his wife! And if pope, bishop, or official[172] should annul any marriage because it was contracted contrary to the laws of men, he is Antichrist, he does violence to nature, and is guilty of treason against the Divine Majesty, because this word stands: "What God has joined together, let no man put asunder" [Matt. 19:6].

Besides this, no man had the right to frame such laws, and Christ has granted to Christians a liberty which is above all the

---

[169] It is to be borne in mind that all that follows is in the nature of advice to confessors in dealing with difficult cases of conscience, and is parallel to the closing paragraphs of the section on the Sacrament of the Bread.

[170] Namely, by officiating at the marriage ceremony.

[171] Namely, by betrothal.

[172] Judge of the bishop's court.

laws of men, especially where a law of God conflicts with them. Thus it is said in Mark 2 [:28]: "The Son of man is lord even of the sabbath," and "Man was not made for the sabbath, but the sabbath for man" [Mark 2:27]. Moreover, such laws were condemned beforehand by Paul when he foretold that there would be men forbidding to marry [I Tim. 4:3]. Here, therefore, those inflexible impediments derived from affinity, by spiritual or legal relationship,[173] and from blood relationship must give way, so far as the Scriptures permit, in which the second degree of consanguinity alone is prohibited. Thus it is written in Lev. 18 [:6-18], where there are twelve persons a man is prohibited from marrying: his mother, stepmother, full sister, half-sister by either parent, granddaughter, father's or mother's sister, daughter-in-law, brother's wife, wife's sister, stepdaughter, and his uncle's wife. Here only the first degree of affinity and the second degree of consanguinity are forbidden; yet not without exception, as will appear on closer examination, for the brother's or sister's daughter—the niece—is not included in the prohibition, although she is in the second degree. Therefore, if a marriage has been contracted outside of these degrees, which are the only ones which have been prohibited by God's appointment, it should by no means be annulled on account of the laws of men. For marriage itself, being a divine institution, is incomparably superior to any laws, so that marriage should not be annulled for the sake of the law, rather the laws should be broken for the sake of marriage.

In the same way that nonsense about compaternities, commaternities, confraternities, consororities, and confilieties must be completely abolished in the contracting of marriage. What was it but the superstition of men that invented this "spiritual affinity"? If one who baptized is not permitted to marry her whom he has baptized or stood sponsor for, what right has any Christian man to marry a Christian woman? Is the relationship that grows out of the external rite or sign of the sacrament more intimate than that which grows out of the blessing of the sacrament[174] itself? Is not a Christian man the brother of a Christian woman, and is she not

[173] Relationship arising from sponsorship at baptism or through legal adoption. Cf. *An Open Letter to the Christian Nobility*, *PE* 2, 128-129.

[174] *res sacramenti*, cf. p. 23 n. 45, above.

his sister? Is not a baptized man the spiritual brother of a baptized woman? How foolish we are! If a man instructs his wife in the gospel and in faith in Christ, does he not truly become her father in Christ? And is it not lawful for her to remain his wife? Would not Paul have had the right to marry a girl from among the Corinthians, of whom he boasts that he became their father in Christ? [I Cor. 4:15]. See then, how Christian liberty has been suppressed through the blindness of human superstition.

There is even less in the "legal affinity," and yet they have set it above the divine right of marriage. Nor would I agree to that impediment which they call "disparity of religion," which forbids one to marry an unbaptized person, either simply, or on condition that she be converted to the faith. Who made this prohibition? God or man? Who gave to men the power to prohibit such a marriage? Indeed, the spirits that speak lies in hypocrisy, as Paul says [I Tim. 4:2]. Of them it must be said: "Godless men have told me fables which do not conform to thy law" [Ps. 119:85].[175] The heathen Patricius married the Christian Monica, mother of St. Augustine; why should that not be permitted today? The same stupid, or rather, wicked severity is seen in the "impediment of crime," as when a man has married a woman with whom he previously had committed adultery, or when he plotted to bring about the death of a woman's husband in order to be able to wed the widow. I ask you, whence comes this cruelty of man toward man, which even God never demanded? Do they pretend not to know that Bathsheba, the wife of Uriah, was wed by David, a most saintly man, after the double crime of adultery and murder? [II Sam. 11:1-27]. If the divine law did this, what are these despotic men doing to their fellow servants?

They also recognize what they call "the impediment of a tie," that is, when a man is bound to another woman by betrothal. Here they conclude that, if he has had sexual relations with a second woman, his engagement to the first becomes null and void. This I do not understand at all. I hold that he who has betrothed himself to one woman no longer belongs to himself. Because of this fact, by the prohibition of the divine law, he belongs to the first with whom he has not had intercourse, even though he has had intercourse with the second. For it was not in his power to give the latter what was

[175] Vulgate version.

no longer his own; he has deceived her and actually committed adultery. But they regard the matter differently because they pay more heed to the carnal union than to the divine command, according to which the man, having plighted his troth to the first, is bound to keep it forever. For whoever would give anything must give of that which is his own. And God forbids a man to transgress and wrong his brother in any matter [I Thess. 4:6]. This must be observed over and above all the ordinances of all men. Therefore I believe that such a man cannot with a good conscience live in marriage with a second woman, and this impediment should be completely reversed. For if a monastic vow makes a man no longer his own, why does not a pledge of mutual faithfulness[176] do the same? After all, faithfulness is one of the precepts and fruits of the Spirit, in Gal. 5: [22], while a monastic vow is of human invention. And if a wife may claim her husband back, despite the fact that he has taken a monastic vow, why may not an engaged woman claim back her betrothed, even though he has intercourse with another? But we have said above[177] that he who has plighted his troth to a girl may not take a monastic vow, but is in duty bound to marry her because he is in duty bound to keep faith with her; and this faith he may not break for any ordinance of men, because it is commanded by God. Much more should the man here keep faith with his first betrothed, since he could not plight his troth to a second except with a lying heart; and therefore did not really plight it, but deceived her, his neighbor, against God's command. Therefore, the "impediment of error" [178] enters in here, by which his marriage to the second woman is rendered null and void.

The "impediment of ordination" is also the mere invention of men, especially since they prate that it annuls even a marriage already contracted. They constantly exalt their own ordinances above the commands of God. I do not indeed sit in judgment on the present state of the priestly order, but I observe that Paul charges a bishop to be the husband of one wife [I Tim. 3:2]. Hence,

---

[176] *fides data et accepta.* Luther here regards the *fides* of Gal. 5:22 as *Treue* or "faithfulness." In his New Testament he later translates it as *Glaube* or "faith."

[177] Cf. p. 79.

[178] With fine sarcasm Luther here plays off one impediment against another. "Error" generally meant cases of mistaken identity or false information concerning prior marital status. Cf. *WA* 10^{II}, 285.

no marriage of deacon, priest, bishop or any other order can be annulled, although it is true that Paul knew nothing of this species of priests and of the orders we have today. Perish then those cursed man-made ordinances which have crept into the church only to multiply perils, sins, and evils! There exists, therefore, between a priest and his wife a true and indissoluble marriage, approved by the divine commandment. But what if wicked men in sheer despotism prohibit or annul it? So be it! Let it be wrong among men; it is nevertheless right before God, whose command must take precedence if it conflicts with the commands of men [Acts 5:29].

An equally lying invention is that "impediment of public decency," by which contracted marriages are annulled. I am incensed at that barefaced wickedness which is so ready to put asunder what God has joined together that one may well recognize Antichrist in it, for it opposes all that Christ has done and taught. What earthly reason is there for holding that no relative of a deceased fiancé, even to the fourth degree of consanguinity, may marry his fiancée? That is not a judgment of public decency, but ignorance[179] of public decency. Why was not this judgment of public decency found among the people of Israel, who were endowed with the best laws, the laws of God? On the contrary, the next of kin was even compelled by the law of God to marry the widow of his relative [Deut. 25:5]. Must the people of Christian liberty be burdened with more severe laws than the people of legal bondage?

But, to make an end of these—figments rather than impediments —I will say that so far there seem to me to be no impediments that may justly annul a contracted marriage except these: sexual impotence, ignorance of a previously contracted marriage, and a vow of chastity. Still, concerning this latter vow, I am to this day so far from certain that I do not know at what age such a vow is to be regarded as binding, as I also said above in discussing the sacrament of baptism.[180] Thus you may learn, from this one question of marriage, how wretchedly and desperately all the activities of the church have been confused, hindered, ensnared and subjected to danger through the pestilent, ignorant, and wicked

[179] An untranslatable pun: *non iustitia sed inscitia.*
[180] Cf. pp. 80-81.

ordinances of men, so that there is no hope of betterment unless we abolish at one stroke all the laws of all men, and having restored the gospel of liberty we follow it in judging and regulating all things. Amen.

We must therefore speak of sexual impotence, in order that we may the more readily advise the souls that are laboring in peril.[181] But first I wish to state that what I have said about impediments is intended to apply after a marriage has been contracted. I mean to say that no marriage should be annulled by any such impediment. But as to marriages which are yet to be contracted, I would briefly repeat what I have said above.[182] If there is the stress of youthful passion or some other necessity for which the pope grants dispensation, then any brother may also grant a dispensation to another or even to himself, and following that counsel snatch his wife out of the power of tyrannical laws as best he can. For with what right am I deprived of my liberty by somebody else's superstition and ignorance? If the pope grants a dispensation for money, why should not I, for my soul's salvation, grant a dispensation to myself or to my brother? Does the pope set up laws? Let him set them up for himself, and keep hands off my liberty, or I will take it by stealth!

Now let us discuss the matter of *impotence.*

Consider the following case: A woman, wed to an impotent man, is unable to prove her husband's impotence in court, or perhaps she is unwilling to do so with the mass of evidence and all the notoriety which the law demands; yet she is desirous of having children or is unable to remain continent. Now suppose I had counseled her to procure a divorce from her husband in order to marry another, satisfied that her own and her husband's conscience and their experience were ample testimony of his impotence; but the husband refused his consent to this. Then I would further counsel her, with the consent of the man (who is not really her husband, but only a dweller under the same roof with her), to have intercourse with another, say her husband's brother, but to keep this marriage secret and to ascribe the children to the so-called putative father. The question is: Is such a woman saved and in a saved state? I answer: Certainly, because in this case an error,[183]

[181] Cf. p. 98 n. 169. [182] Cf. pp. 96-98. [183] Cf. p. 101 n. 178.

ignorance of the man's impotence, impedes the marriage; and the tyranny of the laws permits no divorce. But the woman is free through the divine law, and cannot be compelled to remain continent. Therefore the man ought to concede her right, and give up to somebody else the wife who is his only in outward appearance.

Moreover, if the man will not give his consent, or agree to this separation—rather than allow the woman to burn [I Cor. 7:9] or to commit adultery—I would counsel her to contract a marriage with another and flee to a distant unknown place. What other counsel can be given to one constantly struggling with the dangers of natural emotions? Now I know that some are troubled by the fact that the children of this secret marriage are not the rightful heirs of their putative father. But if it was done with the consent of the husband, then the children will be the rightful heirs. If, however, it was done without his knowledge or against his will, then let unbiased Christian reason, or better, charity, decide which one of the two has done the greater injury to the other. The wife alienates the inheritance, but the husband has deceived his wife and is defrauding her completely of her body and her life. Is not the sin of a man who wastes his wife's body and life a greater sin than that of the woman who merely alienates the temporal goods of her husband? Let him, therefore, agree to a divorce, or else be satisfied with heirs not his own, for by his own fault he deceived an innocent girl and defrauded her both of life and of the full use of her body, besides giving her an almost irresistible cause for committing adultery. Let both be weighed in the same scales. Certainly, by every right, fraud should recoil on the fraudulent, and whoever has done an injury must make it good. What is the difference between such a husband and the man who holds another man's wife captive together with her husband? Is not such a tyrant compelled to support wife and children and husband, or else to set them free? Why should not the same hold true here? Therefore I maintain that the man should be compelled either to submit to a divorce or to support the other man's child as his heir. Doubtless this would be the judgment of charity. In that case, the impotent man, who is not really the husband, should support the heir of his wife in the same spirit in which he would at great expense wait on his wife if she fell sick or suffered some other ill; for it is by his fault and not by his wife's that she suffers this ill. This I have set forth to the best of my ability, for the strengthening of anxious consciences, because my desire is to bring my afflicted brethren in this captivity what little comfort I can.[184]

As to divorce, it is still a question for debate whether it is allowable. For my part I so greatly detest divorce that I should prefer bigamy to it[185]; but whether it is allowable, I do not venture to decide. Christ himself, the Chief Shepherd, says in Matt. 5 [:32]: "Every one who divorces his wife, except on the ground of unchastity, makes her an adulteress; and whoever marries a divorced woman commits adultery." Christ, then, permits divorce, but only on the ground of unchastity. The pope must, therefore, be in error whenever he grants a divorce for any other cause; and no one should feel safe who has obtained a dispensation by this temerity (not authority) of the pope. Yet it is still a greater wonder to me, why they compel a man to remain unmarried after being separated from his wife by divorce, and why they will not permit him to remarry. For if Christ permits divorce on the ground of unchastity and compels no one to remain unmarried, and if Paul would rather have us marry than burn [I Cor. 7:9], then he certainly seems to permit

[184] Several factors ought to be considered in evaluating the two preceding paragraphs, a much criticized section which Wace and Buchheim have omitted altogether from their translation: (1) Couched in the language of the scholars only, this Latin treatise was not intended for popular consumption but rather as a guide for bewildered and confused priests, who were called upon in the confessional to give practical advice and spiritual comfort to troubled souls (cf. p. 98 n. 169). (2) The impediment of impotency was, even according to Roman church law, sufficient ground for declaring a marriage null and void. (3) But the legal process of securing an annulment demanded such an involved procedure for establishing proof that it was equally unpleasant for both parties. (4) Then, as now, divorce under any circumstances was absolutely forbidden by Roman church law. (5) As an alternate to an impossible legal solution, Luther's suggestion of a secret marriage was not without precedent; common law in parts of Westphalia and Lower Saxony, for example, prescribed that a man who could not perform his conjugal duty was required to seek satisfaction for his wife through a neighbor (Jacob Grimm, *Weisthümer* [Göttingen, 1842], III, 42, 48, 70, 311). (6) That Luther's position did not involve any unconditional license for frustrated wives to engage in extra-marital liaisons, as his malicious interpreters promptly inferred, is underscored in his *Sermon vom ehelichen Leben* of 1522, where he scores the offending husband even more severely than he does now ("when I was still shy"). *WA* 10II, 278-279. Cf. Buchwald, *op. cit.*, II, 482 n. 4, and Woolf, *op. cit.*, p. 303 n. 2.

[185] As he actually did later in the case of Henry VIII and Philip of Hesse, considering it to be the lesser of two evils insofar as it was not without divinely sanctioned precedent in the Old Testament

a man to marry another woman in the place of the one who has been put away. I wish that this subject were fully discussed and made clear and decided, so that counsel might be given in the infinite perils of those who, without any fault of their own, are nowadays compelled to remain unmarried; that is, those whose wives or husbands have run away and deserted them, to come back perhaps after ten years, perhaps never! This matter troubles and distresses me, for there are daily cases, whether by the special malice of Satan or because of our neglect of the Word of God.

I, indeed, who alone against all cannot establish any rule in this matter, would yet greatly desire at least the passage in I Cor. 7 [:15] to be applied here: "But if the unbelieving partner desires to separate, let it be so; in such a case the brother or sister is not bound." Here the Apostle gives permission to put away the unbeliever who departs and to set the believing spouse free to marry again. Why should not the same hold true when a believer—that is, a believer in name, but in truth as much an unbeliever as the one Paul speaks of—deserts his wife, especially if he intends never to return. I certainly can see no difference between the two. But I believe that if in the Apostle's day an unbelieving deserter had returned and had become a believer or had promised to live again with his believing wife, it would not have been permitted, but he too would have been given the right to marry again. Nevertheless, in these matters I decide nothing (as I have said), although there is nothing that I would rather see decided, since nothing at present more grievously perplexes me, and many others with me. I would have nothing decided here on the mere authority of the pope and the bishops; but if two learned and good men agreed [Matt. 18:19-20] in the name of Christ and published their opinion in the spirit of Christ, I should prefer their judgment even to such councils as are assembled nowadays, famous only for numbers and authority, not for scholarship and saintliness. Therefore I hang up my lyre[186] on this matter until a better man confers with me about it.

Ordination

Of this sacrament the church of Christ knows nothing; it is an invention of the church of the pope. Not only is there nowhere

[186] This is an allusion to the fact that he is writing a "prelude." Cf. Ps. 137:2.

any promise of grace attached to it, but there is not a single word said about it in the whole New Testament. Now it is ridiculous to put forth as a sacrament of God something that cannot be proved to have been instituted by God. I do not hold that this rite, which has been observed for so many centuries, should be condemned; but in sacred things I am opposed to the invention of human fictions. And it is not right to give out as divinely instituted what was not divinely instituted, lest we become a laughingstock to our opponents. We ought to see that every article of faith of which we boast is certain, pure, and based on clear passages of Scripture. But we are utterly unable to do that in the case of the sacrament under consideration.

The church has no power to make new divine promises of grace, as some prate, who hold that what is decreed by the church is of no less authority than what is decreed by God, since the church is under the guidance of the Holy Spirit. For the church was born by the word of promise through faith, and by this same word is nourished and preserved. That is to say, it is the promises of God that make the church, and not the church that makes the promise of God. For the Word of God is incomparably superior to the church, and in this Word the church, being a creature, has nothing to decree, ordain, or make, but only to be decreed, ordained, and made. For who begets his own parent? Who first brings forth his own maker?

This one thing indeed the church can do: It can distinguish the Word of God from the words of men; as Augustine confesses that he believed the gospel because he was moved by the authority of the church which proclaimed that this is the gospel.[187] Not that the church is therefore above the gospel; if that were true, she would also be above God, in whom we believe because the church proclaims that he is God. But, as Augustine says elsewhere,[188] the truth itself lays hold on the soul and thus renders it able to judge

[187] "Against the Epistle of Manichaeus Called Fundamental" in *The Nicene and Post-Nicene Fathers of the Christian Church*, ed. Philip Schaff (Buffalo, 1887), Series I, IV, 131. Migne 42, 176. Luther gives a fuller interpretation of the meaning of Augustine's statement in *A Reply to the Texts Quoted in Defense of the Doctrines of Men* (1522). *PE* 2, 451-453.

[188] "The Trinity," 9, 6, 10, ed. John Baillie, *et al.*, *The Library of Christian Classics* (Philadelphia, 1955), VIII, 64. Migne 42, 966.

most certainly of all things; however, the soul is not able to judge the truth, but is compelled to say with unerring certainty that this is the truth. For example, our mind declares with unerring certainty that three and seven are ten; and yet it cannot give a reason why this is true, although it cannot deny that it is true. It is clearly taken captive by the truth; and, rather than judging the truth, it is itself judged by it. There is such a mind also in the church, when under the enlightenment of the Spirit she judges and approves doctrines; she is unable to prove it, and yet is most certain of having it. For as among philosophers no one judges the general concepts, but all are judged by them, so it is among us with the mind of the Spirit, Who judges all things and is judged by no one, as the Apostle says [I Cor. 2:16]. But of this another time.

Let this then stand fast: The church can give no promises of grace; that is the work of God alone. Therefore she cannot institute a sacrament. But even if she could, it still would not necessarily follow that ordination is a sacrament. For who knows which is the church that has the Spirit? For when such decisions are made there are usually only a few bishops or scholars present; and it is possible that these may not be really of the church. All may err, as councils have repeatedly erred, particularly the Council of Constance,[189] which erred most wickedly of all. Only that which has the approval of the church universal, and not of the Roman church alone, rests on a trustworthy foundation. I therefore admit that ordination is a certain churchly rite, on a par with many others introduced by the church fathers, such as the consecration of vessels, houses, vestments, water, salt,[190] candles,[191] herbs,[192] wine,[193] and the like. No one calls any of these a sacrament, nor is there in them any promise. In the same manner, to anoint a man's hands with oil, or to shave his head and the like is not to administer a sacrament,

[189] Cf. p. 27 n. 55, and p. 28 n. 58.

[190] Used in connection with baptism.

[191] Used on Candlemas, Feast of the Purification of Mary, February 2.

[192] Used on the Feasts of the Assumption of Mary, August 15; and of St. Peter's Chains, August 1.

[193] Not the sacramental element, but the wine consecrated on the Feast of St. John, December 27, and drunk as a remembrance of John at the time of weddings, dying, and departing on a journey. Cf. Buchwald, *op. cit.*, II, 489 n. 2.

since no promise is attached to them; they are simply being prepared for a certain office, like a vessel or an instrument.

But you will say: "What do you do with Dionysius,[194] who in his *Ecclesiastical Hierarchy* enumerates six sacraments, among which he also includes ordination?" I answer: I am well aware that this is the one writer of antiquity who is cited in support of the seven sacraments, although he omits marriage and so has only six.[195] But we read nothing at all about these "sacraments" in the rest of the fathers; nor do they ever regard them as sacraments when they speak of these things. For the invention of sacraments is of recent date.[196] Indeed, to speak more boldly, it greatly displeases me to assign such importance to this Dionysius, whoever he may have been, for he shows hardly any signs of solid learning. I would ask, by what authority and with what arguments does he prove his hodge-podge about the angels in his *Celestial Hierarchy*—a book over which many curious and superstitious spirits have cudgeled their brains? If one were to read and judge without prejudice, is not everything in it his own fancy and very much like a dream? But in his *Theology*, which is rightly called *Mystical*, of which certain very ignorant theologians make so much, he is downright dangerous, for he is more of a Platonist than a Christian. So if I had my way, no believing soul would give the least attention to these books. So far, indeed, from learning Christ in them, you will lose even what you already know of him. I speak from experience Let us rather hear Paul, that we may learn Jesus Christ and him crucified [I Cor. 2:2]. He is the way, the life, and the truth; he is the ladder [Gen. 28:12] by which we come to the Father, as he says: "No one comes to the Father, but by me" [John 14:6].

---

[194] Dionysius, the Areopagite, was the pseudonym of the unknown author (*circa* 500, in Syria?) of the neoplatonic writings, *Of the Celestial Hierarchy, Of the Ecclesiastical Hierarchy*, and *Of Mystical Theology*. J. P. Migne (ed.), *Patrologiae, Series Graeca*, vol. 3. Luther was among the first to question the high repute and ancient origin which tradition had assigned to these writings when it identified their author with Paul's convert of Acts 17:34.

[195] Omitting marriage, confirmation, and penance, Dionysius mentions six sacraments: baptism, eucharist, unction, ordination of priests, ordination of monks, and burial rites. Schaff-Herzog, *op. cit.*, X, 142.

[196] The system of seven sacraments was first generally accepted on the authority of Peter Lombard, and was first made official doctrine by the Council of Florence, 1439. Buchwald, *op. cit.*, II, 490 n. 2.

Similarly, in the *Ecclesiastical Hierarchy,* what does this Dionysius do but describe certain churchly rites, and amuse himself with allegories without proving anything? Just as has been done in our time by the author of the book entitled *Rationale divinorum.*[197] Such allegorical studies are for idle men. Do you think I should find it difficult to amuse myself with allegories about anything in creation? Did not Bonaventura by allegory draw the liberal arts into theology? [198] And Gerson even converted the smaller Donatus into a mystical theologian.[199] It would not be difficult for me to compose a better hierarchy than that of Dionysius; for he knew nothing of pope, cardinals and archbishops, and put the bishop at the top. Who has so weak a mind as not to be able to launch into allegories? I would not have a theologian devote himself to allegories until he has exhausted the legitimate and simple meaning of the Scripture; otherwise his theology will bring him into danger, as Origen[200] discovered.

Therefore a thing does not need to be a sacrament simply because Dionysius so describes it. Otherwise, why not also make a sacrament of the [funeral] processions, which he describes in his book, and which continue to this day? There will then be as many sacraments as there have been rites and ceremonies multiplied in the church. Standing on so unsteady a foundation, they have

---

[197] William Durandus (1237-96), bishop of Mende. His book, written in 1296, is the standard authority for the laws, ceremonies, customs, and symbolism of thirteenth-century Roman rites and vestments. *Catholic Encyclopedia, op. cit.,* V, 207.

[198] In his *De reductione artium ad theologiam,* the Franciscan Bonaventura (1221-1274) sought to relate all human knowledge to theology. All the arts and sciences were found to have points of contact in Scripture; and their several activities were regarded as parables of heavenly processes. Buchwald, *op. cit.,* II, 491 n. 4.

[199] Donatus (*circa* 350 A.D.), famous Latin grammarian, whose *Ars Minor* was the favorite medieval textbook. The chancellor of the University of Paris, John Gerson (1363-1429), published a *Donatus moralisatus seu per allegoriam traductus,* a mystical grammar, in which the noun was compared to man, the pronoun to man's sinful state, the verb to the divine command to love, the adverb to the fulfilment of the divine law, etc.

[200] Cf. p.30 n. 65. Woolf regards Luther's anti-allegorical insistence on the plain sense of Scripture as his greatest single contribution to modern biblical scholarship, and sees a most excellent example of his exegetical method on pp. 117-123 in this volume where he is discussing extreme unction. Cf. Woolf, *op. cit.,* 312 n. 1.

nevertheless invented "characters"[201] which they attribute to this sacrament of theirs and which are indelibly impressed on those who are ordained. Whence do such ideas come, I ask? By what authority, with what arguments, are they established? We do not object to their being free to invent, say, and assert whatever they please; but we also insist on our liberty, that they shall not arrogate to themselves the right to turn their opinions into articles of faith, as they have hitherto presumed to do. It is enough that we accommodate ourselves to their rites and ceremonies for the sake of peace; but we refuse to be bound by such things as if they were necessary to salvation, which they are not. Let them lay aside their despotic demand, and we shall yield free obedience to their wishes, in order that we may live in peace with one another. It is a shameful and wicked slavery for a Christian man, who is free, to be subject to any but heavenly and divine ordinances.

We come now to their strongest argument. It is this: Christ said at the Last Supper: "Do this in remembrance of me" [Luke 22:19; I Cor. 11:24-25]. "Look," they say, "here Christ ordained the apostles to the priesthood." From this passage they also concluded, among other things, that both kinds are to be administered to the priest alone.[202] In fact, they have drawn out of this passage whatever they pleased, as men who would arrogate to themselves the liberty to prove anything whatever from any words of Christ. But is that interpreting the words of God? I ask you: is it? Christ gives us no promise here, but only commands that this be done in remembrance of him. Why do they not conclude that he also ordained priests when he laid upon them the office of the Word and baptism, and said: "Go into all the world and preach the gospel to the whole creation, baptizing them in the name, etc." [Mark

[201] The so-called *character indelibilis,* peculiar gift of ordination, meant that "once a priest, always a priest." This "indelible mark" received authoritative statement in the bull *Exultate Deo* (1439). Eugene IV, summing up the decrees of the Council of Florence, says: "Among these sacraments there are three—baptism, confirmation, and orders—which indelibly impress upon the soul a character, i.e., a certain spiritual mark which distinguishes them from the rest." The Council of Trent (1563) further defined the correct Roman teachings as follows: "The Holy Synod justly condemns the opinion of those who assert that the priests of the New Testament have only temporary power, and that those once rightly ordained can again be made laymen, if they do not exercise the ministry of the Word of God." *PE* 2, 68 n. 5.

[202] Cf. pp. 20-28.

16:15; Matt. 28:19]. For it is the proper duty of priests to preach and to baptize. Or, since it is nowadays the chief, and (as they say) indispensable duty of priests to read the canonical hours,[203] why have they not discovered the sacrament of ordination in those passages in which Christ commanded them to pray, as he did in many places—particularly in the garden, that they might not enter into temptation? [Matt. 26:41]. But perhaps they will evade this argument by saying that it is not commanded to pray; it is enough to read the canonical hours. Then it follows that this priestly work can be proved nowhere in the Scriptures, and thus their praying priesthood is not of God; as, indeed, it is not.

But which of the ancient Fathers claimed that in this passage priests were ordained? Where does this new interpretation come from? I will tell you. They have sought by this means to set up a seed bed of implacable discord, by which clergy and laymen should be separated from each other farther than heaven from earth, to the incredible injury of the grace of baptism and to the confusion of our fellowship in the gospel. Here, indeed, are the roots of that detestable tyranny of the clergy over the laity. Trusting in the external anointing by which their hands are consecrated, in the tonsure and in vestments, they not only exalt themselves above the rest of the lay Christians, who are only anointed with the Holy Spirit, but regard them almost as dogs and unworthy to be included with themselves in the church. Hence they are bold to demand, to exact, to threaten, to urge, to oppress, as much as they please. In short, the sacrament of ordination has been and still is an admirable device for establishing all the horrible things that have been done hitherto in the church, and are yet to be done. Here Christian brotherhood has perished, here shepherds have been turned into wolves, servants into tyrants, churchmen into worse than worldlings.

If they were forced to grant that all of us that have been baptized are equally priests, as indeed we are, and that only the ministry was committed to them, yet with our common consent, they would then know that they have no right to rule over us except insofar as we freely concede it. For thus it is written in

[203] The stated daily prayers, fixed by canon, and contained in the breviary. The seven hours are respectively: matins (including nocturns and lauds), prime, tierce, sext, nones, vespers, and compline.

I Pet. 2 [:9]: "You are a chosen race, a royal priesthood, and a priestly royalty." Therefore we are all priests, as many of us as are Christians.[204] But the priests, as we call them, are ministers chosen from among us. All that they do is done in our name; the priesthood is nothing but a ministry. This we learn from I Cor. 4 [:1]: "This is how one should regard us, as servants of Christ and stewards of the mysteries of God."

From this it follows that whoever does not preach the Word, though he was called by the church to do this very thing, is no priest at all, and that the sacrament of ordination can be nothing else than a certain rite by which the church chooses its preachers. For this is the way a priest is defined in Mal. 2 [:7]: "The lips of a priest should guard knowledge, and men should seek instruction from his mouth, for he is the messenger of the Lord of hosts." You may be certain, then, that whoever is not a messenger of the Lord of hosts, or whoever is called to do anything else than such messenger service—if I may so term it—is in no sense a priest; as Hos. 4 [:6] says: "Because you have rejected knowledge, I reject you from being a priest to me." They are also called pastors because they are to pasture, that is, to teach. Therefore, those who are ordained only to read the canonical hours and to offer masses are indeed papal priests, but not Christian priests, because they not only do not preach, but they are not even called to preach. Indeed, it comes to this, that a priesthood of that sort is a different estate altogether from the office of preaching. Thus they are hour-reading and mass-saying priests—sort of living idols called priests—really such priests as Jeroboam ordained, in Beth-aven,[205] taken from the lowest dregs of the people, and not of Levi's tribe [I Kings 12:31].

See how far the glory of the church has departed! The whole earth is filled with priests, bishops, cardinals, and clergy; yet not one of them preaches so far as his official duty is concerned, unless he is called to do so by a different call over and above his sacra-

[204] Cf. *An Open Letter to the Christian Nobility. PE* 2, 69. The fullest development of Luther's doctrine of the spiritual priesthood of believers is to be found in his writings against Emser (cf. p. 12 n. 4), especially his *Answer to the Superchristian, Superspiritual, and Superlearned Book of Goat Emser of Leipzig* (1521). *PE* 3, 310-401. Cf. also *The Misuse of the Mass* in this volume, pp. 127-230.

[205] Cf. p. 88 n. 153.

mental ordination. Every one thinks he is doing full justice to his ordination by mumbling the vain repetitions of his prescribed prayers and by celebrating masses. Moreover, he never really prays when he repeats those hours; or if he does pray, he prays them for himself. And he offers his mass as if it were a sacrifice, which is the height of perversity because the mass consists in the use made of the sacrament. It is clear, therefore, that the ordination, which, as a sacrament, makes clergymen of this sort of men, is in truth nothing but a mere fiction, devised by men who understand nothing about the church, the priesthood, the ministry of the Word, or the sacraments. Thus, as the "sacrament" is, so are the priests it makes. To such errors and such blindness has been added a still worse captivity: in order to separate themselves still farther from other Christians, whom they deem profane, they have unmanned themselves, like the Galli, who were the priests of Cybele,[206] and they have taken upon themselves the burden of a spurious celibacy.

To satisfy this hypocrisy and the working of this error it was not enough that bigamy should be prohibited, that is, the having of two wives at one time, as it was forbidden in the law (and as is the accepted meaning of the term); but they have called it bigamy if a man marries two virgins, one after the other, or if he marries one widow. Indeed, so holy is the holiness of this most holy sacrament that no man can become a priest if he has married a virgin and his wife is still living. And—here we reach the very summit of sanctity—a man is even prevented from entering the priesthood if he has married a woman who was not a virgin, though he did so in ignorance or by unfortunate mischance. But if one has defiled six hundred harlots, or violated countless matrons and virgins, or even kept many Ganymedes, that would be no impediment to his becoming bishop or cardinal or pope. Moreover, the Apostle's word "husband of one wife" [I Tim. 3:2] must now be interpreted to mean "the prelate of one church," and this has given rise to the "incompatible benefices."[207] At the same time the pope, that

[206] The eunuch priests of Cybele, "the Great Mother," ancient Phrygian nature goddess, were known as Galli. They ran about with dreadful cries, beating cymbals and cutting their flesh with knives.

[207] The Fourth Lateran Council of 1215 had decreed that no one could simultaneously hold two offices involving pastoral care. The clever and lucrative ways in which the popes legally circumvented this statute Luther describes in *An Open Letter to the Christian Nobility*. *PE* 2, 91-96.

munificent dispenser, may join to one man three, twenty or a hundred wives, that is, churches, if he is bribed with money or power, that is, "moved by godly charity and constrained by the care of the churches" [II Cor. 11:28].

O pontiffs worthy of this venerable sacrament of ordination! O princes, not of the catholic churches, but of the synagogues of Satan [Rev. 2:9] and of darkness itself! I would cry out with Isaiah [Isa. 28:14], "You scoffers, who rule this people in Jerusalem"; and with Amos 6 [:1], "Woe to those who are at ease in Zion, and to those who feel secure on the mountain of Samaria, the notable men of the first of the nations, that go in with state into the house of Israel, etc.!" O the disgrace that these monstrous priests bring upon the church of God! Where are there any bishops or priests who even know the gospel, not to speak of preaching it? Why then do they boast of being priests? Why do they desire to be regarded as holier and better and mightier than other Christians, who are merely laymen? To read the hours—what unlearned men, or (as the Apostle says) men speaking with tongues [I Cor. 14:23] cannot do that? But to pray the hours—that belongs to monks, hermits, and men in private life, even though they are laymen. The duty of a priest is to preach, and if he does not preach he is as much a priest as a picture of a man is a man. Does ordaining such babbling priests make one a bishop? Or blessing churches and bells? Or confirming children? Certainly not. Any deacon or layman could do as much. It is the ministry of the Word that makes the priest and the bishop.

Therefore my advice is: Begone, all of you that would live in safety; flee, young men, and do not enter upon this holy estate, unless you are determined to preach the gospel, and can believe that you are made not one whit better than the laity through this "sacrament" of ordination! For to read the hours is nothing, and to offer mass is to receive the sacrament. What then is there left to you that every layman does not have? Tonsure and vestments? A sorry priest, indeed, who consists of tonsure and vestments! Or the oil poured on your fingers? But every Christian is anointed and sanctified both in body and soul with the oil of the Holy Spirit. In ancient times every Christian handled the sacrament with his hands as often as the priests do now.[208] But today our superstition

[208] Cf. 25-26.

counts it a great crime if the laity touch either the bare chalice or the corporal; not even a nun who is a pure virgin would be permitted to wash the palls[209] and the sacred linens of the altar. O God! See how far the sacrosanct sanctity of this "sacrament" of ordination has gone! I expect the time will come when the laity will not be permitted to touch the altar—except when they offer their money. I almost burst with indignation when I contemplate the wicked tyrannies of these brazen men, who with their farcical and childish fancies mock and overthrow the liberty and glory of the Christian religion.

Let everyone, therefore, who knows himself to be a Christian, be assured of this, that we are all equally priests, that is to say, we have the same power in respect to the Word and the sacraments. However, no one may make use of this power except by the consent of the community or by the call of a superior. (For what is the common property of all, no individual may arrogate to himself, unless he is called.) And therefore this "sacrament" of ordination, if it is anything at all, is nothing else than a certain rite whereby one is called to the ministry of the church. Furthermore, the priesthood is properly nothing but the ministry of the Word—the Word, I say; not the law, but the gospel. And the diaconate is the ministry, not of reading the Gospel or the Epistle, as is the present practice, but of distributing the church's aid to the poor, so that the priests may be relieved of the burden of temporal matters and may give themselves more freely to prayer and the Word. For this was the purpose of the institution of the diaconate, as we read in Acts 5 [6:1-6]. Whoever, therefore, does not know or preach the gospel is not only no priest or bishop, but he is a kind of pest to the church, who under the false title of priest or bishop, or dressed in sheep's clothing, actually does violence to the gospel and plays the wolf [Matt. 7:15] in the church.

Therefore, unless these priests and bishops, with whom the church abounds today, work out their salvation [Phil. 2:12] in some other way; unless they realize that they are not priests or bishops, and bemoan the fact that they bear the name of an office whose duties they either do not know or cannot fulfil, and thus with prayers and tears lament their wretched hypocritical life—unless they

[209] Covers for the chalice.

do this, they are truly the people of eternal perdition, and the words of Isa. 5 [:13f.] are fulfilled in them: "Therefore my people go into exile for want of knowledge; their honored men are dying of hunger, and their multitude is parched with thirst. Therefore Hell has enlarged its appetite and opened its mouth beyond measure, and the nobility of Jerusalem and her multitude go down, her throng and he who exults in her." What a dreadful word for our age, in which Christians are swallowed up in so deep an abyss!

According to what the Scriptures teach us, what we call the priesthood is a ministry. So I cannot understand at all why one who has once been made a priest cannot again become a layman; for the sole difference between him and a layman is his ministry. But to depose a man from the priesthood is by no means impossible, because even now it is the usual penalty imposed upon guilty priests. They are either suspended temporarily, or permanently deprived of their office. For that fiction of an "indelible character"[210] has long since become a laughingstock. I admit that the pope imparts this "character," but Christ knows nothing of it; and a priest who is consecrated with it becomes the life-long servant and captive, not of Christ, but of the pope, as is the case nowadays. Moreover, unless I am greatly mistaken, if this sacrament and this fiction ever fall to the ground, the papacy with its "characters" will scarcely survive. Then our joyous liberty will be restored to us; we shall realize that we are all equal by every right. Having cast off the yoke of tyranny, we shall know that he who is a Christian has Christ; and that he who has Christ has all things that are Christ's, and can do all things [Phil. 4:13]. Of this I will write more,[211] and more vigorously, as soon as I perceive that the above has displeased my friends the papists.

The Sacrament of Extreme Unction

To this rite of anointing the sick the theologians of our day have made two additions which are worthy of them: first, they call it a sacrament, and second, they make it the last sacrament. So it is now the sacrament of extreme unction, which is to be

[210] Cf. p. 111 n. 201.

[211] These basic ideas received expanded treatment about six weeks later in *The Freedom of a Christian. LW* 31, 329-377.

administered only to those who are at the point of death. Since they are such subtle dialectitians, perhaps they have done this in order to relate it to the first unction of baptism[212] and the two subsequent ones of confirmation and ordination. But here they are able to cast in my teeth that, in the case of this sacrament, there are on the authority of the apostle James both promise and sign, which, as I have maintained all along, do constitute a sacrament. For the apostle says [Jas. 5:14-15]: "Is any among you sick? Let him call for the elders of the church, and let them pray over him, anointing him with oil in the name of the Lord; and the prayer of faith will save the sick man, and the Lord will raise him up; and if he has committed sins, he will be forgiven." There, they say, you have the promise of the forgiveness of sins and the sign of the oil.

But I say: If ever folly has been uttered, it has been uttered especially on this subject: I will say nothing of the fact that many[213] assert with much probability that this epistle is not by James the apostle, and that it is not worthy of an apostolic spirit; although, whoever was its author, it has come to be regarded as authoritative. But even if the apostle James did write it, I still would say, that no apostle has the right on his own authority to institute a sacrament, that is, to give a divine promise with a sign attached. For this belongs to Christ alone. Thus Paul says that he received from the Lord [I Cor. 11:23] the sacrament of the Eucharist, and that he was not sent to baptize, but to preach the gospel [I Cor. 1:17]. And nowhere do we read in the gospel of the sacrament of extreme unction. But let us also pass over this point. Let us examine the words of the apostle, or whoever was the author of the epistle, and we shall see at once how little heed these multipliers of sacraments have given to them.

In the first place, if they believe the apostle's words to be true and binding, by what right do they change and contradict them? Why do they make an extreme and a special kind of unction out of that which the apostle wished to be general? For the apostle

212 In the order for baptism, just after the Creed, the child was anointed with oil on chest and shoulders. Buchwald, *op. cit.*, II, 501 n. 1.

213 Eusebius (*circa* 275-340) classed it among the *antilegomena* or contested writings. Jerome (*circa* 340-420) says it was regarded as pseudonymous in the Latin church. Luther's contemporaries, the humanist Erasmus and the Catholic Cajetan, both contested its authenticity. See *LW* 35, 395 n. 47.

did not desire it to be an extreme unction or administered only to the dying, but he says expressly: "Is any one sick?" He does not say: "Is any one dying?" I do not care what learned discussions Dionysius has on this point in his *Ecclesiastical Hierarchy*.[214] The apostle's words are clear enough, on which he as well as they rely; but they do not follow them. It is evident, therefore, that they have arbitrarily and without any authority made a sacrament and an extreme unction out of the words of the apostle which they have wrongly interpreted. And this works to the detriment of all other sick persons, whom they have deprived on their own authority of the benefit of the unction which the apostle enjoined.

But this is even a finer point: The apostle's promise expressly declares: "The prayer of faith will save the sick man, and the Lord will raise him up, etc." [Jas. 5:15]. See, the apostle in this passage commands us to anoint and to pray, in order that the sick man may be healed and raised up; that is, that he may not die, and that it may not be an extreme unction. This is proved also by the prayers which are used even to this day during the anointing, because the prayers are for the recovery of the sick man. But they say, on the contrary, that the unction must be administered to none but the dying;[215] that is, that they may not be healed and raised up. If it were not so serious a matter, who could help laughing at this beautiful, apt, and sensible exposition of the apostle's words? Is not the folly of the sophists here shown in its true colors? Because here, as in so many other places, it affirms what the Scriptures deny, and denies what the Scriptures affirm. Why should we not give thanks to these excellent masters of ours?[216] Surely I spoke the truth when I said that they never uttered greater folly than on this subject.

Furthermore, if this unction is a sacrament, it must necessarily be (as they say) an "effective sign"[217] of that which it signifies and promises. Now it promises health and recovery to the sick, as the words plainly say: "The prayer of faith will save the sick man, and the Lord will raise him up" [Jas. 5:15]. But who does not

---

[214] Cf. p. 109 n. 194.
[215] All editions have *discessuris*, "departing," but *WA* 6, 568 n. 35, suggests *decessuris*, "dying."
[216] Cf. pp. 11-12.
[217] Cf. pp. 64-65.

see that this promise is seldom, if ever, fulfilled? Scarcely one in a thousand is restored to health, and when one is restored nobody believes that it came about through the sacrament, but through the working of nature or of medicine. Indeed to the sacrament they ascribe the opposite effect. What shall we say then? Either the apostle lies in making this promise or else this unction is no sacrament. For the sacramental promise is certain; but this promise fails in the majority of cases. Indeed—and here again we recognize the shrewdness and foresight of these theologians—for this very reason they would have it to be extreme unction, that the promise should not stand; in other words, that the sacrament should be no sacrament. For if it is extreme unction, it does not heal, but gives way to the disease; but if it heals, it cannot be extreme unction. Thus, by the interpretation of these masters, James is shown to have contradicted himself, and to have instituted a sacrament in order not to institute one; for they must have an extreme unction just to make untrue what the apostle intends, namely, the healing of the sick by it. If this is not madness, I ask you what is?

The word of the apostle in I Tim. 1 [:7] describes these people: "Desiring to be teachers of the law, without understanding either what they are saying or the things about which they make assertions." Thus they read and follow everything uncritically. With the same carelessness they have also found auricular confession in the apostle's words: "Confess your sins to one another" [Jas. 5:16]. But they do not observe the command of the apostle, that the elders of the church be called, and prayer be made for the sick [Jas. 5:14]. Scarcely one insignificant priest is sent nowadays, although the apostle would have many present, not because of the unction, but because of the prayer. That is why he says: "The prayer of faith will save the sick man, etc." [Jas. 5:15]. I have my doubts, however, whether he would have us understand "priests" when he says "presbyters," that is, "elders." For one who is an elder is not necessarily a priest or a minister. We may suspect that the apostle desired the older, graver men in the church to visit the sick, to perform a work of mercy, and pray in faith and thus heal him. Yet, it cannot be denied that the churches were once ruled by older persons, chosen for this purpose without these ordinations and consecrations, solely on account of their age and long experience.

Therefore I take it that this unction is the same as that practiced by the apostles, of whom it is written in Mark 6 [:13]: "They anointed with oil many that were sick and healed them." It was a rite of the early church, by which they worked miracles on the sick, and which has long since ceased. In the same way Christ, in the last chapter of Mark [16:18], gave to believers the power to pick up serpents, lay hands on the sick, etc. It is a wonder that they have not made sacraments of those words also, for they have the same power and promise as these words of James. Therefore this extreme —which is to say fictitious—unction is not a sacrament, but a counsel of James, which anyone who will may follow; and it is derived from Mark 6 [:13], as I have said. I do not believe that it was a counsel given to all sick persons, for the church's infirmity is her glory and death is gain [Phil. 1:21]; but it was given only to such as might bear their sickness impatiently and with little faith, those whom the Lord allowed to remain in order that miracles and the power of faith might be manifest in them.

James made careful and diligent provision in this case by attaching the promise of healing and the forgiveness of sins not to the unction, but to the prayer of faith. For he says: "And the prayer of faith will save the sick man, and the Lord will raise him up; and if he has committed sins, he will be forgiven" [Jas. 5:15]. A sacrament does not demand prayer and faith on the part of the minister, since even a wicked person may baptize and consecrate without prayer; a sacrament depends solely on the promise and institution of God, and requires faith on the part of the recipient. But where is the prayer of faith in our present use of extreme unction? Who prays over the sick one in such faith as not to doubt that he will recover? Such a prayer of faith James here describes, of which he said at the beginning of his epistle: "But let him ask in faith, with no doubting" [Jas. 1:6]. And Christ says of it: "Whatever you ask in prayer, believe that you receive it, and you will" [Mark 11:24].

There is no doubt at all that, even if today such a prayer were made over a sick man, that is, made in full faith by older, graver, and saintly men, as many as we wished would be healed. For what could not faith do? But we neglect this faith which the authority of the apostle demands above all else. Further, by "presbyters"—

that is, men pre-eminent by reason of their age and faith—we understand the common herd of priests. Moreover, we turn the daily or temporally unrestricted unction into an extreme unction. And finally, we do not obtain the result promised by the apostle, namely, the healing of the sick, but we render the promise ineffective by doing the very opposite. And yet we boast that our sacrament, or rather figment, is established and proved by this saying of the apostle, which is diametrically opposed[218] to it. O what theologians!

Now I do not condemn this our "sacrament" of extreme unction, but I firmly deny that it is what the apostle James prescribes; for his unction agrees with ours neither in form, use, power, nor purpose. Nevertheless, we shall number it among those "sacraments" which we have instituted, such as the blessing and sprinkling of salt[219] and water. For we cannot deny that any creature whatsoever may be consecrated by the Word and by prayer, as the apostle Paul teaches us [I Tim. 4:4-5]. We do not deny, therefore, that forgiveness and peace are granted through extreme unction; not because it is a sacrament divinely instituted, but because he who receives it believes that these blessings are granted to him. For the faith of the recipient does not err, however much the minister may err. For one who baptizes or absolves in jest,[220] that is, one who does not absolve so far as the minister is concerned, nevertheless does truly baptize and absolve if the person to be baptized or absolved believes. How much more will one who administers extreme unction confer peace, even though he does not really confer peace so far as his ministry is concerned, since there is no sacrament there! The faith of the one anointed receives even that which the minister either could not give or did not intend to give. It is sufficient for the one anointed to hear and believe the Word. For whatever we believe we shall receive, that we really do receive, no matter what the minister may or may not do, or whether he dissembles or jests. The saying of Christ holds good: "All thing are possible to him who believes" [Mark 9:23], and again: "Be it done for you

[218] *bis diapason.* In his *Adagia,* Erasmus explains the intense degree of separation and conflict connoted by this originally Greek phrase. It describes the relationship between two things that are worlds apart, unalterably opposed, and most sharply to be distinguished. *CL* 1, 509 n. 1.

[219] Cf. p. 108 n. 190.

[220] Cf. p. 64 n. 122.

as you have believed" [Matt. 8:13]. But in treating the sacraments our sophists say nothing at all of this faith, but only babble with all their might about the virtues of the sacraments themselves. They will "listen to anybody and can never arrive at a knowledge of the truth" [II Tim. 3:7].

Still it was a good thing that this unction was made the extreme or "last" unction, for thanks to that, it has been abused and distorted least of all the sacraments by tyranny and greed. This one last mercy, to be sure, has been left to the dying—they may be anointed without charge, even without confession and communion. If it had remained a practice of daily occurrence, especially if it had cured the sick, even without taking away sins, how many worlds, do you think, would not the pontiffs have under their control today? For through the one sacrament of penance and the power of the keys, as well as through the sacrament of ordination, they have become such mighty emperors and princes. But now it is a fortunate thing that they despise the prayer of faith, and therefore do not heal any sick, and that they have made for themselves, out of an ancient ceremony, a brand-new sacrament.

Let this now suffice for these four sacraments. I know how it will displease those who believe that the number and use of the sacraments are to be learned not from the sacred Scriptures, but from the Roman See. As if the Roman See had given these "sacraments" and had not rather received them from the lecture halls of the universities, to which it is unquestionably indebted for whatever it has. The papal despotism would not have attained its present position, had it not taken over so many things from the universities. For there was scarcely another of the celebrated bishoprics that had so few learned pontiffs as Rome. Only by violence, intrigue, and superstition has she till now prevailed over the rest. For the men who occupied the See a thousand years ago differed so vastly from those who have since come into power, that one is compelled to refuse the name of Roman pontiff to one group or the other.

There are still a few other things which it might seem possible to regard as sacraments; namely, all those things to which a divine promise has been given, such as prayer, the Word, and the cross.

For Christ has promised, in many places, that those who pray should be heard; especially in Luke 11 [:5-13], where by many parables he invites us to pray. Of the Word he says: "Blessed are those who hear the Word of God and keep it" [Luke 11:28]. And who can count all the times he promises aid and glory to those who are afflicted, suffer, and are cast down? Indeed, who can recount all the promises of God? Why, the whole Scripture is concerned with provoking us to faith; now driving us with commands and threats, now drawing us with promises and consolations. In fact, everything in Scripture is either a command or a promise. The commands humble the proud with their demands, the promises exalt the humble with their forgiveness.

Nevertheless, it has seemed proper to restrict the name of sacrament to those promises which have signs attached to them. The remainder, not being bound to signs, are bare promises. *Hence there are, strictly speaking, but two sacraments in the church of God—baptism and the bread.* For only in these two do we find both the divinely instituted sign and the promise of forgiveness of sins. The sacrament of penance, which I added to these two,[221] lacks the divinely instituted visible sign, and is, as I have said,[222] nothing but a way and a return to baptism. Nor can the scholastics say that their definition fits penance, for they too ascribe to the true sacrament a visible sign, which is to impress upon the senses the form of that which it effects invisibly. But penance or absolution has no such sign. Therefore they are compelled by their own definition either to admit that penance is not a sacrament and thus to reduce their number, or else to bring forth another definition of a sacrament.

Baptism, however, which we have applied to the whole of life, will truly be a sufficient substitute for all the sacraments which we might need as long as we live. And the bread is truly the sacrament of the dying and departing; for in it we commemorate the passing of Christ out of this world, that we may imitate him. Thus we may apportion these two sacraments as follows: baptism may be allotted to the beginning and the entire course of life, while the bread belongs to the end and to death. And the Christian should use them both as

[221] Cf. p. 18.
[222] Cf. p. 59.

long as he is in this mortal frame, until, fully baptized and strengthened, he passes out of this world, and is born into the new eternal life, to eat with Christ in the kingdom of his Father, as he promised at the Last Supper, when he said: "Truly, I say to you, I shall not drink again of this fruit of the vine until it is fulfilled in the kingdom of God" [Matt. 26:29, Mark 14:25, Luke 22:18]. Thus he clearly seems to have instituted the sacrament of the bread with a view to our entrance into the life to come. For then, when the purpose[223] of both sacraments is fulfilled, baptism and bread will cease.

Herewith I conclude this prelude, and freely and gladly offer it to all pious souls who desire to know the genuine sense of the Scriptures and the proper use of the sacraments. For it is a gift of no mean importance, to know the gifts that are given to us, as it is said in I Cor. 2[:12], and what use we ought to make of them. For if we are instructed with this judgment of the spirit, we shall not mistakenly rely on those things which are wrong. These two things our theologians never taught us; indeed, they seem to have taken pains to hide them from us. If I have not taught them, I certainly managed not to conceal them, and have given occasion to others to think out something better. It has at least been my endeavor to set them both forth. Nevertheless, "not all can do all things."[224] To the godless, on the other hand, and those who in obstinate tyranny force on us their own teachings instead of God's, I confidently and freely oppose these pages. I shall be completely indifferent to their senseless fury. Yet I wish even them a right understanding. And I do not despise their efforts; I only distinguish them from what is sound and truly Christian.

I hear a rumor that new bulls and papal maledictions are being prepared against me, in which I am urged to recant or be declared a heretic. If that is true, I desire this little book to be part of the recantation that I shall make; so that the arrogant despots might not complain of having acted in vain. The remainder I will publish very soon; please Christ, it will be such as the Roman See

[223] *res sacramenti,* cf. p. 23 n. 45, above.

[224] Virgil *Eclogues* viii, 63.

has never seen or heard before. I shall give ample proof of my obedience.[225] In the name of our Lord Jesus Christ. Amen.

"Why doth that impious Herod fear
When told that Christ the King is near?
He takes not earthly realms away,
Who gives the realms that ne'er decay."[226]

---

[225] The remainder of Luther's "recantation" was *The Freedom of a Christian*. In *An Open Letter to Pope Leo X*, which accompanied it, he gave ample proof of his obedience. *LW* 31, 327-377.

[226] The eighth stanza of Coelius Sedulius' *Hymnus acrostichis totam vitam Christi continens* (beginning *A solis ortus cardine*), of the fifth century. Stanzas 8, 9, 11, and 13 were used as an Epiphany hymn, which Luther translated on December 12, 1541—"*Was fürchtst du, Feind Herodes, sehr.*" The above translation is taken from *Hymns Ancient and Modern*, No. 60. Woolf, *op. cit.*, 329, has this translation from *The English Hymnary:*

Why, impious Herod, shouldst thou fear
Because the Christ is come so near?
He who doth heavenly kingdoms grant
Thine earthly realm can never want.

THE MISUSE OF THE MASS

1521

Translated by Frederick C. Ahrens

INTRODUCTION

Luther's theological position with reference to the Roman mass had reached its culmination in his book of October, 1520, entitled *A Prelude on the Babylonian Captivity of the Church.* The largest section of that book is devoted to the mass, which Luther calls "The Sacrament of the Bread." It shows that Luther has now reached the high ground of opposition to the official position of the church. He is strongly opposed to the withholding of the cup from the laity, the doctrine of transubstantiation, and the idea of sacrifice in the mass. Luther did not change these views, but he did afterwards elaborate them more positively, and all of the other five treatises presented in this volume are in substance elaborations of the views he set forth in *The Babylonian Captivity.*

The Misuse of the Mass was for the most part a German translation of a book that first appeared in Latin under the title, *De abroganda missa privata Martini Lutheri sententia.*[1] Both the Latin and the German manuscripts were written by Luther late in 1521, while he was in the Wartburg, and were published in January, 1522.

After his experience before the Diet of Worms, Luther was convinced that the Roman church itself would not undertake any of the changes that he felt were absolutely necessary to restore the evangelical character of the church, and that he must himself make a beginning of these practical reforms.

On the first of August, 1521, Luther wrote from the Wartburg to Melanchthon that when he got back to Wittenberg he intended to make changes in the celebration of the Lord's Supper that would make it correspond to Christ's institution of it. That led some of his impatient friends in Wittenberg and elsewhere in Saxony to move into action. Gabriel Zwilling, one of the Augustinian monks, and Andreas Karlstadt, a university professor, began a movement to stop saying masses and to administer the Lord's Supper in both kinds. They were particularly zealous against the Roman understanding of the mass as a sacrifice, and in this they felt they had a clear warrant in Luther's teaching and writing.

[1] *WA* 8, 411-476.

These innovations caused much disturbance in Wittenberg, and in October it came to the attention of the Elector Frederick the Wise. There were investigations, conferences, theses, debates, committees and reports. The Elector advised against the changes, but in Wittenberg there were two parties on the issue, and the disturbance continued. Luther in the Wartburg was informed about the events taking place in Wittenberg, probably through the pen of Spalatin. During the summer and autumn of 1521 he worked on a Latin treatise which he called *The Abrogation of the Private Mass.* If the idea of a sacrifice is removed from the mass, so that the mass is no longer a good work which avails for the reconciliation of the sinner with God, then the private mass, said without the presence of a worshiper, is a veritable abomination. On November 1, which was All Saints' Day and a festival occasion in Wittenberg, Luther wrote from his seclusion to Spalatin expressing the wish that private masses might be done away with, or at least diminished in number. Nine days later he sent Spalatin the manuscript of his Latin treatise with the expectation that Spalatin would have it published.

When Luther made his short secret visit to Wittenberg on December 4, he was surprised to find that Spalatin had not taken any steps to publish the book for fear it would increase the revolution in Wittenberg. So Luther immediately, while yet in Wittenberg, wrote a sharp letter to Spalatin in Lochau telling him that if the manuscript were not published forthwith, a more severe book would be written and published. Within a few weeks, before the middle of January, 1522, the book had come from the press of the Wittenberg publisher, Melchior Lotther.

Luther addressed his Latin treatise to his brother monks of the Augustinian order in Wittenberg. He expressed his joy that they had begun to abrogate the abomination of the mass. At the same time he said he was afraid that some of the brothers were not strong enough in their convictions to stand fast when they would have to face the persecution and attacks that were sure to come. To strengthen and comfort them and any others who were opposed to the abuses of the mass, and to give wider and more explicit statement of his views on the subject, he had written this book. With the manuscript sent to Spalatin on November 10, he wrote: "In this book that I am sending, I am endorsing the abrogation of masses."

The treatise is divided into three parts. The first part points out that the false conception of the mass is built on a false conception of the priesthood. According to the New Testament every Christian is a priest; and the priestly office is one of preaching, not of making sacrifice. The second part discusses the mass itself. The Words of Institution, examined individually and collectively, forbid any interpretation of the mass as a sacrifice; they speak rather of a promise given by God, to be received in faith by men. In refuting the arguments of his opponents Luther expresses himself plainly on the subjects of the canon of the mass, saints, purgatory, and spirits of the dead. The wholly polemic third part contrasts the papal priesthood with the priesthood of Christ. The former, with its laws, has extinguished the gospel, and actually perverted each of the Ten Commandments to mean exactly the opposite of what God intended. An avowedly allegorical comparison of church and synagogue is made, not to buttress, but pointedly to illumine the argument.

A German translation of the treatise was begun as soon as the Latin manuscript had been sent to Spalatin. It was completed no later than November 25. The many differences between the original Latin and the German version can be accounted for by the fact that when he made the German translation Luther no longer had the Latin copy but only his notes and his recollection of it.

The German version was widely reprinted and soon became a target for Roman Catholic assaults. For at least five years opponents continued to publish tracts against Luther's treatise. Luther did not take the time to answer these counterattacks concerning the mass, but his friends wrote in his defense, and a considerable literature marked the path of this little book down the years. It helped to make clear that when Luther had assailed the sacrifice of the mass he had attacked the very citadel of the Roman position. Luther always found special satisfaction in this treatise, and in his Table Talk during his later years he expressed a certain preference for it and remarked that he would not retract anything that he had written in the book. On one occasion (December 12, 1538), when he was asked about the speed with which he wrote, he referred to this treatise of 1521 and said: "In conceiving my books I am really in the pains of labor, for I ponder carefully all the lines of argument in each separate part of the book and even the individual words, because the conception of such books is a matter of great concern to me; and such was the case with the book on *The Abrogation of the Mass*."

The German text of the treatise, from which this English translation has been made, is in *WA* 8, 482-563.

THE MISUSE OF THE MASS

To my dear brethren, the Augustinians at Wittenberg, I, Martin, wish the grace and peace of our Lord Jesus Christ.

I have been informed both orally and in writing, my dear brethren, that you are the very first to have taken steps to do away with the abuse of the mass in your assembly. Although it has pleased me greatly, because I regard it as evidence that the word of Christ is at work in you and that you have not received it in vain, nevertheless, out of Christian love, which leaves nothing undone, I am deeply concerned that not all of you have taken such a great and noteworthy step with equal steadfastness and good conscience. I will not mention how the bishops and priests of Baal daily terrify the consciences of those who are weak in faith, now with papal bulls, now with indulgences,[1] now with brotherhoods[2]; one arrests the married priests[3]; one does this and the other that miracle, and everyone does the most terrible things he can.

But what will happen when throughout the world you suffer all kinds of derision, insults, viciousness, and dishonor from everyone, even from the pious, clever, holy, and wise; and are regarded as blasphemers because you alone, and so few of you at that, have dared to change the whole spiritual and human order contrary to all human reason? It is indeed an extremely great undertaking to resist such a long-established custom and the opinion of all men, to suffer patiently their accusation, judgment, and condemnation, and to stand immovable in the face of such a storm of winds and waves. I know well that if you are built on the rock no violence

---

[1] A reference to the attempt of Cardinal Albrecht of Mainz to revive the sale of indulgences in his home town of Halle. *WA* 8, 482 n. 1.

[2] Sodalities, or associations of laymen for devotional purposes. Luther scored their multiplicity, immorality, and spiritual pride in *A Treatise Concerning the Blessed Sacrament* (1519); he regarded the communion of saints as the one fundamental brotherhood. *PE* 2, 8, 26-31, 137 n. 1.

[3] A married priest, Seidler, had been arrested in Stolpen by his bishop, Johann von Schleinitz.

of water and wind can harm you, but if you stand upon the sand a great and speedy fall will overtake you [Matt. 7:24-27].

I myself experience daily how extremely difficult it is to lay aside a conscience of long standing, one that has been fenced in by man-made ordinances. O with how much greater effort and labor, even on the basis of the Holy Scriptures, have I been barely able to justify my own conscience; so that I, one man alone, have dared to come forward against the pope, brand him as the Antichrist, the bishops as his apostles, and the universities as his brothels! How often did my heart quail, punish me, and reproach me with its single strongest argument: Are you the only wise man? Can it be that all the others are in error and have erred for so long a time? What if you are mistaken and lead so many people into error who might all be eternally damned? Finally, Christ with his clear, unmistakable Word strengthened and confirmed me, so that my heart no longer quails, but resists the arguments of the papists, as a stony shore resists the waves, and laughs at their threats and storms!

Because I felt and considered these things within me, I wanted to write this letter to you for the comfort and strengthening of the weak, those who cannot bear the storm and violence of the opponent and of their own despairing consciences. For such consciences must be treated with faith and trust, so that we not only look upon the judgment of the whole world as straw and chaff, but also that in death we may be adept in fighting against the devil and all his might, even against the judgment of God, and with Jacob prevail against God [Gen. 32:28] through such a strong faith. The weak in faith may indeed disregard the derision and ridicule of the world and pretend not to hear it; but who can so protect himself against the devil and the stern judgment of God that he does not feel them? The world can do no more than denounce us as heretics and unbelievers; it cannot make us heretics. Our consciences will make us sinners before God in many ways and damn us eternally unless they are well guarded and protected at every point by the holy, mighty, and true Word of God—that is, built on the only rock [Matt. 7:24-25]. Whoever does that is sure of his cause and cannot fail, nor waver, nor be betrayed. Such a sure, impregnable fortress we seek and desire.

For these reasons I will prepare a special little book on the mass which should be useful to everyone who wishes it. For I can well see that the books which I have written on the subject so far[4] have not yet made a sufficient impact because the bishops oppose them; so that as often as the word of truth is renewed, exalted, and repeated, so often the paperhangers condemn and suppress it. We ought also to pray the Lord to send out laborers into his harvest [Matt. 9:38], and his angels to gather out of the kingdom of God all causes of sin [Matt. 13:41], which are now very many. This one great cause of sin is now at hand; if we could remove it, then we should have removed not only one, but all, because this is the foundation and fountainhead of all the rest. May the Lord Jesus strengthen and keep your hearts and minds [Phil. 4:7] in a true, right, unsimulated faith and divine love, amen. From my wilderness, on St. Catherine's Day [November 25], 1521.

I stipulate publicly that I wish neither to hear nor to see the foolish senseless persons who will cry out, saying that I write and teach against the ordinances of the church, against the doctrines of the fathers, against old and proven traditions and the long-standing customs, usages, and practices of the church. Likewise I despise all human teaching and the precepts of the Parisian Sodom,[5] which, as Peter says, are none other than destructive heresies [II Pet. 2:1]. If only the lunacy[6] would cease to plague them for one hour, they would themselves recognize (since they prove their whole case without the Word of God) that they are not depending upon divine sayings, but only upon human ones.

Thus it is contrary to human reason, not to mention the divine Scriptures, to found and build an article of faith on human fancies, for the holy sacraments and articles of faith rightly demand that they be founded and preserved only through the divine Scriptures,

---

[4] *A Treatise Concerning the Blessed Sacrament* (1519), *PE* 2, 9-31; *A Treatise on the New Testament that is the Holy Mass* (1520), *PE* 1, 294-326; *The Babylonian Captivity of the Church* (1520), in this volume, pp. 3-126.

[5] The University of Paris, following the lead of Cologne and Louvain (cf. p. 14 n. 14), sprang to the defense of Roman church doctrine and condemned the teachings of Luther on April 15, 1521. The leading scientific authority of the medieval church and scholastic theology, it had withheld judgment in the growing controversy until incited by *The Babylonian Captivity of the Church* to speak out. Julius Köstlin, *Martin Luther*, 3 Auflage; (Elberfeld, 1883), I, 482.

[6] *Mondsucht*. Cf. Matt. 17:15.

as Moses abundantly testifies in Deuteronomy. Why then do they think that they can alienate me from the divine Word with their own fancies, that is, human laws and teachings; as if they did not know that the saints had often sinned during their lifetime and erred in their writings? They are even so foolish as to set up and accept the words and deeds of the saints as a sure, unfailing rule of faith. In addition, their own law, which is really no law at all, makes such human sayings suspect when it says: "Whoever is once found to be wrong will always be regarded and considered to be wrong."[7]

Since the fathers have often erred, as you yourself confess, who will make us certain as to wherein they have not erred, assuming their reputation is sufficient and should not be weighed and judged according to the divine Scriptures? They have (you say) also interpreted the Scriptures. What if they erred in their interpretation, as well as in their life and writings? In that way you make gods of all that is human in us, and of men themselves; and the word of men you make equal to the Word of God.

For these reasons the stupid sophists, the unlearned bishops, monks and priests, and the pope with all his Gomorrah[8] should know that we are not baptized in the name of Augustine,[9] Bernard,[10] Gregory,[11] Peter or Paul [I Cor. 1:13] nor yet in the name of the Parisians,[12] but in the name of Jesus Christ, him alone. Only the crucified one and none other do we acknowledge as our master. Paul does not wish that we believe him or an angel, unless Christ lives and speaks in him [Gal. 1:8, 12]. We know indeed what the fathers, the decrees, the customs, and the folly of the people include and contain. What need have we in addition for the masters of Paris to write and say: "Such an article is an abomination. This one is contrary to the faculty of Paris, that one is contrary to their

[7] *Semel malus semper praesumitur* [*esse*] *malus. Decretalium Bonifacii VIII*, lib. v, tit. XII: *de regulis juris*, reg. 8. *Corpus Iuris Canonici, op. cit.*, II, col. 1122.

[8] Luther often called the universities by the names of Sodom and Gomorrah, names which were synonymous with vice and wickedness since the days of Abraham (Gen. 18-19). Cf. p. 135.

[9] Cf. p. 19 n. 32.

[10] Cf. p. 77 n. 135.

[11] Cf. p. 55 n. 108.

[12] Cf. p. 135 n. 5.

established articles," and more of the like—a boast that only female children and rude blockheads can make?

We will not listen to this: "Bernard lived and wrote thus"; but only to this: "He was supposed to live and write according to the Scriptures." We are not asking how the saints lived and wrote. They were all preserved through this prayer: "Forgive us our debts" [Matt. 6:12]; as Ps. 31 [:6] says: "For this shall every saint pray at the opportune time." We refuse to concede as true and just, that the saints were forgiven by means of a prayer which was itself sinful and in error; which is what the papists are doing when, as Ps. 60 [62] says, they support themselves upon a leaning and tottering wall [Ps. 62:3], whereas God alone should be a support, as the same Psalm testifies so often [Ps. 62:1-2, 5-7].

I have stated, that one does not ask how the saints have lived and written, but how the Scriptures indicate that we ought to live. The quesion is not about what has been done, but about how it is supposed to be done. The saints could err in their writings and sin in their lives, but the Scriptures cannot err, and whoever believes them cannot sin in his life. We accept indeed those saints whose praise comes not from men but from God [Rom. 2:29]; not those whom the pope raises up, but those whom God raises up, Whose oxen and birds they are, killed and made ready for the marriage feast of Christ, his son [Matt. 22:2-4]; that is, those whose life and teaching the divine Scriptures praise, such as the patriarchs, prophets, and apostles. Them alone and no others can we surely believe and cling to, and thus be preserved.

Part I

How faithfully the pope treats and interprets the Holy Scriptures we are shown by the beginning of his decretal,[13] where he quotes from Heb. 10 [7:12]: "For when there is a change in the priesthood, there is a change in the law as well." Thereby he claims to prove that Christ transferred his priesthood to St. Peter, when he ascended to heaven, and St. Peter transferred it to the pope.

[13] *Decretalium Gregorii IX,* lib. i, tit. II: *de constitutionibus,* cap. 3. *Corpus Iuris Canonici, op. cit.,* II, col. 8.

While he is still a priest, who ought to be reading the law, he claims to have the power of making laws and statutes. What a noble beginning and proper foundation for his priesthood and his laws! As the foundation is, so are these priests; and as the priest is, so is the law—each quite worthy of the other.

How quickly God can put to shame his Caiaphas and Balaam with their self-made fancies so that already at the outset—as unwittingly as Caiaphas [John 11:49-52]—they have revealed to all the world what the devil wanted to accomplish in the world through the pope and his laws. How infamously has Satan betrayed himself, against his will, in that through the pope in this beginning[14] he has told the truth, namely, that he wished to change Christ's priesthood as well as His law. This he has now done; indeed he has obliterated them both so that now the pope and no longer Christ is the priest, so that the pope's laws and not Christ's laws now lead and guide us. The desolating sacrilege stands in the holy place [Matt. 24:15] and rules over us in place of Christ; instead of Christ, the king of truth, stands the idol of lies and all error [II Thess. 2:3-12]. And this desolating sacrilege has fulfilled and accomplished abundantly what he promised in this beginning.

First, let us deal with the priesthood. Every true Christian really ought to know that in the New Testament there is no outward, visible priest, except those whom the devil has exalted and set up through human lies. We have only one single priest, Christ, who has sacrificed himself for us and all of us with him. Peter speaks of this in I Pet. 3 [:18]: "Christ died once for our sins, the righteous for the unrighteous, that he might bring us—dead in the flesh but alive in the spirit—to God." And Heb. 10 [:14] says: "For by a single offering he has finished and perfected for all time those who are sanctified."

This is a spiritual priesthood, held in common by all Christians, through which we are all priests with Christ.[15] That is, we are children of Christ, the high priest; we need no priest or mediator other than Christ. "Every priest (Heb. 5 [:1]) is appointed in order that

[14] *The Decretals of Gregory IX*, intended to supplant all previous canonical collections, and promulgated as official canon law on September 5, 1234, contains on page 4 (out of 928 pages) the particular decree to which Luther refers.

[15] Cf. p. 113 n. 204.

he might pray for the people and preach." Thus every Christian on his own may pray in Christ and have access to God (Rom. 5 [:2]) as Isaiah has proclaimed in chapter 65 [:24]: "It shall come to pass that before they call I will answer, and while they are yet speaking I will hear them." Thus also every Christian is himself taught and instructed by God (Isa. 54 [:13]): "And I will grant that all your children shall be taught by God." And Jer. 31 [:34]: "No longer shall one man teach or instruct the other, saying, 'Know the Lord,' for they shall all know me, from the youngest of them to the oldest." And Isa. 11 [:9]: "The earth is full of the knowledge of the Lord as with water of the overflowing sea." Hence it comes that Christ says in John 6 [:45]: "It is written in the prophets, 'And they shall all be taught by God.'"

Through these testimonies of the Scriptures the outward priesthood in the New Testament is overthrown; for it makes prayer, access to God and teaching (all of which are fitting and proper to a priest) common to all men. Why does one need a priest, if one does not need a mediator and a preacher? Are we supposed to establish and maintain a priesthood devoid of function and office? Indeed, Christ alone and no other is the mediator [I Tim. 2:5] and teacher of all men. And there may even be added those taught by God [John 6:45] who can therefore themselves mediate and preach, but who are not yet priests, that is, Christians. Thus it follows that the priesthood in the New Testament is equally in all Christians, in the spirit alone without any roles or masks, as Paul says in Gal. 5 [3:28]: "In Christ Jesus there is neither Jew nor Gentile, neither male nor female, neither master nor servant; for you are all one in Christ."

Now let us continue, and gather together the testimony of the shameless Gomorrah by which they have erected and consolidated their priesthood on the basis of the New Testament, so that we may stop up the shameless mouths of the rude blockheads. The first witness is Peter in I Pet. 2 [:1-5]: "Put away all malice, guile, and envy. Speak evil of no man. Like newborn babes, long for the unadulterated spiritual milk, that by it you may grow up to your salvation, for you have tasted the kindness of the Lord. Go to that living stone, rejected by men but in God's sight chosen and precious; and like living stones be yourselves built upon him, to be a holy priesthood and to offer spiritual sacrifices acceptable to God through

Jesus Christ." And a little further on [I Pet. 2:9]: "You are a chosen people, a royal priesthood, a holy people, dearly bought, that you may declare the might of him who called you out of darkness into his marvelous light."

The second witness is Rev. 5 [:10]: "Thou hast made us kings and priests to our God, and we shall reign on earth."

The third is Rev. 22 [20:6]: "Over such the second death has no power but they shall be priests of God and of his Christ, and they shall reign with him a thousand years."

Although this Book of Revelation is hardly of such significance as to be useful for citing in controversy, yet I wanted to confront our opponents with some evidence from it, which certainly ought to be understood by all Christian people, to the effect that they are all kings and priests. For all Christian people admit that all of these passages cannot possibly have reference to visible kings. Neither may they therefore be construed to be speaking of visible priests. And apart from these passages this word "priest" is not even mentioned by so much as a single letter in the whole New Testament.

Before I say any more I want to nettle the tin gods and buffoons of this world, the pope with his priests. You noble priests, show us one jot or one tittle in all the Gospels and Epistles of the apostles to the effect that you are or deserve to be called priests more than other Christian people, and that your priesthood is different from that which is common to all Christians. What are you waiting for? Will you not show us? Are you too deaf to hear, you lifeless portraits of a priest? I just want to give you a piece of advice: Go to Paris; they will show you instead of the Scriptures their masterful manmade sentiments and will say: This idea is heretical because it casts dishonor upon the priestly estate; and let this masterful pronouncement be to you an article of faith.[16] Where do you get that, you priests of idols? Why have you stolen our common name from us and appropriated it to yourselves? Are you not thieves

[16] Luther translated and published the judgment spoken against him by the theologians of Paris (cf. p. 135 n. 5) to let its weaknesses speak for themselves. It included a catalogue of the objectionable articles, each followed by an unsupported summary condemnation. Among the very first to be cited were these: All Christians are priests, and have equal power with respect to preaching, the sacraments and the keys; to which Paris simply responded: this is "detrimental to the priestly estate, and heretical." *WA* 8, 273.

and robbers [John 10:1, 8] and blasphemers of the church of Christ, who have stolen and taken by force from the other Christians the holy common name and so shamefully misused it for your own power, pride, lust, and avarice? Where do you get that, you idols? Show us by testimony from the Scriptures that you are priests and are properly called such. You are indeed insufferable burdens to the world; priests you are not. You hypocrites and robbers, do you see also what you have deserved?

Here I am mindful of that worthy priest of god—the god Baal—who has written against me in German, a boorish, unlearned ass, so completely shameless in lying, so evil and poisonous in slander, that he is good for nothing better than to write for the pope and his priests. He would not put up with my attacking the holy popish priesthood in this manner, and writes in his book[17] that the words of Peter [I Pet. 2:9] mentioned above ["You are a royal priesthood"] are to be understood as referring to two kinds of priesthood: first, to the spiritual priesthood which is common to all Christians; and second, to the "outward" priesthood, as only the anointed and tonsured—that is, the ordained—priests are called. Therefore the anointed and tonsured priesthood is well-founded in the Holy Scriptures, he says.[18]

Here I ask: To whom did St. Peter say these words? Did he not say them to all Christians, in that he bids them to long for the genuine, pure spiritual milk and in it grow up and increase to their salvation? [I Pet. 2:2]. To grow up and increase in grace, does not this pertain to all Christians? And following that, are not all Christians to be built upon Christ into a holy priesthood? [I Pet. 2:5]. In addition, he distinguishes the holy priesthood from that which is not holy, as we see before our very eyes that the popish priesthood generally is not holy but made up of knaves. Because the words of Peter are spoken to all Christians, if he wishes the anointed and tonsured priesthood to be comprehended therein, it follows that the holy, pious women and children are also tonsured and anointed priests. For Peter's words apply to all Christians of whichever priesthood; they make the priesthood common to all Christians. O, what a worthy patron of the tonsured and well-oiled idols!

[17] Emser's *Quadruplica* (1521). Cf. p. 12 n. 4.

[18] Cf. Luther's reply to Emser, *WA* 8, 247-254.

Let this be the first assault upon the fictitious popish priesthood: how strong and mighty an assault it is, let every pious Christian judge. Here all the splendor and pomp of the popish mass comes to naught; for if the priesthood is nothing, as has now been clearly shown, then its laws also are necessarily nothing. For priesthood and law change together [Heb. 7:12]. If now the priesthood and the law are nothing, then the sacrifices and the works which are supposed to take place through the priest according to the law will amount to even less. From this it follows that the pope's law is sheer deceit and falsehood; the papal priesthood is nothing but a mask and outward show, and the papists' mass, which they call a sacrifice, is idolatry and a shameful misuse of the holy sacrament.

In all this no one need have any doubt, for it is proved that this priesthood is found nowhere in the Scriptures. Therefore it is an addition of the devil. For no one changes, adds to, or takes away from a man's testament, as Paul says [Gal. 3:15]; much less should one add anything to God's testament or change it. Now it has been plainly demonstrated that this priesthood and the mass are additions to God's word and testament. Therefore I conclude on unshakeable grounds and with a good conscience that to offer mass as a sacrifice, and to have anointed and tonsured priests as is now the custom, is nothing else than to slander and deny Christ and to abrogate and remove his priesthood and all his law.

Pertinent here are all passages of Scripture in which the Holy Spirit forbids adding to or subtracting from the Word of God, such as Prov. 30 [:5]: "Every word of God is a fiery shield to those who put their hope in him. Do not add to his words, lest he punish you, and you be found a liar." And Deut. 4 [:2]: "You shall not add to the word which I command you, nor take from it"; and I Pet. [4:11]: "If anybody speaks, let him speak as though it were the word of God, etc." What need is there to recount all that the prophets, Christ, and the apostles say against the law and teaching of men! It is manifest, as John 8 [:47] says: "He who is of God hears the words of God," and John 3 [:31]: "He who is of the earth . . . of the earth he speaks."

I am well aware that when those who have a weak conscience read or hear this, and still see such a vast number of monasteries and churches in which innumerable masses are held daily, they will be loath to believe that so many people should be damned and daily fill the world with so many sins. Because surely the whole world maintains that everyone can and may be aided by masses, as by a good work, and that the world has been preserved until now by the merit of the masses. For it seems incredible to them that God should have abandoned the world for so long a time.

But what is one to do? It is sure, established by the Holy Scriptures, which alone are to be believed even if all the angels taught otherwise [Gal. 1:8] and were to go to ruin with heaven and earth [Luke 21:33]—it is established by God himself that the mass-saying priesthood is not instituted by God. Will you not believe God rather than the world? Is God not greater than the world? Is it not written and proclaimed that the last time shall be a dangerous time, a time of wrath [Luke 21:22-23], so that the world will be filled with error and the chosen ones be on the verge of being misled [Matt. 24:24], a time of which God himself says that he will scarcely find faith on earth? [Luke 18:8]. Do you think that these are frivolous words, and that they can be reconciled with our cursed security in which we live without any fear of God, as if it did not concern us? Thus, before knowing or becoming aware of it, we fulfil the prophecies of Christ and the apostles, just as the Jews fulfilled the Scriptures and crucified Christ before they realized it.

For these reasons we should fortify our consciences and adhere firmly and steadfastly to the words of God. For they teach us that the mass-saying priesthood is nothing in the sight of God, so that in this last persecution of the church, the like of which has never been or ever will be, we may recognize the unfathomable wrath and patience which is proper and fitting to divine majesty alone. It is hard to believe that God should have patiently endured so long throughout the world the daily horrible misuse of the most salutary sacrament of his body and blood. Such is the patience which his divine majesty has reserved and kept until these last days of ours. Incomprehensible also is the terrible wrath of God, the fact that every day so many souls are eternally corrupted and damned. This wrath too he has saved up until the last days, in order to kindle the eternal wrath of his judgment which is soon to come.

Alas for us poor, miserable men of the last days. We still live with such a sense of security that we want to appease God with accursed idolatry and lies and outward show and want to merit heaven for others with ourselves! It is a fearful thing that I am saying. Would to God that I were lying, but alas it is all too true! It is an irrefutable conclusion that in the New Testament there can be no outward priests who are tonsured and set apart from the laity. Those who now exist do so without any basis in Scripture or vocation from God, that is, they are simply of the devil. "And one does not take the honor upon himself, but he is called by God, just as Aaron was" (Heb. 5 [:4]).

For this reason I conscientiously advise all priests that from now on they repent, abandon the mass, and become laymen again, or else learn to use the mass rightly, that they may as soon as possible escape the terrible wrath of God. Therefore the stupid sophists and papists may choose whichever they will: let them prove their priesthood from the Scriptures or else admit that they are nothing else than camouflages of the devil and accursed idols. For whatever does not have its origin in the Scriptures is surely from the devil himself. All the works of God, especially those having to do with salvation, are thoroughly set forth and attested in the Scriptures, so that no one can have any excuse [Rom. 1:20].

It is in vain and without basis that they say: "All that the church ordains and establishes is ordained and established by God, whose spirit the church has; therefore the mass-priests cannot be from the devil." Who will show us this church, since it is hidden in the spirit and only a matter of faith when we pray: "I believe in the holy Christian church, etc."? But now the bishops and professors have instituted the mass-priests; and even if they were saints, who will assure us that they did not err in this? Since it is now clearly evident that they have erred and done violence to the faith, how will our conscience be sure that it was the real church which instituted this order of priests?

This fact, however, constrains us and makes us sure, namely: that a real Christian knows that the church never ordains or institutes anything apart from the Word of God. Any church that does is no church except in name only, as Christ says in John 10 [:27, 5]: "My sheep hear my voice; they do not hear the voice of strangers, they flee before them; for they do not know the voice of strangers." It is not God's Word just because the church speaks it;

rather, the church comes into being because God's Word is spoken. The church does not constitute the Word, but is constituted by the Word. A sure sign, by which we may know where the church is, is the Word of God, as Paul writes in I Cor. 14 [:24-25], telling how an unbeliever falls on his face and declares that God is really among them, because he hears them prophesy. It is not the church which moves him, but the Word of God—by which he is overcome and called to account, and the secrets of his heart are disclosed, as Paul says further in the same passage. He does not say that the man falls down and declares that they prophesy because God is really among them. For how could he know that? Likewise, how can we ourselves know where the church is, if we do not hear her prophesying and the witness of the Spirit? It is certain that the church and those in whom God truly dwells do prophesy; but it is uncertain where the church is which is capable of prophesying unless it does actually prophesy. Therefore whatever is ordained apart from the word of God is ordained not by the church, but by the synagogue of the devil under the name and title of church. May this be sufficient for the first assault!

The second assault which is equally strong and powerful is taken from the New Testament, where Paul says concerning the priest and his office (Rom. 12 [:1]): "I appeal to you by the mercies of God, to present your bodies as a sacrifice, holy, living, and acceptable to God, which is your rational worship." Here no one can deny that at this point he is describing the priestly office, which is nothing else than a rational sacrifice; not the offering of irrational cows or calves, as in the law, but the sacrificing of one's self to God. This, however, is supposed to be common to all Christians; therefore all Christians must be priests. What will you answer to this, you miserable pope?

In this saying of Paul we have not only a statement of what the new priesthood is, but also of what its office and sacrifice should be, namely that they should put themselves to death and offer themselves to God as a holy sacrifice. With this word Paul has clarified and explained all the sacrifices of the law. Christ, the highest Priest, first sacrificed himself [Heb. 9:11-12], and through his new priesthood fulfilled the priesthood of the law and all its offices, and has become an example to all his children and priests, so that they might follow in his footsteps [I Pet. 2:21]. With this Peter also agrees, (I Pet. 2 [:5]): "Like living stones be yourselves built into a holy priesthood, to offer spiritual sacrifices acceptable to God through Jesus Christ."

Is this not meant to refer to all Christians? Are not all Christians built like living stones on Christ, and so built upon him that they are priests who sacrifice not irrational animals, but themselves, after the example of Christ—spiritual sacrifices, when in the Spirit they put to death the deeds of the body? (Rom. 8 [:13]). What will our poor miserable idols and counterfeits say to this? Does Peter here also make two kinds of sacrifice, just as the mouth of falsehood has invented two kinds of priests for him? We are all commanded to make this sacrifice, whatever kind of persons we may be; therefore the priestly office is incumbent upon all of us. Hence it is clear that we are all priests.

Beyond this there is yet another sacrifice which is equally common to all, of which Ps. 51 [:17] speaks: "The sacrifice of God is a broken spirit," and Ps. 29 [50:14, 23]: "Offer to God a sacrifice of thanksgiving, which will honor me," and Ps. 4 [:5]: "Offer the sacrifice of righteousness and put your trust in the Lord," and Heb. 13 [:15]: "Through him let us continually offer up a sacrifice of praise to God, that is, the fruit of lips that praise his name," and Hos. 14 [:2]: "Take away all iniquity; accept that which is good (that is, cease to punish us and seize the good that you give us) and we will render to you the calves of our lips," and Ps. 116 [:16-17]: "Thou hast loosed my bonds. I will offer to thee the sacrifice of thanksgiving." Everyone can see that these offices are not offices of the anointed and tonsured priesthood; nor can anyone lie so unashamedly as to say that they belong spiritually to everyone, but actually only to the tonsured. It belongs properly to all who live under the cross to slay and kill themselves and the lusts and desires of the Adam in them, so that this sacrifice of praise will be as the smoke and fragrance of the sacrifices of the law.

This much is to be found in the Scriptures concerning the new priesthood under Christ and its sacrifices and offices. What are you waiting for now, you poor papists? "Call upon your god, perhaps he is not at home, or asleep; he is a god, he will hear you" [I Kings 18:27]. Tell us, you priests of Baal: Where is it written, that the mass is a sacrifice, or where has Christ taught that one should offer consecrated bread and wine to God? Do you not hear? Christ has sacrificed himself once [Heb. 7:27; 9:25-26]; henceforth he will not be sacrified by anyone else. He wishes us to remember his sacrifice. Why are you then so bold as to make a sacrifice out of this remembrance? Is it possible that you are so foolish as to act upon your own devices, without any scriptural authority? If you make a sacrifice out of the remembrance of his sacrifice, and sacrifice him once more, why do you not also make another birth out of the memory of his birth, so that he may be born once more?

So too, when you remember the Resurrection, make another resurrection of that and awaken him once more. And when you remember the blind who have received sight, cause him continually to give sight to the blind. And in a like manner renew all the works of Christ, when you remember them. I fear, however,—rather, unfortunately I know—that your sacrifice is a second sacrifice of Christ, as is foretold in Heb. 6 [:6]: "They crucify on their own account the Son of God afresh and hold him up to contempt," so that your sacrifice is nothing else than the crucifying of Christ again and again.

With this second assault the popish mass with all its splendor and divine service has been overthrown once and for all. A pious Christian should never consider anything to be a sacrifice when he knows for certain that before God or according to the Scripture it is not, nor ever can be, a sacrifice. He should call a sacrifice only that which God in the Scriptures calls by that name, and nothing else. How can a more terrible daring and boldness be imagined than when you say that this is a sacrifice and divine service, which God does not call a sacrifice or divine service? What else is this but creating a god after our own ideas and ordaining and instituting divine things according to our own reason? Does it not mean setting up and ordaining laws, customs, priesthood and divine services by our own might, without God's command, and demanding from God that he confirm this action and permit himself to be instructed by us as to the manner and means with which one should serve and worship him?

This is the madness of the people of Israel, against which all the prophets cry out with one accord, that they have worshiped God according to their own pleasure. This is why God says that they made an idol out of him, although he strictly forbade them to make any image or likeness [Exod. 20:4; Deut. 5:8]. That is, they should consider him to be not what it pleased them to believe, but what he commanded them to believe; and they should do nothing except what he had ordained and appointed for them to do. In short, it is the most horrible and frightful misuse that one can imagine or express, for it is equivalent to the denial of God himself and of his first, highest and noblest commandment. Let the papists, therefore, show cause for their sacrifice from the Scriptures; or else they really ought to know that with their masses they are practicing worse idolatry than the Jews or heathen do now, or have ever done.

The Scriptures, which know nothing of the present-day mass, cannot deceive us, but our own reason and custom can easily deceive. So all devout Christians are careful to sacrifice nothing to God in their masses, but use the mass as God has instituted it in the Holy Scriptures. Since we rely on the sure Scriptures, we can neither err nor sin by not regarding and using the mass as a sacrifice. The papists cannot act correctly or well, because in things so important, divine, and necessary to salvation they abandon the sure, undeceptive Scriptures and follow their own unsure, deceptive thoughts; acting not merely without, but contrary to, all Scripture and the divine command. O brother, flee and leave the accursed priesthood of the pope!

Thirdly, let us overthrow the pope's priesthood by means of the office which Christ gave and entrusted to the apostles. For a priest ought to preach, as is written in Zechariah [Mal. 2:7] in the second chapter: "The lips of a priest should utter nothing but the law and wisdom of the Lord, for he is the messenger of the Lord of hosts." He is supposed to mediate between God and men: make sacrifice to God on behalf of men, and teach and instruct men on behalf of God. Here the papists think that they have acquired the exclusive prerogative of teaching the others, as Pope Pelagius expresses himself in the decree: "Whoever is the authority has the right to command; the rest should and must obey." In addition they cite the words of Christ: "He who hears you hears me, and he who rejects you rejects me" [Luke 10:16].

Notice here that just as they have invented their own priesthood and sacrifice, unknown and foreign to the true Christian, they have also invented and introduced a new un-Christian office of preaching. In order that this may be known and evident to all men, I will show from the beginning with incontrovertible Scripture that the only true, genuine office of preaching, like priesthood and sacrifice, is common to all Christians. Paul says in II Cor. 4 [3:6]: "Who has made us able ministers of the new testament, not of the letter, but of the spirit." These words St. Paul spoke to all Christians, that he might make ministers of the Spirit out of all of them. A minister of the Spirit preaches grace, forgiveness of sins, just as a minister of the letter preaches the words of the law. The latter function belongs to Moses, the former to Christ. Peter speaks to all Christians: "That you may declare the might of him who called you out of darkness into his marvelous light" [I Pet. 2:9]. Since all Christians are called out of darkness, each one is bound to declare the might of Him who has called him.

We readily admit that not many of you are to preach at the same time, although all have the power to do so. When Paul said in Acts 4 [14:12]: "Barnabas, be still!" was Barnabas therefore not supposed to have the power to preach? "But all things should be done decently and in order" (I Cor. 14 [:40]). By this the universality of the office of preaching is not abolished; indeed, it is strengthened thereby. For if all men did not possess the prerogative of preaching and only one had the right to speak, what need would there be to command and keep order? It is precisely because they all have the right and power to preach that it becomes necessary to keep order.

Let us therefore examine Paul's words, for in this passage with mighty thunderbolts he smashes to bits the pope's lies regarding authority and the power to preach. Thus Paul speaks [I Cor. 14: 27-31]: "If any speak in a tongue, let there be only two or at most three, and each in turn; and let one interpret. But if there is no one to interpret, let each of them keep silence in church before the people, and pray to God by himself. Let two or three prophets speak, and let the others weigh what is said. If a revelation is made to one among those who are listening, let the first be silent. For you can all prophesy, so that all may learn and all be encouraged." What will you say against this, you idols and counterfeits of the pope? Paul says that they can all prophesy, and in an orderly way, one after the other; so that one who is sitting by or listening may rise if a revelation is made to him, and the first, who is preaching, is to be silent and yield to him, and all who preach or lecture are to allow the listeners to judge and be subject to them. Where are you now, Pelagius, with your proud, insolent, slanderous tongue, daring with puffed-up cheeks to say in your fleshly law: "Where the authority is, namely the spiritual authority, there is the right to command; upon the rest devolves of necessity the matter of obedience."

The devil himself has proclaimed this through your mouth in opposition to Christ, who is speaking through Paul. By divine might Christ has made you and everything that is yours subject to everyone. He has given to everyone the right and power to weigh and decide, to lecture and preach. Yet you venture on your own wicked authority to subjugate everything to yourself, and to exalt yourself above everyone, like Lucifer.[19] You falsely allot to yourself alone the right to speak and judge, contrary to God and the Scriptures! Away, you villain; all Christians have a good and perfect right to lecture and preach from the Scripture, even if you should burst.

It now follows that they have misapplied the words of Christ: "He who hears you, hears me, etc." [Luke 10:16]. For they have used these words to serve their own pride, pomp, and power with the same treachery as they have misapplied the prophet's words: "Touch not my anointed ones" [Ps. 105:15]. The prophet is speaking of God's anointed when he says "my anointed ones": those whom God has sanctified and anointed by the Holy Spirit in their hearts and by his divine grace in their souls. The papists apply it to those whom the pope and the bishops anoint with oil merely on the outermost part of four fingers. O malice of all malice against the Holy Scriptures! The anointed ones of God include all real true Christians, but the pope calls those the anointed ones of God who most zealously serve the devil and the world with greed and pride. Thus the pope misapplies the order that all Christians, that is, those who teach of Christ, are to be heard; for he applies it only to his apostles, who teach nothing but the devil. And whoever despises this devil is said to have despised Christ.

Now you can see how, under the name and title of the common

[19] The Lucifer of Isa. 14:12 (Vulgate and KJV) has been commonly but wrongly identified since the third century with the Satan of Luke 10:18.

Christian office, they have set up for themselves their own office of perdition, just as they have introduced a spurious priesthood and sacrifice and error under the name and title of the right and true sacrifice and priesthood. Just as they have robbed the church of its true office, the Word of God, with their stolen and pilfered office, so they have also completely suppressed and extinguished the right and true priesthood and sacrifice with their invented and lying priesthood.

Here we wish to add another witness (John 6 [:45]): "They shall all be taught by God." If all are taught by God, then not merely the tonsured and anointed ones are taught by God. Indeed, no one is less taught by God than these lost, tonsured idols. If all Christians are taught by God, all of them certainly have the Spirit and the Word of God. Hence not only the layman, but even the pope, is subject to the one who is taught by God, unless he refuses to be subject to the Spirit and the Word of God. Even the angels, indeed all creatures in heaven and earth, must and shall yield to the one who is taught by God, and believe him; for he will not be yielding to or opposing a human being, but God himself, who teaches him. The foolish, stupid idols of the pope still dare to boast that the pope is above the council and is lord of the whole world. What else is this than to say that the pope is over the one who is taught by God, and that he is over God himself; so that the prophecy of Paul is fulfilled: "A man of sin and a son of perdition, who opposes and exalts himself against every so-called god or object of worship" [II Thess. 2:3-4].

Now, however, the papists quote to us the saying of Paul (I Cor. 14 [:34]): "The women should keep silence in the church; it is not becoming for a woman to preach. A woman is not permitted to preach, but she should be subordinate and obedient." They argue from this that preaching cannot be common to all Christians because women are excluded. My answer to this is that one also does not permit the dumb to preach, or those who are otherwise handicapped or incompetent. Although everyone has the right to preach, one should not use any person for this task, nor should anyone undertake it, unless he is better fitted than the others. To him the rest should yield and give place, so that the proper respect, discipline, and order may be maintained. Thus

Paul charges Timothy to entrust the preaching of the Word of God to those who are fitted for it and who will be able to teach and instruct others [II Tim. 2:2]. The person who wishes to preach[20] needs to have a good voice, good eloquence, a good memory and other natural gifts; whoever does not have these should properly keep still and let somebody else speak. Thus Paul forbids women to preach in the congregation where men are present who are skilled in speaking, so that respect and discipline may be maintained; because it is much more fitting and proper for a man to speak, a man is also more skilled at it.

Paul did not forbid this out of his own devices, but appealed to the law, which says that women are to be subject [Gen. 3:16]. From the law Paul was certain that the Spirit was not contradicting Himself by now elevating the women above the men after He had formerly subjected them to the men; but rather, being mindful of His former institution, He was arousing the men to preach, as long as there is no lack of men. How could Paul otherwise have single-handedly resisted the Holy Spirit, who promised in Joel [2:28]: "And your daughters shall prophesy." Moreover, we read in Acts 4 [21:8-9]: "Philip had four unmarried daughters, who all prophesied." "And Miriam the sister of Moses was also a prophetess" [Exod. 15:20]. And Huldah the prophetess gave advice to pious King Josiah [II Kings 22:14-20], and Deborah did the same to Duke Barak [Judg. 4:4-7]; and finally, the song of the Virgin Mary [Luke 1:46-55] is praised throughout the world. Paul himself in I Cor. 11 [:5] instructs the women to pray and prophesy with covered heads. Therefore order, discipline, and respect demand that women keep silent when men speak; but if no man were to preach, then it would be necessary for the women to preach.

For this reason we are firmly convinced on the basis of the Holy Scriptures that there is not more than one office of preaching God's Word, and that this office is common to all Christians; so that each person may speak, preach, and judge, and all the rest are obliged to listen. Since the Scriptures know of no other office of the Word of God we ask the pope's idols, whence and from whom

[20] *Denn es gehortt tzu dem geyst, wer predigen wil,* . . . . Cf. in the original Latin version of this treatise: *Exigitur autem ad loquendum ultra spiritum*. . . . *WA* 8, 424.

they have that office which is incumbent upon them alone and is not to be common to all. Go ahead, you delicate papists, you noble priests of Baal, and show us one iota in the Scriptures concerning your office and priesthood!

Perhaps you will bring forth that inflated, un-Christian decree of Pelagius: "Where the authority is, there is also the right to command"? Go and consult the blasphemers at Paris and Louvain;[21] meanwhile we shall overthrow your office and priesthood together with its sacrifice, now for the third time, and say openly, surely, and most confidently on the basis of divine authority and Scripture: Because you rule without the Word of God, you are priests of the devil and your office and priesthood were brought into the world through the devil, so that he might suppress and extinguish the one salutary office of the Spirit and the Word of God. That is why you condemned the teachings of Huss,[22] because it was not fitting to hear about Christ and learn of him from everybody, but the whole world had to hear only about the devil and learn of him from you accursed blasphemers. Hence you teach the poor people nothing but what is worthy of you and your office. You have extinguished and condemned the gospel. You preach Aristotle and your falsehoods, and in all your books and writings there is nothing but the devil himself.

This we say of you freely, unafraid, and without any hesitation, unless you can show us where your office of the priesthood is founded in the Scriptures. But when will that come about? We have demonstrated sufficiently from the Scriptures that everything which is not the word of Christ is a lie of the devil, as Christ says in John 8 [:44]: "When he lies, he speaks according to his own nature." Is that not clear enough, that truth has to be spoken by God alone, and that whoever speaks out of or according to his own nature is lying and deceiving? The pope with all his adherents says everything on his own authority, without that of the Scriptures. Therefore, as his priestly office is, so is also his sacrifice. His priests, his laws, his works are nothing but vain lies of the devil. Let any Christian person, therefore, look upon the innumerable throng of monks and priests, with their masses, offerings, laws, doctrines and

[21] Cf. p. 135 n. 5.
[22] Cf. p. 27 n. 55.

all their works, and he will see nothing but the devil's own folk and servants—an unbelieving people of perdition, for whom the wrath of God is reserved eternally [II Pet. 3:7].

I maintain that with these three arguments it has been demonstrated sufficiently to every real Christian that this popish priesthood and sacrifice of the mass is surely the devil's work, with which he has led and betrayed the world into error. From this everyone can see that there is nothing Christian in what they do, and that they have invented and fabricated the mass merely for their own greed and honor, to the disgrace and dishonor of the holy testament of Christ. For this reason nothing in this world should be so studiously avoided and despised as these fine-appearing spiritual counterfeits, masses, services, faith and clergy. And it would be much better to be a devil and a murderer than a priest or monk.

Let us further consider these noble high priests—who now shamelessly dare to call themselves princes, namely the bishops—so that we may see and recognize the whole body of the devil with all its members. Here again I should like to renew my premise, which ought to be maintained intact by every Christian, that everything which occurs outside the Scriptures, especially in matters pertaining to God, comes from the devil. God showed this in Nadab and Abihu [Lev. 10:1-3], when he did not wish the strange fire to be offered, and in this way vehemently condemned the conduct of divine matters otherwise than he himself has commanded. "I will show myself holy," he says, "among those who are near me" [Lev. 10:3]. How much more will he condemn and grow angry if one not only makes some new thing without scriptural authority, but also extinguishes his command and institution, as when unbelieving Ahaz made the brazen altar into a sundial and set the altar of Damascus in God's temple.[23]

The same is happening with our proud crowned bishops, of whom God knows nothing at all. Indeed, there is no folk on earth who can be more opposed to God than these idols and counterfeit bishops. They are not only without divine institution, but are indeed elevated and set up to rule in direct contradiction to God.

[23] II Chron. 28:22-25. Luther is following an ancient tradition in assuming that Ahaz had the bronze altar of II Kings 16:14 made into the sundial of Isa. 38:8. Buchwald, *op. cit.*, II, 204 n. 2.

To those who believe the Scriptures I will expose and clearly prove this. The idols who deny the Scriptures believe only in the decrees, and you cannot tell them anything that they will believe unless you tell them outright falsehoods, in which their minds and hearts are wholly steeped.

The Difference Between Christian and Papal Bishops

Paul says to his disciple Titus: "This is why I left you in Candia,[24] that you might complete what I left unfinished, and appoint elders in every town as I directed you, men who are blameless, the husband of one wife, whose children are believers and not open to the charge of being profligate. For a bishop, as God's steward, must be blameless," etc. [Titus 1:5-7]. Whoever believes that here in Paul the Spirit of Christ is speaking and commanding will be sure to recognize this as a divine institution and ordinance, that in each city there should be several bishops, or at least one. It is also evident that Paul considers elders and bishops to be one and the same thing, for he says: Elders are to be appointed and installed in all cities, and that a bishop shall be blameless.

Paul does not give the name "elder," however, to the tonsured and anointed idols, but to the honest pious citizens in a city, men of good conduct and repute; they are to become bishops, and several of them in every city, as the Greek text clearly states here, and in Phil. 1 [:1]: "Paul and Timothy, servants of Christ Jesus, to all the saints in Christ Jesus who are at Philippi, with their bishops and deacons: grace and peace, etc." Philippi was a single city and had many bishops, whom Paul greets here. Similarly in Acts 20 [:28] Paul sent a message to the single city of Ephesus and summoned the elders of the congregation to him, saying to them among other things: "Take heed to yourselves and to the people over whom the Holy Spirit has made you bishops, to feed his sheep, which he obtained with his blood." Now Ephesus was one city; and Paul calls the elders in their congregation bishops, and says that the Holy Spirit has appointed many of them.

---

[24] Chief port on the northern coast of Crete, by which name the entire island is sometimes called.

What reply can you, poor wretches, make to these three thunderbolts from heaven? I implore you, Christian friend, for God's sake, do not let yourself be moved one whit by the golden crowns and pearl mitres, red hats and cloaks, gold, silver, precious stones, mules, horses and retinue, with all the glory, ornament and splendor of the popes, cardinals and bishops, those lost sheep; but believe Paul in the Holy Spirit: these are not bishops, but idols, puppets, camouflages and wonders of the wrath of God. You have heard that Paul's bishops are honorable married men, as many of them in a city as are needed to care for the people. These words are not words of the church, nor of the councils, nor of the fathers, nor even of those Gomorrahs,[25] Paris and Louvain, but words of the Holy Spirit and of Jesus Christ, indeed, of the divine majesty.

Even if all the angels and the whole world preached to the contrary, why should it move you? Should you not consider and regard their words as if a goose hissed at you, compared to the supreme divine majesty? But since none oppose these words except unbelieving, un-Christian, unlearned apes and counterfeits of men, the most useless folk on earth, hardly worthy of wearing the mask of a bishop, why should you fear them or be frightened by them, and not rather regard and consider them as blots and blemishes (as Peter calls them) [II Pet. 2:13] on the whole world, with all their laws, lies, pomp, customs, and usages.

Come on, you monstrous abominations of the world, and show cause why you should have yourselves called bishops! The Holy Spirit appointed several bishops in one city, but each one of you is over several cities, and a single pope wants to be bishop over all the cities of the world; by whose command or authority? By the devil's own, who through you opposes the Holy Spirit and that which He has instituted. What do you have to say to that, you blasphemers?

For these reasons we are firmly and irrefutably resolved that according to the Holy Scriptures and the institution of the Holy Spirit you are bishops neither in name nor in fact, but destroyers and suppressors of the bishops and of the Holy Scriptures which teach us how to appoint bishops. You are indeed bishops by the vocation and appointment of the devil and his apostle, the pope, fittingly called creatures of the pope and not of the Holy Spirit: as

[25] Cf. p. 136 n. 8.

the creator is, so is the creature. Are you not yet frightened to hear that you are bishops not only apart from God's will but contrary to his divine command and institution? That is to say, not one of you ever considers what is fitting and proper for a bishop. You seek nothing but honor and wealth, how you may live well and have good times, and fatten yourselves for the slaughtering-block of the eternal judgment of God.

Therefore, give us proof of your episcopate from the Scriptures! Since you cannot do it, we recognize and assert on behalf of God and the Holy Spirit that you are puppets of the world who have assumed the title and name of bishop by force and eradicated the true bishops and offered vinegar and gall to Christ in his last thirst, and to his church. We are compelled to regard you thus by the Holy Spirit, who in Paul appoints and ordains the bishops; and also by the fact that there is nothing more unlike a true episcopal state, indeed, nothing more contrary and opposed to it, than your worldly estate and princely life and conduct.

Lest one think that Paul is the only person who describes and pictures what kind of birds the bishops are, let us look at St. Peter (I Pet. 5 [:1-4]): "I, as a fellow elder and witness of Christ, a partaker with you in all suffering and future glory, exhort the elders among you: Tend the flock of Christ's sheep that is under you, not by constraint but willingly, not for the sake of money, nor as masters of the inheritance; but be examples to the flock, so that when the chief Shepherd comes you will obtain the unfading crown." You see here that in one flock there are to be many elders and bishops, just as Paul ordered, who are not to rule but serve the sheep. They are slaves of another inheritance, namely of Christ [Col. 3:24] and not lords. The pope, however, with his dear, faithful and reverent followers, wants to be lord of the properties, bodies, and souls of all men, and treats them more harshly than any tyrant or heathen treats his possessions; and that they call feeding the sheep of Christ!

Finally, when the apostles were quarreling over seniority, Christ said (Luke 22 [:25-26]): "The worldly kings exercise lordship over them; and those in authority are called gracious lords. But not so with you." Here I will set up each Christian as a judge between Christ and the pope. Christ said and ordained that the bishops, who now have more honor, wealth, and power than worldly kings and princes, and who exercise this power against every man, should not be thus. But the pope has commanded and appointed that they should be thus. If you hold over against one another the words of the prince, Christ, and of his vicar, the pope, you will see and recognize which is Christ and which is the Antichrist, which are the true bishops and which are counterfeits. Woe to us miserable men, that in these last days of wrath we must live—yes, piteously perish—under the counterfeits and idols, the rude, unlearned blockheads and ravenous wolves [Matt. 7:15], without any bishops and priests.

For this reason we recognize and assert on behalf of God the Holy Spirit that Christian bishops are honorable, married, mature, good men, learned in the word of truth [II Tim. 2:15], many in a single city, who are chosen by the neighboring bishops or by their own people. They might be the very ones whom we now call parish priests, and their chaplains and deacons, if only they were not—to please their superior idols—misusing the mass, being forced to keep silent concerning the gospel, and perishing in false vows of celibacy, till no episcopal function is left for them to carry out. This is a divine decision and the Holy Spirit's method and manner of appointing bishops, such as SS. Spiridion,[26] Augustine, and Ambrose.[27] Those who are over many cities, however, do nothing more than at times wear a pearl mitre, consecrate wood and stone with water and incense, and baptize bells, because they have set themselves up contrary to the divine institution and the Scriptures. They are the mockery of the devil, God's enemies, and soon to be eradicated with their prince and creator, the pope, by the coming of our Savior, amen. Since all this is confirmed and demonstrated by the divine Scriptures and the Word of God, a pious soul must despise this whole Babylonian crowd,[28] and all its splendor and might, with a good conscience, freely, surely, and unafraid.

There is present still another part of the devil's retinue, the great countless crowd of monks, who want to be neither priest nor

---

[26] Bishop of Trimithus in Cyprus, one of the bishops most celebrated in popular legends among those attending the Council of Nicaea, 325 A.D.

[27] Ambrose (340-397), bishop of Milan, zealous champion of orthodoxy against the Arian heresy.

[28] Cf. p. 6.

laymen, a new sea-monster concocted, created, and compiled by the devil himself out of all the components of treachery. Insofar as they are priests, what we have said of the priesthood and its sacrifice and office applies to them also. Insofar as they are monks, however, with their foolish, ungodly, and impossible vows, which have never yet been kept by anyone, they require a book of their own. That book I will save until the proper time[29] in order that this present one may not be too long. It is enough now that we know that a Christian people is undivided, without any distinctions of sects or persons, a people among whom there is to be no layman, no cleric, no monk, no nun—no differences at all, all being married or celibate as each one pleases. There is also no essential difference between bishops, elders, and priests on the one hand and laymen on the other, nothing to distinguish them from other Christians except that the one has a different office which is entrusted to him, namely, to preach the Word of God and to administer the sacraments; just as a mayor or judge is distinguished from other citizens by nothing except that the governing of the city is entrusted to him. The same persons who have introduced such sects[30] among the Christian people and divided them into clergy and laity so that some are tonsured and some are not, and the tonsured are partly monks and partly priests, and the monks are even divided among themselves according to a variety of garbs and diets; the same persons who invented these things have severed and cut to pieces the unity of the Christian people.

These persons are the very same ones who have destroyed the church and the Word of God, and with the old serpent's cunning have torn the minds and hearts of Christians from the unity in Christ Jesus, as Paul says in Corinthians [II Cor. 11:3]. Therefore the name of bishop or priest is not the name of a sect, but the name of an office. Priest is the equivalent of elders; bishop is the equivalent of overseer. Out of these the ungodly men have made ranks and dignities. Paul calls them elsewhere dispensers, ministers of Christ, servants of God, and provosts.

Let this suffice for the present concerning their ungodly priesthood, sacrifice, and service. It will serve to instruct every pious

[29] Cf. p. 81 n. 146.
[30] Cf. p. 73 n. 128.

person sufficiently, so that when he recognizes and sees that he is a priest of the devil and of his apostle, the pope, he will soon desist from it and make every effort to become a priest of Christ and his holy church, or else become a layman again and pay no heed whatever to the fictitious character,[31] the anointed and oiled fingers, the tonsured head and the pharisaical dress of these miserable priests. For these are all the devil's priests, not God's. Therefore, what they have vowed they have vowed not to God, but to the devil, to whom no vow is to be kept unless you would set aside and break the vow of the living God. Let them boast of their long spears and short swords. Let them boast that their fathers instituted such pomp, honor, and splendor through inspiration of the Holy Spirit. We will boast of nothing but the Holy Scriptures, continually mindful that the Holy Spirit cannot contradict himself, for he is not a God of discord, but a God of peace and harmony [II Cor. 13:11].

Because we have clearly shown that their whole system is contrary to the divine and Holy Scriptures, we will not believe that their pomp, honor, and splendor are from the Holy Spirit until they convince us that the Holy Spirit contradicts himself or has retracted his Scriptures. Only thus can they establish that their cause is inspired by the Holy Spirit, as we have established through the Scriptures that ours is inspired by the Holy Spirit. We scorn papal bulls and human dreams, but the Holy Scriptures we venerate. If they despise the Holy Scriptures, let them go and worship their water bulls.[32] Christ says: "He who is not with me is against me" [Luke 11:23]. We say: All that is not with the Scriptures is against the Scriptures. Their priesthood and its sacrifice and office, their episcopate, are not with the Scriptures, as shown above; therefore they are necessarily against the Scriptures and thus against God. But what is against God is the work of the devil.

See with what great cunning the devil has slyly brought such abomination, such ungodly ranks and sacrifices into the world, under the semblance and name of priesthood and sacrifice! Since the Christian church has nothing better and nobler than priests, preachers, and the mass, the devil wanted to do his damage under

[31] Cf. p. 111 n. 201.
[32] Cf. p. 77 n. 137.

the semblance of these things; and through the wrath of God he has accomplished it. His priesthood has indeed yielded profit. When the mass was proclaimed a sacrifice he easily drew the world's money and goods to himself. Through riches he has injected into the mass greed, honor, pride, wantonness, and all the villainy and malice which we now see before our eyes, until the true genuine priesthood has been extinguished and the whole world no longer knows of anything but the mass-priests and their sacrifice. By this all men are cheated, because they have no other knowledge or hope of how to attain forgiveness of sins and eternal life except only with their money. So the devil has achieved his wish and purpose and has accomplished so much with his ungodly priesthood that even many holy men have not only failed to understand this error, but have even strengthened it by word and deed.

Thus the true mass and the true priesthood have fallen and have been completely eradicated, so that instead of faith they have preached outward works, which even a sinner and rogue can do. The fruit and power of the true, genuine sacrifice is suppressed and exterminated, so that no one cares to endure or bear the cross as being affliction, agony, pain and all that vexes us; but everyone prefers to live in peace and calm, not in sorrow and travail but in idleness. Hence the glory and honor of the true priesthood is extinguished and in its stead an idol of human law and human doctrine is set up, so that the prophecy of Paul is fulfilled, which he sets forth in II Tim. 3 [:1-9]: "But understand this, that in the last days there will come times of stress. For men will be lovers of self, lovers of money, proud, arrogant, blasphemers, disobedient to their parents, ungrateful, not heeding God's service, inhuman, not keeping compacts, slanderers, profligates, unmerciful, haters of good, treacherous, reckless, swollen with conceit, blind, lovers of pleasure rather than lovers of God, having the appearance of being believing Christians but denying His power. Avoid such people. For among them are those who make their way into households and capture women burdened with sins and follow various desires and lusts, always learning and never arriving at a knowledge of the truth. As Jannes and Jambres opposed Moses, so these men also oppose the truth. They are men of corrupt mind, incapable of faith; but they will accomplish nothing henceforth, for their folly will be plain to all, as was that of those two men."[88]

Part II

Concerning the Words of the Mass, which Prove that the Mass is not a Sacrifice

In the first part I have overthrown the devil's ungodly, un-Christian priesthood and also proved that the mass may not be called a sacrifice. I have stopped up the mouths of the opposition so that they can bring up nothing in the way of counter-argument but their own dreams, customs, human wickedness and violence, all of which, as everyone knows, are worthless in divine matters and in establishing the faith.

In addition I have consoled those whose consciences are weak and have instructed them so that they may know and recognize that there is no sacrifice in the New Testament other than the sacrifice of the cross [Heb. 10:10] and the sacrifice of praise [Heb. 13:15] which are mentioned in the Scriptures; so that no one any longer has cause to doubt that the mass is not a sacrifice. Now, after this bickering, I wish in the second part to demonstrate the same thing through peaceful teaching and without any bickering, and to build neatly on the foundations which I have laid, treating of the mass, not with our own words, as the devil's priests do with respect to their own mass, but with the divine words with which Christ himself instituted it. Let us therefore examine the original institution of the mass and the words of its founder.

First, it is written in Matt. 26 [:26-28]: "As they were eating, Jesus took bread, gave thanks, and broke it, and gave it to the disciples and said, 'Take and eat; this is my body.' And he took the cup, gave thanks, and said, 'Drink of it, all of you; this is my blood of the new testament, which will be poured out for many for the forgiveness of sins.'"

Second, it is written in Mark 14 [:22-24]: "As they were eating, Jesus took bread, and blessed, and broke it, and gave it to them,

[88] II Tim. 3:8 names two Egyptian magicians of Exod. 7:11, 22.

and said, 'Take and eat; this is my body.' And he took the cup, gave thanks and gave it to them, and they all drank of it, and he said, 'This is my blood of the new testament, which will be poured out for many.'"

Third, it is written in Luke 22 [:19-20]: "He took bread, gave thanks, broke it, gave it to them, saying, 'This is my body, which is given for you. Do this in remembrance of me.' And likewise the cup after supper, saying, 'This is the cup of the new testament in my blood, which will be poured out for you.'"

Fourth, it is written in I Cor. 11 [:23-25]: "For I received from the Lord what I also delivered to you, that the Lord Jesus on the night when he was taken captive took bread, thanked God, broke it and said, 'Take and eat, this is my body, which is given for you, and do this in remembrance of me.' In the same way also the cup, when he had eaten, saying, 'This is the cup of the new testament in my blood. Do this, as often as you drink it, in remembrance of me.'" Here you see that Paul and Luke agree almost word for word.

Here I beg each one who reads this little book to believe most firmly that these four men were not drunk or mad when they were writing and speaking these words; but, filled with the Holy Spirit [Acts 2:4, 15], they wrote the truth of the matter, so that everyone may believe these words surely without wavering, cling to them firmly, and trust freely that they will stand even against all the power of the devil.

Next I would also desire to have you believe that, although he said, did, and instituted all these things at night, during and after supper, Christ was not drunk or mad like other men, but that he instituted nothing except by divine power and wisdom. And although that desire seems ridiculous, yet the anger and wrath of the papists and the miserable senseless folly of the ravenous wolves at Paris, Louvain, and other universities forces me to it. They are all so blind and obdurate that they despise Christ, his apostles and evangelists, and the whole of the Scriptures, and take nothing to heart. They want us to be senseless with the senseless ones, to abandon God's Word and works, and together with them to boast of and cling to human words and works. They cry out: the fathers, fathers, fathers; the church, church, church; the councils, councils, councils; the decrees, decrees, decrees; the universities, universities,

universities! With these frothy water bulls they dare to demand that all heavenly and divine wisdom and the thunderbolts of the Holy Spirit should yield to them, and if they do not yield, they want immediately to burn and condemn everything.

What do they indicate with all this wrath, wickedness, and violence except that Christ and his apostles were drunk or mad in their words and works, and that Christ said things of less import than those said by men, and that it is more secure to build and to rely on the fathers, councils, schools and on the canon laws—which err and have often erred, as they themselves admit—than to build and to rely on Christ? Of course, they are not putting their hearts into any defense of the fathers, councils, etc. They are simply buttressing their own position and conduct—which they have taken from the fathers and councils without rightly understanding them—whereby the world is defrauded of body, soul, and property. They are simply extinguishing and eradicating the truth.

Let us meanwhile cling to the divine words firmly and with confidence, even if it vexes the pope or the bishops and their whores and knaves; and let us see whether the divine words quoted above admit that the mass be called a sacrifice.

In the first place, let us pay no heed to the irreligious religion which those foolish people have invented and persuaded the whole world to believe, namely, that the words of consecration have been kept secret[34] and their use and knowledge entrusted to no one but the priests, and to them only after they have celebrated mass. These words, after all, should fittingly have been common knowledge to all people, because the faith, consolation and salvation of all people is contained in them, as I will show. Likewise they have given strict and stern commands that whoever omitted the little word *enim* or *eterni*[35] was committing a great and weighty mortal sin—I should judge, one weighing a hundredweight! Not that I should find it pleasing for the form[36] of the sacrament to be changed

[34] Cf. *The Abomination of the Secret Mass* (1525) in this volume, pp. 310 and 314.

[35] A conjunction and a non-scriptural adjective, both quite minor words from the Latin liturgical text used for the consecration of the wine. See the text itself in *PE* 6, 126. Luther omitted the adjective both in his own rendering of the Words of Institution (pp. 36-37) and in his translation of the canon of the mass (p. 319), allowing the scriptural term "New Testament" to stand without further embellishment.

[36] Cf. p. 62 n. 118.

by the whim of any human being, but such wickedness and daring hurts me: that these rogues dare to make necessary articles of faith out of things which are not commanded, and by their own devices make sins out of things in which there can be no danger or sin. They terrify and corrupt those who have weak consciences, so that they extinguish the spirit of Christian freedom and arouse in us the craven spirit of fear [Rom. 8:15].

No sin, be it adultery or murder, is deemed and considered to be so grievous and weighty as when someone omits the word *enim*. They have not noticed that the Holy Spirit studiously arranged that no evangelist should agree with another in exactly the same words. Yet these evangelists ought to have been more in agreement, or else they would have sinned more than we in the form of the sacrament.

The papists have also made it an unforgivable sin if anyone touches the sacrament except with anointed fingers or tongue, although it does not move them at all if a fly creeps over it, or if it is touched by the chalice or corporal. In other words, they do not consider the human body a worthy creature of God, or else they are insane and mad. It would be a similar sin if someone by chance swallowed a drop of water; he would be unworthy of the sacrament on that day. O senseless folly! It is not right, they say, for a man to take anything into his mouth before receiving the body of Christ. That would be a fine thing: then no mist or air could enter a Christian's mouth, unless the body of Christ had entered first; and one would have to forbid the priests to breathe air until after the mass. Yet Christ and his disciples held mass after the evening meal; and it is a common occurrence that after a man has eaten moderately his mouth, head, and breath are purer and more alert than when he is quite empty and thus heavy with sleep and dishevelled.

We scorn such arbitrary religion as men have invented without Christ's word and command. Not that one might not or should not do these things; but when one attempts to make it a sin to omit them, when one tries to capture and frighten consciences, we cannot and will not tolerate it. Let him who wishes observe them, but voluntarily and without coercion. Let him know that he cannot sin by omitting them, as Christ and the apostles did not sin therein. One commits sin only in that which occurs contrary to Christ's word and institution: that which the counterfeits consider to be a form of divine service, namely, to misuse the mass so horribly and make a sacrifice and good work of it, thereby condemning and suppressing faith and the right usage, so that the words may be fulfilled which are spoken of the ungodly: "They are in great fear, where no fear is" [Ps. 53:5]. So by the just judgment of God they have sin and hell in those things, in which grace and all salvation are; and they make righteousness and salvation, where there is sin and the greatest damnation. Thus God is perverse with the crooked, etc. (Ps. 18 [:26]).

I have written at such length on this subject because I wanted to indicate that it is no wonder that they dared to make a sacrifice out of the mass, these people who are swayed by such foolish, godless dreams that they pervert everything and do nothing aright in this sacrament, so that their use and practice is not only open to suspicion but should be avoided by all men. What good could they possibly accomplish by and in the mass, while they are extinguishing the faith and remembrance of Christ and erecting in their stead a sacrifice and a good work? Let us now treat the statements of the holy gospel one by one, and see what they teach us to believe concerning the mass.

The works and examples of Christ and of the apostles should be plentiful enough, because we believe that all the works of Christ occurred as an example to us, as he himself says: "For I have given you an example, that you also should do as I have done to you" [John 13:15]. And at this point he foresaw the wolves that would come, when he said: "Do this in remembrance of me" [I Cor. 11:24-25]. What are they to do? What I am now doing with you. But what is he doing? Is he blessing bread and wine in a golden chalice or golden chasuble, with all the ornaments and trappings that we use today? No, he takes bread and wine and with the word which he speaks he makes of them his body and blood and gives it to his disciples to eat.

If now someone were to follow this simple manner and leave out everything which men have invented and added, you should not denounce him as a heretic unless you would call Christ himself a heretic. He will not hold up to you the words of the pope, or the Gomorrahs, or the fathers, but Christ's own words: "Do this in remembrance of me" [I Cor. 11:24-25]. And if you hear this and cannot show that they are acting otherwise than as Christ did, you, together with Paris, will be considered a rude ass or a blasphemer. It may be that the Greeks[37] or Bohemians[38] use this plain, simple method, and perform what Christ here says: "Do this"; and that on the other hand at Rome the unlearned, ungodly water bulls sit on precious golden royal thrones—the pope, cardinals, bishops, monks and priests, with their schools, Paris and Louvain, together with their beloved sisters, Sodom and Gomorrah. When they now see that poor, lowly, and despised group doing this they become very angry, turn up their noses, twist their mouths, stretch out their hands and say: The heretics are not adhering to the form and manner of the Roman church, neither do they believe the articles of faith which the holy faculty at Paris and its sisters have made. And they are all well pleased with what they do because there are so many of these unlearned counterfeits and blockheads; even though they do not have one word of the Scriptures they think that all their actions must be right, as if they could not err.

What will you do in this situation? Will you follow the great and excellent crowd in their spite against God's law and leave the smaller group who are in the right, when you see God's Word and work here and see nothing there but human dreams and human might? For that reason you may be certain that Christ directs his eyes to the place where people act and live according to his Word, even if there were no more than two who turned away from those with whom his Word is not present. Even if there were as many popes, cardinals, and bishops as there are stars in the sky and leaves in the forest, dressed in pure gold, pearls, and jewels and riding on nothing but mules and donkeys, should you not for the sake of the Word of God and the supreme divine majesty of Christ simply consider all these idols and counterfeits to be nothing but filth and dirt? Why are you afraid of these effeminate, frivolous priests, as long as you have Christ with you and act according to his word? Does not John say of him: "He who is in us is greater than he who is in the world?" [I John 4:4].

Therefore let the wolves and counterfeits condemn your actions

[37] Cf. p. 24 n. 47.
[38] Cf. p. 20 n. 38.

and set up sacrifices of which they know nothing; let them cite the fathers, councils and long usage of all men. For yourself be content with your Christ alone and his little flock, for of him you know for certain that he did not sacrifice bread and wine in his last supper. He will not condemn you because these men have condemned you; he will crown you because you have followed him and not these men. You have the word and work of Christ, hold it out before all the devils. What do they have? Pearl mitres, red hats, tonsured heads, golden rings with big, broad seals; with these they confirm all their acts and on these the Christian faith now depends. If they lost all this, they would have as much of a bishop's character as the miller's donkey.

Therefore let every real Christian take to heart the example of Christ, and be assured that it is neither fitting nor proper for any angel, much less for human bulls and billows,[39] to make out of the sacrament of God something which Christ himself did not make. And even if it were possible to do so, it would not be advisable for a Christian person to deviate from the example of Christ and make innovations in such important matters without an example. Why did Christ show us the way with his words and works, and preach to us, if we are permitted to undertake or begin anything without his word and work? Why did he come into the world at all, if it is not sufficient for us to follow him in that which he taught us?

We do not condemn the practice of conducting the sacrament with chasubles and other ceremonies; but we do condemn the idea that they are necessary and indispensable and are made a matter of conscience, whereas all things which Christ did not institute are optional, voluntary, and unnecessary, and therefore also harmless. To make a sacrifice of the sacrament, however, is not to make a ceremony, but to change completely its nature and character. This is not merely to act without example; it is to act contrary to the word and example of Christ—something which even Christian freedom cannot excuse, since it is the most damnable idolatry and blasphemy.

---

[39] *Bulgen*, an old German word for "waves." Luther uses it here as another term of reproach because of its alliteration with *Bullen*, and because he regards the latter anyway as mere "bubbles on the water." Cf. p. 77 n. 137. Cf. Buchwald, *op. cit.*, II, 219 n. 2.

In the second place, it is evident that the words of Christ are true, with which he solemnly promises: "This is my body, which is given for you. This is the cup, a new testament in my blood, which is poured out for you." Even Paris, that mother and source of all error, cannot say otherwise than that these are words of promise, incorporating in themselves the pledge of his promise, the body and the blood of Christ in the bread and wine. We are promised the body of Christ and the pouring out of his blood for the forgiveness of sins, which is the new testament.

To this promise belongs faith, namely, that I believe that I shall receive what is promised to me, and a pledge of the promise whereby promise and faith are joined together. Where there is no promise, there is no faith; and where there is no faith, the promise is nothing. And since God clearly makes this promise to us gratis, without any merit or work on our part (for otherwise it would not be a promise, but a reward or recompense), the promise is therefore received and accepted only by faith, without any works; otherwise our works would merit the promise. Therefore one satisfies the promise by faith; and the faith is satisfied by the promise. For works cause one to forget the promise and consider it as nothing; the promise, on the other hand, demands no works, but is satisfied with faith.

For this reason we shall find or see in these words nothing but the promise of Christ and the faith of man. Not one iota about a sacrifice is indicated in them, for sacrifice and promise are further apart than sunrise and sunset. A sacrifice is a work in which we present and give to God something of our own. The promise, however, is God's word, which gives to man the grace and mercy of God. So it is not merely false, but also incomprehensible to human reason to make out of God's promise a human sacrifice, and out of the word of divine majesty a work of a lowly creature. Between the word of God and our work there is no similarity at all, not to speak of their being identical. When Christ commanded us to do this in remembrance of him he wanted nothing more from us than that with the promise and pledge we should exercise ourselves daily in faith. This is why he instituted this sacrament and gave it to us, for the human soul will be nourished more and more if one frequently remembers this gracious promise. Now you see how blind and perverse the papists are in making out of the promise of God a human work, whereby they themselves acknowledge that they have no idea of what the Sacrament of the Altar is or what Christ accomplished and indicated by it. They offer a work; Christ demands faith. They give to God; Christ promises to men. Could anything more foolish be invented or imagined?

If a prince were to allot his property to you and give you a written testament of his last will as a pledge, and he did this out of kindness and goodness because of your poverty, demanding nothing from you except that you love him and accept the testament with gratitude and joy and keep it intact; and if you were to go and offer the testament back to him, so as to increase his property and not your own, and you wished to be honored as a benefactor, while he would be disgraced by accepting something from you, a poor beggar: would you not be considered mad and foolish and lacking in understanding? Or if you understood what you were doing, would you not be ridiculing and mocking the prince out of pride and malice? This is the situation with the papist clergy when compared to the divine majesty because they consider the mass a sacrifice and presume to enrich God with his own promise. O abomination of all abominations!

In the third place, the words read thus: "He took the bread, thanked God, broke it and gave it to his disciples." He did not say: He took the bread and raised it up before God, to show that he had offered it to God and not given it to men. Here the counterfeits will hardly be so senseless and ignorant of the language as to dare to say that "giving to the disciples" is the same as "offering to God." Much less can "take" mean the same as "offer," when he says "he took"; for this indicates that he took the bread to himself in order to use it. For if he wanted to bless the bread and give it to the disciples, he would have to take it in his hands, because he could not break it and give it with his feet. Neither is a sacrifice indicated in the fact that he blessed bread and wine or gave thanks, otherwise he would also have sacrificed the five barley loaves and the two fish [John 6:11], which he took in his hands, blessed or gave thanks, and gave them to his disciples, using the very same form and manner, except that he did not say "This is my body," that is, he did not change the loaves into his body. Likewise "bless" and "give thanks" is a sign and testimony that something is received and given from God, not that we offer or give anything to God.

He who sacrifices prays and asks God that he would graciously accept his sacrifice, etc. He who gives thanks, however, does not pray that it will be acceptable, but rejoices that something is given to him and that he has received it. So you may see how all the words oppose the idea that the mass is a sacrifice given to God, and show that it is a blessing and gift of God given to men, which they are to accept and receive from God, thanking, praising and blessing him for it; and not pray that God will accept it.

Here you can clearly see that the manner and method which they now hold in the mass does not agree with the gospel at all. All three Evangelists, and Paul with them, agree that Christ took the bread, broke it, and gave it to the disciples. They do not say whether he himself ate or drank of it. Since "breaking" and "giving to the disciples" is nothing else than dividing the blessed bread into many parts and distributing them to the others, no mass, if it is to conform to the institution and example of Christ, should be held unless the sacrament is broken and distributed among many by the priest. If a mass is held in any other way it is not a Christian mass, but directly contrary to Christ's ordinance and institution.

What will you say to this, you poor mass-holders? Should not this passage of Scripture fittingly move all of you to cease holding mass, since no one anywhere follows Christ and his institution, except those who bring the sacrament to the sick, or those who administer it publicly without taking it themselves? The latter follow Christ's example best, for they take it in their hands and break it and give it to the others, whose ministers they are; just as Christ, the minister of others, does not take the sacrament himself but administers it to the others. The mass-holders, however, divide the sacrament into three parts: one for the living, the second for those in purgatory, and the third for the saints in heaven. They are not clever enough to know that no saint requires either faith, sacrament, or promise, for they possess and have attained their promise and the promised inheritance. The mass-holders pretend to divide the sacrament, but actually they keep all three parts for themselves, rob the people, and give none of it to anyone. Now compare them: these Antichrists and Christ! The latter breaks the bread and gives some of it to everyone. The former break it but give none of it to anyone, keeping it for themselves alone; they have merely invented a semblance of breaking. What has become of the word of Christ, "Do this"? Why do they act differently and in opposition to Christ? So it is safest to hold no papal mass at all, for which there is neither the example nor the institution of Christ, but when you have blessed and distributed the bread, to take it yourself from another; just as no one baptizes himself or gives himself absolution, but is baptized or absolved by somebody else.

Since this is now clear and evident, we have no need at all of the insights of the Parisians, who say: It is contrary to the doctors of the Holy Scriptures, and injurious to the holy faculty; it defames and dishonors them.[40] The words of the gospel stand there absolutely immovable: "He broke and gave it to his disciples, do this." He does not say: He kept it and took it himself, do this. If they had retained this usage of the sacrament it would never have become a sacrifice; just as one does not call it a sacrifice when the pastor administers and gives the sacrament to the sick or to others who ask for it. But when they substituted for the breaking and distribution of the sacrament the keeping and taking of it by one's self, and called the minister a priest, that is when the sacrifice was invented so that the holy priest would have something to do at the altar and would not stand there idle. And if anyone wishes to serve himself, let him not take it alone, but break it and give it to the others also, so that he may be doing something that is in conformity with the example and institution of Christ. They are words which neither lie nor deceive, but which can make our consciences secure, if you adhere to them, believe them and follow them, even though the whole world thinks and speaks to the contrary.

In the fourth place, he said "take." Not only did Christ indicate by his work and example that the mass it not a sacrifice but a gift of God; he also confirmed it with his word when he commanded them to take it. Why did he not say: Offer it? "Take" does not mean here to offer or give property not your own to somebody else. It means to take to yourself, use and enjoy your own property which has been given you. When he says "take" he makes you thereby possessors of the gifts which he has given and broken. Therefore

[40] Cf. p. 140 n. 16.

the word "take" does not admit of anything being sacrificed. It indicates rather that the gift which you take comes to you from God.

What can possibly be said against this? Will Sodom and Gomorrah still accuse us of presuming to be the only ones who understand the Scriptures? Come, show us a different interpretation and suppress this one! It is not enough that you say: This is a stumbling block. We know well that Christ and his word will be found to be a stumbling block [Cor. 1:23; I Pet. 2:8].

In the fifth place: "Eat and drink." That is all that we are to do with the sacrament. Therefore he breaks it, gives it, and tells us to take it, so that we eat and drink it and in so doing remember him and besides proclaim his death. Likewise Paul knew of no other work in this sacrament than eating and drinking, when he repeated the words of Christ: "As often as you eat this bread and drink the cup, you proclaim the Lord's death until he comes" [I Cor. 11:26]. Here Paul does not command us to sacrifice anything or do anything but only to take, eat, and drink. But what we eat and drink we do not sacrifice; we keep it for ourselves and consume it. Still we are not ashamed to make a sacrifice out of that which we eat and drink, in direct contradiction to these clear and incontrovertible words.

The nature and character of burnt offering in particular is that one gives it wholly to God and allows men to have nothing of it at all; but if it was a common or sin offering, one gave a part of it to God and a part to men [Lev. 1:9, 2:1-3]. Why then do we eat and drink all the bread and wine and leave none of it to God? And if it is to be the best and highest sacrifice, why do we not leave all of it to God? So where is the sacrifice here? It is not enough to prate and say: Christ is sacrificed by us under the bread and wine. We still take Christ to ourselves under the bread and wine, even though nothing is supposed to be taken from the sacrifice of the Lord.

To sacrifice to God and to be consumed by us are not compatible ideas. The Levites, indeed, took the offerings of the people of Israel, but they did not eat any of that which was to be sacrificed to God. Consequently, if we offer our bodies [Rom. 12:1] and praise to God, we donate and entrust them to God completely and hold back nothing for ourselves, so that it may be a true, genuine spiritual sacrifice. Therefore the pope's sacrifice is a marvelous and abominable innovation, just as he and all his followers, laws and actions are innovations that are unfounded in the Scriptures. We eat it completely, and offer it completely to God; that is as much as to say that when we offer it, we do not consume it, and when we consume it, we do not offer it. Hence, since we do both, we do neither. Who ever heard of such foolishness? It is all self-contradictory; one argument overthrows the other, and we must of necessity conclude that this sacrament cannot possibly be a sacrifice. Be angry, men of Louvain and Paris, and refute this for us!

In the sixth place: "This is my body, this is the cup of my blood." Here Christ gives us a pledge and token of his promise, as God has always done in his promises. To Abraham he gave circumcision [Gen. 17:10] as a token of the promised son. When he promised Noah that He would be the God of his children and would never again destroy the earth by water He gave him the rainbow in the clouds as a sign [Gen. 9:11-13]. And He continued to confirm all his promises by signs, so that Isaiah in the same manner bade King Ahaz to ask for a sign from God when He promised him that He would redeem the people from the power of the king of Syria and Samaria [Isa. 7:10-11]. The same custom is still practiced among men: pacts, vows, and promises are confirmed by means of seals and witnesses as well as by words and letters. If one makes a promise to anyone, he shakes hands with him on it. If one gives his bond for anything a seal is attached, so that the promise and bond will be firmly kept.

The same is true here also: in order that we may be certain of this promise of Christ and truly rely on it without any doubt, he has given us the most precious and costly seal and pledge, his true body and blood under bread and wine—the very same as that with which he obtained for us the gift and promise of this precious and gracious treasure, surrendering his life that we might receive and accept the promised grace.

How can we then, out of this pledge and seal of God given to us as a gift, make a sacrifice and work of our own? Who among men would be so foolish as to sacrifice the seal on a letter, in which something is promised to him, to the one who makes the promise?

Rather he takes it and keeps it and confidently anticipates the reception of that which has been promised to him. Thus we hold that God is obligated to us because of the boundless pledge that he has given us; and we hope with certainty and with great joy in our hearts that he will fulfil what he has promised us and what he has confirmed with such a precious pledge and seal. And you, godless crowd, adherents of the pope, would teach us to make sacrifices instead and give away these boundless gifts and joys!

Who would not be deeply grieved and hurt in his heart that these cruel soul-murderers obscure for us this unspeakable love of God, weakening the assurance of our hearts and driving away this confidence? They set up God's wrath in the place of God's love, and works instead of faith; and they make us afraid and unsure in all that we do.

For, when they make a sacrifice out of the mass, do not we become uncertain whether our sacrifice is pleasing to God or not? There is none among all the mass-holders who would dare to say: I am sure that my mass-holding is pleasing and acceptable to God. And they all continue in this uncertain delusion and keep on sacrificing Christ and do not know what they are doing, because they let the promise of the true God slip from them and are led hither and thither by their uncertain sacrifices and works.

Furthermore, he who sacrifices wishes to reconcile God. But he who wishes to reconcile God considers him to be angry and unmerciful. And whoever does this does not expect grace or mercy from him, but fears his judgment and sentence. Whoever is to go to the sacrament with profit must believe and firmly insist that he has a kind and gracious God who loves him so very deeply that He has voluntarily given to him His greatest and dearest treasure. Nothing can be more directly opposed to the profitable use of the sacrament than the teaching of the papists and these harmful consciences who believe that God is angry and needs to be appeased by this sacrifice. But if God were not so gracious and merciful, he would never have poured out so rich a treasure and given us such a precious gift.

Judge from this into what great danger the mass-priests have led us with their sacrifice, so that we have turned our treasure that gives us life and salvation into something that gives us death and damnation, the certain into the uncertain, faith into doubt, in short, divine love and grace into anger and hate. We consider the Father to be an enemy, and have confused heaven with hell, the highest with the lowest.

If, however, you recognize that this sacrament is a promise and not a sacrifice, you are not uncertain and are aware of no anger. You are always certain that God is trustworthy and cannot lie [Num. 23: 19], that he keeps his promise. And as he promises and shows himself to be gracious and merciful, so you will find him to be, if you hold and believe him to be thus. And if you notice that he promises you nothing but grace, then you will understand with a light and joyous conscience that he demands nothing from you in the way of gift or sacrifice, but that he lovingly entreats and encourages you to accept his gift. If you wish to make sacrifices, however, you must necessarily have a burdened conscience which believes that God demands much from you by way of sacrifice; and because of your great concern you will see no good thing for you to receive. So it comes about that where there should be only rejoicing of heart toward God, there is instead nothing but fear, care, anguish and misery. And this is exactly what the raging devil wished to obtain through this godless sacrifice.

In the seventh place: "Which is given for you. Which is poured out for you for the forgiveness of sin." Here is indicated the promised grace—remission of sins. O what a sweet and mighty promise! It can admit of no sacrifice. Body and blood are given in order that we whose sins are forgiven us may have salvation! These are the precious goods and gifts, which are proffered and given to you in this sacrament. How is it possible for an angry, ungracious God to do this? Must he not rather be a kind, solicitous Father? What greater gift could he have promised than forgiveness of sins, which is nothing other than grace, peace, life, inheritance, eternal honor and blessedness in God? And you, ungodly papist, see in this sacrament a different god, one who is to be reconciled.

Do you not see by now that all who make sacrifice in this sacrament, as often as they do so, commit idolatry? For they do not have in the sacrament a true God, but make and invent for themselves a false god of their own minds, a god who is angry and requires reconciling, one who simply cannot and may not be present in this sacrament. And God is truly angry with you, just as you believe. For you have no faith in the sacrament, that is in the promise of Christ. You are truly a heathen and a Jew—only in name and title a Christian and only by virtue of your tonsure a priest—except that you sin much more grievously against the gifts promised in this sacrament, and you embitter and enrage God much more by your sacrifice, than they do. Otherwise, in disbelief you are certainly equal to the heathen and the Jew.

In order to remove this delusion from your minds Christ himself indicated in his own words how he was to be reconciled, when he said: "Which is given for you. Which is poured out for you." Therefore desist from your accursed and harmful reconciliation. There are not several ways to reconcile God, but one way alone. His majesty is much too high to be reconciled by the blood of all the men on earth and the merit of all the angels. The body of Christ is given and his blood poured out, and thereby God is reconciled, for it was given and poured out for you—as he says: "for you"—so that he may avert from us the wrath of God which we by our sins have deserved. And if the wrath is gone then the sins are forgiven. Therefore he says it shall be given and poured out for the forgiveness of sins. If the body were not given and the blood not poured out, then the wrath of God would remain upon us and we would retain our sins.

Here you see clearly that no work of satisfaction or sacrifice of reconciliation is of any use; only faith in the given body and the shed blood reconciles. Not that faith does the reconciling in and of itself, but it lays hold on and obtains the reconciliation which Christ has performed for us. Much less can your foolish work or sacrifice, which takes place without Christ and without faith, procure anything from God, unless it be even greater wrath and displeasure. Therefore this much stands fast: the body is given for you; you cannot give or offer anything for the forgiveness of sins, but it is given to you gratis. But this gift of God in us is not given to Christ gratis; for it and for our sake he gave his body and life, in order that we should love him and, rejoicing in the divine mercy, be grateful that he has given to us unworthy and undeserving people such an unspeakable treasure of his blessings. Therefore the priests are neither to sacrifice nor give anything to God in this sacrament, but only to believe and accept from God.

Hence it follows that one cannot hold mass for another. What do I care if all the papists believe and practice otherwise! They will never root out the faith. We are also well aware that it is proclaimed in the gospel and the epistles that the priests shall mislead the whole world with their error. The words of divine majesty will not mislead or deceive us, even in the midst of death. They demand no more of us than faith, for they are pure, unadulterated, gracious promise. But each person must have his own faith in this promise and be convinced in his own heart that it will come to him as God has promised. This cannot take place on behalf of anyone else. I cannot believe for you, just as you cannot believe for me. Therefore I cannot cause you to share in the promise of God; your own faith must do this, as is written: "He who does not believe will be condemned" [Mark 16:16]. But the shameful mass-priests who set up brotherhoods for the sake of money and hold masses for the living and the dead, only deceive the foolish people and draw them into hell after themselves, and with their lives rob the people of their money and property.

From this it must be clear to every one what is the secret and hidden basis of it all. It is common knowledge to every one on what foundation the bishoprics, cathedral chapters, monasteries, churches, and the whole realm of the priests are based and built, namely, on holding masses, that is, on the most abominable idolatry on earth, on shameful lies, on the perverted, godless misuse of the sacrament, and on a disbelief worse than that of the heathen. Thus it has also come about through the just judgment of God that all their money and property are used for nothing but vain pomp, harlotry and gluttony; they are idle, have good times, are of no use to anyone, either to God or the world, and are obedient only to the Roman idol, as is also fitting. This is the appropriate reward for him who has invented this godless priesthood.

But there is one thought which consoles them, and on which they rely; they think it impossible that all of them should be in error and Luther alone be right; just as Zedekiah struck the only prophet of God, Micaiah [I Kings 22:24], and thought it impossible that all the other phophets should lie, and that this one alone should have the Spirit of God. It is indeed a fine premise, which one bases on size and number over against the clear, pure Word of God. What else but lies should please the liars, who are founded on nothing but lies? With what should they more fittingly be at enmity than with the Word of God, which puts them and their lies to shame?

In the eighth place: "A new testament." See, Christ himself calls the mass a testament. How then can it be a sacrifice? If Louvain, Paris, and the devil's kingdom at Rome all together were wise enough to know their logic, I would dispute with them concerning the nature and character of a sacrifice and a testament, to see whether they would finally perceive the difference between a testament and a sacrifice.

However, because they base their unfounded undertaking only on the profusion of cowls and tonsures, disregarding clear reason and the divine word, I shall let them go on, and let the donkeys wait for their cries; I shall proclaim to devout Christians our scripturally based testament. Between a testament and a promise there is this difference: a testament is made by someone who is about to die; a promise, however, is made by someone who expects to continue living. Thus the Epistle to the Hebrews [9:16-17] says: "For where a will is involved, the death of the one who made it must be established. For a will takes effect only at death, since it is not in force as long as the one who made it is alive."

Since God in the Scriptures again and again calls his promise a testament he means to announce thereby that he will die; and again, in calling it a promise he means to announce that he will live. And thus, by that one word he wanted to make us understand that he would become man, die; and yet live eternally—though with that we are not concerned at the moment. A testament is nothing but the last will of one who is dying, telling how his heirs are to live with and dispose of his properties after his death. I will now be very brief, because I have written concerning this in my work on the Epistle to the Galatians.[41] Four things are necessary in a complete and proper testament: the testator, the oral or written promise, the inheritance, and the heirs; and all of these are clearly visible to us in this testament. The testator is Christ, who is about to die. The promise is contained in the words with which the bread and wine

---

[41] *WA* 2, 518-521.

are consecrated. The inheritance which Christ has bequeathed to us in his testament is the forgiveness of sins. The heirs are all the believers in Christ, namely, the holy elect children of God—wherefore Paul in Titus 1 [:1] calls the Christian faith the faith of the elect.

Now note the deception of the priests, who have made a sacrifice of the testament. God bequeathes and gives something to us, but they sacrifice something to him. That is nothing else than to denounce God as a liar or regard him as a fool, for calling it a testament. For whoever makes a sacrifice out of it cannot consider it to be a testament, because it is impossible for a sacrifice to be a testament. The former we give, the latter we take; the former goes from us to God, the latter comes from God to us; the former occurs through us, the latter without us. What need is there for me to relate all the differences between that which we take and that which we give, when even the irrational beasts can see and grasp the distinction?

It is of no use for the papists and sophists to seek a loophole and say: It may well be a testament if one applies it to us, but applied to God it is a sacrifice. There is, they say, a single God and a single church, between which only the testament mediates from above and the sacrifice from below. Yes, I confess that applied to the god of the papists, who is a false god and only a god of their minds, it is a sacrifice; but applied to our God, the true, genuine God, it can be nothing but a testament.

Secondly, they do not regard Christ as a testator because they neither recognize nor accept the testament. For in it they wish not to receive anything from God, but only to give and sacrifice to him. They will not recognize him as a beneficent giver of his goods, but only as an insatiable jailer, who demands from us goods and works which are not his own.

Thirdly, they deny the inheritance, for they are not seeking the forgiveness of sins, as a free gift which Christ procured for us with his body and blood, but they want to earn and attain their own new kind of forgiveness of sins with their sacrifices and works. These holy ones must work so that they will not receive the grace and mercy of God as gifts. Beyond that, each one wants to prepare and make himself worthy of such a sacrament with many prayers, confessions and other works, so that he may be quite pure on arrival, with nothing left over to be forgiven. In this way they mock the blood of Christ which is poured out for the forgiveness of sins. All this comes about because they know of no sin except that of the evil will and intention to sin; all other desires and lusts of the heart are for them natural drives or imperfections which do not need Christ. So it happens that the papists get quite pure through an assumed or invented repentance, and no longer need the testament of the forgiveness of sins. So they go forth in purity to that place where no one ought to go except the one who needs forgiveness of sins.

Fourthly, they also deny the heirs. For the heirs are only those who believe the testament. But the mass-priests make their own heirs, who rely on their own sacrifices and works, namely, those of restless and frightened conscience who not only do not believe but do not even know that they ought to believe. For they do not know that this is a promise and a testament which demands only faith, but they think that it is a sacrifice brought about by works. So you see that the papists are completely blinded and have no inkling of what the sacrament is, what fruits, benefits, and advantages it brings, or how it should be used.

This knowledge and wisdom of theirs concerning the sacrament you find in all their books, sermons, and songs, and in all the writings in which they treat of the sacrament. They call it words of consecration, not words of a testament. And here they take great pains to make it credible that no bread remains, that it is annihilated, in order to make place for the body of Christ. No one is at all concerned to speak and preach to the people about faith and the testament. Nothing is thought to be so offensive and heretical as when one disregards their foolish and poisonous caricatures and delves into the subject of faith and the testament.

There is now in vogue that song of the feast of Corpus Christi[42] which is patched together from many passages of Scripture; in it the Scriptures are so forced and pulled in by the hair that God's worst enemy must have composed it, either that or it is the dream

[42] Festival observed on the Thursday after Trinity Sunday in celebration of transubstantiation (cf. p. 29 n. 61). Luther is referring to stanza 22 of the Prose appointed in the Roman Missal, and to certain of the versicles, antiphons, and responses appointed in the Breviary's liturgical offices for the festival. Cf. *The Roman Breviary*, trans. John, Marquess of Bute (London, 1908), III, 226-229.

of a poor senseless idiot. Here Melchizedek is remembered, who offered bread and wine [Gen. 14:18]; then the lamb comes into it which the people sacrificed of old [Exod. 12:5-6], and the cake of Elijah [I Kings 19:6], the manna of the fathers [Exod. 16:15], and Isaac, who was to be sacrificed [Gen. 22:2], and I don't know what has not been thought of. All these have had to serve as figures of the sacrament. It is a wonder that he did not include Baalam's ass [Num. 22:21] and David's mule [I Kings 1:38]; they could have had no less significance to the stupid ass than these other stories and figures.

In addition, the pope also enters with great pomp in the lessons at matins, so that everyone thinks that he will proclaim nothing but the rich treasure of faith and testament. He does begin, but immediately falls back upon Aristotle's art, treating of bread, of its whiteness and roundness, and of the annihilation of the bread. After this is over and the poor people are still hungry, indeed have heard only vain straw and chaff instead of the Word of God, the holy father grants them rich and bountiful indulgence. Yet the pious man dares to say in his preface that he could weep when he regards the gracious kindness of the divine majesty.

Now see whether Aristotle should not be despised, who after his death makes the pope so learned, pious, and holy that he weeps for holiness! Alas poor me, that I must see and hear that through God's unspeakable wrath such devil's abuse and mockery is to be preached to poor miserable Christians as serious, wholesome doctrine! Who weeps at this? Who are the ones, who in these days of wrath will make themselves a wall before God for the people of Israel? [Ezek. 22:30].

And in conclusion, let all Christians, especially priests, take heed lest they make a sacrifice out of the testament. The Old Testament, which was given by the angels [Acts 7:53], cannot be called a sacrifice, because it is a word of law, which was not sacrificed, but confirmed by the sacrifice of irrational animals. The angels gave the law. The people received it; they did not sacrifice it. Much less can the New Testament, instituted by Christ himself, be a sacrifice, because it is a word of promise and grace, which is not sacrificed, but perfected and confirmed by the sacrifice of Christ on the cross. Now if he were a godless fool who considered the Old Testament, the law which is given and accepted, to be a sacrifice, how much more a fool would that person be who calls the New Testament a sacrifice, when it is the promise of the grace of Christ, which is given and accepted. And just as it was commanded that one should zealously preach the law to the people and instil it into their hearts, so Christ commanded that the New Testament also should be proclaimed publicly to all men everywhere. For in it the sum of the whole gospel is contained, as Paul says: "For as often as you eat this bread and drink the cup, you proclaim the Lord's death" [I Cor. 11:26].

For if you ask: What is the gospel? you can give no better answer than these words of the New Testament, namely, that Christ gave his body and poured out his blood for us for the forgiveness of sins. This alone is to be preached to Christians, instilled into their hearts, and at all times faithfully commended to their memories. Thus the godless priests have made words of consecration out of them and concealed them so secretly that they would not reveal them to any Christian, no matter how holy and devout he has been. It was fitting for this priesthood that they should in this way suppress and extinguish the Word and faith throughout the world, in order that by their secret masses they might show what they are doing openly throughout the whole world.

Therefore these words, as a short summary of the whole gospel, are to be taught and instilled into every Christian's heart, so that he may contemplate them continuously and without ceasing, and with them exercise, strengthen, and sustain his faith in Christ, especially when he goes to the sacrament. And this is what the minister is indicating when he elevates the host and the cup. He is not referring to any sacrifice with as much as a single word, which is what would have to happen if it were a sacrifice. Actually, it would make no difference if there were no elevation, for that is something men have invented; Christ did not institute it.

It may well signify, however, that just as this pledge of the promise of Christ is elevated in order that the people may thereby be inspired to faith, so the Word should be preached publicly to the people in order that everyone may hear the testament and see the pledge, and through both be attracted and aroused to faith and strengthened in it.

I am also amazed that these clever people do not consider the fact that Christ instituted and perfected this sacrament in an inn, not in the temple, that it was on a table, not on an altar; while the law of Moses strictly forbade the making of any sacrifice outside of the temple [Lev. 17:8-9]. And the apostles (Acts 4 [2:46]) who everywhere else adhered to the law, broke bread in the houses, not in the temple. So even Christ wished thereby to preclude any possibility of his healing gift becoming a sacrifice.

It is my opinion, however, that the elevation has influenced them to make a sacrifice of it. But what becomes of the wafers which are consecrated for the people and which are not elevated? What difference is there between a priest and a layman in receiving the sacrament, except that the priest consecrates the bread and gives it to the people? If the sick and others attending the sacrament sacrifice nothing, why do the foolish priests make a sacrifice out of it, even though they take from it no more than the laymen do? God has preserved the poor simple people, but to those who have made themselves priests and set themselves above the rest he has given a distorted mind [Rom. 1:28], so that they should lose the common Christian faith.

Let this be sufficient for the present concerning these salutary words. It should be enough for every devout Christian (I would hope) so that without any doubt he will consider the mass to be a sure and trustworthy testament, and not a sacrifice.

Now let us give an answer to their invented fable that the mass is a sacrifice, although their fable should rather be despised than refuted inasmuch as we have received our assurance through the words of God. But we are obliged in all respects to serve those whose consciences are lowly and weak, so that they may everywhere be secure, firm, and immovable in faith, and neither tremble nor waver.

First, they throw up to us the secret mass, which they call the canon.[43] In it there are the words[44]: "these gifts, holy and unspotted sacrifices," and further on: "a holy offering, a pure offering and an unspotted offering, etc." But to bring that up is simply to cry: fathers, fathers, canon law, canon law, church, church—which is

[43] Cf. p. 41 n. 88. and p. 51 n. 102.
[44] For the text quoted see pp. 314 and 320.

their customary procedure whenever they wish to lead us from the Word of God to human words and doctrine. But if in return one shoves the Word of God under their noses, they cry out with their ears plugged tight: You do not understand it correctly; one must believe the interpretation of the fathers. Thus under the name of the fathers they eradicate the Word of God. Therefore we also say and cry out just as steadfastly: gospel, gospel, Christ, Christ.[45] Why should we not rely as much on Christ and his gospel as they rely on the fathers and the canon law and appeal to them?

When now they throw up to us their canon, let us cry out the way they do: You do not understand the canon; it has to be interpreted. Who will render a decision in this quarrel and contention? If they say: The words in the canon are clear and manifest and need no glosses, then we in return also say: The words of the gospel are clear and plain and need no glosses. And whatever they boast and say concerning their human doctrines and laws, we will boast and say so much the more concerning the gospel of Christ, our God, until both sides must cease boasting and crying out. Then we shall also be victorious. For they themselves must confess that all creatures in heaven and earth, and everything which is not gospel, must yield to the gospel; and this they cannot concede or claim of their canon laws and the fathers, namely, that to them everything which is not fathers or canon law must yield. Therefore we have already won. We say that the canon, because it is a human word and work, shall yield to the gospel and give place to the Holy Spirit.

And even if I wanted to support the canon, as I used to do, I will none the less now do honor not to the canon, but to the gospel, and give credence to it beyond any doubt. As the jurists say, I will interpret the canon's obscure words against it and not support it at all. I also wish to say further, as the parable in the Gospel relates [Luke 14:7-9]: Because the canon was invited to the marriage feast and sat down in a place of honor, it shall now get up with shame and give place to Christ, its master, and sit in the lowest place, as it should properly have done in the beginning. And why should I regard the canon so highly? It has been demonstrated above that the mass-priests talk nonsense in more than one place in the mass. It is no wonder, therefore, that the canon often contains nonsense.

[45] A passage which much displeased Emser. Cf. *WA* 8, 409.

Moreover, who can fail to see that it is compiled by a babbler who did not have the Spirit of God? Of what use are so many superfluous words, namely: "the presents, the gifts, the sacrifices, the pure offering, the holy offering, the unspotted offering," etc.? In these things as well as others it is quite vulnerable. Yet the priests have exalted it above all the articles of faith; they regard it higher than the gospel, which too in their eyes is a joke in comparison with the canon. They treat it in their characteristic manner, busying themselves with the inflating of human doctrine and law while despising the divine words, zealously keeping the little things which are of no importance while neglecting that which contains the salvation and blessedness of man. Therefore, at this point I reject and condemn the canon as an enemy of the gospel. And if they should say that the church could not err, we shall not listen; for the mass-priests are not the church.

Second, they throw up to us the holy fathers who used this canon and considered the mass to be a sacrifice, such as Gregory, Bernard, Bonaventura,[46] and others. To this I answer that nothing is more dangerous than the works and lives of the saints which are not founded in the Scriptures. Since it is evident that the righteous man falls seven times [Prov. 24:16] and the saints sin in many ways, who will convince us that this which they have practiced and carried out without the Scriptures is not sin? Here I praise St. Anthony,[47] who faithfully advised and commanded that no one should undertake any work not founded in the Scriptures. Indeed it is safer to regard anything the saints did without warrant of Scripture as a sin, rather than to hold it up as a good example. Neither will you offend any of the saints by considering as sins those works which they did without assurance and foundation in the Scriptures; for they know that they are sinners. But you will offend God and the saints if by their example you fall and break your neck.

Christ too wishes us to cling to his true and certain words and

[46] Bonaventura (1221-1274), scholastic theologian at Paris, general of the Franciscan order.

[47] St. Anthony (*circa* 250-356), the first Christian monk, regarded as the father of Western monasticism. In a collection of legendary lives of the saints, compiled by Jacobus de Voragine (*circa* 1230-1298), he is quoted as saying: "In whatever you do, obey the commandments of Holy Scripture." *The Golden Legend of Jacobus de Voragine, op. cit.*, Part One, 101.

not to the works of men. Thus in Ps. 4 [:3] we are told that God does marvelous things with his saints, and in Ps. 68 [:35]: "He is marvelous in his saints,"[48] often permitting them to fall and err. Moses and Aaron sinned. David and Solomon fell; likewise St. Peter even after the coming of the Holy Spirit when, on account of the Jews, he lived among the Gentiles like a Jew [Gal. 2:12]. And how long does God permit them to live in sin, before he converts them and makes them righteous? Do they not all sing at once: "Before I was afflicted I went astray?" (Ps. 119 [:67]). Likewise: "I said in my transgression, 'all men are liars'" [Ps. 116:11]. David sinned in the midst of his misfortune, when he believed the flatterer Ziba against Mephibosheth [II Sam. 16:3-4]. Lot sinned with his daughters in his time of greatest need [Gen. 19:33-35]. In addition, who is aware of his sins? The saints themselves speak of that in Ps. 19 [:12]: "Who can discern his errors? Cleanse thou me from my hidden faults." Only the minutest portion of a man's sins is ever recognized, even by the saints.

There is a twofold reason, however, why sins do not harm the saints, though the ungodly choke on them. The first is that the saints have faith in Christ. They are completely immersed in it. Through it (although they unknowingly do many things that would damn the ungodly) they always rise up again and are preserved. Indeed, they fall into no evil, as Solomon says [Prov. 24:16]. It is incredible to those who have not experienced it how powerful and mighty faith is, especially in sin. Because the ungodly do not have this faith, they sin, even if they were to do all the good works of all saints.

The second reason is that the saints are so wise through faith that they depend solely upon the mercy of God and regard their works as nothing; indeed, they confess from the bottom of their hearts that they are simply useless works and sins. This confession and humility prevents them from being destroyed in their sins, ignorance, and error; for God cannot abandon such humble persons, much less fail to be merciful to those who recognize their own nature. Such was Bernard, when in the throes of death he said: "I have wasted my time, for I have lived a damnable life." Such

[48] In his German Bible, as here, Luther's rendering of both these Psalm verses follows rather closely the Vulgate version.

was Augustine, when he says: "Woe to all men's lives, however holy they may be, if they should be judged without mercy." [49]

Do we not see in Augustine many errors, which he retracts, which would all have damned him if he had not been preserved by his faith? Most of them are contrary to faith, but his confession and fear of God made them harmless to him. Whoever follows them now does so to his ruin, which is the case with many who follow the sayings of the fathers indiscriminately as if they were divine truth. From this it is clear that the saints err at times, even while they believe. That is, they are not as yet perfect; but by virtue of their faith, already begun and still increasing, they are not lost. Lost rather are those who accept their error as truth and follow it as an example, though it will do no good whatsoever to follow any saint beyond the warrant of the Scriptures.

If the saints did not err in faith and truth, why then did Peter teach growth in faith and knowledge of Christ [II Pet. 3:18], and why did Paul teach growth in Christ, so that we might no longer be like children, tossed to and fro and carried about by every wind of doctrine? [Eph. 4:14]. To the extent that we are lacking in faith, to that extent error and unbelief are in us; which is why even the saints at times live and act according to the necessity and penury of this life.

Although these same works are harmless to the saints, for the ungodly who build upon their works and sacrifices they are nevertheless damaging and destructive examples. For the ungodly wish to learn from the saints only their works and not their faith, although the Epistle to the Hebrews, chapter 13 [:7], commands us to consider the lives of the saints, yet in such a manner as to imitate their faith. But our papists say: Bernard did thus, therefore we should do thus; Augustine did thus, therefore we should do thus. These are the unclean animals, who neither chew the cud nor have cloven hooves [Lev. 11:3-8; Deut. 14:6-8], who perceive only the works and rush upon them with great confidence.

The same thing has happened to them with the sacrifice of the mass, and is doubtless still happening to many devout Christians, namely, that in the simple faith of their hearts they hold mass and deem it to be a sacrifice. But because they do not rely on the

[49] *Confessions,* Book IX, Chap. 13. Migne 32, 778.

sacrifice—indeed, they consider all that they do to be sin, and depend solely on the pure mercy of God—they are preserved, so that they are not destroyed in this error.

Now when the mass-priests follow these people without having their faith, lift high their sacrifice and serenely sell it to others, they deserve to be charged with this error and to be eternally damned for following the saints. For God examines, searches, and judges the hearts and minds [Ps. 7:9], that is, the inner desire. Hence it comes that God remits and forgives an error to one man which he condemns in another, because their hearts are unequal in faith and humility.

That the saints were of such a sort as I have described is shown by the act of Bernard, when he said to his faint-hearted brother: "Brother, go and hold mass on my faith," and when he did so, he was benefited.[50] You see that this holy man performed all his acts in faith, which is what prevents anyone from perishing in his error, no matter how great the error may be. I know, however, that this will displease and vex the papists very much; but that does not concern me as long as I may be able to serve usefully and profitably the poor consciences whom they are torturing so miserably.

Now that we have recognized the error, it is not fitting that we should continue to err by regarding the mass as a sacrifice, for this would be sinning against the whole faith and our own conscience. Here no faith, no confession could excuse us. You cannot say: I will err in a Christian fashion. A Christian error is one that occurs out of ignorance, as in the case of those whom the Apostle in Rom. 14 [:1] commands us to tolerate in their weakness. So it is not fitting that we should despise or condemn those who as yet do not know or recognize their error (since they live by the mercy of God), until they do recognize their error. One should do this however: reveal the error to every man and no longer consider it as truth, so that the sins of the ungodly will not be increased and no offense will be given to those who have weak consciences.

Concerning such error of the saints and their dangerous example Christ speaks in Matt. 24 [:24]: "They will show signs and wonders, so as to lead astray, if possible, even the elect." Here Christ does not mean that his elect will not err, for what great

[50] *Exordium magnum Cisterciense*, dist. II, cap. 6. Migne 185, 419.

danger would that be, if none of the elect should be exposed to danger? This, however, is his meaning, as we pray in the Lord's Prayer: "And lead us not into temptation" [Matt. 6:13]; not that we are not to be tempted, but that when temptation comes, we are to remain steadfast in faith and not let temptation get the upper hand. So it is here too: the elect will not be led into error. Not that they will not err, indeed, the danger will be so great that they will err with the ungodly; but they will neither persist nor remain in error, although they will escape only with great difficulty and effort. That is what Christ means: they will lead the elect, that is the saints, into error if possible; and they [the saints] will err with the ungodly who mislead them, until it seems that they are going to remain in error and be destroyed. We see it in Gregory, Bernard, Bonaventura, Francis, Dominic[51] and their adherents. These greatly honored the pope because they did not recognize him and the nature of his rule, believing all his life and actions to be godly and Christian, ordained by God; although his estate with the entire parliament and all its laws and decrees is manifestly contrary to the gospel. They did not even apply the gospel against the pope and his realm in the case of great and notable errors. Is it not un-Christian to believe that the rock in Matt. 16 [:18] is the pope? Is it not un-Christian to regard the sea [Matt. 14:29] as the human race, over which Peter and the pope are to walk, that is, to rule? Is it not un-Christian that the little word "feed" [John 21:15-17] should signify the honor, power, and might of the pope? And although there are many such errors on the part of the saints, yet they were not aware of them but clung to a simple, unsophisticated Christian faith; which is why God forgave them their errors.

Those who know and recognize error, and nonetheless cling to it as if it were no error, are following the fathers. But they will not reach the place where the fathers are, because they are following what the fathers finally abandoned—and in abandoning attained mercy. They follow it as if it were an article of faith; they persist in it to the very end.

Third, they throw up to us a great many examples of spirits and also of holy men who appeared and pleaded that one should

[51] Cf. p. 77 n. 135.

come to their aid with masses and thereby deliver them.[52] Here I will state freely that whatever spirits go about, making a noise, screaming, complaining, or seeking help, are truly the work of the devil; by which he attempts to take the holy sacrament from us Christians, alienate us from it, and use us for his mischief, scorn, and mockery. For he saw plainly that through this single sacrament the Word of God and faith were fruitfully planted, grew and increased, whereby his accursed realm of darkness was destroyed and laid waste. Therefore he has used all his tricks and wiles to the end that he might obliterate and extinguish this powerful sacrament. He has brought matters to a point where the mass is held mostly for the dead, although it was given and instituted as a consolation only for living Christians. From this the mass-priests have become rich and have annexed for themselves all the properties of the whole world.

For this reason I wish to prove that the spirits who go about saying that they are blessed or damned are not human souls. In the first place, there is no instance of this in the Holy Scriptures, and all that occurs outside the Scriptures, whether it be done by angels or men, is and ought to be suspect. For God wishes his Word alone to be our lamp, which is to shine in this dark world for us, as Peter says [II Pet. 1:19]; and as Ps. 119 [:105] says: "Thy word is a lamp to my feet and a light to my path." And Christ says in John 8 [:12]: "I am the light of the world." Who will follow where the lamp and this light do not shine? He will surely walk in darkness, as Christ says: "He who follows me, will not walk and wander in darkness"; by which he shows beyond any doubt that he who goes where Christ has not gone before, is wandering in darkness.

It may be that St. Gregory was the first to write that the dead have appeared and desired help.[53] Who will make us certain that he and his followers were not deceived? And that it is not safe to believe him is clear from the verses here cited, and especially from

[52] All Christians bound for salvation were obliged first to spend some time in purgatory in order to be purged by fire of their sins. This time of anguish could be shortened, not by the victim himself, but only by those still living on earth, who through their sacrifices could prevail upon God for a quicker release. Cf. Buchwald, *op. cit.*, II, 178.

[53] *Dialogorum*, lib. iv, cap. 40. Migne 77, 396-397.

what Christ says, that the elect are to be led astray and deceived [Matt. 24:24], and from the passage where Paul warns us so faithfully against powerful and mighty errors [II Thess. 2:3-12].

Therefore it is much safer utterly to disregard purgatory, than to believe St. Gregory in this; for in the latter there is great danger, in the former there is none. He may well have been deceived, as Christ says. In addition, he does and says everything without the Scriptures. For God gives no signs without his divine Word. First he speaks, then he gives signs. And as Mark [16:20] says, he confirms his Word by signs following it, not preceding it. And the prophet Amos [3:7] says: "Surely the Lord God does nothing without first revealing it to his servants, the prophets." The Epistle to the Hebrews in the second chapter [Heb. 2:4] says, "God also bore witness by signs and wonders and various miracles and by distribution of the Holy Spirit"; but always he caused his healing, divine Word to precede. For miraculous signs are divine confirmation and evidence of the divine Word, just as the seal of a letter is a confirmation. Therefore you should be certain, on the basis of the Scriptures, that any signs which occur by themselves, apart from the Word, are signs of the devil, with which God permits your faith to be tempted.

Since you are now quite certain that one should believe nothing except that which God demands, why do you not scorn these poltergeists, no matter who speaks of them? Without any sin or danger to your soul you can utterly disregard them. And you must not fear that you will offend God by doing so, for he wishes you to believe and trust in his Word alone. Why would you wish to believe them, and expose yourself to such danger without need or cause? Another good reason to consider them actually spectres of the devil is that they are not worthy of belief. God never produces such things as ought not to be believed; that is characteristic only of frivolous and deceitful spirits. God's works are serious works, which (if they are proclaimed to you by his Word and ministers) you have to believe. God surely would not have caused Christ to be born, suffer, and rise again, unless it had first been proclaimed and written repeatedly by the prophets.

So it is also obvious that Gregory was deceived with respect to the soul of his steward. He had found three gulden among the steward's papers after his death and so had excommunicated him, producing great (though useless) fear and terror among the brothers. He buried the steward as a condemned man, and the gulden with him, then afterwards released him from purgatory by saying thirty masses.[54] Who cannot see that here the devil deceived this holy man with a very childish error? Nevertheless, because of his faith and humility the error did not cause his condemnation. It was the crafty devil who lied and invented the story about the steward, that he had to suffer in purgatory on account of the three gulden and then be released by the saying of thirty masses. The devil's purpose was that those signs and wonders might continue whereby the elect are to be led astray and that the results of the error might have the effect of a punishment upon unbelievers [II Thess. 2:9-12]. Who will believe that the steward acted against God, when perhaps he left the three gulden lying among his papers by chance? For if he had wished to steal he could have stolen much more and hidden it secretly elsewhere. And even if he had done so out of selfishness, he would have transgressed only against human laws. Gregory, a holy man but too superstitious in many respects, found here occasion to frighten consciences and strengthen human doctrine and institutions—in which the devil is only too eager to aid, as Paul says in II Timothy 3,[55] for he knows very well that thereby faith succumbs and works are exalted.

Similarly it is doubtless also the devil's doing in the case of St. Severinus,[56] who after his death said that he had to endure insufferable torture—not because he had sinned against God's commandment or human law, but because, due to the pressure of many affairs, he had recited the seven canonical hours[57] in the morning, all at one time in immediate succession, rather than each one separately at the proper, stated time.[58] It is a shame that the devil should deceive and mislead the church of Christ with such childish foolishness. Yet by it he advances his own enterprise with such earnestness among the saints of God. He has succeeded to such an

[54] *Dialogorum*, lib. iv, cap. 55. Migne 77, 420-421.

[55] Perhaps a reference to II Tim. 2:26.

[56] Apostle of the land of Noricum between the Danube and the Alps, died 482. Buchwald, *op. cit.*, II, 248 n. 1.

[57] Cf. p. 112 n. 203.

[58] *Petri Damiani opusculum XXXIV*, cap. 5. Migne 145, 578.

extent that the papists dare to say: The church cannot err; as if Christ were lying when he says that the elect (who alone are the church) are to be led astray [Matt. 24:24]; or as if the church were not the church because it happened to sin or err, when indeed Christ is daily cleansing it of its sins and errors, like the branches of the vine [John 15:2]; or as if the faithful and holy ones never sinned. O you hard-hearted, foolish, blind men! This mischievous devil had no other intent in this sham-fighting than that the works of love which are commanded by God should be suppressed and scorned, and human commandments and laws be held in high honor, awe, and repute.

Indeed, St. Severinus might not only have been permitted to interrupt his prayers because of his manifold business, but he might even have neglected them altogether; since, by serving the people, he was being obedient to the commandment of God, where Paul commands slaves to obey and serve their earthly masters in singleness of heart [Eph. 6:5; Col. 3:22]. All the angels are supposed to yield to God's commandment; how much more ought human laws to yield! Indeed, I even hold that those who pray the seven hours without sincere desire and joy in God sin much more in his sight than those who neglect to pray them. They are simply hypocrites, who pretend to pray and speak to God, though that is the last thing they are really doing; they are merely tempting God and mocking him. This is what the devil wanted from St. Severinus, that he should cause such countless mockeries and blasphemies of God, and in addition false, frightened, bad consciences throughout the world. And this he has accomplished and achieved. For now they consider no sin so great in their priesthood as when the priests neglect the stated prayers, while in truth there is scarcely any sin greater than this wearisome and spurious worship, which takes place in all churches and monasteries with howling and screaming; so that the sin is of the same character as the priesthood.

O unhappy Christians that we are! We seize upon the legends and examples of the saints, without recognition of the spirit. We rely upon human doctrine and wandering spirits, putting God's Word last and scorning the advice of the Holy Spirit, who says through Paul [I Thess. 5:21]: "Test everything; hold fast what is good." And Peter says [I Pet. 4:11]: "Whoever speaks, let him speak it as the word of God. Whoever has an office, let him render service by the strength which God supplies." He wishes nothing to be said among Christians except that which we hold with certainty to be the Word of God. Nothing is to transpire or be done unless it is certain that God is the author and doer of it. This is what Paul intends in Rom. 12 [:6]—"If any one has the gift of prophecy, let him prophesy in accordance with the faith"—that the words of all men are to be valued and judged according to faith. And in Rom. 15 [:18], he ventures to speak nothing except what Christ has wrought in him. Yet we poor creatures leave God's Word and follow our own opinion. We order, we institute, we bid and forbid, we do and omit whatever pleases us. Then we say: The church has done it, and the church cannot err, for it is ruled by the Holy Spirit. So in the name of the church we fill the whole world with mighty error and downright lies. Would to God that I had the time to cleanse the legends and examples, or that somebody else with a higher spirit would venture to do it; they are full, full of lies and deception.

Because we are Christians, we should really know henceforth the devil's thoughts, and believe that the poltergeists are not the souls of men but simply devils who act and speak as if one could redeem them; that they make a jest and mockery out of the holy sacrament and testament of God, extinguish the faith, and try to establish and buttress that abominable rummage sale of the mass (which has now taken the upper hand everywhere). Try this. Show your faith. And you will see that these spirits will immediately cease from their foolishness and spookery.

If all this fails to move you to believe nothing unless it is founded in the Scriptures, then be moved by the fact that the Scriptures forbid and condemn communication with the spirits of the dead. In Deut. 18 [:9-14] Moses says: "Israel, when you come into the land which the Lord your God gives you, see that you do not learn the abominable practices of the people which is now in it. There shall not be found among you any one who burns his son or his daughter as an offering, any one who practices divination, a soothsayer, or an augur, or a sorcerer, or a charmer, or a medium, or a wizard, or a necromancer. All this is an abomination to the

Lord, and because of these abominable practices your God will annihilate them, etc."

This divine commandment we, like the Jews, have scorned and rejected, when we hear that it is an abomination before God to ask anything of the dead, as if God were not among us, and could not or would not tell us all the things that we should know and have to know, and we are yet dissatisfied with his words. Is it any wonder, therefore, that he deserts us who have deserted his commandment, and lets us fall into error?

See, therefore, that these cannot be good spirits which wish to tell us of the actions and mode of life of the dead. A good spirit is obedient to the commandment of God, who does not wish us to know what happens among the dead. This is why the Holy Spirit himself keeps this commandment of God so strictly that not a single instance of spirits of the dead is found in the entire Scriptures; indeed, they forbid believing these spirits. That Samuel was brought up by a medium or wizard [I Sam. 28:8-14] was surely a spectre of the devil, not only because the Scriptures in that place declare that it was done by a woman who was filled with devils (just as though one ought to believe that the souls of the saints which are in the hand of God [Wisd. of Sol. 3:1] and in Abraham's bosom [Luke 16:22] were in the power of the devil and of evil persons), but also because Saul and the woman when they inquired of the dead were clearly acting contrary to this divine commandment. Against this commandment the Holy Spirit cannot and may not act, nor let his saints act; nor yet help or approve those who do act against it.

The Scriptures do not expressly state whether it was really Samuel or not; they only call him Samuel. This proves that the Scriptures put the matter as it was in the heart of Saul, who did not know but that it was Samuel; and the spirit skilfully spoke all the words of Samuel and added more to them. The Holy Spirit, however, intends that we should be warned and armed by this commandment, which he had previously delivered and described, so that we might know that whatever happens contrary to it does not proceed from a good spirit or from the children of a good spirit. For similarly in II Sam. 1 [:2-16] the Scriptures introduce the servant of Saul who came to David and said that he had slain Saul;

and this he related with such an appearance of truth that David believed him and had him put to death because he had slain God's anointed. The Scriptures do not say here whether he is lying or telling the truth, but they wish us to recognize his lies from the passage in the last chapter of I Sam. [31:4] (where they previously described the death of Saul as it occurred). Whoever does not seek it in this place will surely believe that this servant is telling the truth. So also in this counterfeit reawakening of Samuel the Scriptures refer us to the true commandment of God as written in Deut. 18 [:11].

This commandment is renewed by Isaiah in chapter 8 [:19-20], who says: "And when they say to you: 'Let us consult the mediums and wizards, who chirp in their wizards' way,' then answer: 'Should not a people consult their God? To the dead on behalf of the living? To the law and to the testimony! If they do not speak thus they shall not live to see the morning light.'" Here you see clearly that one should not consult or inquire except from his God, from His law and testimony. Whoever does otherwise will not see the dawn. And it specifically condemns the living who desire to consult and inquire from the dead. It says: "To the dead." That is in the Hebrew style which puts it: "I ask to God, I ask to the dead." In our language that is the same as saying: "I inquire of God, I inquire of the dead." Thus the living asking the dead is the same as the best asking the least; it is like a man taking advice from a piece of wood. Let the people of God inquire of a higher and better source, namely from their God. Not that every person should expect a special answer from heaven, but he should inquire of the Lord his God, in His law, in the Scriptures. And Christ himself confirms this when he tells in Luke 16 [:29] how Abraham spoke with the rich man and would not allow anyone to be sent from the dead to the living for the purpose of teaching them, but referred them to the Scriptures, saying: "They have Moses and the prophets, let them hear them." This agrees very well with Isaiah [8:20], who refers us to the law and the testimony, by which he has demonstrated sufficiently that when the dead appear to the living it is neither from God nor by God's command, and that we should be satisfied with the Scriptures.

Therefore we should with utter confidence hold up before the poltergeists these three witnesses of Scripture: first, Moses, who says: you shall not inquire of the dead [Deut. 18:11]; second, Isaiah [8:19-20]: you shall consult the law and the testimony rather than the dead; third, Abraham and Christ: "They have Moses and the prophets, let them hear them" [Luke 16:29]. And we are not to let ourselves be moved by the great number of vigils,[59] masses or anniversaries,[60] churches and altars, which are all founded and erected upon the words and answers of these poltergeists. For you can see that all of it stands and depends upon the devil's lies and the signs and wonders of false Christs and apostles (which Christ announced beforehand [Matt. 24:24-25]) so that they might fill the world with horrible idolatry which cries to heaven and causes God's last judgment to press closer with great, unbearable wrath.

Since it has been demonstrated sufficiently by all this that through the work of the devil, to the deception of the whole world, and contrary to the gospel, contrary to faith, and contrary to love, the mass has been made into a sacrifice, and that it has now on valid grounds been overthrown, we who desire to be Christians ought to aid in doing away with such masses. We should not merely look on when some pious people use them without sin in Christian error. We should make a real effort to revive the manner and form in which Christ instituted the mass, so that only a single mass is held each Sunday, as is presently done on Easter day. To this mass all those should come who hunger and thirst after this food, that is, all devout, believing Christians, contrite and fearful consciences who desire with all their hearts to become righteous and whole. All who lead a carnal life should be excluded from it. And the death of Christ should be proclaimed publicly through the Word; he should be remembered. And there should be prayer and thanksgiving in the congregation. On the basis of the Acts and Epistles of the apostles, that is obviously how it is to be arranged.

[59] Night services held in the cloisters.

[60] Cf. p. 36 n. 81.

PART III

Concerning the Pope's Priests, Laws, and Sacrifices

It has been sufficiently proven, in what has already been said,[61] that the damnable and horrible priesthood of the papists has come into the world through the devil, and that by this action our Christian priesthood has been destroyed and eradicated, as the pope, the one high priest of this priesthood, promised in the beginning of his decretal,[62] saying that he would take the priesthood of Christ away from him and transfer it to himself. Nevertheless, we will recognize this even better when we see and hear that he has also done away with Christ's laws, and made and ordained new laws fitting and appropriate for his devilish priesthood. Therefore let us see again how the laws were taken away and others put in their place. Perhaps the holy foundations upon which the faith of the Sodoms and Gomorrahs at Louvain and Paris rest will also be brought to light here.

Every kind of priesthood has its own law, according to which it operates; and each one differs in its laws from the laws of any other priesthood, as the apostle so correctly said [Heb. 7:12]: "When there is a change in the priesthood, there is necessarily a change in the law as well." For there can be no priesthood without a law, likewise no law without priests; namely a law by which our consciences may be instructed how to conduct themselves toward God, just as worldly laws govern men in temporal affairs. Every priesthood has also its own sacrifice, works, and priests; they are set forth and described in its law according to which one does good or evil, right or wrong, and so becomes a sinner or a saint. And among the priests there is one who is the chief one. All of this was already true in the priesthoods of Vesta, Jupiter, Bacchus, Apollo, etc.

The same now holds true also under the rule of the pope.

---

[61] Cf. pp. 137-138.

[62] Cf. p. 137 n. 13.

Each diocese has its bishop, as the highest among its priests. Similarly its laws and customs, its punishments and sins, which they call *statuta synodalica*, are different from those of another diocese. The bishops justify this with Ps. 45 [:9]: "The queen has stood at your right hand in a golden dress adorned with many colors." This allegorical coat of many colors, which Peter calls the varied gifts of grace of the Holy Spirit [I Pet. 4:10], these counterfeits take to mean their temporal external differences, which have been invented and devised by men. That is the way in which they are accustomed to deal with the Scriptures. For such a method the verse in Jer. 2 [:28] would be more appropriate: "O Judah, you have as many idols as cities." So it is throughout the entire realm of the pope. The pope is called, and he truly is, the highest and greatest bishop when he stands upon his tower at Babylon, in which he also sits and rules; he is the holiest person upon earth, a true apostle of that master according to whose will he lives and moves, namely the devil in hell.

Now among all these varieties of priesthood not more than two have been instituted by God. One was the outward priesthood in the Old Testament, which is called Levitical, in which Aaron was the high priest. Its laws are the books of Moses. Its sacrifices were irrational animals and physical things. Its sins and righteousness were in external things: holy garments, eating, drinking, days, places, vessels, persons—things which could give neither grace nor life to the soul. The second priesthood is a Christian spiritual priesthood, in which the high priest is Christ alone, blessed, living and eternal; which is why his whole priesthood and everything in it is eternal, holy, and living.

His law is faith, that is, a living spiritual flame, by which hearts are set afire, born anew and converted through the Holy Spirit, so that they desire, will, do, and are exactly what the law of Moses expressly commands and requires. Jer. 32 [31:33] says of it: "I will put my law within their souls and I will write it upon their hearts, etc." And Paul in II Cor. 3 [:3]: "You are a letter from Christ delivered by us, written not with ink but with the Spirit of the living God, not on tablets of stone but on tablets of human hearts." Paul in Rom. 4 [3:27] calls it a law of faith; and in Rom. 8 [:2], the law of the Spirit of life. In II Cor. 4 [:13] he calls the preachers of faith ministers of the Spirit. For the living Word of Christ, when preached, imparts the Spirit, who writes the law of God in our hearts with living fire, as happened to Cornelius in Acts 10 [:44], and again Gal. 4 [3:2]: "Did you receive the Spirit by works or by the preaching of faith?" Hence the gospel is called a word of life in John 6 [:68].

Similarly Christ's sacrifice is a living sacrifice, his body being sacrificed once on the cross and our bodies being sacrificed daily, a living holy sacrifice, which is a rational service of God [Rom. 12:1]. His works and righteousness are the fruits of the Spirit (Gal. 5 [:19-23]): faith, voluntary chastity, goodness, willing service to one's neighbor, etc. His sins are unbelief, impurity, anger, hypocrisy, idolatry, false religion, and the like. All these things are not just works in appearance only, but they are in themselves good or evil from the heart, either living fruits of the Spirit or living sins. Thus the law of Christ [Gal. 6:2] is a matter not of doctrine but of life, not of words but of being, not of labels but of the content itself. The gospel, however, is a word, through which that life, that being, that content come into our hearts and minds.

Into this holy, glorious, happy, gracious priesthood the devil's swine, the pope, has fallen snout and all; not only defiling it, but completely destroying and suppressing it, and setting up another priesthood, one of his own, stirred together out of all the heathen priesthoods like a stew of abominations. First he divides the priestly people of Christ into clergy and laity. The clergy he calls his religious ones. He intends to be high priest and prince among them. He makes them religious simply by tonsuring them, anointing their fingers with oil, and having them wear long garments. He claims that he is imprinting on their souls an indelible character;[63] actually it is the mark of the beast in Revelation [13]. Thus whoever is the pope's priest is not called a Christian (since to the supreme father the name Christian stinks); rather he is called the tonsured, anointed, marked and well-clothed cleric, and is highly esteemed by the pope. This institution they call holy orders or ordination, one of the seven sacraments, much holier and better than baptism itself.

The pope's law is the canon law, in which he orders, defines,

[63] Cf. p. 111 n. 201.

and prohibits strictly—on pain of mortal sin and eternal damnation—regarding food, drink, clothing, persons, churches, altars, chalices, corporals, books, incense, wax, banners, holy water, reading, singing, fasting, prebends, tribute (and who can recite all the devilishness of Roman holiness?). The first thing in his law is the matter of celibacy of the clergy. Why, hell itself is not so wildly confused as is the law of this priesthood.

Sin, according to the pope, consists in transgression of one of the things here enumerated; it is more highly regarded and more heavily punished than all the sins against God's own commandments. His good works are to observe zealously and fulfil the same devil's commandments. Here they praise obedience to the church and call it the queen of all virtues, without which the other virtues are nothing. His sacrifice is the holy sacrament of the body of Christ and the money of the laity. Behold the noble, precious priesthood! I shall remain silent concerning the accursed, godless, and extreme idolatry which is enough to break the heart of a real Christian. Has there ever been such a foolish, childish, and senseless priesthood even among the heathen? Nevertheless this abomination has suspended the salutary honorable priesthood of Christ and removed it, and in its holy place under its name substituted itself. O dear Lord Jesus, only too truly have you called them false Christians, for they truly are false Christians!

Thus he removes and eradicates our Christian priesthood with this damnable priesthood, for hardly anyone knows of any other priesthood except that of the pope. As soon as anyone hears a priest mentioned he imagines one who is tonsured, anointed and dressed in long garments. Similarly he has rooted out the living law of Christ, which is the Spirit of God, given only through the word of the gospel. But because the pope has permitted only his canon law to be preached it is impossible for the Spirit of God to be given through it. And what is more, they pay no attention to the Spirit, consequently do not recognize him; and they fancy that for salvation it is sufficient just to obey the pope and the Roman bulls and the Roman church.

Hence it is impossible for the gospel and the canon law to rule at one and the same time. The latter restricts and drives away the Spirit; the former brings the Spirit with it. The latter entangles consciences; the former frees them. The latter teaches us nothing but mere childish, foolish, and ridiculous works, with which it eradicates and extinguishes faith; the former, however, teaches us faith. How many Christians are there indeed, who, when they hear the law of Christ mentioned, understand by it faith and the Spirit living in our hearts? How many of them are there who understand obedience to be anything other than submission to the pope, which is contrary to God? The priesthood of Christ (alas and alack!) lies prostrate and quite dead, together with its law, and is scorned, blasphemed and condemned by the accursed double-dealing Jews at Rome. Likewise, when one speaks of sacrifice, no one thinks that it is the crucifixion of Christ and of our old Adam, or the praise of God; everyone understands by it the mass and the money of the laity.

Concerning the sacrifice of the mass we have indeed said enough above, but that the money and property of the laity are not a sacrifice of God even swine and donkeys know. For the pope there are no sins any more, other than anger, envy, hate, pride, unchastity, robbery. Especially at Rome nothing else is heeded or punished. Indeed, the greatest and most grievous sins, such as unbelief, self-love, hypocrisy, hatred of righteousness, and doubt, he sanctifies through obedience to the church, and rewards them as good Christian works. Woe is me, I am overwhelmed by the countless number of cursed, shameful, and blasphemous incidents and episodes.

Further, no one remembers that true Christian work is to serve one's neighbor, to counsel and aid even one's enemies and do good to them; instead they think it is to endow masses,[64] build churches, eat neither milk nor meat, and as I have said, keep the pope's laws. So you see that Christ's priesthood has less chance of existing with the pope's pseudo-priesthood than death has with life or heaven with hell. Verily, verily, the pope is a regent of Christ; he has driven out Christ and expelled him and put himself in Christ's place as a ruler, and instead of the priesthood of the Spirit he has set up a childish and grotesque priesthood.

[64] People gave sums of money, the interest from which was to assure the reading of a certain number of masses annually for a departed loved one or for the donor himself after his death, to provide assistance for the soul in purgatory. Buchwald, *op. cit.*, II, 259 n. 1. Cf. p. 191 n. 52.

Yet he is not satisfied that this abomination at Rome has suppressed and obliterated Christ, the gospel, faith and Christ's entire priesthood. He reaches back even further into the Old Testament and the priesthood of Aaron. He eradicates and extinguishes the law of Moses also, and sets up in its place new principles and articles of faith, with the aid and advice of the despicable, shameless whores at Louvain, Paris, and Cologne, together with their dear sisters, who are the source and wellspring of all error and heresy on earth.

In order that every man may be aware of these things, however, let us run through the Ten Commandments and see how the pope deals with them, beginning with the last and least commandment. Moses says: "You shall not covet or desire" [Exod. 20:17, Deut. 5:21]; and Paul repeats it in Rom. 7 [:7]. Hence evil desire and covetousness is a sin, as Moses and the divine law have ordained. Over against this the Sodoms and Gomorrahs of Paris and Louvain with their master, the pope, have set up a new principle and article of faith, which reads thus: Evil desire and covetousness is no sin, but a weakness and a failing; and if the flesh rages against the spirit, that is no sin. Therefore it is quite proper, according to the pope's new ten commandments, to have evil desire and covetousness without sinning.

And Moses and God have lied, as have all who agree with Moses when he said: "You shall not have evil desire and covetousness." If you reject Moses, however, you also reject Christ; because those who have such evil desire are defended and immediately freed by the pope, and have no need of Christ's grace. That, I believe, is freeing Barabbas and crucifying Christ [Matt. 27:26; Mark 15:15].

Second, Moses says: "You shall not bear false witness" [Exod 20:16; Deut. 5:20], and by this he has forbidden all lies. But wnat does the pope set up and ordain over against this? With all his might he tears up all vows, promises, treaties, oaths, and alliances which have been made without papal authority and confirmation, especially when they are damaging or detrimental to the bellies of his clergy, their privileges, incomes and rents, and their harlotry. Thus the pope's will and pleasure are enough to release one from keeping any pledge or promise; for the supreme impeccable authority, the prince of this world [John 14:30], sits in the pope's heart[65] and hatches out nothing but young devils. Thus the commandment of God is obliterated and any man may safely lie and deceive, as long as he has the pope's authority and permission to do so. And the Parisians really help matters by writing and saying that it is not commanded to love your enemies and do good to them [Luke 6:27],[66] and if you have promised or pledged anything to them you dare not keep it, but may safely, freely, and without sin deny it and even bear false witness. For to keep faith is a work of love, and at Paris you do not owe love to your enemies. If Moses required it in his Ten Commandments, then send him to the dean[67] of Paris, who has decided that it is merely advice and that, if Moses will not yield, he will write an angry letter against him and condemn him without citing any reasons, as the apostles are said to have done.[68] For whatever the holy faculty at Paris says amounts to an article and principle of faith.

Third, Moses says: "You shall not steal" [Exod. 20:15; Deut. 5:19], and by this all unrighteous acquisition of property is forbidden. Over against this the pope says in his commandment: You may indeed keep wrongfully acquired property if you give me a share; I will give you a letter and seal for it—such as the bull he gave to the Cardinal of Mainz, which is now proclaimed and published at Halle.[69] Here you see that God himself, to whom all things belong, will not permit anybody to take or keep somebody else's property. Yet the pope brazenly dares to talk back and tell God to his face: Let him keep it—you keep it, only give me and my cardinals a part of it! And to this new principle and article of faith the Parisians again contribute faithfully with their view of brotherly love as mere counsel. Since it is not necessary to love my enemy, I may with a clear conscience steal and keep his property—for to do my enemy no harm and to return his stolen goods to him is a work

[65] An allusion to the *scrinio pectoris*. According to a decree of Boniface VIII (1294-1303), the Roman pontiff has all laws in "the chamber of his heart." *Licet Romanum Pontifex, Decretalium Bonifacii VIII*, lib. i, tit. II: *de constitutionibus*, cap. 1. *Corpus Iuris Canonici, op. cit.*, II, col. 937. Cf. *An Open Letter to the Christian Nobility, PE* 2, 148.

[66] The theologians at Paris denied Luther's contention that to "turn the other cheek" is not mere counsel but earnest command. *WA* 8, 284.

[67] The top administrative officer of the university.

[68] Cf. p. 140 n. 16; also *WA* 8, 271-272.

[69] Cf. p. 133 n. 1.

of love. If love is not commanded, then neither is any work of love commanded. See, these are the Christian principles and articles of the theologians of Paris!

Fourth, Moses says: "You shall not commit adultery" [Exod. 20:14; Deut. 5:18], and by this all unchastity is forbidden. How the most holy father eradicates this commandment also would take too long to tell. But the devil, working through the pope, is nowhere so raging and senseless as in the matter of chastity and unchastity. In the first place, although he does not expressly forbid chastity or teach fornication, nevertheless, with his intolerable and destructive law of celibacy for all his priests (with which the world is filled everywhere) he causes them of necessity to fornicate; because the grace of chastity is a rare and precious gift, granted to few persons. By forbidding marriage to those who neither can nor should be celibate, what else is he doing but saying in effect: Go ahead and fornicate? They do it too, and he lets it go without punishment. O, who can adequately comprehend this fury of the devil with his accursed ungodly law which destroys so many souls? He does not indeed teach unchastity, but with his law he makes matters so much the worse by forcing the priests to do the impossible, and permits their fornication with impunity, whereby he has increased fornication and sodomy and filled the world with these sins. And I hold that if he had commanded fornication he would not have caused so much unchastity or increased it to such a degree.

Besides this he separates married persons under certain conditions which he has invented, others he joins together again, but in such a way that one party has no power to require the conjugal duty. He recognizes too that some are not inwardly driven to do or discharge their required conjugal duty; but they are supposed to allow the other party to go ahead and secure his own satisfaction. This is nothing else than ensnaring the consciences of people in adultery where none exists. Thus, when he joins them in marriage he forces the one party to commit adultery, and as solace teaches him that he should neither demand nor discharge the conjugal duty with his whole heart. What raging madness is this, that one should join a man and a woman together, naked, and command that they just put up with the conjugal relationship, neither requiring it nor giving it! The devil is delighted and pleased to destroy souls with such impossible laws. What else does this law teach, but: Go ahead, commit adultery, but do it unwillingly!

The devil has been unable to find a disguise here, for this sin is too crude and easily recognized to be made a command under any pretense. Therefore he has gone to the other extreme and with his prohibition made it much more common and uninhibited. For he certainly knew that a celibacy so generally commanded could not possibly be maintained in every case. Therefore, since he could not command it because of open scandal, he undertook to bring it about by means of an impossible law. But what do the Parisians do with their "counsel"[70] in this case, they who are enemies to their enemies? Perhaps because it is a mere work of love (which, as Paul says [Rom. 13:10] fulfils the law) not to sleep with an enemy's wife, daughter or maid-servant, one may indeed commit adultery and practice fornication, but only with the wife or daughter of an enemy.

Fifth, Moses says: "You shall not kill" [Exod. 20:13; Deut. 5:17]. Because this commandment more than all the others demands love of neighbor, the pope and his Gomorrahs hold it in special scorn and derision. Although all anger is forbidden in it, the pope nevertheless orders war and bloodshed, even by his bishops and priests, and boasts that the temporal sword is in his hand and power; and to those whom he orders to wage war he promises heaven on the spot. In short, the pope is the murder-bishop, who blithely commands to strangle and murder as often as he wishes. Here he does not just release Barabbas [Matt. 27:26; Mark 15:15]; he bids them to be Barabbas. To those who wrongfully transgress this commandment of God he promises heaven, as to obedient children. But to love your enemies [Luke 6:27], suffer injustice [I Cor. 6:7], turn the other cheek and give your cloak as well as your coat [Matt. 5:39-40] is the greatest evil according to this fountain of righteousness, and by no means to be done. His decretal[71] says: "The laws permit the use of force to repel force." By this he accomplishes the result that men live and remain in pure

[70] Cf. p. 205 n. 66.

[71] *Decretalium Gregorii IX*, lib. v, tit. XII: *de homicidio*, cap. 18; and tit. XXXVIII: *de sententia excommunicationis*, cap. 3. *Corpus Iuris Canonici, op. cit.*, II, cols. 801 and 890.

envy and hate, which is wholly forbidden by God in this commandment; and he eradicates the cross of Christ throughout the world. I shall remain silent concerning the great wars which the popes have waged against Naples, Venice, the French, and the Germans. Indeed, against whom have these senseless monsters not waged war?

Here the Parisians are a bit more subtle than the pope, although they also tear to pieces this commandment of love. They do not say that it is wrong to love your enemies, do good to them, pray for them, thank those who insult you, offer the other cheek and lend or give gratis; but for them these commandments are merely advice: Yet all these things are included by Christ among his commandments in Matt. 5 [:39-44].[72] For there he opens his mouth and teaches them [Matt. 5:2]—he does not merely give advice—and concludes his speech: "Whoever hears these words and does not do them will be like the man who builds upon sand" [Matt. 7:26]. And in the course of the same sermon he says: Those who do not do these things are no better than sinners and tax collectors [Luke 6:33; Matt. 5:46]. O Paris, you shameless blasphemer, how dare you with your shameless mouth scorn and abuse Christ, the Lord of all creation, and call him a liar? Hence, according to the Parisian rule and principle of faith, it is proper to do no less against this commandment than the pope does. Since not to kill and not to curse are mere works of love, we may safely kill and destroy the honor, property, and bodies of our enemies. There is no difference between the pope and the Parisians, except that the pope orders and commands these things while the Parisians write that they are not wrong and may indeed be done. Therefore the principle of the Parisian faith, if you regard the intent of the devil who speaks through them, is that one may indeed act contrary to the last six commandments without sin.

Sixth, Moses says: "Honor your father and your mother" [Exod. 20:12; Deut. 5:16]. Like all the others, nobody keeps this commandment either; they all break it at will. For example, the youth in Christendom nowadays are all too uninhibited and self-willed. They are miserably neglected, for no one takes any interest in them, nor does anyone take any thought or make any effort to see that they are

[72] Cf. Luke 6:27-35.

taught and raised in a truly Christian way. Especially at the universities and in the common trades they let the young people go their own way without discipline and live in unchastity, gluttony, drunkenness and pride. Thus they fall into all the vices of impurity so that there is no more hope of future reformation. The pope and the bishops attend to their courts and seek only their own honor and profit, when they should be taking care of the young people, watching out for them and looking after them as the most important segment in Christendom. But Paul predicted this when he said: "In the last days they shall be disobedient to their parents" [II Tim. 3:1-2].

Thus the pope and his Gomorrahs have their own peculiar way of transgressing the commandments of God. Do not misunderstand me. I am not attacking the undisciplined evil life at Rome or elsewhere in the universities, where none of God's commandments is kept, where, as among the common herd, each one sins for himself and transgresses the commandments of God in his own person. That is not the point of my quarrel with them. Such evil living, which harms them alone, you just have to tolerate and endure as you do the life and deeds of the common people. Since it is a sin against good morals, something which no one can praise but which is shameful and dishonorable to everyone, there is therefore still hope of repentance and improvement here. The thing I am attacking, the point of my quarrel with them, is that they are ravenous wolves instead of shepherds [Matt. 7:15]. With their doctrine and absurd laws they are breaking to bits and tearing apart not only "the least of these commandments"—such men Christ calls the least in the kingdom of heaven [Matt. 5:19]—but the greatest as well, all at the same time. With this they mislead and ruin the people. With this one does not sin merely against good morals, but against the faith. This sin they praise and preach as Christian truth and a principle of faith. Where that is inculcated into the people and accepted by them there is no longer any hope of repentance and improvement. And what is still more, they promise eternal life to those who follow and adhere to this error, and from those who do not follow they demand pain and punishment. This horrible perverted sin is not something committed by the people; indeed, it is something the people have to countenance and put up with on the part of their bishops, universities, and pastors—a sin immeasurably greater than any adultery or murder. Therefore one cannot be silent here, nor should anyone endure it patiently.

For while they write and say that evil desire in the Ninth and Tenth Commandments is no sin, they pretend at the same time to preach and teach both commandments, although in fact they permit evil desire and thus break the commandment of God. In the Eighth Commandment, where they teach lying and deceiving, they make up an excuse and say it is not lying and deceiving, but obedience to the pope and to the church, and thus also to God; and wish it to be considered a truth and held as a principle of faith by everyone, whether it is fulfilled by works or not.

In the Seventh Commandment they give the appearance of teaching that one should not steal, and they boast of God's commandment. But in truth they do teach stealing by permitting the possession and keeping of wrongfully acquired property. In the Sixth they praise and commend nothing so highly as chastity, but only with words, not with their hearts. For with their intolerable and unnecessary laws and invented cases they occasion greater and more shameful unchastity than the flesh with its ardor and evil desire ever could or would commit. In the Fifth Commandment they loudly cry that one should not kill, so that everyone would think that they mean it from their hearts. But by teaching and preaching that one may be angry with one's enemy, wage war, take revenge on him, break treaties, do evil to him, and also that one may not pray for his persecutors, or thank or praise those who revile us, or give or lend gratis, they are in truth preaching and teaching the transgression of this commandment of God. By writing and preaching that to love one's enemy is mere advice, not a commandment of God, they not only transgress completely the whole law of God, but they openly deny it and preach the very opposite. For Paul says: "The fulfilling of the law is love" [Rom. 13:10].

This is why Paul said of them that in hypocrisy they would preach and teach out-and-out lies [I Tim. 4:2]; and in another place: "They will outwardly pretend to lead a godly life, but deny its power" [II Tim. 3:5]. And Christ said: "False prophets and false Christs will come in my name [Matt. 24:24], and ravenous wolves in sheep's clothing" [Matt. 7:15]. They boast of the way they teach the commandments of God and wish this to be considered an article and principle of faith, although they really teach nothing but the transgression of those commandments. This is why I am at odds with them, as every Christian ought to be: for the sake of the teaching, not just on account of their life and conduct. For, as Demodocus in their beloved Aristotle[73] says: "The Milesians are not without sense, but they do the things that senseless people do," so we may also say: The Parisians and papists are not Ebionites, Montanists, Pelagians,[74] Turks,[75] and Antichrists, but they do the things that all these do.

Nor can any heretics be compared to the Parisians and papists, for there have never yet been any heretics who have so completely suppressed, condemned and denied the whole gospel, the whole law of Moses, the whole faith and Christ, as the Parisians and papists are doing, yet under the semblance of the name of Christ. That is why it was declared that the abominations and dregs of all heretics should finally be brought together in one mass under the Antichrist. With their writings and bulls, the holy faculty of theology at Paris and its dear sisters, Odolla and Olibama,[76] have shown that they themselves are the den of these latter abominations and dregs.

Let us therefore see how the pope and his adherents play and have their sport in this Fourth Commandment. With words he says that one should obey one's parents, but in himself he teaches and commands that one should not obey one's parents. He does this by making obedience to the pope and the church incompatible with this Fourth Commandment and raising such obedience to the pope and the church not only above obedience to parents, but also above that due to kings and princes, indeed, over and against obedience to God himself. How securely and unashamedly he teaches and commands this, and what great reward in heaven he promises if someone out of obedience to the church kills his parents,

[73] *Nichomachean Ethics* VII, 8. *Basic Works of Aristotle, op. cit.*, 1049.

[74] Three sects of the early church, long regarded universally as heretical.

[75] With their militant Mohammedanism, the Turks represented both a political and a religious threat to all western Christendom. Luther published *On War Against the Turk* early in 1529 urging resistance to their invasion, which later that year carried all the way to Vienna. Cf. *PE* 5, 77-123.

[76] Contemptuous names for Cologne and Louvain, probably derived from the names of the licentious sisters in Ezek. 23. Cf. p. 136 n. 8.

not to mention disobeying them or dishonoring them! Did he not incite Emperor Henry IV against his natural father to such an extent that Henry, as an obedient child of the Roman church and of the holy vicar of God, shamefully took his father's empire and his life? [77] How often has the most holy father caused subjects to fall away from their own kings and lords and to become unruly, and taught them obedience least of all? Thus this principle of faith is accepted just like the Parisian articles, that he who is disobedient and unruly toward his parents performs the highest service to God, so long as he acts on the authority and command of the Roman debaucher[78] (I meant to say bishop) and out of obedience to him.

He says that the spiritual father is much higher and greater than the natural father. Actually this damnable sodomite ought to be a "spiritual father" in order to teach everyone to obey his parents and thus acknowledge the commandments of God—except, of course, when the parents command anything contrary to the divine commandments. Instead he teaches that children's obedience to their parents must yield to his wanton purposes according to his desire and pleasure.

Those shameless brothels, the universities, hear this horrible destructive abomination and sit in silence. As obedient children of the church they hear, accept, and follow with humility and customary reverence the words of their whoremaster. As often as it pleases him they permit him with his dissembling, mocking ban to set aside obedience to parents, kings, and princes, as well as all divine and human treaties, alliances, and vows. Whereas every single Christian at the risk of his life (even if he had a thousand necks) ought to resist. For we see the poor, common, unsophisticated people, frightened by his childish and shameful bulls, doing and omitting to do everything that only the damnable Roman villain, prompted by the devil, can think up.

Related to this is the fact that he has imposed laws and restraints upon consciences. He forbids secret marriage; yet, after

[77] In *De abroganda missa privata*, the Latin original from which *The Misuse of the Mass* was derived (cf. pp. 129-132), it was stated correctly (*WA* 8, 465): the son of Henry IV was incited against his father by the pope. The error here is due to a mistake in translating from the Latin to the German. Buchwald, *op. cit.*, II, 268 n. 2.

[78] *Bufen*, i.e., *Buben*, probably chosen for alliteration with *Bischoff*.

it has taken place, he confirms it, against the will of the parents. In this way he teaches children to disobey their parents and marry against their wishes. If he just left parental authority and obedience untouched and commanded the children to obey their parents, there would be no need of this foolish, stupid law concerning secret marriages. Indeed, out of respect for the parents there would be no more of them. And there would never have been any, for the children would have been well aware that their parents would not have tolerated their secret betrothal. Yet the pope clothes and adorns this disobedience not only with obedience to the Roman bishop, as we have said, but also by making of marriage a sacrament, free, yet caught and entangled in countless strings. Thus the pope teaches the commandment of God outwardly with words; but in himself, through his laws, he teaches that one should trample upon it.

Hence parents should know that they have the right and the authority to break the secret betrothals of their children. And the children should know that they are obliged to render obedience in this, and in all things that are not against God; and that their secret betrothals are invalid, unless they afterwards obtain the consent of their parents with humble pleas and entreaties. The pope, the most terrible enemy of God and his laws, they should put behind the door. Tell me one thing: Why did not the children of Israel too betroth themselves in secret? Where does this chapter of the canon law[79] come from, except from the devil?

The same should be true of children who become monks or nuns. Parents should have the power to demand their release from the monasteries if they need them, or if they entered the monasteries against the wishes of the parents, regardless of the hypocritical claim that they have now publicly taken vows, or that they have been consecrated, anointed, tonsured or ordained to the priesthood. What has been done through disobedience to the parents is invalid before God, just as it is invalid if one married person becomes a monk or a nun without the consent of the other.

And just as it is not valid in this case when a person says:

---

[79] The decretals had a specific chapter on secret bethothal. *Decretalium Gregorii IX*, lib. iv, tit. III: *de clandestina desponsatione. Corpus Iuris Canonici, op. cit.*, II, cols. 679-680.

I have entered a holy order for the purpose of serving God, so are the lies of the pope also invalid when he defends the disobedience of children against God's commandment in the matter of religious orders by saying: The service of God is more important than obedience to parents. Religion in a monastic order is not a true service to God, but a spurious substitute for it. True service to God is obedience to God's commandments; otherwise all men would have to become monks, since all men have the same commandment to serve God. For there is no difference among men in the true service of God, but only in the hypocritical service of God invented by men. The hypocritical service must yield to God's command, that is, to the true, genuine service to God, as the crude donkey-heads at Louvain and Paris must themselves admit.

So much for the second table of Moses. Now let us speak of the first, that is, of the first three commandments. I do not know whether to speak or remain silent, so impossible is it for me to express in words the abomination of the papists in these three commandments. Up until now everything has still been a joking matter, in that they have taught and acted only against God's law. In these three commandments, however, they do not merely condemn the law. They also teach and do everything possible or imaginable (except in outward appearance) against God's grace, faith, and the gospel. What more could they do? They not only teach the opposite of God's commandments; they also condemn, burn, curse, revile, and persecute them as being the worst heresy and most terrible blasphemy. And yet they do it all in the name of Christ, to the honor of God, and out of fervent love of faith and of service to God!

Let us begin with the foremost principle of their faith, which reads thus: A man is able to keep and fulfil God's commandments through his own natural powers, if he does as much as in him lies. From this it follows, in the first place, that for our own sakes we have no need of God's grace, because we can do these works by our own strength, as they unashamedly write with express words in their books; but we need it for God's sake because he will not be satisfied that the works of the commandments are merely done, but wants them done in grace. Hence, it follows further that God has been most unjust in closing heaven and opening hell to men, not on account of sin or broken commandments, but on account of God's own arbitrary demands.

Now this is the first honor which the Parisians and all the papists ascribe to God: that God is unjust, and condemns man unjustly without any guilt on his part, and out of criminal malice closes heaven to him. And that they believe this with all their hearts is shown by their own teachings just enumerated, no matter how holy and Christian they pretend to be. How can you with all your heart be kindly disposed toward someone who, without any reason except his own malice, demands superfluous, unnecessary, and impossible things from you, such as they say and preach about God? Thus we must also be baptized, not because it is necessary to overcome sin, since we can overcome sin and fulfil God's commandments by our own natural powers, but because God's malicious desire to manipulate men needlessly demands it.

So we must believe that Christ was crucified on account of such malicious desire, not because we needed it. In short, if you consider us and our natural powers, all that Christ is and all that has been given to us in him has occurred unnecessarily, in vain, and to no purpose; but if you consider God's demand, then it was necessary.

Can you men of Paris deny that you write and preach such things? Are not your books at hand, especially the most recent condemnation,[80] in which you have written stating this precious principle? How can you deny either that all these things follow therefrom? You clearly state that Christ is unnecessary on our account. Therefore you obviously do not consider him to be a "Jesus," that is, a redeemer of men. You consider him rather to be a satisfier of the superfluous demands of the unjust God. Neither has he redeemed us from our sins (since we have none if our free will does all that in it lies); but over and above sins and commandments he has redeemed us from the superfluous demands which burden men so heavily. See, this is the gang of the holy faculty of Paris on the one hand!

On the other hand they have for their faith such a principle as this: Man (if he does as much as in him lies) is certainly able to

[80] Cf. p. 140 n. 16.

merit[81] the grace of God, not that he deserves it, but because it is appropriate. Is this not what you teach us, you holy faculties? By it you teach us that in and of ourselves we can satisfy even the unjust superfluous demands of God; that poor Christ has only the shameful honor of being called, not Jesus or a redeemer of men, but a satisfier of the unjust, superfluous demands of God. For we can now achieve the grace of God ourselves without a mediator, and thus Christ is doubly superfluous and unnecessary, even as far as God is concerned.

I fear no one will believe that such horrible, un-Christian doctrine is being taught and preached in the universities. But I call to witness their books, which are available, and their own consciences, and those who have read their books; they will disclose an abomination that passes all human understanding. As you see, they deny Christ twofold because they exalt so highly our natural powers. What good does it do them, if they confess Christ with their mouths, when they consider him to be doubly unnecessary to us?

Thus you can see that Peter was prophesying of none other than these poisonous papist dregs in I Pet. 2 [II Pet. 2:1-2]: "There will be false teachers among you who will secretly bring in destructive heresies, even denying the Master who bought them, and because of them the way of truth will be reviled." What are these destructive heresies other than the art and doctrine of the universities, which they wish to be considered articles of faith? What are the lying teachers other than the professors of Holy Scripture, the swine, yes, the thorns and thistles in the vineyard of God? Now whoever denies Christ, denies God. For to say that the divine decision and pleasure, by which God sent Christ and made him a Savior, are unnecessary and superfluous is the same as to say that God himself is unnecessary and superfluous. It is the same as saying: There is no God. Now see what has become of the

---

[81] The merit of congruence (*meritum de congruo*), though not strictly meritorious, was fittingly rewarded by God with a "grace freely given" because it was congruous to, or in conformity with, man's best inner nature. Scholastics distinguished this "first grace" from the merit of condignity (*meritum de condigno*) which man attained through cooperation with the aforesaid grace, and which was strictly meritorious in that it secured eternal life and blessedness from God as its just and due reward. Cf. *LW* 21, 288-289.

first three commandments: You shall worship one God, hallow his name, keep the sabbath. The universities say and teach: You shall say that God is to be worshiped, but you shall be your own god! You shall say that one should hallow his name, but exalt your own name! You shall say that one should rest and keep still before God, but accomplish everything by yourself and do not let God work in you!

I cannot explain and expound the commandments here, but this is the conclusion: Because man is conceived and born in sin and is a child of wrath he can do nothing but sin and daily fall deeper and deeper into the wrath of God, until he finally hears and believes that Christ is his Savior and has died for him to redeem him from his sins. Through this hearing, the Spirit of God comes into his heart and he is permeated with God's grace and love, so that he loves God, praises and hallows his name, rests and keeps still and lets God accomplish His own work in him. Thus, no one can fulfil these three commandments without Christ. And yet they consider Christ unnecessary and superfluous, because they say that natural reason, without Christ's help, is able to avoid sin. They raise up and erect in Christ's stead the free will of man, and in God's stead an idol of their own hearts, a destructive heresy. Thus they deny Christ and the whole New Testament and do away with the first three commandments.

Would to God that a rude swine of Paris would come forth and bite open the nut and expose the reason for their condemnation, so that I might more clearly bring to light their misleading, devilish art and show to all men what an un-Christian, accursed abomination is hidden in the universities under the Christian name and title of the doctors of the Holy Scriptures!

At present I cannot proceed further for lack of space in this book and lack of time. Otherwise I would discuss the dispensation of vows, in which the pope goes to such excesses. But I will do this when I write on monastic vows,[82] so that I may deliver the miserable youth from impure celibacy and vows. Now let us compare the Ten Commandments of God and those of the pope so that we may see how in the name of God's law he has done nothing but change and pervert the law, just as in the name of

[82] Cf. p. 81 n. 146.

Christ's priesthood he also displaced and perverted the priesthood. Let us see how he has set up his own law for God's law and his own priesthood for Christ's priesthood, and thus has set abomination in the holy place [Matt. 24:15].

The Ten Commandments

Of God	*of the Pope*
You shall have no other gods.	Say, one shall have no other gods, but have them.
You shall not take the name of God in vain.	Say, one shall not take the name of God in vain, but do so.
You shall keep the sabbath.	Say, one shall keep the sabbath, but do not keep it.
You shall honor your father and mother.	Say, one shall honor his father and mother, but do not; be disobedient to them; kill them.
You shall not kill.	Say, one shall not kill, but do so.
You shall not be unchaste.	Say, one shall not be unchaste, but compel people to be so.
You shall not steal.	Say, one shall not steal, but steal nevertheless.
You shall not bear false witness.	Say, one shall not lie, but lie nevertheless.
You shall not covet your neighbor's wife.	Say, one shall not covet her, but say that it is no sin.
You shall not covet your neighbor's possessions.	Say, one shall not covet anything, but know that it is no sin.

The Priesthood

of Christ	*of the Pope*
Christ is the high priest.	The pope is the high priest.
His law is grace and life.	His law is the canon law.
The sacrifice is a living body.	The sacrifice is the sacrament of the altar and money.

of Christ	*of the Pope*
Good works are to serve one's neighbor.	Good works are to pretend outward piety with singing, fasting, and prayer.
Sin is to omit this.	Sin is to omit this.
The punishment is eternal death.	The punishment is the invented ban.
The reward is eternal life.	The reward is peace and property in this world.
His servants are the preachers of God's Word.	His servants are the proclaimers of bulls.
The consequence is the bearing of the cross with joy.	The consequence is bad consciences.

From this you see that I have made no unjust statements concerning the papist priesthood and its laws. If this is not sufficient I will convince them with their own books that they are the sodomites and scoundrels that I have accused them of being. Therefore you shall also know that the pope is the true, genuine, final Antichrist, of whom the entire Scriptures speak, whom the Lord Jesus has now begun to slay with the breath of his mouth, and whom he will soon destroy and kill with the brightness of his coming [II Thess. 2:8], which we expect.

Let us now ramble through an allegorical interpretation, and compare the synagogue and the church. In the synagogue there was the true, genuine priesthood of Aaron, instituted by God [Exod. 28:1]. Afterwards there was the Beth-aven[88] priesthood of the golden calves, which King Jeroboam erected [I Kings 12:28]; in addition, the priests on the high places [I Kings 12:31]; and the notorious priesthood of Baal, established by King Ahab [I Kings 16:31-32]; and finally the blasphemous priesthood of the idol Molech [II Kings 23:10]. Among all these none is so lightly punished as the priesthood of the high places, and none so speedily and thoroughly as those of Baal and Molech. There were also many other kinds of idolatry, such as Baal-Peor [Num. 25:3-5]; Astarte, the goddess of the Sidonians [I Kings 11:5]; and the idols of the Ammonites and

[88] Cf. p. 88 n. 153.

Moabites [I Kings 11:5-7]. But they were not so common or long-enduring.

So now we say that all true Christian believers are genuine priests in the Christian congregation, as the Levitical priests were in the synagogue. The bishops and their canons are priests of Beth-aven. The older monks and hermits are priests of the high places. But the new monks and mendicant orders are Baalites. Molech refers to the universities, which the Book of Maccabees calls youthful games and Greek glories [II Macc. 4:12, 15].

And just as in those days their great number filled the land, so that even in Elijah's time, among such a vast and countless people, no more than seven thousand were found who were not adherents of the idol Baal [I Kings 19:18], so now too the multitude of godless people has filled and occupied the whole world, so there are no more true priests found now than there were true prophets then. They found safety in numbers, however, and said: God's people does not err; just as one says now: The church does not err. Jeremiah writes of them in the seventeenth chapter: "The law shall not perish from the priest, nor counsel from the wise, nor the Word of God from the prophet" [Jer. 18:18]. And just as some true Levitical priests, prophets, and wise men erred with the rest and were misled, so Christ also foretold [Matt. 24:24; Mark 13:22] that in his church some devout Christians would be misled by this multitude of the ungodly.

Let us therefore consider further their names, nature and character: first, the priests of the high places. They based their priesthood on the example of the holy patriarchs who served God and worshiped him in the high places, as the Samaritan woman says to Christ in John 4 [:20]: "Our fathers worshiped God on this Mount Gerizim, etc." And Amos [5:5] punishes Gilgal, because they were circumcised on the mountain of Gilgal [Josh. 5:8-9]. And others had other places, just as now churches and chapels are built and erected in honor of the saints who are said to have lived there, as at St. Wolfgang, St. Gall, St. Meinrad,[84] and many others.

[84] Wolfgang, bishop of Ratisbon (972-994). Gall (*circa* 550-646), an Irishman who became a hermit at Arbon on the Lake of Constance after 612, whose name is perpetuated there both in the famous Benedictine abbey and in the Swiss canton. Meinrad (d. 861), a hermit whose chapel is regarded as the beginning of the Benedictine abbey of Einsiedeln near Lake Zürich in Switzerland.

This would not be such an evil work if it did not, through misuse, furnish a bad example for superstition and arouse a confidence in works over against faith (which sanctifies alike all cities and all persons everywhere). Hence come the first monks and hermits, who have followed the holy fathers in outward works but have forgotten the faith, and who build only upon outward life and conduct. They sacrifice themselves to God and believe that they are serving God more perfectly than other Christians; whereas, since they live without faith, they are much worse. But those who follow the faith of the fathers can be tolerated, such as the disciples of SS. Benedict,[85] Augustine, and Anthony were in the beginning. Thus too, in former times, the ceremonies conducted in some of the high places did not displease God, such as the great altar of Gibeon in I Kings 3 [:4], upon which Solomon sacrificed, and the high place where Samuel lived and anointed Saul [I Sam. 9:25, 10:1]; because they lived in faith and did all things in faith, and did not merely follow the works of the fathers, as the later monks did and still do. They are downright hypocrites when it comes to God's commandments; for such ceremonies are intended to achieve righteousness in the divine law by means of their own works and without faith.

The priesthood of Bethel, however, cannot be used at all for comparison, for it was completely opposed to the true Levitical priesthood. So the papist priests also, who have issued from human law, are completely contrary not only to faith and the Christian priesthood but also to God's law and its Levitical priesthood—even though they bear the name and title that they alone are the church and the people of God, for their place is called Bethel, that is, a house of God [Gen. 28:19]. And Hosea [4:15; 10:5] was so bold as to change the name and call it Beth-aven, that is, a house of evil or of toil (that is, the righteousness of the ungodly, which tortures consciences). And Hosea had to die on that account; just as now, if some one should change the name of the papists (who claim to be the church of God) and say: They are the synagogue of Satan [Rev. 2:9; 3:9], which they truly are, he would have to be

[85] Benedict of Nursia, died *circa* 543 at Monte Cassino, founder of the Benedictine order.

called a heretic and be burned, for like Hosea he would have blasphemed the church of Bethel.

For this the name Jeroboam is most fitting. In our language it means a superior, a lord, a professor and teacher of the people, one who has the power to teach the people. For the pope says: "Where the authority is, there is the right and power to command." He sets himself above all men and makes of himself a teacher and master, that is, a Jeroboam, of the whole world. The golden calves are his invented doctrines, the holy canon law, in which he promises as much truth of Christian doctrine as did Jeroboam, who also pretended that the true God was honored in the golden calves. It is evident that in the Scriptures idols are to be understood as human doctrines, as the golden calf of Aaron also indicates. For Moses writes that it was fashioned with a graving tool [Exod. 32:4]; that is to say, out of the writings of the bishops and priests come godless doctrines. But the fact that he made two golden calves and set one in Dan to the North and the other in Bethel to the South [I Kings 12:29] signifies that the pope assumes dominion over both the heavenly and the earthly realms, as he writes of himself. He not only presumes to rule consciences in God's stead, but also to judge all kingdoms and decide all things and thereby live according to his own pleasure, resplendent in the North over temporal things and in the South over spiritual things.

Dan means judge; and that is what the canon law is wherever it vaunts itself and claims that all the judges in the world are to obtain their verdicts from the judgment seat of Rome. He is Bethel, however, wherever he sits in God's temple and is exalted above and contrary to God [II Thess. 2:4]. The temple of God consists of the consciences in which he has set his idol and over which he rules authoritatively. Therefore the worshipers of the calves at Beth-aven are none other than the tonsured and anointed priests in long garments, who serve God day and night [Rev. 7:15] according to the canon law of the most holy one. The most holy one is Jeroboam, of whom the Scriptures so often say that he caused the people of Israel to sin; for he blotted out faith and he exalted works, and this is the greatest of sins.

But the priesthood of Baal, that devout (really godless) people, which as Elijah says to Ahab has sold itself to do what is evil

[I Kings 21:20], is the clergy. They imagine that with their three vows[86] they make themselves the bride of God and have a status next to that of God himself; for "Ahab" means father's brother. They also wish to be called nothing else than worthy fathers and brothers, that is in Hebrew: Ahabites. His wife, Isabella or Jezebel, means cohabitation, just as if the Spirit were saying "monastics," that is, the fathers and brothers living together in one house. Baal is the name of an idol and means husband; and their teaching is precisely this, that they bind themselves eternally to God, as a husband binds himself to his wife, with their vows of obedience, which God, after all, has never commanded. In this respect they differ very much from the first monks and hermits, who followed the examples of the fathers voluntarily, without any vows whatever. But these people go beyond the faith and contrary to the faith in marrying themselves eternally to God. And these ceremonies took place in Samaria, which is to say that their rule is bound up with externals: places, clothing, eating and drinking, as we now see it openly in the orders. Samaria means an observance, strict conformity, etc. These priests also cut themselves with swords and lances [I Kings 18:28]; the same is done now when they daily torment themselves with new statutes, and are always learning but never arriving at a knowledge of the truth [II Tim. 3:7].

Ahab believed that with these things he was serving and pleasing the true, genuine God, as is to be inferred from the prophet Hosea [2:16], when God promises: "She will no longer call me Baalim, but Baali"; that is, she will no longer call me "men," but "my husband," meaning that she will honor and worship me with one faith, not with various kinds of works. This these monks also do. They do not see that with their vows they are serving themselves and not God, because we can serve God only with faith, and not with works chosen by ourselves. What he has not commanded and is chosen by us, is already condemned in Deut. 12 [:8]: "You shall not do whatever is right in your own eyes." What we are supposed to do is commanded so abundantly that our self-chosen works are not necessary at all; indeed, they are always contrary to the divine commandments because of the impression they make, just as Baal is contrary to the true God.

[86] Cf. p. 76 n. 134.

The last idol is Molech. This is derived from Malach, meaning "he has ruled, or reigned"; the bishop's slave, whose ear Peter cut off [John 18:10], was called Malchus, a royal slave. This worship is described by Moses [Lev. 20:2-5] and Jeremiah [7:31], who tell how people burned their children, believing that they were doing a great service to God. They did not spare their children, as Abraham did, but engaged in such godless proceedings unbidden and without faith. Therefore Ps. 77 [106:37] says: "They sacrificed their children to the devil, not to God." For everything that we do which is not commanded by God is not done for him, but for the devil; no matter how holy it may seem, it is the devil who inspires it. This represents the universities, in which the largest and best part of our youth is sacrificed like a burnt offering, in order that they should there become learned and very holy. Everyone believes that there is no place under heaven where the youth may be better instructed; even the monks go there. Whoever has not been to the university knows nothing, but he who has been there and studied knows everything. It is held that all divine and human arts are taught in the universities. Everyone believes therefore that he could not send his son to a better place, and that he is doing a great service to God by sacrificing his children there, so that they may be trained and made into preachers, priests, and servants of God who are useful to God and man.

Here belongs Molech, that is, a king. For these people make great lords, doctors, and masters who are skilled in ruling others. We can see before our very eyes how no one can become a preacher or a pastor unless he is a master or doctor, or has at least attended the university. One must first crown the donkey; then he goes forth and rules. And the parents do not see, or if they see they pay no attention to the fact, that nowhere is youth more grossly corrupted and misled, since no one prevents it. That they fall into fornication, gluttony, and other open wickedness is the least of their corruption; but that they are instructed in false, heathenish art and ungodly, human doctrine is the fire of Molech. No one can bemoan that enough, for through it the most devout and clever lads are miserably ruined in the universities. So great is the wrath of God over this valley of Topheth and Hinnom [II Kings 23:10; Jer. 7:31] that those who learn most and best and live in chastity are ruined more miserably than those who learn nothing and live in fornication. For the latter learn nothing which ought to be unlearned again; they are well aware that they are doing wrong. The former, however, absorb poisons of which they can never rid themselves; they hold evil to be good and teach this also to their pupils. All this is what accounts for the fact that the sun of the gospel is darkened and obscured by human teaching.

From this den of murderers proceed the locusts of Rev. 9 [:3-5] who rule the whole world everywhere, both spiritually and temporally. Since the beginning of the world even the devil himself could not have invented anything more powerful to suppress faith and the gospel than the universities. Such evil was bound to arise now at the end of the world; for the world, weighed down with God's wrath on account of its sins, which have taken the upper hand, has inclined itself toward hell and its damnation. The poor people are allowed to hear nothing but what its Molechites have learned in the universities, namely blasphemy, as has been shown earlier in the pope's ten commandments.[87] They do not dare to accept any other kind of preacher or pastor.

Jeremiah [7:31] calls this valley Gehinnam, and from this Christ has taken the name Gehenna.[88] What the name means I do not know. "Ge" means a valley; "Hinnam" may mean various things. Since I do not know how to interpret it I will omit it. I think, however, it may come from the word Jhana, which means to devour and flay, as the mighty lords and usurers devour the people, flay them, and suck them dry. So Gehinnam means a valley of flayers, who, when they should be feeding the people with the living Word of God as shepherds and preachers, instead devour, destroy, and flay the poor people in body, soul, and property with their poisonous, ungodly doctrine. Such are the shepherds which the universities, the synagogues of destruction, give to us.

Hence you see that in this interpretation the church corresponds completely to the synagogue. How few there are who are preserved from this error and destruction. Not only do the best fall into it, but even the chosen ones will be misled by it. Oh miserable people

---

[87] Cf. pp. 218-219.

[88] Matt. 5:22 in the Greek New Testament, derived from the Hebrew *ge ben-hinnom.*

that we are, to live in these last times so securely and unperturbed among all these Baalites, Bethelites and Molechites, all of whom appear to be religious and Christian but who have nevertheless swallowed up the whole world and claim that they alone are the Christian church! Wretched people that we are, we laugh when we should be weeping tears of blood because the children of our people are being murdered so cruelly!

Finally, if all this fails to move anyone, I humbly beg all priests from the bottom of my heart and for the sake of their salvation not to hold mass grudgingly, either out of a sense of duty to its endowment[89] or otherwise for the sake of money. Would to God that I might achieve that much! Let each one, therefore, examine himself and see if he feels so disposed as not to hold mass unless motivated by a sense of duty, or out of obligation to the endowment, or for the presence fee,[90] or for any other reason except true faith; let him not hold mass on any account for the rest of his life, regardless of human ordinances or endowments! It is much better to scorn human endowments and ordinances—there is no sin in that—than to commit sacrilege in this salutary sacrament of the divine majesty. The world is burdened with no greater sin, even if it were not used as a sacrifice, than with the unworthy celebration of the mass by priests and the unworthy reception of the sacrament by the laity, which is all too common throughout the world.

It is the desire of a true faith, however, that one should go to the sacrament because he desires it from his heart and is seeking grace, mercy, and the forgiveness of his sins—because he hungers and thirsts after righteousness. For this precious royal feast benefits, satisfies, and fills a hungry and empty soul. The rich, however, and those who have eaten their fill, who go to it for the sake of profit, honor, or the favor of men, it does not satisfy. It leaves them empty [Luke 1:53] and delivers them with Judas to the devil unto eternal death.

Not that I would wish to confirm the mass by this advice; but, because the custom has taken hold and human doctrines and ordinances have gained such a firm upper hand that it is hardly

---

[89] Cf. p. 203 n. 64.

[90] Associate clergy in some cases received a sum of money for being present. Buchwald, *op. cit.*, II, 284 n. 2.

possible to make any general Christian change in this holy testament, let us at least do this much: Walk in a pure faith and sin less, so that perhaps we may at last be saved with the erring elect [Matt. 24:24]. I see a great many going to the sacrament with spiteful, shocking, impenitent, and contemptuous consciences, who desire only that the mass be held and they will pay what they owe, or that they may receive their presence fees and not be discredited. O what horrible, frightful presumptuousness!

And now, to return to you, my friends at Wittenberg, would to God that this pharisaical scandal might grow and increase among you, and that the papist crowd would say: See, at Wittenberg there is no longer any divine service; they no longer hold mass or play the organ, and they have all become heretics and madmen! Would to God that I might hear the raging Rabshakehs and blasphemers screaming and howling: "Is that not Hezekiah who has removed the high places and altars of God, saying to Judah and to Jerusalem, 'you shall worship before this altar'?" [II Kings 18:22]. Or again, would to God that you were the ones who with Isaiah [36:11] ridiculed their lord Sennacherib, whether he spoke Syrian or Jewish. That masses stop, and the bawling and bellowing in the churches cease will amaze the papists. But that love (which serves its neighbor) [Rom. 13:9-10] and the living sacrifice of our bodies [Rom. 12:1] are blotted out by unchastity, hate, anger, fornication, etc., that they just laugh off, as is fitting and proper for the papist faith and wisdom.

You also have a Beth-aven among you, namely All Saints' Church, which Duke Frederick[91] inherited from his ancestors and, deceived by the papists, has admirably enlarged and improved. How many poor people in Saxony could have been supported by it! He could have made them all his friends by means of the unrighteous mammon, so that if it became necessary they might have received him into the eternal habitations! [Luke 16:9]. On the basis of this example, it is to be feared that the money and property of

[91] Frederick the Wise, Elector of Saxony (1486-1525), had assembled in his church at Wittenberg the choicest collection of relics in all Germany, numbering at the time almost 20,000. Viewers of the collection received indulgences. While officially neutral toward the new faith until shortly before his death, Frederick was firm in his defense of Luther's person and of his rights to freedom and justice.

princes is seldom worthy of being put to Christian uses, just as it is rarely acquired otherwise than in the manner in which Nimrod gained his property and money [Gen. 10:8-9]. But there is by the grace of God one thing that you may well boast of: the prince is no tyrant or fool. He gladly hears the truth and is able to endure it, and he judges no one capriciously. He is no less to be feared by the evil than to be loved by the good. Because in him you are so favored and blessed, you are the more able to complete the work already begun, as those whom God by this occasion has called to it, and to whom he extends his hands.

As a child I often heard in the provinces a prophecy to the effect that Emperor Frederick would deliver the Holy Sepulchre. And as it is in the nature of prophecies that they are fulfilled before they are understood, so they always point to some place other than what the words themselves might indicate before the world. Hence it also seems to me that this prophecy is fulfilled in our prince, Duke Frederick of Saxony. For what other Holy Sepulchre[92] can we understand than the Holy Scriptures, in which the truth of Christ, put to death by the papists, has lain buried; and which the murderous, that is, the mendicant orders,[93] and arch heretics have guarded and protected so that no disciple of Christ might come and steal it away [Matt. 27:64]. For God is as little concerned with the grave in which our Lord lay, which the Saracens possess, as with all the cows[94] in Switzerland.

[92] This identification of Holy Sepulchre with Holy Scripture is found also in the section on *Martinus Luther* in the anonymous contemporary satirical poem *Triumphus Veritatis:*

Ich mein das grab die heilig schrift,
Die unser selen heil an trifft,
Das alt und auch neu testament,
Das billich würt ein grab genent:
Dan warlich drin vergraben ist,
Das götlich wort das got selbs ist,
Welchs in der heilgen junkfrau rein
Ist worden war fleisch, blut und bein.
Ich mein den herren Jesum Christ,
Der einig unser fürsprech ist.

Oskar Schade, *Satiren und Pasquille aus der Reformationszeit* (Hannover, 1863), II, 206-207.

[93] German: *bottel, das ist, die bettel orden. Bottel,* a word chosen for alliteration with *bettel,* designated that functionary of the court who executed the sentence of death by hanging.

[94] In the Latin version (*WA* 8, 476) Luther refers to the oxen mentioned by Paul in I Cor. 9:9, for which God is not concerned.

No one can deny that under Duke Frederick, the Elector of Saxony, the living truth of the gospel has flourished among you. What if I should boast that I had been an angel or Magdalene at the grave? Although he is not an emperor now, it is sufficient for the fulfilment of the prophecy that he was unanimously elected emperor by the electors at Frankfurt,[95] and was truly an emperor if he had wanted to be. Before God it does not matter how long one is an emperor if only he has been one. And although some may think that I am playing a conjurer's trick, I will play on and wonder how it happens that God has willed the awakening of his Word in this forgotten corner of the world. It is a wonder which, as far as I know, no land has experienced, that the towns and villages about Wittenberg, even the citizens, have Hebrew names, like the cities and hamlets about Jerusalem. What is the origin of Ephrata, Hebron, Ressen, Panneck, Globog, Sidon, Jesse, Damascus, Dibon and many others like them? And Wittenberg itself, that is, White Mountain, what else is it but Mount Lebanon? Lebanon means white. Enough of this jest!

It is a serious matter, however, that to us of all people it has been given to see the pure and original face of the gospel. Since you have now become zealots of the Spirit you must spread it out and let others see it. But see to it that you walk in harmony with one another and offer your hand to one another without strife and dispute. If anyone among you is weak in faith, let him eat vegetables and not judge him who eats meat; on the other hand, let him who is strong in faith not despise him who abstains from meat [Rom. 14:1-3].

However, if your neighbor, friend, or enemy becomes irked that

---

[95] On June 28, 1519, at Frankfurt-am-Main, Charles of Spain was elected emperor to succeed his grandfather, Maximilian (d. January 12, 1519). Pope Leo X had vainly sought the election of Francis of France, or even of Duke Frederick of Saxony as a last resort to defeat Charles. Cf. Karl Brandi, *The Emperor Charles V*, trans. C. V. Wedgwood (New York, 1939), pp. 110-111. What precisely transpired in the actual balloting prior to the announced result is not known with certainty. One theory is that Frederick was elected by a vote of 4-3, his own being the deciding ballot; but that his reign lasted only three hours, when Count Ludwig of the Palatinate changed his vote for fear of threats received from Spain. Luther's witness to a unanimous election and a declination by Frederick is supported by parallel testimony of Erasmus and of Spalatin, secretary and chaplain to Frederick. Cf. Paul Kirn, *Friedrich der Weise und die Kirche* (Leipzig, 1926), pp. 132-136.

you are introducing new things, and puts an evil interpretation on your actions according to his human reason and wisdom, be assured that, unless you are a theatrical spectacle to God, angels, and men, you are not yet true Christians. Who will gag every man's mouth, or who will explain to each man individually the true cause of all things? There is a proverb: "Whoever builds on the street has many foremen" [96]; "In every play there are more spectators than actors." [97] These are human words and remain nothing but leaves; they are human judgments and remain water-bubbles.[98] Follow your consciences in God, regardless of the roles or masks of men! I wanted to send you this letter in order to comfort and strengthen you, so that I too might become a fellow-worker with you and share your spirit in Christ. If I have not done this in vain I thank God. May he enrich you and keep you in the knowledge of our Lord Jesus Christ, to whom be honor and praise forever. Amen.

---

[96] Cf. Karl F. H. Wander, *Deutsches Sprichwörter-Lexikon* (Leipzig, 1867), I, 253.

[97] *Ibid.*, IV, 698.

[98] Cf. p. 77 n. 137.

RECEIVING BOTH KINDS IN THE SACRAMENT

1522

Translated by Abdel Ross Wentz

INTRODUCTION

While Luther was in confinement at the Wartburg during the winter of 1521 others proceeded in his absence to introduce at Wittenberg some of the reforms he had been advocating, and some of their own devising. Mass was abolished and the churches closed except for preaching services. Monks left the monasteries, some priests took wives, and communion under both kinds was instituted. Karlstadt, at first moderate in his conduct, had by his teaching sown the seeds of disorder. He branded communion under only one kind as sin, taught observance of the divine institution even if it causes offense, and denounced organs, images, and Gregorian chanting. On Christmas Day, 1521, he preached against pre-communion confessions and then proceeded, attired in street garb, to celebrate an "evangelical" mass by giving communion to the people in both kinds, placing the elements directly into their hands. With even less restraint, Gabriel Zwilling and the Zwickau prophets—Nicolaus Storch, Thomas Drechsel, and Marcus Stübner—also advocated an immediate overturn of established order and practice.

On December 3 some students and other citizens had caused a disturbance in the parish church and driven off the priests who were saying mass. Soon after, other citizens demanded of the city council the abolition of the mass by law, the restitution of the cup to the laity, and the release of those taken into custody in connection with the disturbance of December 3. Christmas Eve in both the parish and castle churches was marked by wild disorders. On January 11 Zwilling and a band of monks destroyed all the altars except one in the convent church and cast out the images. The city council acceded to the popular demands by setting January 24 as the date on which the images should be removed from the parish church. But the excited populace could not wait; it took matters into its own hands, invaded the church, and burned the images and pictures.

Shortly after his secret visit to Wittenberg in December, Luther had written *An Earnest Exhortation for all Christians, Warning*

Them Against Insurrection and Rebellion.[1] It appeared in January, but the disturbances continued. Apparently the time for writing had passed. So in spite of the elector's instructions to remain, Luther set out on March 1 from the Wartburg to return to Wittenberg. There on eight successive days he preached his *Eight Sermons at Wittenberg*[2] dealing with the distinction between essentials and non-essentials, plus proper procedures, in the matter of reforms. He emphasized the sole sufficiency of the Word alone, without force, and the duty of dealing with the weak gently and in love. Karlstadt was silenced, Zwilling admitted he was wrong, and order was quickly restored to Wittenberg.

Luther himself took no steps towards the publication of his *Eight Sermons at Wittenberg*. That was done by others. But he was interested in bringing his ideas on these subjects to the knowledge of a wider circle than that reached by the sermons. Even while he was preaching the eight sermons he seems to have conceived the purpose of writing something for publication. On March 17 he wrote a letter to his friend Nicholas Hausmann in which he indicated the main ideas that he had in mind. The next day, in his answer to an inquiry from Duke John Frederick of Saxony about receiving the sacrament in both kinds and with the hands, Luther wrote that he had started to prepare a manuscript on the subject, and in the same letter he made a very brief summary of the points that were afterwards developed in this treatise.

A week later, in a letter to John Hess at Breslau, he referred to the disturbances at Wittenberg and the reception of the sacrament in both kinds, and closed his letter with these words: "But more about this in the little book that I am writing on the subject." And on March 30 he wrote to his friend George Spalatin: "I have in hand a little work concerning the evangelical form of the communion."

Early in April the manuscript of the little book was completed, and on April 12 the author wrote to John Lang in Erfurt: "My little book which is now in the press explains to the world in greater detail my judgment on all these matters." The next week Luther wrote Zwilling and advised him to read "my newest little book," and

[1] *PE* 3, 206-222.
[2] *LW* 51, 67-97.

a few days later he had Spalatin take a copy to Hans von Berlepsch. Before the end of April, Luther was making reference to the book in his letters to other people. By the middle of May the treatise had reached Nuremberg, and already on the first of June it had been reprinted in Zurich.

In this treatise Luther repudiates hasty reform in the administration of the sacrament. He pleads on behalf of the unenlightened conscience of the rank and file. He does not withdraw any of his previous positions, but asks for moderation in the practical application of those principles. He continues to insist that when the papists withhold the cup from the laity they are "despoiling the sacrament," because Christ instituted it in both elements; and so did Christ's apostle, Paul, practice it. No human creature has the right to enforce a change.

However, Luther goes on to urge delay in introducing this reform in circumstances where the consciences of the people would be offended. The evangelicals, he says, should always be prompted by considerations of love. After all, the elements are not the essence of the sacrament; the Word is the essence, and this can be appropriated through the use of either element alone. The overzealous reformers at Wittenberg, he felt, had made a serious mistake in implementing justifiable reforms, because they had rushed forward without regard to the weak conscience of the ordinary man, whom they should have led on in love toward fuller knowledge. Christ cares more for love than for the elements of the sacrament. The power of the sacrament is the Word.

There is a close relation between the ideas expressed in the *Eight Sermons at Wittenberg* and those set down in this treatise, but the order is not the same in both instances.

Our translation is from the German text in *WA* 10^{II}, 11-41.

RECEIVING BOTH KINDS IN THE SACRAMENT

To all my dear sirs and brothers in Christ: grace and peace from God our Father and our Jesus Christ.

St. Paul calls the holy gospel a word of the cross [I Cor. 1:18], a preaching of foolishness for the heathen and a preaching of offense for the Jews [I Cor. 1:23]. But since by the fathomless mercy of God our Father we have again been blessed with the pure and holy message of the gospel, we have to remind ourselves that for us also the gospel by its very nature is and continues to be nothing else than a word of the cross, a message of foolishness and offense. It is a very precious sign of true faith and doctrine on our part that Satan, through his lackeys, attacks us so bitterly and in so many different ways. If our doctrine were of the world then the world would praise it, as the world has praised the doctrines of the pope. Since it is not of the world, however, but has been given us by God, the world hates us [John 15:19; 17:14].

Now that is the least of our troubles, that the world hates us and persecutes us. Even Satan is not satisfied with that; he plans to exercise his malice within our own ranks. If outwardly we are too strong for his stooges, the papists, he will rend and destroy us inwardly through ourselves. May God our Father prevent him from doing this. Amen. So henceforth we must have regard to ourselves rather than to our enemies from without. As St. Paul says in II Cor. 2 [:11], we know well what he has in mind. Now that he sees he cannot subdue us from the left side, he rushes over to the right side. Formerly he made us too papistic; now he wants to make us too evangelical. But God has commanded us many times in the Scriptures to keep on the straight path and not to turn either to the right or to the left [Deut. 5:32-33; Isa. 30:21]. Indeed the time has now come that we must arm ourselves, and defend ourselves with prayer and teaching, for Satan is about to attack.

Hitherto he has wrestled with me alone through a number of coarse, stupid blockheads who can do nothing but lie and slander. But now they cherish the fond hope that we will destroy ourselves with our own divisions and controversies.

But let us not be discouraged on that account. St. Paul had it a lot worse. Among his followers were false brethren and false apostles. Moreover, all those who were in Asia fell away from him [II Tim. 1:15]; his specially dear friend and disciple Demas also deserted him [II Tim. 4:10]. So we too must expect that some of our own will fall away when the conflict begins. Moreover, when the really crucial battle with the devil begins, within ourselves, we must expect that some of those who are now the spearheads of our movement will fall, be it Luther or someone else. When we fight with Satan, it is no mere academic disputation.[1]

But I know where my teaching comes from and who has sustained me. Moreover, the work is also sufficient confirmation of it. For, although I have not done any of the little signs and wonders, which I might perhaps have done if it had been necessary, yet it may be regarded as a great miracle that Satan's chief representative and highest power, the pope and his retinue, have received such a blow through my work as no secular or religious power could have given them. Even Satan himself knows very well who is the author of my teaching; that is why he rages as he does and resorts to underhanded tricks.

I regret to see that the secular authority,[2] the servant of the papacy, has injected itself into this affair. But if this has to be, we must place our trust in Christ, that he will help us. Since we have defeated and scorned that furious gentleman himself, we shall certainly not be afraid of his angry servant. We are convinced that Christ is Lord over them as well as us, and will stand by those who rely upon his help. Let us pray for them, and ask God to enlighten them in this critical time and to take their hands out of the pope's stew, so that they do not get involved and destroyed with him. For I fear their actions in this matter will make them scratch their heads. Christ does not intend to be frightened because a few

---

[1] This is aimed at Karlstadt. *WA* 8, 12 n. 1.

[2] The Imperial Council and Duke George of Saxony. Cf. p. 246 n. 10.

incensed flunkeys of the pope want to "risk life and property"[3] in such a matter as this. On the contrary Christ figures it is imperative for them to give some thought to how they may save their lives and property from destruction. They have already risked too much. If they can extinguish my teaching, then certainly God has not spoken through me. But it must always be true, as it was from the beginning, that no class has so many fools as the upper classes, as the Greek proverb says: One must be born either a prince or a fool.[4]

I say all this in order that we may not be scared by these various stumbling blocks and hindrances [Rom. 14:13] of Satan. For St. John says: "He who is in you is greater than he who is in the world" [I John 4:4]. So I humbly ask all my dear friends in Christ to receive kindly this instruction and judgment of mine concerning the present disturbance and with earnest prayer help to preserve and further for God's sake this evangelical cause which has now become the common cause of all of us, that light may thereby shine upon the poor souls yet to come, and that we with them may be strengthened in the knowledge of our Lord Jesus Christ. To Him be praise, thanks and glory forever. Amen.

Jesus

Let me first make it clear that in what follows I shall not argue about whether the holy sacrament is to be administered and received in both kinds, or whether the laity have the right to take it in their hands, or whether one has the right to administer it in vessels other than chalices, or in clothes other than the sacramental vestments, or in houses other than churches. In these and other external practices, whether they be opposed to the pope or not, may God preserve us from extended disputes. On the contrary, in such matters we Christians should and will have the right and power to adhere to the institution of Christ in any way that we may

[3] In his proclamation of February 10, 1522, Duke George of Saxony declared that "in this un-Christian affair" he "as a Christian prince" would not hesitate to "risk life and property." *CL* 2, 313 n. 17.

[4] Luther was probably acquainted with the writing of Erasmus entitled: *The Proverb, "One must be born either a king or a fool."* It had been translated into German by Spalatin, and published at Logau in 1520. *Sprichwörter-Lexikon, op. cit.*, II, 1487.

see fit, without regard to the false and fabricated decrees of the churches, church orders, and the raging of all the tyrants, both religious and secular.

Our reason for holding this is based on Him who cannot lie, and who says in Matt. 15 [:7-9], "You hypocrites! Well did Isaiah say of you: 'This people honors me with their lips, but their heart is far from me; in vain do they worship me, teaching the precepts of men'" [Isa. 29:13]. By this a Christian should set his conscience at ease, in the firm conviction that Christ does not lie. And if he does not lie, then it must be true that in this sacrament everything of mere human origin which has been added and believed beyond the original institution of Christ is vain worship, despite all the devils who grumble to the contrary.

Now it is quite certain that it is a mere human addition and teaching that one may not partake of both kinds, nor touch the sacrament with the hands, nor administer it in unconsecrated vestments, or in ordinary houses and vessels. For this sort of prohibition was neither set up nor practiced by Christ or the apostles, nor for a long time thereafter. On the contrary, the exact opposite was the case, as the Gospel writers clearly show. So it is certainly vain worship of God to teach that such things are necessary commandments.

The second reason we base again upon Mark 3[5] and Matt. 12 [:8]: "The Son of Man is lord even of the sabbath." Christ spoke that word because his disciples had the power to break the sabbath. Now every Christian is a brother of Christ, as St. Paul says in Rom. 8 [:17] and Gal. 4 [:7], and as Christ himself testifies in Ps. 22 [:23], for "to all who believe in his name he gave power to become children of God" (John 1 [:12]). Therefore every Christian too is lord over the sabbath, rather over all human commandments, teachings, and ordinances, as Paul also says in I Cor. 3 [:21-23]: "All things are yours, whether Peter or Paul, life or death, all are yours; and you are Christ's; and Christ is God's." For this reason we hold and shall continue to hold that we are lords over all papal and human teachings and commandments; it is for us to determine whether we will follow them or not. Let us just see what all the devils can say or do against that. I believe I am speaking plainly

[5] Mark 2:28; cf. 3:1-5.

now, and that my words are not mine but Christ's. These raging cavaliers are not going to toss our Christ out of heaven, because he who has set him on his right hand [Eph. 1:20] intends to keep him there. We can count on that and reassure ourselves with it, no matter how much their wrath may rage against it.

But we must understand that this Christian lordship of ours, this liberty and power, is purely spiritual. For Christ would have nothing to do with lordship. He was himself subject to worldly power and paid taxes (Matt. 17 [:24-27]). Spiritual freedom, however, means to keep the conscience free. It means that I should not make it a matter of conscience before God whether I break human ordinances, as if I had thereby committed a sin. It also means that I should not make it a matter of conscience when I observe them, as if I had thereby done a good work and merited something before God; for Christ himself calls that vain worship [Matt. 15:9]. On the contrary, I should look upon such human ordinances as I look upon eating and drinking, sleeping and walking, all of which I am free to do or to abstain from doing without hurting or benefiting my conscience. That is to say, faith in Christ is my only good work, life, and service, capable of reassuring my conscience; after that comes love to my neighbor.

The third reason is stated by St. Paul in Gal. 4 [5:13]: "For you were called to freedom, brethren; only do not use your freedom as an opportunity for the flesh, but through love be servants of one another." Christians are also told that they owe nothing except to serve one another in love [Rom. 13:8]. For everything that they have before God and according to conscience they have through faith; they are lords over sin, death, the devil, and all things. Therefore no one can impose any commandment upon them, to which they would be in conscience bound if they were to become righteous, or against which they could commit sin. This is just as true as it is that one cannot impose on a healthy person a commandment about eating and drinking, with respect to which he could become healthy or sick; for he is already healthy, and can become sick, without any such commandment. He is free to take such a commandment or to leave it.

For there is a great difference among these three things: to observe human ordinances, to serve through human ordinances, and to be lord over human ordinances. Christ did not discard the sabbath, but said he is lord over it [Matt. 12:8], so that he might keep it or not keep it. Likewise, he did not discard human ordinances, for how could it have hurt him to wash his hands as the Jews required? [Matt. 15:2]. But he did not feel that he was thereby rendering service. He says it is vain worship of God [Matt. 15:9]; that is, they wanted thereby to bind the consciences of men as if the person who did it was doing God an essential service, one which he was obligated to perform on pain of committing a mortal sin. That is false and misleading. So also in our case, to observe papistic rules where they are not contrary to the will of God would not in itself be wicked, any more than eating and drinking, and so forth. But to insist that one must do these things on pain of disobeying the church and committing a mortal sin, to insist that he who does not do them cannot be saved and is not a Christian but a heretic, and so to ensnare the conscience, that is of the devil himself. Here our liberty is at stake and we say: That is a lie, for in conscience we are lords over such commandments; we do no sin by transgressing them, and we are not righteous for having kept them. That is the way the matter stands.

And so we come back again to the first point, and we speak by the command of our Lord Jesus Christ and in his name, Amen.

Those who have touched the holy sacrament with their hands or have celebrated it without consecrated vestments or vessels, or in ordinary houses—or will so celebrate it in the future, whether at Wittenberg or Eilenburg,[6] in Bohemia or Hungary, in Russia or Prussia—on pain of losing their salvation should not make this a matter of conscience, as if they had done some wicked thing. So far as the act itself is concerned, it is not wrong. Those who have done it should insist upon that, and allow themselves to be put to death ten times rather than repudiate, condemn, or declare it to be wrong—no matter whether the pope, the emperor, the prince, or the devil himself sets up and proclaims ordinances, judgments, and commandments to the contrary. But I am speaking now of the act itself; we shall speak later[7] about its misuse and the persons involved.)

[6] The radical reformer, Gabriel Zwilling, was active in Eilenburg. *CL* 2, 316 n. 18.

[7] Cf. Part Two, pp. 248-267.

The reason for all this is that those who have condemned these things or will yet condemn them cannot prove that they are contrary to Christ's original institution, but must admit that Christ himself and Christendom generally for a long time have done the same things, and have left us free to do them also. On pain of losing his salvation, no one dares to repudiate or censure as wrong, or allow to be censured, what Christ himself and all of Christendom have done in times past. For that would be the same as to deny or condemn Christ together with all the apostles, and all of Christendom when it was at its very best. That the papists decry such practices as heresy,[8] however, and that some raging princes proclaim their Christian zeal by abusing and persecuting those who engage in these practices, is quite fitting. For what else should Caiaphas and Herod better do than to crucify and revile the Son of God?

The other reason is this: they must also admit that the things they emphasize and rage about are mere human regulations or, as they falsely and deceitfully declare, commandments of the church. It will take them a good long while before they ever prove that Christ administered the sacrament in consecrated vessels, clothes, and houses, or commanded that it should be administered in that way, or that it should be placed in the mouth and not in the hands. Therefore, so long as we are Christians, we are lords over such human commandments, so far as our consciences are involved. And we are in duty bound to risk our necks for it and not to give up our liberty. For that would be to deny and condemn Christ who so strictly commanded us to be free. It is not at all in our power to change or surrender our liberty.

They ought to be satisfied that we do not reject their ordinances and ways, and may even keep them. However, when they try to make of them a requirement, as if it could not be done any other way, and when they bind consciences to them and insist that it is heresy to do otherwise, we refuse to tolerate it and shall resist it with life and limb. The conscience must remain free to choose either way in this matter, and our liberty must remain unimpaired. This we must insist upon, and in this we shall have the help of Christ who gave us our liberty and commanded us to keep it.

---

[8] Duke George of Saxony so labelled them in his proclamation of February 10, 1522. *CL* 2, 316 n. 36.

The angry papists write, and they make a big fuss about it, that people have received the sacrament with "lay hands."[9] What do you think of that? Isn't that terrific! Lay hands indeed! Anyone who didn't know them might think they were fulminating in honor of the holy sacrament and out of real Christian motivation. Now if I were to ask them with what kind of mouths they themselves receive the sacrament at Easter, whether they receive it with a lay mouth or with a priestly mouth, perhaps they would say their mouths just then were the mouths of angels or bishops. To such gentlemen I should like to suggest quite humbly, if they are not too thick-skinned to hear me, that if they want to indulge in tomfoolery and act like fools, they should do so in their own affairs and not interfere with God's work and the business of human souls. I am not saying these things in order to undermine anybody's secular authority, but because it is our duty, when they try to fool around with the things of God, to break our silence and to offer objection. Others have grabbed the sacrament with lay hands; but these people, when they try to joke about it like that, are butting in with their lay butts. Still they boast of their great Christian love.

If it is wrong to touch the sacrament with lay hands because the hands have committed sin or are not consecrated, it would be even less proper to receive it with the mouth or to let it enter the stomach or to look at it with the human eye. For neither mouth nor stomach nor eye is consecrated, and more sins are committed with the mouth and the eye than with the hand. Such wise brains will probably go so far as to advise us not to hear or speak God's holy Word in order that the holy Word may not be received with lay mouths or ears. This is the same unreasonable blindness, however, with which Christ used to charge his enemies; so we see with what authority he asserts himself over those who think they have devoured him—they have to shame and punish themselves with their own foolishness.

A Christian should know that there is nothing more holy on earth than God's Word, for even the sacrament itself is constituted and sanctified and consecrated through God's Word, and all of us have received our spiritual birth from that Word and were consecrated as Christians by it. The Word sanctifies everything, and is

[9] The term is found in the *Resolution* of the Imperial Council. Cf. p. 246 n. 70.

above the sacrament (insofar as the sacrament admits of being grasped with the hands). If a Christian nevertheless embraces that Word with his mouth and with his ears and with his heart, yes, with his whole life, why should he not dare also to touch that which is consecrated by the Word? Or should he refrain from touching himself? For he is sanctified by the Word [John 17:17] as well as the sacrament is. This was the way of the Pharisees, concerning whom Christ said in Matt. 23 [:17, 19] that they made the gold more sacred than the temple and the gift more sacred than the altar. It is as if they began to teach that it is a sin to touch the lining of the cup but quite proper to take hold of the cup itself. I wish I could sometime hear something from the papists that they could present without excessive foolishness. But how could those who judge and blaspheme God himself do otherwise?

A Christian is holy in body and soul, whether he be layman or priest, man or woman. If anybody denies that, he speaks blasphemy against holy baptism, the blood of Christ, and the grace of the Holy Spirit. A Christian is a rare and wonderful thing, and God is more concerned about him than about the sacrament. For the Christian was not made for the sacrament, but the sacrament was instituted for the Christian. And yet these blind heads would first of all debate whether he may touch the sacrament, and would even make a heresy out of it. There is no hope for these blind and stubborn pagans who have no idea what it means to be a Christian.

Therefore we also beg those who have received the sacrament in both kinds, in fact if it helps we will command them in the name of our Lord Jesus Christ, that they give themselves no pangs of conscience about the matter as if they had done something wrong or wicked, but forfeit their lives rather than repudiate or disavow it, no matter what pope, emperor, prince, or even the devil may say or do or legislate to the contrary. For in this matter the text of the gospel is so clear that even the papists cannot deny that Christ instituted the sacrament in both kinds and gave them to all of the disciples. Therefore, it is your duty, on pain of forfeiting your salvation, to let nobody deny or disfigure it. For that would be the same as if you were to say that Christ himself had done wrong in this matter and was a heretic because he acted differently from the pope and the raging papists (who claim that they are themselves the church). Shall the papists lay such blasphemy on the works of Christ, and must you praise and honor and justify them with life and limb in order to be a Christian and be saved?

And now see once more with what power the Lord Christ rules over his blasphemers and exposes them through their own cleverness. Orders have been issued by the Regency at Nuremberg that this question concerning the reception of both kinds in the sacrament shall be postponed to a future council.[10] The wise gentlemen do not want to condemn it; yet in the interim they will not permit it, and so condemn it unknowingly. Now what do you think of that? I say, those are real Christians for you! They acknowledge, it is true, that Christ instituted the sacrament and that it is recorded in the gospel. Yet they want to "take under consideration" whether what Christ instituted and did is right or wrong, to be kept or not kept. I wish that Christians would begin to take under consideration whether the gospel is right or wrong, whether it is to be tolerated or not. Christ also commanded that one should not commit adultery. But now I begin to see why the great gentlemen usually regard adultery so lightly: they have probably taken it under consideration, whether it is a good commandment or not.

Since therefore our Lord Christ has publicly shown up the foolishness of his enemies in these matters, the bigwigs both religious and secular, and has indicated that they have acted so childishly and disgracefully that even Claus Narr[11] would be man enough to answer them, we should take comfort and view their raging and folly with quiet contempt. We should not worry about how to answer them, for they know nothing of the grace of God.

---

[10] The Imperial Council of Regency, set up by Charles V in 1521 to act as a central government during his absence from the German nation, under prodding from Duke George of Saxony released a *Resolution und Decisum* at its Nuremberg headquarters on January 20, 1522, in which the neighboring bishoprics of Naumburg, Meissen, and Merseburg were admonished to suppress, by force if necessary, any innovations departing from the traditional manner of celebrating the mass "until such time as . . . a council . . . shall have made a prudent, deliberate, well-grounded and certain declaration of faith." Leopold Ranke, *History of the Reformation in Germany*, trans. Sarah Austin (London, 1845), II, 55-56. See the text of the edict in *St.L.* 15, 2194-2196.

[11] Claus Narr, mentioned by Luther on numerous occasions, was the well-known jester at the Saxon court. A book containing 627 anecdotes about him was published in 1572, as late as 57 years after his death at the age of 90. *WA* 10^{II}, 514.

This the pope has shown clearly enough with his bulls and his papal apologies, and now the raging lords also prove it. We must rather disregard flesh and blood, and consider how we may base our consciences on the pure Word of God alone, so that when we die we can face the devil and stand fast. Dear brother, believe me, for I know from experience, that the devil has no fear of men's words and commands. So if at your death he finds that you base your conscience on human commandments and say: "This is what the pope, the church, the princes, etc., have commanded me," he will annihilate you so completely that not a trace of you will remain. On the other hand, if he finds that you put your trust in the Word of God and say: "This is what Christ has commanded me, there is his Word," you will thereby make the world too small for him.

This is what St. Paul means when he says in Eph. 5 [6:12]: "We are not contending against flesh and blood, but against the spiritual hosts of wickedness in the heavenly places, against the world rulers of this present darkness." But those powers contend only for the purpose either of misleading the consciences of men with craft and doctrine or of destroying them with unfounded fears. No weapon avails against them except the Word of God, that sword of the Spirit [Eph. 6:17]. Therefore, we must always firmly insist upon it that the use of both kinds in the sacrament is right and Christian and evangelical; and whoever says otherwise denies and blasphemes God, whether it be pope, emperor, princes, or even the devil. So we must also assert and preserve our liberty to take the sacrament with our hands or with our mouth, to administer it with and in consecrated or unconsecrated clothes, vessels, and houses, as we please. Whoever denies this liberty, or denounces either alternative as heresy, also denies and blasphemes Christ and his Word, whether it be pope, emperor, princes, or even the devil. We have the pure and clear gospel, as they themselves acknowledge. They have only their own "considerations," as to whether they should hold on to the gospel, and along with the gospel their own views contradicting it. Let the maniacs rave, let them rave!

In short, as St. Paul says to the Galatians, "Even if we ourselves, or an angel from heaven should preach otherwise than what we have preached to you, let him be accursed" [Gal. 1:8]. So I say to you now: In these matters and in all others you must put your trust in God's Word so firmly and with such assurance that even if I myself should become a fool (may God forbid it) and repudiate or deny my teaching, you will not for that reason depart from it but will say: Even if Luther himself or an angel from heaven should teach otherwise, let him be accursed. For you must be Christ's disciple, not Luther's. It is not enough that you say: Luther, Peter, or Paul has said this; but you yourself in your own conscience must feel Christ himself. You must experience unshakably that it is God's Word, even though the whole world should dispute it. As long as you do not have this feeling, just so long you have certainly not yet tasted of God's Word. You still cling with your ears to human mouth or pen and do not cling with your very heart to the Word. You do not know the truth of Matt. 23 [:10]: "You should not call one another masters on earth, for you have one master, the Christ." The Master does his teaching in the hearts of men–through the external word of his preachers, however. The preachers impress the Word upon the ears, but Christ impresses it in the heart.

Therefore, imagine that you are facing death or persecution. I cannot be with you then, nor you with me, but each one of us must then struggle for himself to overcome the devil and death and the world. If at such a time you tried to look around to see where I was, or if I tried to look around to see where you were, and if you allowed yourself to be moved by the fact that I or anybody else on earth had said otherwise, you would be lost already. You would have let the Word depart from your heart. For if you do not cling to the Word but to me or somebody else, there is no help for you. From this you can see what awful destruction of human souls it is to preach to people the doctrines of men, or to fail to preach God's Word in its purity and certainty. Moreover, you can see how few cling to it with their whole heart even when it is preached in its purity and is praised by many. So much for the first part of our discussion.

Part II

If then this is really true and there is no doubt about it, why do people not act accordingly? Yes, you will say to me, why don't you yourself allow it to proceed in Wittenberg, where it has begun, and at other places? My answer is that I regret that it does not proceed, and I deplore the fact that it cannot proceed. A prisoner in custody ought to travel, of course, and even has the authority and the right to do so; but he cannot because the matter is determined not by him but by others who prevent it. Take an illustration: The gospel naturally ought to be preached throughout the whole world, and why is it not? Certainly it is not the fault of the gospel, for it is right and true, profitable and blessed. No, the trouble is that there are not enough people who are qualified to do it. And if a person doesn't have the qualifications it is better to keep silent than to preach; otherwise the preaching will be false and harmful. So also here, the sacrament and the practice which I have described above is right and good, but where are the people who are qualified to begin it and carry it on?

If it were ordered that this practice be used and if a person were to become a Christian merely because he received the sacrament in this way, then nothing would be easier than to be a Christian; even a sow could be a Christian. I have earnestly desired and tried to bring it about that the pope's decree ordering that the sacrament be received annually at Easter[12] be set aside, and that it be left to the free decision of each person, so that he may go to the altar not by compulsion but moved by his own conscience and the hunger of his soul. In this way the terrible, un-Christian misuse of the sacrament and blasphemy of God would be diminished; and henceforth hardly anyone would go to the sacrament, where at present many hundreds are going. So I see that Satan plans to make the use of both kinds in the sacrament just as common as, and even more common than, the pope has made his use of one kind—before the real Christians are actually produced who should be using both kinds. He hopes to make things worse on the right side than on the left. Therefore it is essential that we stay on the correct middle way, and ask God to help us and keep us there, because Satan is after us in dead earnest.

---

[12] The Fourth Lateran Council, 1215, decreed: "Let everyone . . . confess all his sins at least once a year . . . , reverently receiving the sacrament of the Eucharist at least in Paschal time." Heinrich Denzinger, *The Sources of Catholic Dogma*, . . . (St. Louis: Herder, 1957), p. 173.

I defer telling at this point why I have not allowed this use of the sacrament to proceed at Wittenberg, for that is a particular and incidental reason about which it is not necessary to write. Even if it were still more precious and heavenly than it is, I should not help to confirm or strengthen such an undertaking. It is not proper for every individual to begin or to do all things that are right; it is enough that each one do that right thing which is appropriate to himself and incumbent upon him. Where this order is perverted nothing is right, no matter how good it might otherwise be. So I shall only consider that which militates for or against the continuance or discontinuance of this use of the sacrament.

For one thing, this sacrament and the form of its administration is not under our control. It is captive to the laws of the pope just as the golden vessels of the temple were captive in Babylon [Dan. 1:2; 5:2]. And the captivity is such that the conscience of the common man has been so ensnared and his faith so weakened by papal laws and tyranny that he cannot suddenly free himself and be assured in his conscience that the pope's way is wrong and this new usage right and consistent with the gospel. Even I had to apply myself diligently for three full years before I freed my conscience from the pope's laws. I did it by exercising myself in the gospel daily, through preaching, lecturing, observing, discussing, writing, and hearing. How then can the common man be brought out of it so suddenly?

Where such weak persons go and receive both kinds their consciences afterwards hurt them, and they go to confession and admit that they had received the sacrament in both kinds, as if they had thereby committed some evil. There have been cases of this kind, and that is a terrible thing. It is evil compounded, because with such a conscience and such a confession they deny and condemn Christ and his institution. Away with these advocates of both kinds, for their experience accords with the saying of Christ in Matt. 9 [:17]: "No one puts wine into old wineskins; else the wine bursts the skins, and the wine is spilled, and the skins are destroyed." The wine is the teaching of the gospel, and the old wineskins are these weak and antiquated consciences—which is why they cannot get along together. The conscience deteriorates and then denies the teaching which it had embraced.

Yes, I say further, away with the proponents of only one element—and of the sacrament as a whole! Because when they come to die the devil will torment with the gospel those who use only one element, for the gospel ordains both elements. If they don't know how to cope with it they will have to perish. And it will not help for them to plead the papal law and ancient custom. The gospel does not care about pope or custom. That is why I said it is not a question of what is right but of having the right people. It is contrary to the gospel to partake of only one element, and the pope's ordinance cannot be so very generally observed everywhere without terrible destruction of human souls. At the same time, it would do just as much harm suddenly to impose on the whole church the reception of both elements, in accordance with the gospel, when the church consists of such weak, captive consciences.

But you say: What does this lead to? If there is so much danger in both directions with this sacrament, that if we use only one element the devil will plague us with the gospel when we die, and if we use both elements the pope will plague with his ordinances while we live, in what direction are we to go? Let me answer, this is why St. Paul proclaimed that the rule of the Antichrist will bring critical times [II Thess. 2:9]. People will not be able to walk with safety on either side, in the gospel or outside the gospel—not through any fault of the gospel, for the wine is good, but through the fault of the pope. He has caused the consciences of men, the wineskins, to grow old and deteriorate so that they cannot grasp or hold the gospel. Yet they cannot be preserved without the gospel.

So what are we to do? I answer: do nothing except what Christ teaches when he says in Matt. 9 [:17]: "Put the wine into fresh wineskins, and so both are preserved." We must first become coopers and make new vessels before the wine harvest begins and the wine is stored away. The old vessels must be discarded. That is to say, we must preach repeatedly and vigorously against the pope's law of only one element, and hammer home Christ's institution of both elements as set forth in the gospel. But in the meantime we should turn the people away from the sacrament as a whole, whether in one or both kinds, and not drive them to it either at Easter or at Pentecost.[18] In this way we would drop the ordinance of the pope long enough for the people to understand sufficiently how to come to the sacrament of their own accord, without urging or prodding, driven by their own consciences to implore and insist that the sacrament be given to them. One would be able thereby to perceive that the vessels and the wineskins were new and their consciences sufficiently strengthened. And the others, those who are weak, would remain behind in their weak estate until they also became strong.

However, if one orders people to the sacrament or commands or urges and prods them, the whole crowd presses forward and puts the wine into its old wineskin and is destroyed. For that reason it is not possible to set up a general ordinance about who should partake of it, as the pope does; the sacrament will not admit of it. Rather one must first preach everywhere among the people and keep the weak consciences away from it until they are fully instructed in the gospel and humbly come of their own accord, announce themselves to the priest, and out of spiritual hunger ask him for the sacrament. Away with all the others, away from the sacrament, regardless of papal ordinances, church customs, or anything else. For Christ says in Matt. 11 [:12], "The kingdom of God is preached and suffers violence, and men of violence take it by force." That means that one should not bind any person with commandments or ordinances, or entice him toward the gospel with customs or with words; but one should preach freely, and then let people come of their own accord and insist upon it.

But where do we get such preachers? And if we had them, how could we keep the common man from coming to the sacrament at Easter? The ordinance of the pope is too deeply imbedded for us to remove the old wineskins and vessels completely. We must let the old misuse of the sacrament go on for a while yet, until the vessels, at least most of them, have become new and the gospel has taken root among the people.

Now if these old vessels and wineskins consisted only of those people who are against us and who condemn the receiving of the

[18] According to a work by Regino, abbot of Prüm (d. 915), the bishop in his visitation is to ask "if there be anyone who has not gone to Holy Communion three times in the year, that is, at Easter, Pentecost and Christmas." *Catholic Encyclopedia, op. cit.*, IV, 154.

sacrament under both kinds and who plague the consciences of men with papal law and custom, our simple advice in the matter would be this: We should once more condemn their law not only as something that is opposed to the gospel and both kinds in the sacrament, but also as something that, even if it did teach the gospel, would nevertheless oppress the consciences of men and compel them to believe—which is not only senseless and inconsistent with the gospel, but also an impossibility. One should not and cannot compel anybody to believe; one should and can only allow the gospel to draw freely whomever it draws. Out of defiance and opposition to such fools we would therefore use both kinds consistently and exclusively, and tread their ordinances underfoot.

However, there are among the old vessels and wineskins many good hearted, simple, little people, who would like to do what is right and proper if they knew what it was or could grasp it. For that reason we must proceed against the tyrants in this matter in such a way as not to upset and confuse the poor multitude of the rank and file. Faith is supposed to fight against the tyrants, hold fast to the gospel despite their ordinances, and throw such old useless vessels on the junk heap. But love should receive and embrace these weak and simple consciences, and work to make new vessels out of them.

Here we may apply the teaching and example of St. Paul. When he encountered the stubborn Jews who insisted upon circumcision and the law, he took delight in teaching and doing the very opposite; he would not be coerced [Gal. 2:3-5]. But when he came to the weak and simple people he even practiced circumcision [Acts 16:3] and let the law stand, until such time as he might strengthen them and deliver them from the law. Therefore he boasts in I Cor. 12 [9:20]: To the Jews I became as a Jew; to the Greeks I became as a Greek; and yet he says in Gal. 6[14]: In Christ there is neither Jew nor Greek—all this because he refused to tolerate the law and the oppression of consciences. He wanted to be free to do it or not to do it.

We should deal in the same way with the matter before us now. Since we cannot keep the common man away from the sacrament, which is what should be done, until the gospel is understood, we

[14] Gal. 3:28; cf. 6:15.

must have regard for the simple people among them and not let them receive both kinds; or else we must take certain steps to help them in that direction.

The first step is to let the old practice continue. Let the mass be celebrated with consecrated vestments, with chants and all the usual ceremonies, in Latin, recognizing the fact that these are merely external matters which do not endanger the consciences of men. But besides that, through the sermon keep the consciences free, so the common man may learn that these things are done not because they have to be done that way or because it would be heresy to do them differently, as the nonsensical laws of the pope insist. For one must attack rigorously and roughly those tyrants who would ensnare and coerce by means of laws, in order that Christian freedom may remain intact.

The second step is for the priests who celebrate mass to avoid every word in the canon[15] and the collects which refers to sacrifice. For this is not something that we are free to do or not to do, like the things mentioned in the preceding paragraph. It simply must and shall be done away with, no matter who takes offense. The priest, however, can probably avoid these words in such a way that the common man never realizes it and no offense is caused. But if anyone stubbornly refuses to avoid such words, let him do as he pleases and let him answer for himself.

The third step is to emphasize in the sermon the words of the sacrament: This is my body given for you; This is my blood shed for you,[16] and so forth. Let every Christian store these words in his heart and especially keep them before him and meditate upon them when he receives the sacrament or hears mass. For these words are a thousand times more important than the elements of the sacrament; without them the sacrament is not a sacrament but a mockery before God. So the sacrament is in the church of the papists all right, but it is not given to anybody, because they conceal the words and give only the element. That is a horrible thing.

The fourth step is this. If you come to a place where they give the sacrament in only one kind, then take only the one element, as they do. If they give it in both kinds, take both. Don't

[15] Cf. p. 51 n. 102. The text of the canon and collects is on pp. 314-327.
[16] Cf. p. 37 n. 84.

start anything new. Don't set yourself against the multitude either—except to testify (if you are asked) that it is not in harmony with the gospel to receive one element. For one should restore the sacrament in both kinds by means of the gospel, not through acts or ordinances. The common man will learn, not through an act or an ordinance but through the gospel, that both kinds is correct.

If you are disturbed by Christ's institution of both kinds and think it improper to receive only one kind, reason with yourself this way: In the first place, you have, after all, the words of the sacrament and these are the most important part of the sacrament. These words you can take and use just as well whether you receive one element or both elements, or even none at all. So you are in no danger whatever, and yet you do receive the real power of the sacrament. In the second place, it is not your fault that you are receiving only one kind and not observing Christ's institution. You would gladly receive both kinds, but the one element is now taken captive by the ordinance of the pope, with which weak consciences are ensnared. And you must not throw these weak consciences into confusion, but bear with them and instruct them until they also become strong. Just as St. Peter in prison was unable to preach the gospel, as he would have been in duty bound to do; for necessity knows no law.[17] Therefore, in such a case, the law of love is far to be preferred above the institution of both kinds. For Christ is more concerned about love than about the elements in the sacrament.

Now therefore, since Satan has so terribly confused the matter through the ordinance of the pope that one cannot use the sacrament in both kinds without violating the law of love towards weaker consciences, and since one cannot exercise love without violating the institution of both kinds, one must give preference to the exercise of love and for a time overlook the institution. But this does not mean that one denies or condemns the use of the sacrament in both kinds; it simply means that love is something that lays us under obligation and compulsion whereas the reception of the sacramental elements is not a matter of compulsion. One can

[17] According to this proverb, whatever one does out of unavoidable necessity, even though it contravene a law, is not considered a transgression. *Sprichwörter-Lexikon, op. cit.*, III, 1051.

forego them and simply cling to the words. For Christ has not commanded us to partake of the sacrament, but has left it free for any one to partake who wishes to do so, and to do this in both kinds if he can. But in our situation it is not possible to do so on account of the consciences which love is in duty bound to serve.

In saying this I hope I have not confused those who wish to partake of the sacrament under both kinds and are in a position to do so, either privately or openly. But they should avoid calling attention to their individual action, and they should not do it from the common altar or at the same time that those of weak conscience do it in their way. For then those of weak conscience might join in receiving the sacrament in both kinds and follow that by taking the matter to the confessional. And if anyone on our side is so weak that he would dispense with the sacrament altogether rather than partake in one kind, be patient with him also and let him live by his own conscience.

The procedure which I have just described is now in use at Wittenberg; not that I would thereby condemn the former procedure,[18] nor that this procedure accords adequately with the gospel, nor yet that I would in this way help to strengthen the tyranny of the pope, but that I would out of love make this much concession to weak consciences for a time, until we have to a greater extent spread the gospel in the world. I see nothing particularly wrong in what was done except that Satan insisted upon too much haste, bypassed the law of love, and allowed no consideration for the weak. In the end there would then have been new ordinances perhaps less compatible with the gospel than the laws of the pope. The devil is sly: he wants to be either on the right side or on the left. But the gospel wants to proceed along the correct path freely, unencumbered with any ordinance. It wills to be lord over all ordinances, and have the right to observe now this one, now that one. Such liberty, however, cannot be brought speedily to the rank and file of people. Would to God that even the most intelligent comprehended it.

The fifth step is this. I wish, and it ought to be so, that no

[18] The more radical, hasty, forcible introduction of both kinds was enjoined and to a considerable extent effected by Karlstadt, Zwilling and the Zwickau prophets. Cf. the Introduction, p. 233; also p. 129.

mass at all would be celebrated except at such times as the people were present who really desired the sacrament and asked for it, and that this would be only once a week or once a month. For the sacrament should never be celebrated except at the instigation and request of hungry souls, never because of duty, endowment, custom, ordinance, or habit. But it is still too early to begin this practice, because the consciences of the people will not follow me until it has been preached and understood better.

In the meantime I can only advise the chaplains and priests who are under obligation to say masses that they do it as a service of love to the poor misguided consciences; but at the same time that they drop some of the masses, and so quietly in the course of time bring about a change, to the extent that that is possible and they can accomplish it. And I advise them to preach on the subject with confidence, so that such masses may be done away with primarily through the power of the Word.

Some will say: But how then will we care for the sick? Answer: I shall continue to allow the practice of reserving the sacrament for the sick in pyxes; but if the proper use of the mass were to come into general acceptance simply through a clear understanding of the gospel, people would realize that the elements of the sacrament at the time of death are not essential. Since the words of the sacrament are present, on which its power entirely depends, it is enough that a person should receive the elements while he is healthy, and not despise them when he is dying. The papists have made the sacraments so indispensable for dying people, yet they have passed over in silence the words which alone are really indispensable.

The sixth step. The private masses, performed as sacrifices or good works, have been and are to be abolished. On this subject I have written enough in Latin.[19] However, since nobody is to be forced to believe, one should not drag priests away from the altar if they want to hold such masses, but let them answer for it before God. It is enough to preach against such masses and tell the people not to contribute to them and not to endow them or have them

[19] *De abroganda missa privata Martini Lutheri sententia* (1521). *WA* 8, 411-476.

said. Through such preaching they will probably in course of time disappear of their own accord.

The seventh step. I have taught that private confession is not to be required. But neither is it to be prohibited, as I have taught in my little book, "On Confession." [20] This is still my position. For everything that is evangelical or Christian, everything that has to do with faith, should be free, so that people press toward it of their own accord out of love and real desire for it, without law or compulsion. Therefore, if somebody does not like to make confession, let him just steer clear of it. Let him tread underfoot the ordinances of pope, princes and devil, and be content with his private confession before God. But, even though I do not insist upon it, yet I do advise that you make confession gladly before you go to the sacrament, or at least that you do not despise confession. For although the absolution is present in the words of the mass, which is primary, nevertheless you should not for that reason despise the other absolution in the confession. God has given us his absolution richly and in various ways, and no one of them is to be despised for the sake of the others.

For instance, he put an absolution in the Lord's Prayer, that our sins will be forgiven if we forgive our neighbors [Matt. 6:12, 14]. You should not despise that absolution or on that account neglect the Lord's Prayer, simply because there is also an absolution in the mass. Likewise in Ps. 32 [:5] he placed an absolution in the private confession before God, when he says: "I said, 'I will confess my transgressions,' and thou didst forgive the guilt of my sin." This absolution too you should not despise because of the one that is contained in the words of the mass. Moreover, in Matt. 18 [:18] he gives the absolution to all Christians, and says: "Whatever you loose on earth shall be loosed in heaven"; and later: "If two of you agree on earth about anything they ask, it will be done for them" [Matt. 18:19]. So do not despise any absolution that God sets up, whether public or private; the more you have of God's Word the better it is.

The eighth step. Some people have treated the images shamefully, without the knowledge or consent of their rulers and

[20] *Von der Beicht, ob die der Papst macht habe zu gepieten* (1521), especially Part Three. *WA* 8, 164-185.

teachers.[21] They really deserve a stiff punishment. But let Satan be Satan; we will address ourselves to the main subject. To have images is not wrong. God himself in the Old Testament commanded the bronze serpent to be lifted up [Num. 21:8-9], and the cherubim to be placed on the golden ark [Exod. 25:18]. But the worship of images God has forbidden [Exod. 20:5]. It is true that they are dangerous, and I wish there were none of them on the altars. But we cannot prove it right to mutilate and burn them instead of tolerating them. I shall give you my reason for saying this:

The devil and his papists want to appear quite nice, and to have done nothing wrong. Now if you argue that images are being greatly misused and therefore we should have none of them but should mutilate and burn them, they will say: We do not misuse them. And how will you refute them? They will point out that women and wine are also dangerous things and are being misused, and what is there that is not being misused? They will say that you have slandered not the misuse, however, but the images themselves, which could conceivably be used in a proper way. What will you say to this? You see, in this way they will have caught you. And if they break off a single leaf they will claim to have won the entire forest, for they are hungry and watching closely for each opportunity.

So we must be wise in our struggle with the pretty devil. We must permit the images to remain, but preach vigorously against the wrong use of them. We must preach not merely against this particular misuse or danger, the worshiping of images. That is a very small matter. (And they would probably say you are crazy to accuse people of worshiping stone and wood.) But we must preach against the worst misuse of all, of which the papists are guilty to overflowing. I refer to the fact that they place images in the churches because they think they are thereby doing a good work and a service to God. Of course none of them would acknowledge such disbelief, even though it must be present in the heart where real Christian faith is lacking. You see, with a word like that you have quickly done more damage to the images than all the world can do with rifles and swords. When the common man learns that it is not a service to God to place images in the churches, he will

[21] Cf. Introduction, p. 233.

cease doing it of his own accord without your insistence. He will have pictures painted on the walls only because he likes them or for decoration or some other reason that does not involve sin. How did we ever get into this predicament, that men should forbid us to do what God has not forbidden, particularly they who are struggling against human teachings and ordinances?

The ninth step. That priests should marry, and monks and nuns be free to leave their orders, also offends the papists greatly and arouses their wrath beyond measure. That does not matter. I have said above,[22] where one can yield to weak consciences one should do so, in order not to throw them into confusion; but only insofar as it can be done without injury to the things that are essential. For example, that the mass is not an offering or a good work is a previously unheard-of idea, very offensive; but one must not for that reason give it up, no matter who takes offense, whether strong or weak consciences. When Christ was preached, it was also offensive to everybody. Should one for that reason keep quiet about him? Likewise, that it is the devil who has forbidden the marriage of priests and has set up monastic orders is incontrovertibly proved by St. Paul in I Tim. 4 [:3]. Therefore we should and must acknowledge that God has left them free to marry, and they cannot be bound by any vow contrary to God's Word, nor obligated to the teachings of the devil.

He who can restrain himself does well to remain unmarried, but one who cannot is not under obligation to remain unmarried [I Cor. 7:8-9, 36-38]. For he is not supposed to serve his neighbor with a kind of love that condemns the neighbor and destroys his own soul. On the contrary, other people are in duty bound not to take offense at him if he does marry. Necessity knows no law; necessity knows no disgrace; necessity knows no dishonor; necessity knows no offense.[23] If the reception of both kinds were a matter of such necessity, we should pay no attention to the matter of offense or to weak consciences.

It is true, I fear, that there will be some who will get married or leave the orders not out of Christian motivation but because they are glad to have found in evangelical freedom a basis and

---

[22] Cf. p. 253.

[23] *Sprichwörter-Lexikon, op. cit.*, III, 1051, 1053. Cf. p. 255 n. 17.

pretext for their rascality [I Pet. 2:16]. Can we help that? The pope's regulations about chastity have hardly produced a single priest in a thousand who has observed chastity in public, not to speak of the unchastity that is practiced in private. Is it any wonder, then, that some do not make proper use of our gospel? Well, there are gallows and wheels and swords and water; one can easily restrain any evildoer.

Take care what kind of priests get married and what kind of monks or nuns try to leave. They should make the break with a strong conscience so that when they come to die they will be able to stand firmly before the devil. It does not matter that the ignorant and crazy papists murmur against it. But the devil will belabor you in masterly fashion with your vow and force you to confession. He will make your marriage and your liberty to be sin, unless you are thoroughly equipped with the Word of God and can depend upon it and despise him. Therefore, take to heart the saying of Paul in I Tim. 4 [:1-3], where he calls it lies and the doctrines of the devil. You will need this saying. And put your confidence in it, that these are the words of God, who cannot lie. Read well my little book on vows[24] and gird yourself as best you can. It is nothing less than the flagrant murder of souls that the devil has brought to pass through the prohibitions of the pope. By them human souls have been so sorely debilitated that it is very difficult to gird them against such devil's vows.

The tenth step. That men are free to eat eggs and fish and meat every day of the year, and that neither the pope nor the church has the right to set restrictions on certain days or certain foods, is surely true, as is clear from the words of St. Paul in I Tim. 4 [:3]: "forbidding marriage and enjoining abstinence from foods." Since this is a matter in which one may well spare those of weak conscience, however, and since there is no need of propagating it among the simple people who do not yet know of it, I am not sorry that the regulations on abstinence have suffered quite a setback. The papists use this liberty to abstain in a purely arbitrary and wanton manner, against the interests of the simple people and without any improvement in body or soul. Yet in other matters they do not so much as move a finger [Matt. 23:4] to improve Christian

[24] *De votis monasticis Martini Lutheri iudicium.* *WA* 8, 573-669.

conduct, thus making the gospel and the good name of the Christians a subject of scandalous talk, so that people say: Look, they can eat meat on Fridays; how can they be Christians? Well, they did not learn this from us, and yet we must bear the burden of their wrongdoing. Christ will catch up with them some time and rescue his good name from their defamation of it.

What we have taught and intended was to free the consciences of men from the impositions of the devil, who through the pope has laid restrictions on foods and days, on pain of mortal sin and of hell. Now if we have set human consciences free, we should also use them wisely and subject them in service to their neighbor, that we may bring him also to that same freedom of conscience. So, go ahead, stupid, hit the simple people on the head, so they will yell back and say: Look here, I can devour meat, but you, dear pig, you must devour something else.

In short, it is irksome to God and to men that we begin our Christian life with external matters and pass over that which is really inward. We try to prove ourselves evangelical by receiving the sacrament in both kinds and in our own hands, by pulling down images, by devouring meat, by abstaining from prayer and fasting, and that sort of thing. But nobody will lay hold of faith and love, which alone are essential, and in which alone there is any power. Not one of those externals is necessary. But this emphasis upon externals is an enticement of the devil which he uses to mislead the people, so that they leave the pope and yet do not come to Christ. They are neither papist nor Christian, but continue to hang on to external things as much as the papists do.

I have taught in such a way that my teaching would lead first and foremost to a knowledge of Christ, that is, to pure and proper faith and genuine love, and thereby to freedom in all matters of external conduct such as eating, drinking, clothes, praying, fasting, monasteries, sacrament, and whatever it may be. Such freedom is had and is used in a salvatory way only by those who have faith and love, that is, those who are real Christians. On such people we can and should impose no human law—nor permit anyone else to do so—which would bind their conscience. But always we must first have the people who are supposed to possess such liberty, that the wine may be stored and kept in new vessels [Matt. 9:17].

So the rabble plunges in and tries in headstrong fashion to establish such freedom with their fists, not remembering that they are supposed to exercise faith and love. They remain as full as ever of greed, hatred, unchastity, wrath, swearing, and cursing. Let me say emphatically, I do not recognize such people as disciples of Christ. Christian people fight against the devil's work and teaching only with the Word. First they tear hearts and consciences from his grip; then everything else takes care of itself. The apostles never tore down altars among the pagans. St. Paul travelled in a ship that carried as its figurehead the idols called the Twin Brothers,[25] but he did not tear to pieces either the figurehead or the ship. I too have denounced vigorously the idolatry of the pope, more vigorously perhaps than anyone else; but I have never yet laid hands on it, nor asked anyone else to do so except those who have the authority and the power from God. We have done more than enough if we preach against it and set consciences free. We may leave it to God to effect the deed. For it is written in Dan. 8 [:25] that the Antichrist shall be destroyed by no human hand, but by the breath of the mouth of our Lord Jesus [II Thess. 2:8].

Therefore, I ask again that all Christians take my advice concerning the sacrament and all other things. First, since Satan through the ordinance of the pope has thrown the sacrament before swine [Matt. 7:6] by compelling everybody to partake of the sacrament at Easter,[26] whether they believe or not, whether they love or not, and since he has also concealed from them the words of the sacrament, on which faith must depend and nourish itself, let us therefore labor first to raise the sacrament above the level of the swine. We do this, however, only as we dissuade and keep the people from it by teaching and exhortation, so that no one goes to the sacrament out of compulsion by, or obedience to, the pope's ordinance. For the sacrament does not admit of people being compelled or driven to it. Rather, instructed by the gospel, people should request and insist upon it of their own accord, because they are driven by the hunger of their believing hearts.

Second. Now anyone who thinks he has this kind of hunger

---

[25] Acts 28:11. According to Greek and Roman mythology, Castor and Pollux were the guardian deities of sailors.

[26] Cf. p. 249 n. 12.

should see to it that he does not deceive himself. He should make sure that it is no mere desire of the human flesh that prompts him. He should examine his faith and determine whether it is genuine, as St. Paul admonishes in I Cor. 11 [:28]: "Let a man examine himself." This examination, however, covers your whole life. You must find within yourself a smiting conscience which is weighed down with a sense of sin and longs for the grace of God, a conscience that stands in dread of death or hell and longs for strength, a conscience that seeks and takes the sacrament, firmly relying on Christ's word, in order to receive such grace and strength and help. For as I have said, this sacrament requires a hungry, thirsty, oppressed, and anxious soul, that comes of its own accord, conscious of its own need and thirst, with utter confidence, and without regard to the pope's laws or lawlessness. That is the proof of faith; it is an inward matter.

Third. Direct the examination also to your outward life and ask yourself whether you are showing love to your neighbor and are serving him. If you do not find these evidences of faith within yourself, if you are living the same as before, still packed full of unfaithfulness, hatred, envy, wrath, and unbelief, then, dear friend, by all means stay away from the sacrament until you have become a different person. Don't let yourself be driven to it by crowd or custom or the ordinance of the pope. Heavens, if this idea were really put across, it would mean that where thousands come to the sacrament now, scarcely hundreds would come. In this way we would diminish the abominable sins with which the pope has flooded the world through his hellish ordinance, and so we would at last become again a group of real Christians, whereas at present we are almost completely pagan and only Christian in name. Then we should be able to do what is now impossible for us, namely, separate from our number those in whom we see by their works that they have neither faith nor love.

Alas, we are still far from Jerusalem; we have scarcely begun to break out of our captivity in Babylon,[27] and yet we want to act as if we had already arrived at home. Everyone wants to be called Christian, and we have to permit it; but then they do not want to exercise faith and love. Creating sects does not help matters. So

[27] Cf. the first treatise in this volume, especially pp. 12, 17, and 18; also p. 250.

there is nothing else to do but to preach the gospel and to keep people away from the sacrament and all external rites until they feel and show themselves to be Christians and of their own accord press forward first to faith, to love, and then to the external sacrament and things like that. In the meantime we have to let matters take their course. We are in captivity at Babylon, and our enemies are sitting within the temple and using our sacrament and all our possessions. We can only cry out in lamentation as Jeremiah does and in Ps. 137 and pray God to help us to return to our own. Amen.

Finally, I see that I must add a good word of admonition to those whom Satan has now begun to persecute. For there are some among them who think that when they are attacked they can escape the danger by saying: I do not hold with Luther or with anyone else, but only with the holy gospel[28] and the holy church, or with the Roman church. For saying so they think they will be left in peace. Yet in their hearts they regard my teaching as the teaching of the gospel and stand by it. In reality this kind of statement does not help them, and it is in effect a denial of Christ. Therefore, I beg such people to be very careful.

True, by any consideration of body or soul you should never say: I am Lutheran,[29] or Papist. For neither of them died for you, or is your master. Christ alone died for you, he alone is your master, and you should confess yourself a Christian. But if you are convinced that Luther's teaching is in accord with the gospel and that the pope's is not, then you should not discard Luther so completely, lest with him you discard also his teaching, which you nevertheless recognize as Christ's teaching. You should rather say: Whether Luther is a rascal or a saint I do not care; his teaching is not his, but Christ's.

---

[28] Luther regarded the self-styled "Evangelicals" as cowards, the self-styled "Lutherans" as rowdies. *CL* 2, 333 n. 19. Cf. *An Earnest Exhortation for all Christians, Warning Them Against Insurrection and Rebellion* (1522). *PE* 3, 218.

[29] By this time, in 1522, the word *lutherisch* was already in extensive use, not only as a possessive adjective and a predicate adjective, but even in the form of a substantive as the name of a new religious party. It was used first and most particularly by Luther's enemies, but also by his friends (despite his repudiation of it) and by the population generally. Cf. Alfred Goetze, *Lutherisch; "Zeitschrift für deutsche Wortforschung"* III, 183-198.

For you will observe that the tyrants are not out merely to destroy Luther, but to wipe out the teaching. It is on account of the teaching that they attack you and ask you whether you are Lutheran. Here you must be sure not to speak with slippery or evasive words but frankly to confess Christ, no matter who did the preaching—Luther, or Tom, Dick, or Harry. The person you can forget; but the teaching you must confess. Paul also writes thus to Timothy in II Tim. 1 [:8]: "Do not be ashamed then of testifying to our Lord, nor of me, a prisoner for his sake." If it had been enough here for Timothy to confess the gospel, Paul would not have commanded him not to be ashamed also of Paul—not of Paul as a person but of Paul as a prisoner for the sake of the gospel. Now if Timothy had said, I do not hold with Paul or with Peter, but with Christ, when he knew that Peter and Paul were teaching Christ, then he would actually thereby have denied Christ himself. For Christ says in Matt. 10[30] concerning those who preach him: "He who receives you receives me, and he who rejects you rejects me." Why this? Because holding thus with his messengers, those who bring his word, is the same as holding with Christ himself and with his word.

Moreover, let each one see to it that he does not forget to love his enemies, pray for those who persecute him and revile him, and not seek revenge, as Christ teaches in Matt. 6.[31] For these miserable people have already been so terribly punished, and we, I am sorry to say, avenged at such a terrible price, that the time has come for us to plead with God for them, that we may avert the punishment and judgment that is coming upon them—as Christ did for us when in our blindness we too were committing sin. You see how terribly hardened they are in their blindness. They will not listen to us, nor give us a hearing. Neither will they answer, or let us hear from them. Instead they are like the Jews with St. Stephen [Acts 7:57]: they close their eyes and stop their ears, and shamelessly execute their sentence without knowing what they are doing. If you are a Christian you should observe carefully what wrath that brings upon them, what torment and punishment, and therefore how you should intercede for them with God. They act just like the possessed and madmen who say: We shall deal with God so harmfully and

[30] Luther here combines quotations from Matt. 10:40 and Luke 10:16.
[31] Matt. 5:44, 39; Luke 6:27-29.

insolently that he will have to beat us over the head at once. Be assured, they will not continue their madness very long. Just wait a while, and let it suffice that your God makes you this promise: He who touches you touches the apple of my eye [Zech. 2:8]. Help therefore to pray for them. And even if we are not able to save them, let us pray that God may not because of their tyranny and blasphemy take his Word away from the whole German nation, and deprive all the other poor people who really long for it. May God's grace and strength be with you all. Amen.

THE ADORATION OF THE SACRAMENT

1523

Translated by Abdel Ross Wentz

INTRODUCTION

This treatise was published near the end of April, 1523. It was written to clarify a point some people had raised in the light of Luther's rejection of transubstantiation in *The Babylonian Captivity of the Church.* Luther himself did not consider the point very important. But the discussion that followed the publication of that treatise of 1520 indicated that his friends were perplexed and that an explicit statement on his part was called for. In addition, contacts with the Bohemian Brethren, both directly and by correspondence, prompted Luther to speak out on this subject.

The dissertation is addressed to the Bohemian Brethren, whom Luther commonly called Waldenses or Picards. He knew them largely through a catechism which they had published and which came to his attention in 1520 in Bohemian (or Latin) and again in 1523 in Bohemian and German. Luther was not pleased with some of the things he found in the catechism, because they seemed to point in the direction of the radical views with which he had now begun to contend at home. This was true especially of the implications of the catechism concerning the presence of Christ's body in the Lord's Supper, specifically the adoration of the sacrament. The German editions of the catechism dealt in different ways with this matter of adoring the sacrament: some favored it, as Luther did; some rejected it, as did the Brethren; and some ignored it. This irritated Luther and led him to seek more definite information about the position of the Brethren on the matter. But Luther had heard many good things about the Brethren. On the question of the Lord's Supper he was convinced that they were in quite a different class from Karlstadt and the Swiss theologians, and he felt that if they deviated from him somewhat in their teaching about the adoration of the sacrament it would not be too serious a matter, for he no longer regarded it as heresy to refuse such adoration.

But then the subject was forced upon his attention from another source. In wide circles people were reaching the conclusion from *The Babylonian Captivity of the Church* that Luther himself meant to teach that it is not necessary to honor or adore the sacrament. It is possible that some of Luther's opponents were helping to promote this mistaken interpretation in order to discredit Luther as a radical. Luther's friend, Margrave Frederick of Brandenburg, wrote to Luther from Prague in Bohemia, on January 5, 1523, and informed him that people were under the impression he opposed the adoration of the sacrament as a matter of principle. It was clear that many people were waiting for a definite statement from Luther on this point.

In the meantime Paul Speratus, who had been called as an evangelical pastor to Iglau in Moravia, had sent reports to Luther concerning the Brethren and had requested his opinion concerning some of their teachings. He raised specifically the question whether the sacrament on the altar was to be adored, and he reported that the Brethren were opposed to the practice. Speratus also reported that, in his judgment, the Brethren did not hold to the real presence. Luther's first reply to Speratus was dated May 16, 1522. A month later he wrote Speratus again, this time in answer to a series of questions that some of the Brethren, not officially but as individuals, had brought to him in Wittenberg.

Luther desired, however, a more official statement from the Brethren about their teaching, and for that purpose he entered into correspondence with their Senior Lucas. About the middle of December, 1522, an official delegation from Senior Lucas visited Luther in Wittenberg. He also received several official documents that were calculated to clarify the position of the Brethren concerning the sacrament. Among them was the *Apologia* which Luther mentions at the end of the third paragraph of the treatise. From these documents, especially the *Apologia*, and from the delegation, Luther got the clear impression that the Bohemian Brethren, unlike Karlstadt and Zwingli, held that the Lord's Supper is not essentially a religious transaction on the part of the human worshiper but a sacrament in which the communicant receives an objective gift from God. This gratified Luther but he continued to have some misgivings about their interpretation of the Words of Institution and the matter of the real presence. At any rate, the Brethren seemed to him to be sorely in need of instruction, and he was impelled to publish a more complete answer to their questions than his letters to Speratus had provided.

On January 4, 1523, while the deputation of the Brethren was still on Wittenberg, and before receiving the letter from Margrave George, Luther preached on the subject, "Concerning the Adoration of the Sacrament." Perhaps the Bohemian deputation was a part of his congregation as he preached. This sermon became the basis for our treatise, just as the "Eight Sermons" in 1522 had become the basis for the document, *Receiving Both Kinds in the Sacrament*. But before the sermon was sent to the printer Luther added a number of things because of the letter dated January 5 he had received in the meantime from the Margrave. In these added portions of the treatise he uses sharper tones than in the portions that are addressed directly to the Bohemian Brethren, for he had begun to sense that his view of Christ's presence in the Lord's Supper was meeting vigorous opposition from the Swiss.

These circumstances account for the variation in the form of the treatise. The title and the first three paragraphs are a direct address to the Bohemian Brethren. Then follows a portion in which the second person singular is used, as though addressed to a congregation or to Senior Lucas individually. Then the second half of the treatise, the discussion of the specific topic, "The Adoration of the Sacrament," has the tone of a dissertation, and the conclusion returns to the form of a message to a congregation. Luther's mild tone in addressing the Brethren is in striking contrast to the sharp tone he used with Karlstadt and the Zwinglians. That Luther published the treatise in German rather than Latin seems to indicate that he had in mind a larger audience in Germany than among the Bohemian Brethren.

The Brethren made a Czech translation of Luther's treatise. Then under date of September 16, 1523, an answer from Senior Lucas was published by authority of the elders. There followed further correspondence and another deputation to Wittenberg in 1524. Luther gradually came into the clear about the teachings of the Brethren and continued to deal with them in friendly tones. But the Brethren took offense at some of the things they heard from Wittenberg, and the friendly relationship was suspended for a number of years. It was not renewed until 1533. In the meantime

Luther expressed to others the same idea set forth to the Brethren, namely, that the adoration of the sacrament is a matter of indifference and should be left to the individual.

Our translation was made from the German text in *WA* 11, 431-456.

THE ADORATION OF THE SACRAMENT

The Adoration of the Sacrament of the Holy Body of Christ

To my dear sirs and friends, the Brethren who are called Walden sians in Bohemia and Moravia: grace and peace in Christ.

There has come from your midst a little book[1] in German and Bohemian, "Christian Instruction for Young Children," in which among other things it is stated that in the sacrament Christ is not present substantially and naturally, and that he is not there to be adored. This is a matter of real concern to us Germans. For you doubtless know that through your messengers to me I requested that you would prepare a special treatise to clarify this article of faith. For I heard your messengers[2] testify verbally that you unanimously hold that Christ is truly present in the sacrament with his flesh and blood as it was born of Mary and hung on the holy cross, just as we Germans believe.

Now a little book in Latin[3] has been sent to me by Mr. Lucas,

---

[1] The reference is probably to the Waldensian catechism, *Ein christliche Unterweisung der klaynen Kinder jm Glauben durch ein weyss einer Frag.* This "little book" was written by Senior Lucas in 1502 in Bohemian, but it first came to Luther's attention in 1520, probably in Bohemian (or Latin), and then in 1523 in both Bohemian and German. Cf. *WA* 11, 417-418; and Joseph Müller, *Die Deutschen Katechismen der Böhmischen Brüder* (Berlin, 1887), pp. 29 and 49.

[2] In the summer of 1522 Luther was visited in Wittenberg by members of the Bohemian Brethren (Johann Horn and Michael Weiss) who discussed with him this question of adoring the sacrament. Luther learned that his visitors were not official representatives of the Brethren, and he therefore asked them to have the leaders of the Brethren send him "a special treatise" on the matter so that he would know their official position, and he promised to translate it into German. *WA* 11, 418.

[3] This was probably the Latin confession, title unknown, which Lucas afterwards published in German under the title *Von der siegreichen Wahrheit.* Cf. Müller, *op. cit.*, p. 30; and *WA* 11, 418.

but in this matter of the sacrament it is not so clear and unambiguous as I could have wished. For that reason I have not had it translated or published as I had promised, because I am afraid that I should not render correctly some of the obscure words and so not do justice to your meaning. For I have found in my translating that it takes luck to make a precise rendering even when the original is perfectly clear and certain. So, in order to bring the matter to a conclusion and to silence the offense occasioned by the little book which you published in German,[4] I shall set forth this article, for you and for everybody, just as clearly as I possibly can, as we Germans believe it, and as it must be believed according to the gospel. In what I write it will be possible for you to discover whether I have stated your faith correctly, or how far apart we are from each other—in the event that my German is perhaps clearer to you than your German and Latin is to me.

I also asked of your messengers whether there were other matters in which you did not agree with us, in order that your people should not for that reason harbor animosity against us, nor we against you, but that each party should in brotherly fashion advise the other to see whether we may reach a common mind. It is true that I once called you heretics,[5] while I was still a papist; but now I think differently. However, I shall now tell you what pleases me about you and wherein I think you are lacking. What our faith is you can learn from Philip Melanchthon's little book,[6] in which all the principles and main articles of our faith are summarized and proved on the basis of Scripture, just as you have done in your first *Apologia*.[7] But I suppose you will find some

[4] This is the same book as that referred to above, p. 275 n. 1.

[5] As late as 1520, in his *Verklärung D. Martin Luthers etlicher Artikel in seinem Sermon von dem heiligen Sakrament,* Luther distinguished between three parties among the Bohemians, the first of which—the *Pigharten*—he explicitly called heretics, not because they received communion in both kinds, but because among other things they did not believe that Christ's flesh and blood is truly present in the sacrament. *WA* 6, 80.

[6] The reference is to the *Adversus Furiosum Parisiensium Theologastrorum Decretum, Phillipi Melanchthonis Pro Luthero Apologia* (1521). *C.R.* 1, 398-416.

[7] Luther received an *Apologia* from the Brethren at the same time he received the Latin confession. This may have been his second copy of it, however—his "first" having possibly come earlier from Speratus. Since no German or Latin printed publication of such an *Apologia* from the 1520's is known, Luther's copy (or copies) was probably a handwritten manuscript. *WA* 11, 419.

things lacking in the *Apologia* of our Philip, just as we find some things lacking in your *Apologia*.

In the first place, we have often said that the chief and foremost thing in the sacrament is the word of Christ, when he says: "*Take and eat, this is my body which is given for you.*" Likewise also, when he took the cup, he said: "*Take and drink of it, all of you, this is the cup of a new testament in my blood which is shed for you for the forgiveness of sins. As often as you do this, do it in remembrance of me.*"[8]

Everything depends on these words. Every Christian should and must know them and hold them fast. He must never let anyone take them away from him by any other kind of teaching, even though it were an angel from heaven [Gal. 1:8]. They are words of life and of salvation, so that whoever believes in them has all his sins forgiven through that faith; he is a child of life and has overcome death and hell. Language cannot express how great and mighty these words are, for they are the sum and substance of the whole gospel. This is why these words are far more important than the sacrament itself, and a Christian should make it a practice to give far more attention to these words than to the sacrament. But as a matter of fact the situation everywhere is just the reverse of this because of the false teachers. They have depreciated these words in the eyes of the people, hidden them securely besides, and called attention only to the sacrament. The result is that faith has been lost and the sacrament has been turned into a purely external work devoid of faith.

Now, in accord with this distinction between the words and the sacrament, and in view of the greater worth of the words, one must also measure the honor that is to be bestowed on the sacrament. If you accord less honor to the words than to the sacrament itself, it is a sure sign that you do not properly understand the sacrament. For example, if you bow or kneel before the sacrament, and do not do so even much more before the words of the sacrament, especially in your heart, you are really inverting the honors. For that reason it is highly important to lead the people back from the sacrament to the words, and to accustom them to pay much more attention to the words than to the sacrament; then it would be

[8] Cf. p. 37 n. 84.

easy to preach about honoring the sacrament. But where this is not the case, no other kind of preaching will help; there will continue to be nothing but an outward dissembling with respect to the sacrament, with bowing, bending, kneeling, and adoring, but without any spirit or faith.

But the honor which is to be accorded the Word is of two kinds. One kind is external, as when a person writes [its] words with big, beautiful, glowing gold or silver letters, lays it away in beautiful silk cloths, and carefully preserves it. It is external honor also when one cries them aloud and sings them in stately fashion—or out of respect keeps them secret, the un-Christian practice that formerly prevailed. But God and his Word do not care about such childish external honor.

The proper way to honor the Word is to fix it in your heart. The heart is its real gilded ciborium. You accord the Word more precious honor with your heart, than if you were to build a ciborium for the sacrament out of pure gold or the most costly jewels. For it is certainly true that you can have life, righteousness, and salvation without the sacrament, but you cannot have life, righteousness, and salvation without the Word, even though you were to receive the sacrament not only three times a day (as the priests do at Christmas)[9] but even three times an hour.

Now when I say that you should fix the Word of God in your heart I do not mean merely that you should know it and meditate on it. That is nothing. I mean rather that you should regard and esteem it as it ought to be regarded and esteemed. That is, you should hold it to be a living, eternal, all-powerful Word that can make you alive, free from sin and death, and keep you so eternally; that brings with it everything of which it speaks, namely, Christ with his flesh and blood and everything that he is and has. For it is the kind of Word that can and does do all these things, and therefore it should be so regarded. That is its own proper honor. It is not satisfied with any other kind of honor. In short, the proper honor for the Word is nothing else than a genuine faith from the

[9] The number of times a priest was to celebrate mass in any given day was variously prescribed in various periods. Permission to celebrate three times on Christmas had already been attested by Walafrid Strabo (*circa* 808-849). Georg Rietschel, *Lehrbuch der Liturgik* (Berlin, 1900), I, 352.

bottom of one's heart, a faith that holds the Word to be true, that trusts it and stakes its life upon it for eternity.

That is what we have believed and still believe about this sacrament. But in order that we may better understand and grasp it, let us treat the matter more fully and show how so many wanton spirits have taken offense at it. In this way we will see how impossible it is to stay on the right track when the Word is not held in the highest esteem and when faith in it is not exercised.

In the first place, there have been some who have held[10] that in the sacrament there is merely bread and wine, such as people otherwise eat and drink. They have taught nothing more than that the bread signifies the body and the wine signifies the blood of Christ, just as if one were to take a figure from the Old Testament and say: the bread from heaven which the Jews ate in the wilderness *signifies* the body of Christ or the gospel, but the bread from heaven *is* not the gospel or the body of Christ.[11] It is as if I should say of baptism: baptism is a washing of the soul; that is, baptism does not actually wash the soul but merely signifies the washing whereby the soul is washed with the Word of God in faith. Those who teach this view have accorded similar honor to the sacrament by saying: the body of Christ is not there; it merely signifies the body like a symbol.

Now beware of such a view. Let go of reason and intellect; for they strive in vain to understand how flesh and blood can be present, and because they do not grasp it they refuse to believe it. Lay hold on the word which Christ speaks: "Take, this is my body, this is my blood." One must not do such violence to the words of God as to give to any word a meaning other than its natural one, unless there is clear and definite Scripture to do that. This is what is done by those who without any basis in Scripture take the word "is" and forcibly twist it to mean the same as the word "signifies." They sneer at Christ's statement: "This is my body," and say it is equivalent to: "This signifies my body," and so forth. But we should and will simply stick to the words of Christ—he will not deceive us—

[10] Luther is referring to the position of the Dutch jurist, Cornelius Honius (d. 1524 at The Hague), one of the earliest of the *Significatisten*. *WA* 11, 420.
[11] Italics here and on the following pages have been supplied by the editor for purposes of clarity.

and repel this error with no other sword than the fact that Christ does not say: "This signifies my body," but "This is my body."

For if we permit such violence to be done in one passage, that without any basis in Scripture a person can say the word "is" means the same as the word "signifies," then it would be impossible to stop it in any other passage. The entire Scripture would be nullified, since there would be no good reason why such violence should be valid in one passage but not in all passages. In that case one could say: That Mary is a virgin and the mother of God is equivalent to saying that Mary signifies a virgin and the mother of God. Likewise: Christ is God and man; that is, Christ signifies God and man. Likewise Rom. 1 [:16]: the gospel is the power of God and so forth; that is, the gospel signifies the power of God. See what a horrible mess this would lead to. Therefore, since such violence cannot be allowed in other passages of Scripture, it cannot be allowed here either, that Christ's body is signified by the bread; because the words stand there clear, unadorned, and plain: "This is my body"—unless one can adduce clear and definite passages to prove that the word "is" should mean "signifies."

But they may quote the passage in I Cor. 10 [:4], where Paul says: "They all drank the same spiritual drink; for they drank from the spiritual Rock which followed them, and the Rock was Christ." And they may argue: Paul here says Christ was the Rock even though it is clear that Moses struck a physical rock from which they drank [Exod. 17:6]; if then it can be said in this passage that the Rock *is* Christ (which surely can mean nothing else than that the rock *signifies* Christ, because Christ cannot be a natural rock) it can also be said here that this bread *signifies* my body, where the text says: "This *is* my body."

If they argue in that way, one should answer that their reasoning contains two great fallacies. The first is that what they attribute to the statement in St. Paul is not true. St. Paul does not say that the rock which Moses struck is Christ. His words say very plainly: They ate of the same spiritual food of which we eat, and they drank of the same spiritual drink of which we drink, and so forth. Now we certainly do not eat the physical bread from heaven and neither do we drink of the natural rock of which the Jews ate and drank in the wilderness. On the contrary, it is the spiritual bread from heaven and the spiritual rock which are identical for both them and us. Paul makes this clear himself later on when he says: "They drank from the spiritual Rock which followed them, which Rock was Christ" [I Cor. 10:4], as much as to say: "I am not speaking of the physical rock but of the spiritual Rock who had yet to come, and by this expression I mean Christ; he is the true Rock, of whom they have eaten as well as we, because they too have believed in him as well as we."

So you see, they have been wrong in citing Paul's statement on behalf of their error. For it is true that St. Paul says: "Christ was the Rock." He does not say that Christ is *signified* by, but that Christ himself actually *is*, the spiritual Rock—the one signified by that physical rock. That is why Paul was careful to add the word "spiritual" to the word "Rock," so that no one could ever construe it to mean that physical rock. Moreover, he says it was a Rock which was yet to come, from which they drank spiritually; this too cannot be construed to mean the rock in the wilderness. Still it has not helped that St. Paul speaks so clearly and specifically about the spiritual Rock. That is the rock of which the Lord says in Matt. 16 [:18]: "On this rock I will build my church." Now certainly the Christian church cannot be built on a physical rock, but upon Christ himself through the gospel. There it will prevail against all the gates and powers of hell.

The second fallacy in their reasoning is this: Even if they had demonstrated that in this passage of St. Paul or anywhere else the word "is" means the same as "signifies" (which they nevertheless cannot do), they still would not have proved anything. For if one does find that a word has a particular meaning in one passage, that is no reason arbitrarily to impose that same meaning on the word in all other passages. For example, the fact that Christ in Matt. 16 [:18] calls himself a rock would be no warrant for me, every time I find a rock in the Scriptures, to make Christ out of it. Again, it is not proper, merely because Moses struck a rock in the wilderness [Exod. 17:6], for me to make a physical rock out of the rock in Matt. 16 [:18]. How then should one proceed?

One should proceed thus: Every single word should be permitted to stand in its natural meaning; no deviation should be allowed unless faith compels it. Thus the word "rock" in Matt. 16

[:18] I ought to let stand in its natural meaning, that it denotes a physical rock. But faith will not permit that; it forces me away from such a natural meaning and compels me to understand a spiritual Rock. For faith will not permit me to build Christendom upon a physical rock. Therefore when I say in this passage: "Christ is the Rock," the word "is" cannot mean the same as "Christ is *signified* by the rock." It must mean he himself actually *is* the Rock. Furthermore, when I refer to Moses' rock in the wilderness [I Cor. 10:4] and say: "Christ is the physical rock in the wilderness," here faith compels me to understand the word "is" as "signifies," so that it means: "Christ is signified by the physical rock of Moses." For faith does not permit us to hold that Christ, who is a person, is a natural stone.

Likewise with reference to the sacrament. If they want to say that the bread *is* not Christ's body but merely *signifies* it, they should indicate wherein it is contrary to faith for the bread to be the body of Christ and the wine to be his blood. For we also find the same kind of twofold existence in the world of nature. We say properly concerning a red-hot iron: "The iron is fire, and the fire is iron." We do not say: "The fire signifies iron, and the iron signifies fire." In the same way we say also concerning Christ: "The man is God, and God is the man," and not "God signifies the man, or the man signifies God." Since therefore faith permits it and nowhere contradicts it, that the bread is the body of Christ, one should let the word "is" stand in its own natural meaning, and under no circumstances retreat from that position, but hold fast to God's word that the bread is truly the body of Christ.

The second error involves the perversion also of the two phrases, "my body" and "my blood." Indeed, it gives the whole passage a different meaning. It does this by claiming that when Christ says: "This is my body," he means: If you take this bread and wine you will have a share in my body. Thus the sacrament is nothing else than a participation in the body of Christ, or, better, an incorporation into his spiritual body. To implement this process of incorporation he presumably instituted this bread and wine, as a sure sign that the spiritual incorporation is taking place and that the spiritual body is being realized. This is a clever sophistry. It is based on the fact that the Scriptures ascribe to Christ two kinds of body: one a natural body, which was born physically of Mary, just as all other men have bodies; the other a spiritual body, which is the whole Christian church, of which Christ is the head—just as husband and wife are one body and the husband is the head of the wife, of which Paul writes in Rom. 12 [:5] and in I Cor. 12 [:27] and in many other passages.

So they try then to refer Christ's words to the participation in his body. When he says: "This is my body," that is taken to mean: "This is the participation in my body." And they cite for support the statement of Paul in I Cor. 10 [:17], "We who are many are one loaf and one body, for we all partake of the same loaf." Likewise at the same place [I Cor. 10:16] he says: "The cup of blessing which we bless, is it not a participation in the blood of Christ? The bread which we break, is it not a participation in the body of Christ?" They think St. Paul has here elucidated Christ's words. When Christ says: "This is my body," that is supposed to be the same as saying: "This is the participation in my body." That is, he who eats the bread eats not "my body" but "the participation in my body"; along with the others he appropriates the benefits of my body (which is not in the sacrament, but was given for you elsewhere and is now in heaven). By the eating of this bread he has a share in everything that my body has and does and suffers—not by virtue of the bread or the eating, but by virtue of God's promise. It works like the water of baptism, which cleanses the soul not by virtue of the water but by virtue of God's promise, that he who receives baptism with water shall be saved, and so forth.

Such ideas do seem quite attractive to the reason—if you want to let them interpret the words of Paul and of Christ as they please! But this is not Christian teaching, when I intrude my own ideas into the Scripture and compel Scripture to accord with them. On the contrary, the Christian way is to make clear first what the Scriptures teach and then compel my own ideas to accord with them. And who can tolerate it with good conscience when Christ's statement: "This is my body, which is given for you" is interpreted to mean: "This is the participation-in-my-body, which is given for you"? For this interpretation has no basis in Scripture. "My body" is a very different expression, a very different thing, from "the participation in my body."

Since, therefore, the words of Christ: "This is my body which is given for you" stand so clearly in the way and so directly contradict such an interpretation, we should by no means follow this understanding of the sacrament. For even Paul himself, after he has spoken in the tenth chapter [I Cor. 10:16] about the participation in the body, nevertheless in the eleventh chapter [I Cor. 11: 23-24] comes back to the words and speaks just as Christ himself spoke, and says: "I have delivered to you what I have received, that the Lord Jesus on the night when he was betrayed took bread, gave thanks, broke it and said: 'Take and eat, this is my body which is given for you; do this in remembrance of me.'" Here the words are plain and clear, that it is not the spiritual body of Christ which is present, but his natural body. For the spiritual body was not given for us. It was his natural body that was given—on behalf of his spiritual body, which body we are! And it is not proper in this passage for us to make of the word "body" a "participation-in-the-body," and thus arbitrarily, without any basis in Scripture, to proceed in contradiction to such clear words.

But if they rely for support on the statement of St. Paul [I Cor. 10:16]: "The bread which we break is a participation in the body of Christ," one should answer that it is not enough to say such a statement may convey their understanding of it. They must show that it demands and compels such an interpretation. In matters like these, where conscience is involved, one must proceed with certainty, and not simply take a position and say: "It might be interpreted this way." "Might" and "must" are not the same. You have to prove that it *must* be interpreted in this way and no other. So long as you are unable to prove such a "must" your statement and interpretation are not binding. For one could easily give this statement of St. Paul a different interpretation, one which would make you uncertain of yours; then you would be guilty of falsehood and would have to give up the statement because its meaning is not certain.

For someone could well say that St. Paul in this passage is not speaking about the instituting of the sacrament but only about its use and benefit, and that he really means this: Just as those who eat what has been offered to idols are companions of the idols and partake of them [I Cor. 10:20], and just as the priests in the law who eat of the offerings on the altar partake of the altar [I Cor. 10:18], so likewise we who eat of that bread—which is the body of Christ—eat and partake of his body. Thus St. Paul is not here stating what the bread and the cup are (which he does later in the eleventh chapter) but what the eating of the bread and the drinking of the cup are, namely, a participation in Christ's body and blood.

Now even if they were to take their stand firmly on this passage, they still could not stop anybody from saying that St. Paul is here explaining not what the *bread* is but only what the *breaking* of such bread and the drinking of such wine are—in the conviction that the Corinthians already knew what the bread was of which Paul spoke, and he himself explicated it afterwards in the eleventh chapter. This is implied in the words which he uses [I Cor. 10:16]: "The bread which we break." It is as though he were to say: "We have a bread, as you know, such as no other people has, and what that bread is, you know very well. But if we eat this bread, is it not true that we thereby become partakers of the body of Christ? Why then would you make yourselves partakers of idols?" Just as he says, right after that [I Cor. 10:17]: "We are all one loaf and one body for we all partake of the same loaf." Here too he does not say what the bread *is* but what it *bestows*.

Now I have set forth this interpretation as the very minimum, which they cannot overthrow, and against which they cannot maintain their own interpretation. This passage therefore gives them no strong support. For there can be no doubt that the proper and sure interpretation of this passage in St. Paul is this: "The bread which we break is the participation in the body of Christ" means that when we eat such bread we all receive and eat together, one as much as the other, not plain bread but the body of Christ.

Suppose they challenge this interpretation and say that by "participation in the body of Christ" St. Paul means that we partake of all the benefits that Christ achieved in his body, just as those who eat food offered to idols must share in the expiation of all the miseries that the devils possess. We answer: that is true, and it is a good interpretation, but it contributes nothing to the debate and does not really help them. For by it the truth that Christ's body is present is not yet overthrown.

Paul shows that the passage is really to be understood in the sense of participation-in-the-*sacrament* when he says [I Cor. 10:16]: "The bread which we *break* is the participation in the body of Christ." For the "breaking" certainly refers to the act of giving and receiving the sacrament, and so Paul must surely be speaking here of the participation which is had by those who "break" the bread. But not all who "break" have spiritual participation in the body of Christ, even though they all have participation in the sacrament. So St. Paul's statement must mean: The "breaking" of the bread is the participation in the body of Christ. The breaking of the bread is the "participation in the body of Christ," which, according to Hebrew usage, is the same as "participation in Christ."[12] To put it very simply and literally, the breaking of the bread is the distribution of the body of Christ. So the passage is a perfect confirmation of our faith and agrees completely with the words of Christ that the bread *is* the body of Christ.

If they insist upon their opinion and refuse to accept our interpretation, let them go their way. At any rate we have made the passage uncertain for them, if indeed we have not entirely taken it away from them; so that all they have salvaged from it is the desire of retaining their own view even though they cannot do so. If they still think that we have not sufficiently met their argument, at least we can be sure that they will be much further from meeting ours with an uncertain interpretation of a single passage, while we have the perfectly clear statements of three Gospel writers [Matt. 26:26-28; Mark 14:22-24; Luke 22:17-19] and one of Paul [I Cor. 11:23-25] in addition to a clearer interpretation than they have of this passage of theirs [I Cor. 10:16]. For it is not enough simply to say that this passage supports their interpretation. If they would overthrow our interpretation they must also show that the words simply will not admit of our interpretation. This they will not do because the words convey our understanding perfectly; therefore theirs falls flat.

So it is true that we Christians are the spiritual body of Christ and collectively one loaf, one drink, one spirit. All this is achieved by Christ, who through his own body makes us all to be one spiritual body; so that all of us partake equally of his body, and are therefore

[12] In the original this sentence is in Latin: *Ebraico more fractio panis est participatum Corpus Christi, proparticipatio Christi.*

equal and united with one another. Likewise, the fact that we consume one bread and drink makes us to be one bread and drink. And just as one member serves another in such an integrated body, so each one also eats and drinks the other; that is, each consumes the other in everything, and each one is food and drink for the other, so that we are simply food and drink to one another, just as Christ is simply food and drink to us. With words such as these, St. Paul portrayed the riches and the nature of faith and of love, using the very terms appropriate to natural bread and wine [I Cor. 10:17]. For the many grains that are ground together become a single loaf; each grain loses its own form and becomes the flour of another. Likewise, many grapes become one wine; each grape too loses its own form and becomes the juice of the others. Likewise, Christ has become all things to us; and we, if we are Christians, have become all things among ourselves, each to the other [I Cor. 9:22]. What one has belongs to the other, and what one lacks is a matter of concern to each of the others as if he were lacking it himself. Concerning this I have spoken elsewhere at greater length.[13]

The third error is that in the sacrament no bread remains but only the form[14] of bread. Of course, this error is not very important if only the body and blood of Christ, together with the Word, are not taken away—though the papists have earnestly contended and still contend for this their new[15] doctrine. They label as heretic anyone who does not agree with them that it is a necessary truth, that no bread remains there—that monastic fantasy buttressed by Thomas Aquinas[16] and confirmed by the popes.[17] But while they insist so strongly upon this, and that out of pure arbitrariness and without any foundation in Scripture, we shall defy them and hold to the contrary that real bread and wine are truly present along with the

[13] *A Treatise Concerning the Blessed Sacrament* (1519), *PE* 2, 10-19. Cf. also in this volume, pp. 252-253.

[14] Cf. p. 29 n. 61.

[15] Cf. p. 31 n. 67.

[16] "Some have held that the substance of the bread and wine remain in the sacrament after the consecration. But this opinion cannot stand." *The "Summa Theologica" of St. Thomas Aquinas,* Part III, (Q.LXXV, Art. 2), trans. Fathers of the English Dominican Province (London, 1914), p. 267.

[17] The first of 45 errors of John Wycliffe enumerated for condemnation by the Council of Constance on May 4, 1415, was this: "In the sacrament of the altar the material substance of bread and likewise the material substance of wine remain." Denzinger, *op. cit.,* p. 208. Cf. in this volume p. 28 n. 58.

body and blood of Christ. We are glad to be labeled heretic by such imaginary Christians and naked sophists. For the gospel calls the sacrament bread. It says that the bread is the body of Christ. We shall stand by that. We are sufficiently certain, contrary to all the dreams of the sophists, that what the gospel calls bread is bread. If it deceives us, we shall take our chances.

The fourth error is the worst of all and the most heretical. It was invented by the Antichrist, the pope and his followers. This error consists of the fact that they have made of the sacrament a sacrifice and a good work and thereby have deceived everybody. On this error they have built a multitude of endowments, cloisters, churches, and the entire spiritual estate. This has been a commercial fairground for the papists, at which they have sold that work and sacrifice to the whole world, and have claimed to set everything straight with masses and to make satisfaction for everyone. It was not for any good purpose that the devil let the papists retain the body and blood of Christ in the sacrament. On the contrary he has caused them on their commercial fairground to deal with Christ as the Jews dealt with him that night in Caiaphas' house when he had been betrayed into their hands [Matt. 26:57-68]. There would not have been so many and such terrible sins if the sacrament had been entirely renounced, just as those who did not crucify Christ did not commit such great sins as the Jews did who seized him and put him to death.

Although I have dealt many a sharp thrust against this kind of error,[18] nevertheless I am obliged on this occasion also to say a few things about it. To protect yourself against this abominable error you should hold fast to the word that says: "Take and eat, this is my body." This word is the whole gospel. You will observe and understand that it says nothing about a sacrifice or a good work but about a present and a gift, which Christ offers and gives to us, and which we should receive and with faith appropriate and hold fast. He tells you to take and keep, and would you make an offering of it and give it away? How can you say to God: "I give you your Word"? Neither can you say to another person: "I am offering God his Word on your behalf." On the contrary, you should say: "Dear Lord, since you say that you freely give it to me, I receive it with

[18] Cf. pp. 35-57 and 162-198.

gratitude and joy." Just as you cannot make out of the gospel a sacrifice or a work, so you cannot make a sacrifice or a work out of this sacrament; for this sacrament is the gospel.

Therefore, in this matter no one can achieve anything for another person. Each one must believe for himself, just as I must believe all the Gospels for myself. I cannot hear or believe or keep for any one else so much as a single letter of the gospel, even as I cannot be baptized for any one else. But a good work I can always do to another person and for another person. Indeed, I have to do them for somebody else or they are not good works. For example, I can pray for you, serve you, work for you, suffer for you, and so forth. There is a great difference between faith and good works, just as vast as the difference in value between the tree and the fruit. Fruits disappear and return each year, but the tree remains always. Faith also remains always, but works disappear. In such a shameful way have they misled and deceived us that we go looking for good works and fruits when we should be looking for faith and the tree.

Be careful, therefore, to stay on the track. Don't let anyone pull you away from the Word through any statement of man, be it Augustine, Jerome, Bernard, or even an angel [Gal. 1:8]. "The elect will be led astray," says Christ [Matt. 24:24]. Therefore we cannot build on the mere word of one of the elect saints, without Scripture. Christ has warned us faithfully enough, and our own experience has probably taught us, that saintly men can make mistakes and have made mistakes. If our opponents complain that we have degraded and dishonored the sacrament because we have not let it become a sacrifice, then answer that we have not let the sacrament become a sacrifice for the very reason that we do not want to degrade and dishonor it as they do. It is a great degradation of the sacrament when a person ascribes nothing more to it than he ascribes to a good work. No good work can free us of our sins or give us grace or life or salvation. But this sacrament does give life, grace, and blessedness, for it is a fountain of life and of blessedness.

This is enough about the errors in the interpretation of this sacrament. Now we come to the subject at hand, the adoration of the sacrament.

The Adoration of the Sacrament

In John 4 [:20-24], the Samaritan woman asked the Lord where one should worship. Jesus answered her: "Woman, I tell you, the hour is coming when neither on this mountain nor in Jerusalem will you worship the Father. You worship what you do not know; we worship what we know, for salvation is from the Jews. But the hour is coming, and now is, when the true worshipers will worship the Father spiritually and truly, for the Father also seeks such worshipers. God is a spirit, and he who worships him must worship him spiritually and truly."

From these words we understand that there are two kinds of worship: one outward and physical, the other inward and spiritual. It is outward worship when you choose outward places and gestures to express it, as when in the church or before the altar or the sacrament you prostrate yourself, kneel, bend your body, bow your head, look up toward heaven, speak with your mouth and do similar things that can be done outwardly and are signs by which you outwardly acknowledge your God or overlord. But in this passage Christ rejects such worship if it takes place with the idea that it is pleasing to God and is enough in itself without any inward spiritual worship, as the Jews maintained. But where the inward worship accompanies it, it is well and good, as the patriarchs, prophets, apostles, and all the saints have done.

For when Christ says here: "Neither on this mountain nor in Jerusalem will you worship" [John 4:21], he certainly rejects all outward places, but in such a way as to make all places free. His intention is to set consciences free. It is as if he were to say: "I desire that henceforth no outward place shall be regarded as necessary for worship, as when you say that one must worship in Jerusalem or on this mountain, but that all places shall now be free for worship, as has hitherto not been the case. If the spiritual worship is present, you may worship also outwardly, whether you be in Jerusalem or on this mountain, in the house or out in the field, in Persia or in Greece. But hitherto one could worship only in

Jerusalem, or at least facing Jerusalem, no matter what part of the world he was in."

Now where outward worship is all alone, there is downright hypocrisy and actual mockery of God. There our Lord receives the same kind of honor as that which the Jews gave him when during his Passion they knelt before him and said: "Hail, King of the Jews" [Matt. 27:29]. For when there is no spiritual worship, it cannot be meant earnestly and it does not come from the heart. And if it does not come from the heart, it is certainly a mockery of God. Alas, this kind of worship fills the whole world today in all its corners. The mockery is now in full swing which the Jews began during Christ's Passion when they called him the "King of the Jews." For there are so many churches and services of divine worship on every hand, and yet there is scarcely one in a thousand who honor God with spiritual worship. Instead they all mock him with the outward, hypocritical worship. And this mockery of Christ takes place especially in all the masses and in the monstrance at Easter[19] and on Corpus Christi day.[20] For at those times he receives great outward honor, but it is pure mockery because it is without faith.

Therefore, where there is no faith and spiritual worship, it is better to stay far away. And one should not celebrate mass where there are no real and genuine Christians. Until such Christians are present one should abandon the monstrances and the Corpus Christi processions,[21] because there is no need for them; they serve no useful purpose and they only dishonor the sacrament with gross hypocrisy and mockery. Moreover, the monasteries and foundations of charity should be provided with believing priests and monks, or else they should be dissolved. For their chief work is mere outward worship and they think they have accomplished their purpose if they do a lot of outward kneeling, bending, and bowing. And the pope has assigned indulgences[22] to such processions and honoring

[19] Cf. p. 249 n. 12.

[20] Cf. p. 181 n. 42.

[21] The processions associated with this festival, which involved a displaying of the consecrated host for purposes of adoration, though not mentioned in the bull of Urban IV (d. 1264) which decreed the Corpus Christi observance (*Transiturus*, September 8, 1264), were nonetheless of early origin, being endowed with indulgences by Popes Martin V (d. 1431) and Eugene IV (d. 1447). *Catholic Encyclopedia, op. cit.*, IV, 391.

[22] *Ibid.*

of the sacrament, and so has filled the world with Jews who worship Christ in mockery [Matt. 27:29].

The second kind of worship is true and spiritual. It is free in all external matters, so that it does not require the worshiper to use special places or to employ special gestures. For every man can engage in this kind of worship wherever he may be or go or stay, even in the field, or sick in bed, or captive in prison; and not only in the churches or chapels, before the altar, or on his knees. But I suppose there are in reality many people who do not know what is meant by the word "worship" and do not see any difference between praying [*beten*] and worshiping [*anbeten*]. Let us therefore first clarify this distinction; then it will be easier to instruct concerning true worship.

Worship [*anbeten*] is not a matter of the mouth, like praying, petitioning, and pleading. For to pray [*beten*] is really to repeat the words of a prayer such as the Psalms or the Lord's Prayer. But to petition [*bitten*] is to accompany such a spoken prayer with one's own special need and indicate it by name, just as the Lord's Prayer contains seven such petitions, and so forth. To plead [*flehen*] is to go beyond the petition in one's prayer and to admonish God through something that He prizes very highly, such as his mercy, name, honor, truth, or through Christ, and so forth. In addition there is also intercession for others, and praise and thanksgiving. All of this is a work of the mouth.

Worship [*anbetten*] is nothing of the sort. It is not a function of the mouth but of the whole body. It is to bow the head, bend the body, fall on the knees, prostrate one's self, and so forth, and to do such things as a sign and acknowledgment of an authority and power; just as people bow in silence before secular princes and lords, and just as popes, bishops, abbots, and people generally, have themselves honored and adored [*ehrbieten*] by bowing and kneeling, and so forth. Such outward adoration [*ehrbietunge*] is what the Scriptures really mean by worship [*anbeten*]. It is out of a complete misunderstanding that the little word *adorare* is translated "worship" [*anbeten*],[23] because the latter has too strong a connotation of

[23] But Luther rendered *adorare* as *anbeten* in John 4:20-24 in both his translations of the New Testament, 1522 and 1546—perhaps as a concession to "common usage." See the text in *WA*, DB 6, 338-339.

praying with the mouth. Were it not such a common usage, it would still be a good thing if we were to say "adoration" [*ehrbieten*] –or "bowing" [*neygen*] as the Hebrew has it–instead of "worship" [*anbeten*]. We read in the Scriptures that worship [*anbeten*] or adoration [*ehrbieten*] is rendered outwardly both to God and to kings without distinction, just as bowing and kneeling are still rendered outwardly both to God and to men.

From this understanding of outward worship you will also understand what Christ meant by true spiritual worship. It is the adoration or bowing of the heart, so that from the bottom of your heart you thereby show and confess yourself to be his subordinate creature. For from this you see that true worship can be nothing else than faith; it is faith's sublimest activity with respect to God. For no one is capable of such heartfelt confession, adoration, bending, and bowing (or whatever you want to call it) before God in his heart, unless he unwaveringly holds God to be his Lord and Father, from whom he receives and will receive all good things, and through whom, without any merit on his part, he is redeemed and preserved from all sins and evil.

In a word, where there is none of this heartfelt trust and confidence that comes from a true and living faith, concerning which I have spoken so often, there can be no true worship, because there God is not recognized with the heartfelt confidence of faith. Therefore it is also impossible for him to be confessed, honored, and adored. For although people may with their mouths call him God and Father and outwardly adore him, nevertheless the heart is faithless and the result is lies and hypocrisy. But where worship is offered from the heart, there follows quite properly also that outward bowing, bending, kneeling, and adoration with the body. For this reason it is not possible to maintain a distinction in the New Testament between the worship [*anbeten*] of God and that of a man. For people bow, bend, and kneel before both alike; only with respect to God they lift their eyes and faces to heaven. But inwardly in the heart the difference is greater than that between heaven and earth; for the heart holds God to be God, but the prince it holds to be a man.

Now to come back to the sacrament: he who does not believe that Christ's body and blood are present does well not to worship either with his spirit or with his body. But he who does believe, as sufficient demonstration has shown it ought to be believed, can surely not withhold his adoration of the body and blood of Christ without sinning. For I must always confess that Christ is present when his body and blood are present. His words do not lie to me, and he is not separated from his body and blood. And when he lay dead in the grave, he was still Christ and worthy of his honor, even when there was no longer any blood in him. Moreover, we must honor and adore one another, as Paul teaches in Rom. 12 [:10], for the sake of Christ, who dwells in us spiritually through our faith.

It is, of course, true that there is a distinction between Christ sitting on high in heaven, and being in the sacrament and in the hearts of believers. For certainly he ascended to heaven so that men should and must worship him there and confess him to be the Lord, mighty over all things (Phil. 2 [:10-11]). But he is present in the sacrament and in the hearts of believers not really because he wants to be worshiped there, but because he wants there to work with us and help us; just as he also came to earth in the flesh not that men should worship him, but to serve us, as he himself said: "I have not come to be served but to serve and to give my life for many" [Matt. 20:28].

But from this it does not follow that one should not worship him. For many people worshiped him when he was upon earth and he accepted it too, such as the three kings at the manger [Matt. 2:11], the blind man [John 9:38], and many others. Nevertheless, his state at that time was not yet the state of his honor and glory, for which nothing but worship and adoration is fitting. There had to be freedom to worship or not to worship, because no definite command had been given to worship him before he was glorified. That is why he allowed himself to be worshiped at times, and at other times not to be worshiped. Likewise, here in the sacrament and in all believing hearts it should be left a matter of freedom, in order that we may be assured that he gave no command about worshiping him in the sacrament or in believing hearts. Moreover, that is not the reason for his presence there. Nevertheless, one should not withhold from him such worship and adoration either; but freely give it, if the proper time and occasion presents itself, or omit it.

For that reason we say now that one should not condemn people or accuse them of heresy if they do not adore the sacrament, for there is no command to that effect and it is not for that purpose that Christ is present. Just as we read that the apostles did not adore the sacrament since they were sitting and eating at table [Matt. 26:20, 26]. On the other hand, one should not condemn and accuse of heresy people who do adore the sacrament. For although Christ has not commanded it, neither has he forbidden it, but often accepted it. Free, free it must be, according as one is disposed in his heart and has opportunity. Therefore both parties are to be blamed when they take a stand on either of these two sides and quarrel over this matter and condemn one another, and both of them miss the middle way. The first group would like to compel people not to adore the sacrament, as if Christ were not there at all; and the other group would like to compel people to adore it, as if Christ's state of glory were in the sacrament as it is in heaven.

With this kind of quarreling they both get off the track, so that they emphasize the sacrament and neglect the words. The sacrament then becomes a mere work and faith perishes. For while they busy themselves trying to decide how they may properly honor Christ and do him abundant service, they never do get around to considering what he does for them in the sacrament and why he is there and what they are supposed to receive from him, just as if he were there solely for the sake of their worship and service. We have it backwards when in the sacrament we think only of the works that we ourselves might do and accomplish for the sacrament, and pay no attention to the works that the sacrament is supposed to do and accomplish for us.

And so I repeat what I have said above,[24] that a person should note carefully these two things in the sacrament: first, the Word; and second, the bread and wine. The words teach you to give thought and attention to why Christ is present; they will cause you to forget your work and to wait only upon his. For a sacrament is a matter of faith, because in it only the works of God proceed and are effected—through his Word! Therefore, those who consider the sacrament to be thus in the Word will forget both worship and adoration. That is what the apostles did at the Supper [Matt. 26:26]

[24] Cf. pp. 277-278.

and yet without any doubt they were most acceptable and did him the proper honor. They acted just as one does when he hears the gospel, the Word of God—to which the highest honor is nonetheless due because God is nearer in it than Christ is in the bread and wine. Yet no one thinks of bowing before the gospel; instead everyone sits still, and in listening gives no thought whatever to the kind of honor he will do to the Word.

Bread and wine, or the body and blood of Christ, regarded without the words, will teach you to give thought and attention to your own works. They will drive you away from pondering God's work and the reason why he is present, so that you will be quite anxious to do a lot for him, and will not let anything be done for you. Thus the sacrament becomes purely a matter of works. But if you first exercise faith rightly, at the most important point, namely, with respect to the words, then the adoration of the sacrament will afterwards follow beautifully in its own place; and if it did not follow, that would be no sin. But where faith, the most important thing, is not right and is not exercised with respect to the Word, there one cannot teach anybody properly to worship, even if he were to write the world full of books.

Now, therefore, let me describe in order four groups of people. The first are those whose entire interest is in the words of this sacrament, so that they feed their faith; they receive the bread and wine with the body and blood of Christ as a sure sign of that Word and of faith. These are the most secure and the best. They probably seldom descend so low as to bother themselves about worshiping and adoring, for they pay attention to the work God does to them and forget about the works they do for the sacrament.

The second group are those who exercise the right sort of faith, and then descend to their own works and worship Christ spiritually in the sacrament. That is, they bow inwardly with their hearts and confess him as their Lord, who does all things within them; and they prove their inward worship by outwardly bowing, bending, and kneeling with the body.

The third group are those who worship him inwardly only. The fourth group are those who worship him outwardly only. These last are completely worthless, and I have already said enough about them. Nevertheless, you can see that adoration of this sacrament is a dangerous procedure if the Word and faith are not inculcated; so much so that I really think it would be better to follow the example of the apostles and not worship, than to follow our custom and worship. Not that adoration is wrong, but simply because there is less danger in not adoring than in adoring; because human nature tends so easily to emphasize its own works and to neglect God's work, and the sacrament will not admit of that. But what more should I say? For this sacrament and for every work of God there must be Christians. Where there are no Christians, it will be done wrong, please God, whether they adore or not.

There have also been many who have been concerned about how the soul and the spirit of Christ, and thereby the Godhead, the Father and the Holy Spirit, is in the sacrament. It is a wonder they have not included in their concern the angels also and finally the whole world. All these are the thoughts of idle souls and empty hearts, who forget the words and works of God in this sacrament and give themselves over to their own thoughts and words. The more simply you stick to the words of the sacrament the better it will be for you. So let go of their dreams: "concomitantly," "through concomitance," [25] and other things like that. And hold fast to these truths:

First, that you lay hold on the words: "This is my body which is given for you," and so forth. Eat and drink there, and nourish your faith. Then take also the body and blood as tokens of these words of God. And say to yourself: I am not commanded to investigate or to know how God, the Father, the Son and the Holy Spirit, or how the soul of Christ is in the sacrament. For me it is enough to know that the Word which I hear and the body which I receive are truly the Word and body of my Lord and God. Let the subtle and unbelieving sophists inquire about such secondary matters and employ their magic to bring deity into the sacrament.

[25] The Council of Constance on June 15, 1415, declared: "The whole body of Christ and the blood are truly contained under the species of bread as well as under the species of wine." Subsequently the Council of Trent utilized the term *per concomitantiam* in its statement of the official dogma to explain that the body is present under both species "by force of that natural connection and concomitance by which the parts of Christ . . . are mutually united." This accounted also for the presence of Christ's divinity under both species by virtue of its "hypostatic union with His body and soul." Denzinger, *op. cit.*, pp. 211, 267.

The body which you receive, the Word which you hear, are the body and Word of him who holds the whole world in his hand and who inhabits it from beginning to end. Let this be sufficient for you.

This is our view on the adoration of the sacrament. Whether it agrees with yours, you will best be able to determine. We know of nothing to teach us differently, for the words of the gospel are clear and potent: "This is my body," and so forth; "This is my blood," and so forth. So we have no desire to forbid proper honor to the body of Christ, but we want to be free—to adore where it is not profitable or necessary. But the thing that we emphasize as of the utmost importance is faith in the words of the sacrament.

But, as I have said above,[26] I want to indicate what I like in your *Apologia* and statement of faith and what I think is lacking. I do this in order to make your position and ours very clear and in order that we may daily draw nearer to each other.

First, I bear you witness (although you do not need it) that you have the right idea of God, namely, that there is one God and three persons, God the Father, God the Son, and God the Holy Spirit; in one and the same substance, majesty, power, work, and honor; who created the heavens and the earth.

Second, that neither the Father nor the Holy Spirit but only the Son, our Lord Jesus Christ, became man, was conceived by the Holy Spirit, was born of the Virgin Mary, and for our trespasses [Rom. 4:25] suffered under Pontius Pilate, died, was buried, descended into hell, and on the third day rose again for our justification [Rom. 4:25], ascended to heaven, sits on the right hand of God, and from there will come to judge the living and the dead. Thus it is not our work or merit or satisfaction that takes away our sins and earns us grace for eternal life, but solely his merit and the work that he has done for us.

Third, that the Holy Spirit drives home this merit of Christ and makes it operative in us, so that it was not done and is not preached in vain. For thereby a holy Christian church comes into being, which is the entire congregation of all those persons, wherever they may be, living or dead, who through the operation of the Holy Spirit partake of Christ's merit, suffering, and resurrection. To this congregation and to every member of it belong the keys, the power

[26] Cf. p. 276-277.

to forgive sins, and to proclaim the gospel—privately, and publicly if one is required to do so by others having equal authority. Through this office of preaching and of forgiving sins, souls are resurrected here from sins and from death, and confidently await also the resurrection of the body and life everlasting through the same Holy Spirit who has now begun this in the soul.

These are the chief articles of the Christian faith. Where necessary they are sufficient for salvation, and without them no one can be saved. In these articles I find nothing blameworthy in you, and your *Apologia*[27] is correct.

Fourth, it is, of course, quite right that you make nothing of the pope and bishops, as is now the case also among us, nor of human ordinances or traditions. For at Easter[28] only unleavened bread should ever be eaten, as Moses says [Exod. 12:15-20], and as Paul in I Cor. 5 [:7] interprets it in terms of the gospel.

Fifth, I am pleased that you make nothing of purgatory and all those things that are based upon it—the masses, vigils, foundations, altars, cloisters, and all its spreading corruption. For certainly no one is required to believe that there is a purgatory, because God has said nothing about it. Even if God did make a purgatory for some people, about which nobody knew but they themselves, that is his prerogative. It would not be necessary on that account to believe in purgatory, for God's judgments are concealed from us and in this matter we are not commanded either to know or to believe.

Sixth, I certainly would not call you heretics, as our sophists do, because you do not honor or call upon the mother of God or any of the saints, but cling alone to the only mediator, Jesus Christ, and are satisfied that in heaven as well as on earth each one is obligated to pray for the other. For there is nothing in the Scriptures about the intercession of dead saints, nor about honoring them and praying to them. And no one can deny that hitherto through services for these saints we have gone so far as to make pure idols out of the mother of God and the saints. We have placed more confidence in

---

[27] Cf. p. 276 n. 7.

[28] Luther is alluding to the papal requirement of annual communion at Easter as illustrative of the kind of "old leaven" which must be "cleansed out" according to Paul's gospel.

them, on account of the services and works which we have done for them, than we have placed in Christ himself, with the result that faith in Christ has perished.

As to that which I find lacking in you, I would not conceal it from you either. But I ask you very earnestly to take it kindly from me. For if I did not do this, by way of service to you, you might well think that I am holding something back from you. And you also will have the right, in fact it will be an obligation upon you, in return, to set forth frankly the points in which you think we are lacking. For we feel that God has given us a good clear light, but we are pretty weak in following it and adorning it with our lives and works. If my papist opponents had been able to permit the friendly pointing out of their mistakes and if they had not opposed me, in return, with wantonness and violence, this whole business would not have developed, and their authority and honor would probably still remain. But I expect much better things from you than I received from those fellows, because you are reasonable people. So I shall go ahead.

First, concerning the sacrament of Christ's body I have indicated sufficiently above what I miss in you. However, we have not yet been able to bring into practice among ourselves such a proper Christian administration of the sacrament in both kinds, nor to set up among ourselves such practice of doctrine and love and such a well-ordered life, as we hear is the case among you. We are still immature and things proceed slowly among us. But pray for us.

Second, as I hear from your messengers, the sacrament of baptism is properly observed among you. But I am much concerned because you baptize young children on the basis of future faith, which they are supposed to learn when they come to understanding, and not on the basis of present faith. For you hold (as they tell me) that the young children do not have faith; nevertheless you baptize them. On this point I have said it would be better not to baptize any children anywhere at all than to baptize them without faith, since in such procedure the sacrament and God's holy name are taken in vain [Exod. 20:7], and to me that is a serious matter. For without faith the sacrament should not and cannot be received, or if it is received, it works greater injury.

Over against this we hold the words of Christ: "He who believes and is baptized" and so forth [Mark 16:15]. Before one baptizes, or at least at the same time, faith must be present. Else we make of baptism a mere mockery of God's majesty, as if his majesty were present there offering grace and no one were accepting it. Therefore it is our judgment that through the faith and prayer of the church young children are cleansed of unbelief and of the devil and are endowed with faith, and thus are baptized; because this also is the gift that was given to the children through the circumcision of the Jews. Otherwise, Jesus would not have said in Matt. 19 [:14]: "Let the children come to me, for to such belongs the kingdom of heaven." But without faith no one has the kingdom of heaven.

And if anyone is able to overthrow this judgment of mine (though I do not believe it can be overthrown) I would rather teach that children should not be baptized than (as I have said) that they should be baptized without faith. For one should not take God's name in vain [Exod. 20:7], even if the salvation of the whole world depended on it.

Third, I am rather pleased that you speak so discriminatingly about faith as to say it is one thing to believe about God, and another to believe God, and still another to believe in God. Thus, the demons also believe [Jas. 2:19] about God, that he has created all things, that he became man, that he died and did everything for us. Again, to believe God is to believe that what he has spoken is true. But to believe in God is to follow God with love and good works, and so forth.

Whether you have here a correct understanding of faith, I am unable to determine. Your words still sound as though they ascribe a good deal to works. It is doubtless true that to believe in God is the only true and living faith, which is created within us not by our strength but by God's Spirit. Likewise, that this kind of faith is active in the works of love and falls back upon God and becomes like him, is also correct. But the real nature of faith is not yet thereby described, because works are still kept in view.

This is what we think. When the Holy Spirit makes us aware of the work of Christ and of his merit, outwardly through the gospel and inwardly through his gift, when he bestows this merit upon us and causes us to believe in it, then this faith is nothing else than a living trust and confidence in the merit that Christ has bestowed upon us. We rely upon it from the bottom of our hearts, without doing any works of our own. We are confident that it is not our own works but the work and merit of Christ that destroys our sins, overcomes death, and swallows up hell. This means that no work is required in order to believe in God or to have a true and living faith. Rather it is this living faith in God which subsequently does good works to one's neighbor, as Christ has done to him.

And in fact, that this is the nature of true faith one can easily learn by considering the nature of false faith and unbelief. For we observe in those who have faith in the mass that they are safe all day when they have heard a mass. They do nothing additional to establish their security because they are satisfied with having heard mass. They stand on that, and afterwards do as they please. And even if they also did something to establish their security, yet they would ascribe it to the mass alone if they are saved. The same thing is done by all others who go about with blessings, magic, and false faith.

So much the more must it be the case in this regard with respect to true faith, that we can be helped not by anything that we do but only by that in which we believe, namely, God and his Word. Our works cannot add anything to faith or to its power. But this matter cannot now be discussed at length. Perhaps we shall make more progress in the discussion if we instruct one another with Holy Scripture. For we don't want to destroy one another by fire as the papists do.[29] When they can no longer give answer or cite reasons for their faith, they defend themselves with fire like the Chaldeans [Dan. 3:8-21] and can say nothing more than: "You are a heretic; bring the fire." But we shall listen to the Scriptures as they are presented by each side.

Fourth, you still have the seven sacraments from the church of the papists, although the Scriptures have no more than the two[30] —baptism and the table of the Lord. Although in such matters we must be patient with those who are weak, nevertheless we cannot

[29] The bull, *Exsurge Domine*, which threatened Luther with excommunication, also included a demand to burn his books. Publication of the bull in Rome (June 15, 1520) and other places was accompanied by such bonfires. Cf. *LW* 31, 381.

[30] Cf. pp. 18 and 109.

continue forever to teach that there are seven sacraments. As you well know, a sacrament must have two things for sure, God's Word and the external sign that has been duly instituted, and these we find only in the two sacraments which I have mentioned above. Now it is certainly too much if we equate things instituted by men with things instituted by God. It would seem to follow that you cannot with good conscience reject some human ordinances, especially the pope's, if you accept certain of his institutions as necessary to saving faith. For you know that faith must and will rest on nothing else than on the sure Word of God.

Fifth, I am pleased to know that you yourselves choose your own servants and attendants (whom we call priests and parsons) to teach the Word of God and administer the sacraments, after you have proved them learned, upright, and devout. But it is still damaging to the gospel that you require them to go unmarried. This gives the impression that marriage is too despicable an estate to permit one to wait upon God in all kinds of divine service. However, voluntary chastity is not a general gift, as is preaching and teaching. Although I was glad to hear that you do not forbid anyone to marry, yet I regret that a married person is made to desist from the office of preaching. That is still a place where we fall into the danger of sinning. But it would be more Christian to let that estate remain free also. For, although we are Christians, nevertheless we are not better than Abraham and all the patriarchs, and surely they were as fully Christians and preachers as we are. And as marriage did not hinder them, much less ought it surely to hinder us.

These are the items in which I am conscious of your still lacking something with reference to the plain doctrine of the gospel. And of these I regard as most important the one in which I have remarked concerning faith and works. For although I do not know whether your position is right or not, nevertheless I see that your statement on the matter does not make it clear, beyond the possibility of misunderstanding, that you attribute life, justification, and salvation to faith alone and without works. You seem to have trouble with the statement of St. Paul that love is greater than faith [I Cor. 13:13], and with the words of St. James [2:24] about works, and so forth.

Of course, it may well be, as your messengers say, that your case sounds very much better in your Bohemian language than you have been able to put it in Latin. Perhaps for that reason we may have understood some articles differently from the sense in which you really hold them. At the moment I will not deny that. But we know Latin and German well enough to set forth our position so that you and everybody can understand what we mean, to the end that even if we cannot ascertain how far from us or how near to us you stand, at least you will be able to ascertain how far from you or how near to you we are. In this way we shall reach the gist of the matter, and become one.

And further, if I could bring it to pass among you, I should like to ask that you do not neglect the languages but, since it would not be difficult for you, that you have your preachers and some of your gifted boys learn Latin, Greek, and Hebrew well. I know for a fact that one who has to preach and expound the Scriptures and has no help from the Latin, Greek, and Hebrew languages, but must do it entirely on the basis of his mother tongue, will make many a pretty mistake. For it has been my experience that the languages are extraordinarily helpful for a clear understanding of the divine Scriptures. This also was the feeling and opinion of St. Augustine[81]; he held that there should be some people in the church who could use Greek and Hebrew before they deal with the Word, because it was in these two languages that the Holy Spirit wrote the Old and New Testaments.

Herewith I commit you to the grace of God, and I humbly ask that you dear brethren will not take this writing of mine with scorn, as if I had taken delight in censuring your errors. On the contrary, since you know that you are regarded as the worst kind of heretics, I would bear witness that you are much nearer to the gospel than any others that are known to me. I know very well that with this statement I shall be bringing hatred down upon my head, but I am

[81] In "Christian Instruction" (*De doctrina Christiana*), Book Two, Chap. 11, Augustine writes: "Men who know the Latin language . . . have need of two others in order to understand the Sacred Scriptures. These are Hebrew and Greek, by which they may turn back to the originals if the infinite variances of Latin translators cause any uncertainty." John J. Gavigan (trans.), "The Writings of Saint Augustine," IV, 73. In *The Fathers of the Church* (New York, 1947).

now accustomed to that, by God's grace, and I expect nothing else in this matter. For I hear that by God's grace there is such a fine, virtuous outward manner of life among you that you have none of the revelling that we have among us, none of the excessive eating and drinking, swearing and cursing, gaudiness and social evils, but that each one must maintain himself with his own work if he can. I understand also that you do not have such greedy gluttons as we have, and that you do not let anyone starve either. So I could not forbear, out of a sense of Christian duty, to indicate to you what I think is still lacking in your inner life, the life of faith and doctrine. I should like to hear and see that it is utterly pure. For we who dwell in the midst of Sodom and Gomorrah and Babylon do not see how we could bring about externally such a fine, virtuous manner of life (unless God helps us further). Nevertheless we do have the plain and true doctrine of the gospel as a clear light in the midst of a perverse and crooked generation of darkness [Phil. 2:15]. This light we would gladly communicate to everyone. We in turn should like to learn from everyone, and we do expect to learn from you.

The grace of our Lord Jesus Christ be with you [Rom. 16:20; I Thess. 5:28]. Amen.

THE ABOMINATION OF THE SECRET MASS

1525

Translated by Abdel Ross Wentz

INTRODUCTION

For about two years Luther had been trying to get rid of the mass in the churches of Electoral Saxony and especially in Wittenberg. Beginning in March, 1523, and continuing until he achieved his purpose, at least in Wittenberg, near the end of December, 1524, there were numerous sermons and letters dealing with this matter. But nowhere in all these documents is there the slightest indication that Luther intended to publicize his success in abrogating the mass in Wittenberg or that he was about to publish a special treatise dealing with the secret mass.

Nor do we find in Luther's letters of 1525 or 1526 any evidence about the date of this treatise. The clearest lead concerning the time of its publication is found in the close parallel between the text of this treatise and the text of a sermon that Luther preached in Wittenberg on November 27, 1524.[1] In this sermon Luther made his final and successful attack upon the canons and prebendaries in Wittenberg demanding the abrogation of the mass. The sermon was taken down by the indefatigable George Rörer, and it is almost certain that Luther had Rörer's manuscript of the sermon in his hands when he wrote this treatise for publication. After the introduction the order of the thought and, for the most part, the order of the sentences is the same in the treatise as in the sermon.

As early as December 11, 1524, a letter was received by Luther's friend, Stephan Roth, then in Wittenberg, in which the writer, an artist in Freiberg, expressed the earnest hope that the ideas set forth in the sermon of November 27 might be given wider circulation through the printed page. This may have given Luther the suggestion that he write a special treatise on the subject. It certainly proves that this treatise had not yet been published at that time.

Internal evidence seems to indicate that this little book was written shortly after the successful termination of Luther's efforts to get rid of the mass in the church in Wittenberg. In the very first

[1] *WA* 15, 764-774.

sentence of the Preface he refers to his many sermons and letters in the effort to abrogate the mass, and he seems to imply that the effort has succeeded. Further on, in the third paragraph, he makes clear reference to the local situation in Wittenberg when he writes concerning the people whom he seeks to enlighten in this treatise that "they live with us in the same city and the same community, and enjoy with us all kinds of outward association."

In establishing the exact date for the publication of this treatise we have further help from two of Luther's enemies. In the beginning of his Preface, Luther makes vigorous denial of the charge by the papists that he has sought to arouse the common people to insurrection and rebellion. This led his opponent, Jerome Emser, theologian at Leipzig, to write and publish a pamphlet with the title: "Answer to Luther's Abominable Attack on the Sacred Secret Mass; also, How, Where and with What Words Luther in his Books has Advised, Written and Urged Insurrection." The printed pamphlet is dated 1525, and from its references to contemporary events it is clear that its author knew of Luther's treatise no later than June 26 of that year.

Moreover, Emser's prince, Duke George of Saxony, another opponent of Luther, in his correspondence with Luther's prince, Elector John, refers to Luther's "book against the office of the holy mass," and to another writing of Luther's which he calls, "a little book against rebellion." This latter is clear reference to Luther's "Admonition to Peace, Concerning the Twelve Articles of the Peasants in Swabia," [2] and this "Admonition" was probably written between April 17 and 20, 1525.

It is safe to conclude, therefore, that our treatise was written and published some time during the first three months of 1525.

In this little book Luther attacks what was always a fixed part of every mass, the "canon." For the Roman Catholic it was so holy that the priest read it in a whisper. To Luther it was very offensive. In this treatise he calls it the *Stillmesse*, i.e., the silent mass or the secret mass. By publishing this little book he sought to drag it out of its corner and exhibit its abomination to all readers.

Our translation is from the German text in *WA* 18, 22-36.

---

[2] *WA* 18, 291-334.

THE ABOMINATION OF THE SECRET MASS

The Preface

I have often preached and written about the disgraceful masses of the papists and what one should do to get rid of them. And our lords, the papists, have found fault with us and complained that we intend to foment insurrection. Very well, let it go; let them tell that lie about us also; they have surely told worse lies. For since they shamelessly dare to blaspheme and insult the divine majesty every hour with their abominable masses and idolatries, what does it matter that they charge us poor humans with lies?

But according to my understanding it is no insurrection when a person undertakes and accomplishes something through the duly constituted authorities, as I have always done myself and taught others to do.[1] For I have never taught that the unauthorized masses or anyone without authority should break in and change things. Neither have I ever commanded that anyone should enter their houses with the sword or otherwise harm them, but I have used all diligence to prevent that and have admonished the responsible officials. I have never told anyone that, having been taught by the Word of God, he should proceed on his own accord to give up these abominations or change them. So it was not necessary to invent such a groundless charge against me. But, as I have said, let it go: it cannot hurt me.

But now to come to our subject. The learned people know and understand quite well what the mass is, and why I would like to be rid of it. But that the simple people and the unlearned also may have a better understanding of it, I am obliged to bring it out

[1] Cf. *An Earnest Exhortation for all Christians, Warning Them Against Insurrection and Rebellion* (1522). *PE* 3, 206-222.

further into the light of day, so that men can grasp what it is. For I fear that people still hold it to be true and do not believe that it is such an abomination as we say, else they would have a different attitude toward doing something about it. For if I did not know and see it plainly, if it had only been told to me, I too could not have believed that it is such a very shameful thing or that God could be so angry as to let such a plague arise in Christendom. And I particularly lament that, although it is so clearly written and preached that they could easily read or hear it, yet they simply stop their ears and will neither hear nor see what is intolerable for them. If it were weakness and lack of understanding we might wink at it and not hold it against them. But because they are stubborn and don't want to understand, but let it go on among us and make us look on while they blaspheme and insult God, we cannot and shall not continue to be patient with them. For, since they live with us in the same city and the same community, and enjoy with us all kinds of outward association, we should ultimately be obliged to carry on our shoulders the responsibility for their deliberate blasphemies, as those who acquiesced in these things and did nothing about them, as we well might have done; so St. Paul says in Rom. 2[2]: "They also deserve to die who approve those who practice them."

So I shall do my part and warn everyone to avoid such an abomination as he would avoid the worst kind of devil; and those who have power to prevent it I shall admonish to do so. And that each one may see and understand, I shall also repeat word for word the canon of the mass, which is held to be the best and most important part of the mass. From this it will be clear to everyone what blind and stubborn blasphemers our papists are.

But first I want to remind each one of the ground on which our faith and all our preaching rests. I shall repeat it briefly. But I preach now only to those who accept the gospel as the Word of God and nothing else, for those who still do not know that or are in doubt about it will not accept this ground of our faith. Well, you have heard in the gospel and learned from it that the problem of our salvation from sin, death, the devil, and an evil conscience, the problem of attaining true righteousness before God and eternal

[2] Rom. 1:32 cited according to the Vulgate version.

life, is by no means solved or helped with works or laws, no matter what they may be or may be called. For God will accept no other mediation and no other mediator than his only Son, whom the Father sent into the world and whom he caused to shed his blood for the sole purpose that he might thereby obtain for us the treasure of faith.

That, briefly, is the sum total of the gospel that we preach. And if anyone seeks another way to be freed from his sins and stand before God, he blasphemes and insults God and accuses him of lying, as if he had let his Son shed his blood in vain and his death had accomplished nothing and was of no importance. For this is what God insists on and nothing else, that no one shall stand before him except by that innocent blood alone. And if anyone undertakes some other method, such as his works or order or station in life, he shall belong to the devil much more than anyone else. For it is a very serious matter with God and he will have no jest made of it, because for this purpose he gave his Son to die. For that reason we know and have no other sacrifice than that which he made on the cross, on which he died once for all as the Epistle to the Hebrews [9:12, 26] says, and thereby put away the sins of all men and also made us holy for eternity.

That, I say, is our gospel, that Christ has made us righteous and holy through that sacrifice and has redeemed us from sin, death, and the devil and has brought us into his heavenly kingdom. We have to grasp this and hold it fast through faith alone. We have preached this and reiterated it so often that everyone can know it well and can conclude from it that all our own works undertaken to expiate sin and escape from death are necessarily blasphemous. They deny God and insult the sacrifice that Christ has made and disgrace his blood, because they try thereby to do what only Christ's blood can do.

Now if this gospel is true, then everything that offers another way or another sacrifice must be false. But in the mass the papists do nothing but continually ride the words "we offer up, we offer up" and "these sacrifices, these gifts." They keep completely quiet about the sacrifice that Christ has made. They do not thank him. Indeed, they despise and deny his sacrifice and try to come before God with their own sacrifice. Dear reader, what will God say if you try in this way to come before him? He will say, "Must I therefore become your fool and liar? I have presented you with a sacrifice, my own Son, which you ought to receive with thanks and great joy. Yet you dare to come before me and say nothing about it, as if you did not need him, and so you despise the most precious treasure that I have in heaven and on earth. What do you think I should give you as a reward for this?" If God were the devil himself, such conduct would be insult enough. How long this abomination has been practiced in the world, and is still incessantly practiced, in so many daily and innumerable masses; and up to the present God has withheld his wrath! Now that we know and understand this matter, however, we may no longer keep quiet and endure it, else we should draw upon ourselves horrible wrath and punishment. I wanted to say this at the outset by way of warning.

Now we shall recount the words that the papists secretly read in the secret mass which they call the canon, the words which they hold to be so high and holy that they forbid the laity to know them. In this way we shall expose the devil and stand him up to the light for you, so that everyone may see what a terrible abomination the repulsive devil is carrying on every day and everywhere in the secret mass.

HERE BEGINS THE DEAR CANON OR SECRET MASS

"We humbly beseech Thee, most merciful Father, through Jesus Christ, Thy Son, our Lord, that Thou wilt deign to be pleased with and bless these gifts, these presents, these holy unspotted sacrifices, which we offer Thee especially for Thy holy universal Christian Church. Give Thy Church peace, protect her, help her, rule over her throughout the whole world, as well as Thy servant N., our Pope, and N., our Bishop, and all the true believers and those who hold to the Christian and Apostolic faith."

See, there stands the priest and has before him a host or wafer of simple bread and a cup of wine, and he talks with God and asks him to regard the wafer as so precious and worth so much that it may serve as a sacrifice before God on behalf of all Christendom. Does not this blaspheme the blood of Christ, that bread and wine are regarded as highly as Christ's own blood? Nobody notes or observes what a blasphemy this is. How dare you, miserable man, come so shamelessly before the high majesty of God in a way that would be proper enought if he were a sow? Should he have any regard for the gifts and the sacrifice, which are nothing but yet unconsecrated bread and wine? Shall we offer God a little bread and wine and ask him to accept it on behalf of all Christendom? And shall we say of it that it is a holy unspotted sacrifice? If it is holy and unspotted, why should God have regard for it and bless it? But if he should regard it and be pleased with it and bless it, why then do you call it an unspotted holy sacrifice? Is it not the same as if you were to say, God should let himself be reconciled by means of bread and wine, when in reality it is nothing more than any other bread of which everybody eats? Yet you say it is holy and is presented to God as a sacrifice, and you afterwards eat of it yourself. Would you offer such a thing for the entire holy Christian church and all believers?

Now is it not sufficient insult and blasphemy that a sinful human being presumes to take and offer up bread and wine for all holy Christians everywhere? It is rather the devil who tells you to say that. Should you offer up for all Christendom what God has bought through the blood of his own Son? What could or would they offer up? Has not the sacrifice for the whole world already been made through Christ? What are they doing then? Would you plead on behalf of devout Christians, when you yourself are a rascal and a blasphemer? And you do nothing more than offer up a little bit of plain bread and wine. If one really opened his eyes and took a look at this abominable blasphemy going on every day and everywhere, it would break his heart. When they say these words: "We offer thee this on behalf of the whole world and beseech Thee that Thou wilt deign to be pleased with it," it is equivalent to blaspheming and saying to God publicly before the whole world: "We have to help Christendom with bread and wine; it is a barefaced lie when you say that the blood of your Son alone is sufficient." This is what we have to put up with, as we hear and see each day how they so shamelessly insult God and call him a liar that it would be no wonder if the earth were to swallow up both them and us. This they hear and see themselves, as they have the text before their eyes, so that they cannot deny it. Yet they are so stiff-necked and stubborn that one cannot tell them anything or help them.

This is one part of the abomination, that they offer bread and wine to God as a pure sacrifice and yet they beseech God to be pleased with it and bless it. In this way they lie hundreds and thousands of times, because they are so blind and they do not know themselves what they are saying. For God himself says in Mal. [1:11]: "My sacrifice, that is offered to me throughout the world, pleases me well."

In addition, the canon adds needless superfluous words, just as if the "true believers" were something different from those who hold to the apostolic and universal Christian faith. But by apostolic faith the devil means the faith of the papists, as if the mass were of benefit only to those papists (and that is true, too); he does not want it to benefit me and other devout Christians. But let us go on.

PRAYER FOR THE LIVING

> **"Remember, O Lord, Thy servants, men and women, N. and N., and all who are here present, whose faith and devotion are known to Thee, for whom we bring our offerings to Thee, or who themselves bring their own offerings to Thee, this sacrifice of praise on behalf of themselves and all their loved ones for the redemption of their souls, for the hope of their salvation and welfare, and who pay their vows to Thee, the eternal, living and true God."**

Here the priest includes "those who are here present," that they are supposed to offer with him the plain bread and wine, and he says the same thing also about those who have faith. May God spare us this: we will have no part of it, but run while we can. For what purpose do they make their offerings? "For the redemption of their souls, etc." Behold, is not this a raging, mad, and foolish people? If they have faith, as the canon itself says, why should their souls need redemption? Or are they still in bondage to the devil? Just see, dear Christians, how the devil has reinforced the thing in defiance of God and the whole world. It is no wonder that God has blinded the people so completely that they accuse themselves of lying and yet are so blind that they do not see it, but even regard it as a great service to God. Is it not exactly the same as if I should say: Christians stick in their sins and are not redeemed, and yet are without sin and are redeemed; or: Those whom Christ has redeemed with his blood, that is, Christians, are not redeemed and are not Christians, but we will make ourselves Christians and redeem ourselves with a piece of bread and a drink of wine? With such abominable lies and blasphemies they dare to come boldly before God, and think that for that reason he should crown them. That is the second part, and now they go on from the living to the dead.

During the consecration the canon includes the following wicked and inappropriate prayer, that certainly does not in the slightest fit into the mass.

> **"Those who have fellowship and honor the memory, especially of the highly to be praised and ever Virgin Mary, the Mother of God and of our Lord Jesus Christ, and also of Thy blessed apostles and martyrs, Peter, Paul, Andrew, James, John, Thomas, James, Philip, Bartholomew, Matthew, Simon and Thaddaeus, Linus, Cletus, Clement, Sixtus, Cornelius, Cyprian, Lawrence, Chrysogonus, John and Paul,[3] Cosmas and Damian, and of all Thy saints, through whose merit and intercession wilt Thou vouchsafe to us that in every way we may be guarded through the help of Thy protection, through the same Christ our Lord. Amen."**

Christ instituted his body and blood as a remembrance of him [I Cor. 11:24-25], and for our fellowship who live here upon earth. But this fool of a canon makes of it a remembrance and fellowship of the departed saints, and sets them up as intercessors and mediators precisely at the very moment and in the very function when it is dealing and should be dealing with the sole mediator, Christ; thus it leads us from Christ to the saints. Is not that a horrible and shameful thing? Oh, the holy canon! One can see clearly that it has been collected and compiled by mad, unlearned priests.

Then follows a prayer.

DURING THE CONSECRATION

> **"Therefore we pray Thee, O Lord, graciously to receive this offering of our service, and of all Thy family, and to dispose our days in Thy peace, and also to save us from eternal damnation, and command us to be numbered among the multitude of Thy elect, through Christ our Lord. Amen."**

---

[3] John and Paul are here two Roman martyrs, not the apostles.

There the priest once more offers up bread and wine, and precisely in order that they may be saved from eternal damnation and be numbered among the elect. All that, too, the bread and wine is supposed to accomplish. For Christ's blood and death do not avail here for such salvation. Let each one ponder what an abomination that is! Yet we are supposed to pray it, and because it is such a very holy thing the laity are not supposed to hear it, as if it were all a heavenly thing. Let us go on.

A PRAYER

> **"Which offering, we beseech Thee, O God, in all things to make blessed, accredited, effective, reasonable and acceptable, that it may become for us the body and blood of Thy most beloved Son, our Lord Jesus Christ."**

At that point the priest then proceeds to consecrate the elements. I don't know what to make of these words. The foolish canon does not know itself what it is saying. It quotes from Paul's letter (Rom. 12 [:1]) that the sacrifice is to become "reasonable,"[4] but not until it has become the body and blood of Christ. Then, too, it is to become "accredited and blessed" although the canon has already in a previous petition called the bread and wine a holy unspotted offering. That will surely please God that I pray him to give heed to my petition and thereby for the first time be gracious to his Son and bless him and make him acceptable—when it is really through him that we are blessed and sanctified! How could one more completely blaspheme and insult him? If this were the only thing in the accursed canon, it alone would be abomination enough, that they dare to take it upon themselves to reconcile Christ and his pure and holy blood—when it is really through it that all sins are blotted out and washed away! And where Christ's blood is not present man's entire nature and all his being is accursed as an enemy of God and the devil's own. For is that not basically the same as saying that Christ's blood is not pure, yes, that it belongs to the devil? Else why does the canon pray that God should cleanse it? So you see clearly enough that the mass is nothing but a terrible and abominable blasphemy against God.

---

[4] *rationabile* (rational) in the Vulgate.

Here he takes the host in his hands and says:

"Who the day before He suffered took the bread in His holy and venerable hands and lifting up his eyes toward heaven gave thanks to Thee, O God, His almighty Father, blessed and broke it and gave it to His disciples, and said: Take and eat of it, all of you, for this is my body."

Thus run the noble words which Christ himself spoke. These they have scribbled in too, but they leave out what Christ added:[5] "which is given for you" [Luke 22:20]. They make no reference to these words because they know of something better to give for themselves, namely, a piece of bread and a drink of wine. But they have added the little word *"enim,"* [6] and they say it means the same as "truly." They have written many books about it, and decreed that whoever omits it commits a mortal sin. Yet they themselves have left out the best and most precious words, just so that they may keep quiet about the sacrifice which Christ has made. That is an omission which is not a sin!

Here he lays the host down
and lifts up the cup and says:

"In the same way, when they had eaten supper, He also took this excellent cup in His holy and venerable hands, and gave Thee thanks again, blessed and gave it to His disciples, and said: Take and drink of it, all of you, for this is the cup of my blood, of the New[7] Testament, a mystery of faith, which is poured out for you and for many for the forgiveness of sins. As often as you do this, you shall do it in memory of me."

Here he sets the cup down

This part of the sacrament they have reserved for themselves alone, and they have denied it to us laity in spite of the fact that the text says "Drink of it, all of you" [Matt. 26:27]. And they add here, from the words of Christ, "which is shed for you [Luke 22:20]

[5] Cf. Luther's own rendering of the Words of Institution on p. 37.
[6] A Latin conjunction meaning "for." Cf. p. 164 n. 35. Cf. also Luther's repudiation of those radical reformers who insisted on omitting the offensive conjunction. *LW* 40, 173.
[7] Luther does not even translate the non-scriptural adjective *eterni* ("and eternal"). Cf. p. 164 n. 35.

for the forgiveness of sins" [Matt. 26:28]. Perhaps these words are supposed to apply only to them. Earlier in connection with the bread, which is the only element they give to us, these words are not allowed to stand. Let us proceed.

> **"Wherefore, O Lord, we Thy servants, but also Thy holy people, remember Christ Thy Son, our Lord, both His holy passion and also His resurrection from hell, likewise also His glorious ascension into heaven, and offer to Thy excellent majesty of Thy gracious presents and gifts, a pure offering, a holy offering, an unspotted offering, the holy bread of eternal life and the cup of eternal salvation."**

See, here the canon comes again to the offering, for now the bread has become the body of Christ. The canon calls it a holy bread and a cup of salvation. How foolishly it does talk of the matter! But we want to do it the honor of giving it the best interpretation and not make it too wicked. The priest offers up once again the Lord Christ, who offered himself only once [Heb. 9:25-26], just as he died only once and cannot die again or be offered up again [Rom. 6:9-10]. For through his one death and sacrifice he has taken away and swallowed up all sins. Yet they go ahead and every day offer him up more than a hundred thousand times throughout the world. They thereby deny, both with their deeds and in their hearts, that Christ has washed sin away and has died and risen again. This is such an abomination that I don't believe it could be sufficiently punished on earth if it rained pure fire from heaven [Luke 9:54]. The blasphemy is so great that it must simply wait for eternal hell-fire [Matt. 18:8-9].

A PRAYER

> **"Upon which look with gracious and favorable countenance and let them be pleasing to Thee, as Thou wert pleased with the gifts of Thy righteous servant Abel and the sacrifice of our patriarch Abraham and that which Thy most high priest Melchizedek offered unto Thee, a holy sacrifice and unspotted host."**

Here again the priest prays for the offering, that God should be gracious to his Son and be pleased with him. And so a miserable man becomes a mediator between God and Christ, his dear Son. O what an abomination! In addition, the canon cites examples from the holy fathers, whereby they actually confess very clearly that the flesh and blood of Christ are unclean. For since they pray for it and the prayer is seriously intended, they certainly must be saying that it is not under God's favor. Were it under God's favor, why should one pray for it? Therefore, this prayer not only denies the blood of Christ, but actually treads it under foot. Christ's blood is supposed to sanctify and reconcile us, but we try to do that for it instead. Still they will not do him the honor of seeing it that way. Moreover, the blood of Christ is presumed to have no greater validity than the offerings of Abel [Gen. 4:4] and Abraham [Gen. 22:2] and Melchizedek [Gen. 14:18], all of which are purified through this sacrifice of Christ. Then, too, it is a great big lie that Melchizedek sacrificed bread and wine; but of that we have also spoken elsewhere.

Here he bows and says:

"We humbly beseech Thee, Almighty God, command that this be carried by the hands of Thy holy angel to Thy altar on high in the sight of Thy divine majesty, so that all of us who shall partake at this altar of the communion of the body and blood of Thy most holy Son may be filled with all heavenly blessing and grace, through the same Christ our Lord. Amen."

Here you see that there is no faith at all in the sacrifice of Christ. The priest tries to do everything himself, simply through his prayer. The canon speaks as if the congregation received the sacrament with the priest—as it really should—but then flatly contradicts itself and lets the people imagine that God has an altar in heaven to which the angel is supposed to carry the sacrament with his hands; yet the priest later eats and drinks it himself, as Christ also instituted it. That, I think, is blind, crazy, and senseless. But then everything really ought to be pretty much twisted around, since without the holy Word of God there cannot be so much as a single good syllable.

COMMEMORATION OF THE DEAD

"Remember also, O Lord, Thy servants, men and women, N. and N., who have gone before us with the sign of faith and repose in the sleep of peace. For these and all who rest in Christ we pray, O Lord, that Thou wilt grant a place of refreshment, light, and peace. Through the same Christ our Lord. Amen."

Now the priest comes again to the dead. This part is worth money, so that they do not say mass in vain. He prays for these who respose in the sleep of peace and rest in Christ and have the sign of faith. If that is true, why should you pray for them? Are you not a madman and a fool? If they have rest and peace, why or how should the priest refresh them and give them peace? So they of necessity contradict themselves, talking out of both sides of their mouth at the same time. They have no idea what they are saying or what they are talking about.

Here he beats his breast somewhat loudly and says:

"And also us sinners, Thy servants, who hope in the multitude of Thy mercies, wilt Thou grant some part and fellowship with Thy holy apostles and martyrs, with John, Stephan, Matthias, Barnabas, Ignatius, Alexander, Marcellinus, Peter, Felicitas, Perpetua, Agatha, Lucy, Agnes, Cecilia, Anastasia, and with Thy saints, into whose fellowship admit us, we beseech Thee, not as one who regards merit but as one who forgives. Through Christ our Lord."

Here the priest comes back at last to the living, but mixes with them the saints in heaven. His attention is centered there. He does not need the portion and fellowship of the Lord Christ besides. He wants to consort only with the saints, even though Christ has not obtained a share or fellowship or portion such as the saints have, but the whole treasure that he gives in heaven and on earth, yea everything that he himself is. And here you pray only for a share and worthless portion among the saints! They have also patched together again at this point a register of saints. There really ought to be not saints but only devils there—as indeed there are, under the names of saints.

"Through Whom, O Lord, Thou dost always create, sanctify, quicken, bless, and give to us all these good things. Through Him, and with Him, and in Him hast Thou, O God, Almighty Father, in the unity of the Holy Spirit, all honor and glory."

The vain babbler speaks again of many but takes it himself alone. Christ instituted the breaking of bread that it should be given and distributed to many. Yet here it is said that the bread is broken, but it is given to no one, and he who breaks it does not himself know what he does or why. And he affirms again that through their petition God daily sanctifies and quickens the body of Christ for the poor sinner.

> "For ever and ever." Response: "Amen."
>
> "Let us pray: We who have been taught by the salutary command and divine instruction make bold to say, Our Father, Who art in heaven, and so forth." Response. "And deliver us from evil."
>
> "We pray Thee, O Lord, deliver us from all past, present and future evils, and through the intercession of the blessed, highly to be praised and ever Virgin, the Mother of God, Mary, and of Thy blessed apostles Peter and Paul, and Andrew and all the saints, graciously give us also peace in our days, that we may have the help of Thy mercy, that we may always be free from sins, and that we may be secure against every kind of affliction."

So the saints must come to reconcile us with God, and not only us but even Christ himself. They would have good days without affliction. Well, God has heard that prayer and given the papists good days. But woe to them!

Here he breaks the host
first into two parts and says:

> "Through the same our Lord Jesus Christ, Thy Son, our Lord,"

Then he breaks the one part
into two parts and says:

> "Who liveth and reigneth with Thee in the unity of the Holy Spirit, God."

Then he elevates somewhat
the third part with the cup and says:

> "For ever and ever." Response. "Amen."

Then he makes the sign
of the cross over the blood and says:

> "The peace of the Lord be with you always." Response. "And with thy spirit."

Here he lays a piece of the host in the blood and says:

"May this commingling and consecration of the body and blood of our Lord Jesus Christ nourish us who receive it unto eternal life. Amen." [8]

Here the fool speaks again, of many who partake, but then partakes of it himself alone. And it is another blasphemy when he says that he commingles the body and blood of Christ with each other. I should like to know how one can mix the body and the blood, which really are one Christ. Bread and wine he commingles to be sure. But it is much worse that he calls it a consecration of the body and blood, just as if there were something about Christ that needed consecrating. Moreover, he adds that the commingling shall nourish those who partake unto eternal life. That is to say, the work itself is supposed to do it. What becomes of the words, in which that life resides? You see, everything depends on us and on the sacrifice!

Now he prays again for peace, bows before the body of the Lord and says:

A PRAYER

"Lord Jesus Christ, Who hast said to Thine apostles, 'My peace give I unto you, peace I leave with you,' regard not my sins but the faith of Thy church, and give her peace according to Thy will and hold her together, Thou Who livest and reignest, God for ever and ever. Amen."

Here for once he is wise; he confesses that he has no faith and asks God to regard the faith of the church. On this faith they depend and with it they try to justify their abomination. But God has struck them blind so that they think, and pride themselves on the thought, that they need not have faith because it is enough that the church has faith. And yet at this point nothing is more essential than that each one shall have faith for himself. Moreover, they say that the sacrifice and work is in itself well pleasing to God;

---

[8] Luther does not here record or comment upon the Agnus Dei which follows at this point in the canon. Cf. *The Formula of the Mass* (1523), *PE* 6, 91; and *The German Mass* (1526), *PE* 6, 183, both of which retain it intact.

even though the person is not pleasing, yet the sacrifice is pleasing! They thereby pass judgment upon themselves, because they receive the sacrament unworthily, with no more faith than a dog, and yet have guarded well their prerogative to grab and keep the money without any obligation to be righteous. At this point the canon has a long appendix full of senseless prattle; it never does get to the real subject.

Here he kisses the altar

A PRAYER

"Lord Jesus Christ, Son of the living God, who according to the will of the Father and through the cooperation of the Holy Spirit hast through Thy death given life to the world, redeem me through this Thy holy body and blood from all my iniquities and from all evil, and grant that I may always cleave to Thy commandments, and let me never be separated from Thee, Who with the same God the Father and the Holy Spirit livest and reignest for ever and ever. Amen."

The body and blood are supposed to do it through prayer, but faith in the Word must avail nothing!

A PRAYER

"May the taking of Thy body, Lord Jesus Christ, which I, though unworthy, presume to receive, redound not to my judgment and condemnation, but profit me according to Thy goodness as a shield of spirit and body, and be received as a healing potion, Thou Who livest and reignest with God the Father, and so forth."

This little prayer might pass if there were added, "As Thou hast spoken to me and commanded me to believe," so that the Word of God were brought in.

Here he takes the paten
with the body of Christ and says:

"I shall take the heavenly bread and call upon the name of the Lord."

These are all inopportune words that lead from faith to works.

Then he beats his breast three times
and says:

"Lord, I am not worthy that Thou shouldst come under my roof, but speak the word only and my soul will be healed."

Here he reverently takes[9] the body and signs himself with it and says:

"The body of our Lord Jesus Christ preserve my soul to everlasting life. Amen."

Here he takes the cup and says:

"What shall I render to the Lord for all His bounty to me? I will take the cup of salvation and call upon the name of the Lord. I will call upon the Lord with praise, and so I shall be saved from my enemies."

Then he drinks the blood and says:

"The blood of our Lord Jesus Christ preserve my soul to everlasting life."

Here he sticks on a patch from Ps. 116 [:12-13], and acts as though he would now repay God by taking the cup. That he takes the bread first is inconsequential; with the cup, however, he expects to repay everything. Dear fellow, go ahead, make sport, insult and blaspheme while you can. God has hitherto been able to bear it, and this he would never have done if he had not had in mind soon to overthrow them.

The prophet David says in Ps. 116 [:13] that God has helped him out of every adversity, and therefore he will give completely in return and will offer his cup, which is his modest portion, and will endure whatever God lays upon him and out of love to God will do and bear whatever he should.

This the fool applies here to his offering and his receiving of the sacrament.

When he has received the blood he says:

"What we have received with the mouth let us also receive with the heart, and the temporal gifts will become for us a heavenly medicine. Amen.

[9] That is, he communicates himself after crossing himself with the consecrated host. *PE* 6, 132 n. 15.

"Lord, grant that Thy body which I have received and Thy blood which I have drunk may cleave to my inner man, and that no spot of vice remain in me, who have been refreshed with the pure and holy sacrament."

That is the mass. Now here is the last part, when he is about to leave the altar.

When the mass is finished and the benediction has been pronounced, he bows before the middle of the altar and says this prayer; after which he kisses the altar:

"Be pleased, O Holy Trinity, with our service, and grant that the sacrifice which I have offered, though so unworthily before the eyes of Thy Majesty, may be pleasing to Thee and through Thy mercy atone for me together with all for whom I have offered it. Through Christ our Lord. Amen."

As he began, so he concludes, always making an offering and praying that it may be pleasing. The good Christ is not pleasing to the Father unless the holy canon comes and makes him pleasing, in that the offering reconciles him with God. And so again Christ is dead and of no avail, since only the work is supposed to forgive sins and obtain favor with God so that he is gracious to Christ and to us.

You see, there you have heard the holy secret mass, so that you may know what it is and may be shocked by it and may cross yourself as you would before the devil himself. Since now by God's Word and grace this abomination has been brought to light and its folly has been made plain to everyone, as Paul says (I Tim. 3 [II Tim. 3:9]), so that the great Babylonian whore has been uncovered before and behind, we should first thank God and then earnestly pray him to take away this abomination everywhere and exterminate it. For if we do not pray and show him our gratitude, and help to curtail this despicable practice, if we simply look on while God's name is blasphemed in this way, we too will have to bear the same guilt and punishment as they do. For when a shameless rogue on the street openly blasphemes, curses, or insults God, and the authorities tolerate it instead of punishing it severely as they ought, in the sight of God they are participating in such wickedness. In some countries it is forbidden to curse and swear. How much more ought the secular rulers to take action in this matter with restraints and punishments, because in the mass such blasphemies and insults are as evident and take place as publicly as if a rogue were blaspheming on the street. If the one is punishable, the other also is punishable.

Therefore, dear Christians, let us flee from such an abomination; and let us agree that it is possible through the duly constituted authorities to remove this blasphemy of God, so that we need not hang the sins of others about our own necks. For the authorities are responsible for the prevention and punishment of such public blasphemy of God, but if they tolerate it and simply look on where they could be preventing it, God will not wink at such conduct but will terribly punish both the blasphemers and those who approve them, so that the punishment will be more than they can bear. I have done my part. I have faithfully counselled. I have warned everybody. I cannot answer for those who do not follow me.

God give us his grace. Amen.

THE SACRAMENT OF THE BODY AND BLOOD OF CHRIST—AGAINST THE FANATICS

1526

Translated by Frederick C. Ahrens

INTRODUCTION

Luther preached three sermons for the purpose of preparing his congregation at Wittenberg for the celebration of the Lord's Supper on Easter Sunday of 1526. The first sermon was delivered on March 28, the day before the sacrament, and the other two on March 29. The first two dealt with the Lord's Supper and included a brief orientation on the view of the Swiss theologians concerning the sacrament. The third sermon, however, after opening with a short statement concerning "the fruit of the sacrament," dealt more with the confession of sins.

These sermons were not intended for publication, and some six months passed before they appeared in print. A whole string of circumstances combined to bring about their publication in late September or early October of 1526.

As early as 1524 Zwingli had begun to declare his view of the sacrament, first privately and then in print. In November of that year he wrote a letter to Matthew Alber, the pastor at Reutlingen, inviting him and his people to accept the Zwinglian view of the sacrament. This letter Zwingli published the following March and its publication was regarded as a definite challenge to Luther. The following August Zwingli's letter was answered by John Bugenhagen, Luther's colleague at Wittenberg. Since Luther himself did not accept the challenge to combat, the pastor and people of Reutlingen sent messengers to Wittenberg near the end of the year to secure Luther's opinion on this question of the Lord's Supper. Thereupon Luther wrote a letter to the Christians at Reutlingen strongly controverting the views of Karlstadt and Zwingli and admonishing the Reutlingen congregation to resist the devil and to continue steadfast in the words of Christ. This letter was published January 4, 1526. It was the first of several preliminary skirmishes that Luther fought with the Swiss "fanatics" in 1526 concerning the meaning of the Lord's Supper. The great battle itself did not burst into flame until the following year.

Another minor encounter in 1526 was Luther's Preface to the

German translation of a Latin document composed by Brenz on behalf of a number of Swabian pastors to refute the position of Oecolampadius. The document is known as the Swabian Syngramma. It was published in January, 1526, and Luther was greatly pleased with it. The German translation by Agricola together with Luther's preface appeared in June. The preface warned against the "new dreams about the sacrament" and again urged steadfastness in the words of Christ.

A little later a second German translation of the Syngramma appeared, apparently with Luther's encouragement, and it carried a second and more emphatic preface by Luther because by this time (September, 1526) the Swiss were claiming Luther's assent to their views.

One more skirmish, and probably the immediate occasion for the publication of our treatise against the fanatics, was a letter that Luther wrote on September 13, 1526, to John Herwagen in Strassburg. Herwagen had published a four-volume translation into German of *Luther's Exposition of the Epistles and Gospels.* The translation was made by Martin Bucer. In the course of the publication the translator seems to have been converted to Zwingli's view of the sacrament, and in the fourth volume of his translation he took occasion to present the Swiss view in refutation of Luther's view. Luther's letter to the publisher protested against this procedure and demanded that any future editions of his *Exposition* include also his letter of protest.

About the same time Luther's attention was called to a document from the hand of the Zurich theologian, Leo Jud, a friend of Zwingli and Oecolampadius, in which he attempted to show that Luther was really in agreement with the Swiss view.

Without prompt and definite answer from Luther himself these publications threatened to mislead Luther's followers. Moreover, it had become quite evident that Luther's friends as well as his opponents were trying to bring him to some major expression of his views on the sacrament. However, Luther's other obligations just then kept him too busy to write out a complete answer to the Swiss view and a detailed explanation of his own position. So it was felt that a useful purpose would be served by the immediate publication of the sermons preached the preceding March, because it would show how earnestly he was warning his own congregation against the fanatics.

It is uncertain what part Luther himself had in the publication of this "sermon." Two copies of the three sermons he preached at Easter, 1526, are extant; apparently they were written down by his hearers. A comparison of these two copies with the text of the "sermon" published six months later indicates that a number of additions were made in preparing the materials for publication. These additions do not in all cases fit into the logic of the sermons themselves. This lack of continuity suggests that it was not Luther himself who prepared the sermons for publication. Certainly Luther could not have regarded them as a systematic polemic against the Swiss theologians. They were clearly intended as popular instruction for the laity and were adapted to the educational and doctrinal background of his Wittenberg congregation. It is therefore unlikely that Luther himself would have added to the title the phrase, "Against the Fanatics." Nor would he have chosen a title that covers only the first two of the sermons unless he had intended to omit the sermon about the confession of sins.

Moreover, Luther wrote no preface to the document, as he would most probably have done if he had participated in its publication. When his friends later urged him to take part in the debate of 1526 it seems that he never referred them to this treatise as the answer to their wishes. And he does not mention the document, even when he lists his writings against the fanatics.

On the other hand, it would be too much to suggest that Luther did not know of the publication of this "sermon" at the time it was published, or that he did not consent to its publication. It is significant that he did not complain when his opponents attacked it as his own publication. At any rate, it served to touch off the major battle on the subject that developed the following year, and it may be regarded as the prelude to his longer and more spirited defenses of his views on the Lord's Supper.

Our translation is from the German text in *WA* 19, 482-523.

THE SACRAMENT OF THE BODY AND BLOOD OF CHRIST—AGAINST THE FANATICS

In this sacrament there are two things that should be known and proclaimed. First, what one should believe. In Latin this is called the *objectum fidei*, that is, the work or thing in which one believes, or to which one is to adhere. Second, the faith itself, or the use which one should properly make of that in which he believes. The first lies outside the heart and is presented to our eyes externally, namely, the sacrament itself, concerning which we believe that Christ's body and blood are truly present in the bread and wine. The second is internal, within the heart, and cannot be externalized. It consists in the attitude which the heart should have toward the external sacrament. Up to now I have not preached very much about the first part, but have treated only the second, which is also the best part But because the first part is now being assailed by many, and the preachers, even those who are considered the best, are splitting up into factions over the matter, so that in foreign lands a large number are already pouncing upon it and maintaining that Christ's body and blood are not present in the bread and wine, the times demand that I say something on this subject also.

At the outset I will say this, however: if anyone is thought to be engulfed in such an error, I would earnestly advise him to abstain from the sacrament until he emerges from his error and becomes strong in the faith. For we have before us the clear text and the plain words of Christ: "Take, eat; this is my body, which is given for you. Drink of it, all of you, this is my blood, which is poured out for you. Do this in remembrance of me" [Matt. 26:26-28; Luke 22:19-20]. These are the words on which we take our stand.[1] They are so simply and clearly stated that even they, our adversaries, must confess that it is difficult to interpret them otherwise. Yet they pass these clear words by and follow their own thoughts, making darkness for themselves in the midst of the bright light.

If anyone wishes to pursue a true course and not come to grief, let him beware of the clever idea, inspired by the devil in this matter everywhere, that he may suck the egg dry and leave us the shell, that is, remove the body and blood of Christ from the bread and wine, so that it remains no more than mere bread, such as the baker bakes. In accordance with this clever idea our opponents mock us at their pleasure, charging that we are eaters of flesh and drinkers of blood and that we worship a baked God.[2] In former times that desperate renegade, Averroes,[3] who had himself been a Christian, similarly mocked and slandered the faithful, maintaining that there is no people on earth more despicable than the Christians, because they devour their own God, which no other people had ever done. Was this not an exquisitely clever saying? Such are the tricks which the devil is playing against us nowadays everywhere.

Now God is the sort of person who likes to do what is foolish and useless in the eyes of the world, as Paul says in I Cor. 1 [:23]: "We preach Christ crucified, a stumbling block to the Jews and folly to the Gentiles." And again: "For since, in the wisdom of God, the world did not know God through wisdom, it pleased God through the folly of what we preach to save those who believe in him" [I Cor. 1:21]. Well then, if anyone does not believe this, let him believe accordingly that it is mere bread, or a batch of bread.[4] Anyone who has failed to grasp the faith may thenceforth believe whatever he likes, it makes no difference. Just as when someone is

---

[1] Cf. p. 37 n. 84.

[2] In his *Billiche Antwort* of July 18, 1526, a reply to the Swabian Syngramma and Luther's preface to it, Oecolampadius defended his use of the terms *gotsfleischesser* and *gotsblutsauffer* to describe his opponents, and *brötenen* and *gebachnen* to describe their God. *WA* 19, 457 n. 2.

[3] Averroes (1126-98) was an Arab physician and philosopher whose commentary on Aristotle had a wide vogue in the Middle Ages and did much to revive the study of Aristotle.

[4] *Schusselbrod,* as much bread as is put into the oven at one time. *WA* 19, 484 n. 4.

on the point of drowning, whether he drowns in a brook or in the middle of a stream, he is drowned just the same. So I say of these fanatics: if they let go of the word, let them believe whatever they like and squabble as long as they like. It has already happened that six or seven sects have arisen over the sacrament, but all of them under the delusion that Christ's flesh and blood are not present.

This comes about, I maintain, because in the first place they have not adhered to the words, and then because they have followed their own thoughts and have seen that if Christ were present in the bread and wine and were distributed so widely everywhere and if each person were to eat this Christ, that would be an awkward situation. This has been their first thought. Hence they have a colored glass before their eyes, and therefore the words must mean what they think. This is what all factious spirits do: they first concoct an opinion. If it pleases them, they then attempt to force the Scriptures to agree with it. But whoever derives the right faith from the words will believe like this: Whether Christ enters into the bread or the cup or into whatever he will, God grant that as long as I have the words, I will not seek or speculate any further; what he says, I will keep. Thus the believer envelops himself in the Word, will not let himself be turned aside from it, and is also thereby sustained.

For we are not so simple-minded that we do not understand the words. If these words are not clear, I do not know how to speak German. Would I not understand, if someone were to place a roll before me and say: "Take, eat, this is white bread"? Or again, "Take and drink, this is a glass of wine"?[5] Therefore, when Christ says: "Take, eat, this is my body," even a child will understand perfectly well that he is speaking of that which he is offering. It is a natural way of speaking that when someone points to a thing, we know what he is saying. If I should now make this word obscure and invent some subtlety concerning it, I would only be confusing myself. These words are quite clear and explicit: take bread, give thanks, break, give, bid them eat and drink, this is my body, this

[5] The shorter of the two sermon copies, which is almost entirely in Latin, at this point has the German phrase: "*das ist wittenbergisch bier.*" Cf. *WA* 19, 475, 481, and 485.

is my blood. The fanatics really knock themselves out struggling with these words. First they come up with a notion of their own; then they have to interpret the words according to what each one has dreamed up. For this reason we stick closely to the words and close our eyes and senses, because everyone knows what "this is my body" means, especially when he adds "given for you." We know what Christ's body is, namely, that which was born of Mary, suffered, died, and rose again.[6]

Now they have two points in particular which they bring up against us. First, they say it is not fitting that Christ's body and blood should be in the bread and wine. Second, it is not necessary. These are about the best foundations that they have to build on. Let us look at them.

To the first point I might say equally well that it is not reasonable that God should descend from heaven and enter into the womb; that he who nourishes, sustains, and encompasses all the world should allow himself to be nourished and encompassed by the Virgin. Likewise, that Christ, a king of glory [Ps. 24:10], at whose feet all angels must fall and before whom all creatures must tremble, should thus humble himself below all men and allow himself to be suspended upon the cross as a most notorious evil-doer and that by the most wicked and desperate of men. And I might conclude from this that God did not become man, or that the crucified Christ was not God. Thus they say it is not fitting that God should perform in the sacrament so many wondrous deeds that he does not perform anywhere else. For what we believe, they consider to be incongruous; they regard it as tremendous miracles, that the single body of Christ is in a hundred thousand places, wherever bread is broken, and that the massive limbs should there be so concealed that no one sees or feels them. But they do not see that these are vain and useless thoughts. If one wished to apply this kind of measurement, one would be forced to allow no creature to exist.

If it were possible and I should measure all creatures and describe them in words, you would see wonders just as great, nay, even greater, than in this sacrament. Behold the soul, which is a single creature, and yet at the same time is present throughout the

[6] The longer of the two sermon copies, the one by Rörer, adds: "he does not say 'is my stone, or table' but 'my body.'" *WA* 19, 500.

whole body, even in the smallest toe, so that when I prick the smallest member of the body with a needle, I affect the entire soul, and the whole man quivers. Now, if one soul can be present at one time in all the members—though I am unable to explain how that happens—should Christ not be capable of being present at one time in all places in the sacrament?

Again, my soul can think and speak simultaneously, and while speaking see, hear, feel, etc., and at the same time digest food into blood, flesh, bone, urine and feces. No one considers this a miracle, because we see it daily and are accustomed to it. The only thing that those people lack is that they have never observed any creature rightly, as we shall hear further.

Look at a grain of wheat in the field, and tell me how it comes about that the stalk grows out of the earth from a single seed and bears so many kernels on the ear, and gives each one its own form. Moreover, in a single kernel there are many, many miraculous works, which they neither perceive nor pay any heed to. Again, how does it happen, that I have only two eyes, and yet I am able to take in the heads of all men at one time with the sight of my eyes? Indeed, I can do it just as well with one eye as with two. Thus one eye can focus upon a thousand kernels, and on the other hand, a thousand eyes can focus on one kernel.

Take the word which I am speaking as a further example. The voice is a poor, miserable thing, to be reckoned as the least of creatures, not more than a breath of wind. As soon as the mouth ceases speaking, the voice is gone and is no more, so that there can be nothing weaker or more perishable. Yet it is so mighty, that I could rule a whole country with my voice. How does it come about, then, that I may capture so many hearts with words? I have a small voice, and there are several hundreds or thousands of ears, yet every single ear perceives the complete and entire voice. I do not distribute it, so that each ear has only a part of it, but each one has all of it. The fanatics see this, and do not consider it a miracle. Indeed, if we had never seen it, it would be the greatest of miracles. Now, if my voice can accomplish this so that it fills all ears, with each one receiving as much of it as the other, and my word is distributed so widely, should not Christ be able to do so all the more with his body? How much easier it is with a glorified body than with a bodily voice! You will find many more such miracles among the creatures, so that anyone who examines a creature rightly will not permit himself to be led astray by this article.

Again, I preach the gospel of Christ, and with my bodily voice I bring Christ into your heart, so that you may form him within yourself. If now you truly believe, so that your heart lays hold of the word and holds fast within it that voice, tell me, what have you in your heart? You must answer that you have the true Christ, not that he sits in there, as one sits on a chair, but as he is at the right hand of the Father. How that comes about you cannot know, but your heart truly feels his presence, and through the experience of faith you know for a certainty that he is there. Now I can accomplish this again, that the one Christ enters into so many hearts through the voice, and that each person who hears the sermon and accepts it takes the whole Christ into his heart. For Christ does not permit himself to be divided into parts; yet he is distributed whole among all the faithful, so that one heart receives no less, and a thousand hearts no more, than the one Christ. This we must ever confess, and it is a daily miracle. Indeed, it is as great a miracle as here in the sacrament. Why then should it not be reasonable that he also distributes himself in the bread?

But what happens when I bring Christ into the heart? Does it come about, as the fanatics imagine, that Christ descends on a ladder and climbs back up again? Christ still sits on the right hand of the Father, and also in your heart, the one Christ who fills heaven and earth. I preach that he sits on the right hand of God and rules over all creatures, sin, death, life, world, devils and angels; if you believe this, you already have him in your heart. Therefore your heart is in heaven, not in an apparition or dream, but truly. For where he is, there you are also. So he dwells and sits in your heart, yet he does not fall from the right hand of God. Christians experience and feel this clearly. But those people see none of these things, great as it is that Christ dwells thus in the heart and imparts himself completely in every heart and is distributed through the Word. Therefore, whoever can believe this does not find it difficult to believe also that his body and blood are in the sacrament. For if you try in this way to measure that wondrous sign with the measuring-rod of thought and reason, you will at last reach the point where you must also say that Christ does not dwell in the hearts of the faithful.

Now see, as I have said, how much the poor bodily voice is able to do. First of all it brings the whole Christ to the ears; then it brings him into the hearts of all who listen and believe. Should it then be so amazing that he enters into the bread and wine? Is not the heart much more tenuous and elusive than bread? You will probably not attempt to fathom how this comes about. Just as little as you are able to say how it comes about that Christ is in so many thousands of hearts and dwells in them—Christ as he died and rose again—and yet no man knows how he gets in, so also here in the sacrament, it is incomprehensible how this comes about. But this I do know, that the word is there: "Take, eat, this is my body, given for you, this do in remembrance of me." When we say these words over the bread, then he is truly present, and yet it is a mere word and voice that one hears. Just as he enters the heart without breaking a hole in it, but is comprehended only through the Word and hearing, so also he enters into the bread without needing to make any hole in it.

Take yet another example. How did his mother Mary become pregnant? Although it is a great miracle when a woman is made pregnant by a man, yet God reserved for him the privilege of being born of the Virgin. Now how does the Mother come to this? She has no husband [Luke 1:34] and her womb is entirely enclosed. Yet she conceives in her womb a real, natural child with flesh and blood. Is there not more of a miracle here than in the bread and wine? Where does it come from? The angel Gabriel brings the word: "Behold, you will conceive in your womb and bear a son, etc." [Luke 1:31]. With these words Christ comes not only into her heart, but also into her womb, as she hears, grasps, and believes it. No one can say otherwise, than that the power comes through the Word. As one cannot deny the fact that she thus becomes pregnant through the Word, and no one knows how it comes about, so it is in the sacrament also. For as soon as Christ says: "This is my body," his body is present through the Word and the power of the Holy Spirit. If the Word is not there, it is mere bread; but as soon as the words are added they bring with them that of which they speak.

Moreover, we believe that Christ, according to his human nature, is put over all creatures [Eph. 1:22] and fills all things, as Paul says in Eph. 4 [:10]. Not only according to his divine nature, but also according to his human nature, he is a lord of all things, has all things in his hand, and is present everywhere. If I am to follow the fanatics who say that this is not fitting, then I must deny Christ. We read of Stephen in Acts 7 [:56] that he said: "I see the heavens opened, and Jesus standing at the right hand of the Father." How does he see Christ? He need not raise his eyes on high. Christ is around us and in us in all places. Those people understand nothing of this. They also say that he sits at the right hand of God, but what it means that Christ ascends to heaven and sits there, they do not know. It is not the same as when you climb up a ladder into the house. It means rather that he is above all creatures and in all and beyond all creatures. That he was taken up bodily, however, occurred as a sign of this. Therefore he now has all things before his eyes, more than I have you before my eyes, and he is closer to us than any creature is to another. They speculate thus, that he must ascend and descend from the heavens through the air, and that he lets himself be drawn down into the bread when we eat his body. Such thoughts come from no other source than from foolish reason and the flesh. We must understand that it is not the words which we speak that draw him down. They have been given to us rather to assure us, that we may know we shall certainly find him.

Although he is present in all creatures, and I might find him in stone, in fire, in water, or even in a rope, for he certainly is there, yet he does not wish that I seek him there apart from the Word, and cast myself into the fire or the water, or hang myself on the rope. He is present everywhere, but he does not wish that you grope for him everywhere. Grope rather where the Word is, and there you will lay hold of him in the right way. Otherwise you are tempting God and committing idolatry. For this reason he has set down for us a definite way to show us how and where to find him, namely the Word. Those people, who say that it is unreasonable for Christ to be present in the bread and wine, do not know or see this at all, because they also do not understand what Christ's kingdom is, and the sitting at the right hand of God. If Christ were not with me in dungeon, torture, and death, where would I be? He is present there through the Word, although not in the same way as here in the sacrament, where through the Word he binds his body and blood so that they are also received corporeally in the bread and wine. If we believe the one, it is easy also to grasp and believe the other. Heaven and earth are his sack; as wheat fills the sack, so he fills all things. And as a seed bears a stalk, an ear, and many kernels; or again, as a single cherrystone cast into the ground brings forth a tree which bears many blossoms, leaves, inner and outer bark, and cherries; or again, as my voice reaches so many ears; much more is Christ able to distribute himself whole and undivided into so many particles.

Now because the fanatics do not see this, they come up with their man-made opinion to the effect that God is thereby performing some kind of hocus-pocus. Well, let them just go on making fools of themselves; but you cling to the thought that Christ, as I have said, does all these things through the Word, just as the wonders which he daily thereby performs are countless. Should he not through the same power know how to do these things also here in the sacrament? He has put himself into the Word, and through the Word he puts himself into the bread also. If he can break into the heart and spirit and dwell in the soul, he must have much easier access to the material object because the heart is much more tenuous and elusive. But he retains the lesser miracles in order that through them he may remind us of the greater ones. For that he enters the heart through faith is a much greater miracle than that he is present in the bread. Indeed, it is for the sake of faith that he uses that very bread or sacrament. If we would bear this in mind, we would not talk so much of miracles in the sacrament. But if we wanted to follow after and think of God with our reason we should have to say of faith too that no man is able to believe. For God is too far beyond all reason. Hence, to sum it all up, what those people keep saying—that because it is not in accord with reason it is not true—we shall simply turn about and say the opposite: God's Word is true, therefore your notions must be false. Is it necessarily unreasonable, just because it seems unreasonable to you and you think that the Word must be wrong and your ideas valid?

The other argument which they bring up is that it is not

necessary. So Christ has to let himself be taken to school and taught by them. The Holy Spirit hasn't hit it right. For this is what they say: If I believe in Jesus Christ, who died for me, what need is there for me to believe in a baked God? Wait and see, he will bake them when the time comes, so that their hides will sizzle. Who says this? God or a human being? A man says it. Why? Because Satan has taken possession of them; they have learned no more than to speak and preach the words: "Christ died for us, etc.," but in their hearts they do not feel it in the least. Do you wish to instruct God as to what is necessary and unnecessary, and have him decide according to your notions? It is better for us to reverse this and say: God wishes it thus, therefore your notions are false. Who are you, that you dare to speak against that which God regards as necessary? You are a liar, and therefore God is true [Rom. 3:4].

You might as well tell me also that because faith alone justifies, Christ is not necessary. So let us say to God: You had sin, death, devil, and everything in your power; what need was there to send down your Son, and permit him to be treated so cruelly and to die? You could indeed have allowed him to remain on high; it would have cost you only a word, and sin and death would have been destroyed, along with the devil. For you are certainly almighty. Again, let us conclude that Christ was not born of the Virgin, and say: Of what use was it? Could not God have caused him to be born of a man just as well, and still be fashioned so that he would have been conceived without sin and have remained innocent? Indeed, let us even go further and say that it is not necessary that Christ be God. For through God's power he could just as well have risen from the dead and saved us, even if he had been purely human. Thus the devil blinds people, and the result is, first, that they are incapable of seeing any work of God in the right light, and second, that they also fail to regard the Word, and accordingly want to find out everything with their own minds. If you were to search out everything about a kernel of wheat in the field, you would be so amazed that you would die. God's works are not like our works.

Therefore you should reply to these opponents: What is it to me, whether it is necessary or not? God knows well how it shall be and why it must be thus. If he says that it is necessary, then all creatures must be silent. But because in the sacrament Christ says in clear words: "Take, eat, this is my body, etc." it is my duty to believe these words, as firmly as I must believe all the words of Christ. If he handed me a mere straw and spoke these words, I should believe it. Therefore one must close mouth, eyes, and all the senses and say: "Lord, you know better than I." The same is true of baptism. The water is baptism, and in baptism is the Holy Spirit. So you might also say: "Why is it necessary to baptize with water?" But the Spirit says so, do you hear? Here is God's will and Word; adhere to it, and let your opinions go.

See, these are the two reasons they give for saying one should not believe that Christ's body and blood are in the sacrament. They are also the best reasons they can find, and the second one in particular they delineate at length. These are reasons, nevertheless, of the sort that sway devout hearts today, and have done so in the past. I myself have pondered much, what necessity there was in it, and how so great a body could be in so small a piece of bread, and how it could yet be undivided and whole in every particle. But if they examine a kernel of wheat or a cherrystone, it can well teach them manners. For why does God feed us through the bread, or under the bread, when he could do so just as well by the mere Word alone, without the bread? Why does he not create men as he created Adam and Eve, in a moment; he takes so long a time in doing it, in that man and woman must come together and the child must be trained so long with labor and effort. But he says: "What is that to you? [John 21:22]. I made Adam and Eve in this way at the beginning, but now I do not will to do it in this way any longer. I once caused a son to be born of the Virgin, and that also I do not will to do again." Thus those people would bind God by their laws, which is just as if I were to say: "Why have you given him a large body and me a small one? Why do you give this one black hair and that one blond, or this one brown eyes and that one gray?" Let this then be the sum of it: See only that you pay heed to God's Word and remain in it, like a child in the cradle. If you let go of it for a moment, then you fall out of it. This is the devil's sole aim, to tear people out of it and to cause them to measure God's will and work by human reason.

Those, I say, are still reasonable souls who concern themselves with the two points which I have touched on above; they can still be helped. The rest, however, are vain fanatics who proceed to force the words of Christ open and shut like pincers. Indeed, they are arch-fanatics, and do not have a leg to stand on. Those two points at least have some standing in the eyes of reason. But from the way in which the latter tear and twist the words, reason can well see that they are fools. There are only three words: "This is my body." So the one [Karlstadt] turns up his nose at the word "this" and severs it from the bread, claiming that one should interpret it thus: "Take, eat,—this is my body"; as if I were to say: "Take and eat; here sits Hans with the red jacket."[7] The second [Zwingli] seizes upon the little word "is"; to him it is the equivalent of "signifies." The third [Oecolampadius] says, "this is my body" means the same as, "this is a figure of my body." They set up these dreams of theirs without any scriptural basis. These fanatics do not disturb me, and are not worthy that one should fight with them. Some of them are crude, grammatical fanatics; the others are subtle, philosophical fanatics. Let them go, therefore, and let us adhere to the words as they read: that the body of Christ is present in the bread and that his blood is truly present in the wine. This does not mean that he is not present in other places also with his body and blood, for in believing hearts he is completely present with his body and blood. But it means that he wishes to make us certain as to where and how we are to lay hold of him. There is the Word, which says that when you eat the bread you eat his body, given for you. If the Word were not there, I would not pay any heed to the bread. Let this suffice for the first part.

PART II

Now that we have preserved the treasure, and not allowed the kernel to be taken out of the shell[8] so that we have only chaff left instead of grain,[9] we must now preach on the second part, namely, how one should make use of the sacrament and derive benefit from

[7] The shorter sermon copy at this point adds in Latin: "and behold the bread, I have money in my purse." *WA* 19, 498.
[8] Cf. *Sprichwörter-Lexikon, op. cit.*, IV, col. 78, *Schale,* No. 2.
[9] Cf. *Ibid.*, II, col. 1542, *Korn,* No. 53.

it. For it is not sufficient that we know what the sacrament is, namely, that Christ's body and blood are truly present, but it is also necessary to know why they are present and for what reason they are given to us to be received.

But here is where our opponents cause anguish. The devil cannot leave it alone; he must besmirch God's works and words. If he cannot tear it away completely, he makes an empty nut[10] of it. The pope took away from us one element of the sacrament. These people, however, leave us both elements; but they make a hole in the nut,[11] in order that we may lose the body and blood of Christ. In addition, both sides permit the right use to be lost from sight.

Thus we say now: Formerly we tortured ourselves with anxiety as to how we might approach this sacrament worthily. This worthy approach we now call the use of the sacrament. Then one advocated self-torment with many arduous works, with fasting and confession, and prepared one's self for it in such a way that it was used merely as a good work. The papists went that far with it, but still it remained intact. It is by grace that with respect to the gospel, the Scriptures, baptism, and the sacrament the thing has remained, as it is in itself. But the proper use of it they have destroyed and taken away from us. This use we must revive and preserve, as we have done heretofore. For when I was preaching against the misuse I did not foresee the heresy which is now gaining the upper hand; I merely contested with them concerning the proper use.

This is what I have taught: that one should not use the sacrament as a good work. They believed that whoever had confessed properly and knew of no mortal sin upon his conscience and so went to the sacrament was doing a precious, holy work, through which he merited heaven. If you wish to make the right use of it, you must not receive it in such a way that you say: "This I have done," just as if you had fasted or kept watch. But you ought to believe, not only that Christ is present with his body and blood, but also that he is given to you. You should always stand upon the words: "Take, eat, this is my body, which is given for you. Drink, this is my blood, which is poured out for you. Do this in remembrance of me." In these words his body and blood

[10] Cf. *Ibid.*, III, col. 1076, *Nuss*, No. 112.

[11] Cf. *Ibid.*, III, col. 1074, No. 78; and col. 1077, No. 129.

are given to us. So there are two things to be believed: that it is truly present, which the papists also believe; and that it is given to us, which they do not believe, and that we should use it as a gift.

There you hear it, expressed in clear German: he commands you to take his body and blood. Why? For what reason? Because the body is given for you and the blood is poured out for you. Here they have great anguish to inflict upon us, these new preachers of ours, in that they deprive us of this also, and in so cruel a manner that I believe the devil is trying his utmost and that the day of judgment is not far off. I should rather be dead than hear Christ so scorned and abused by them. They say that it is only a sign, by which one may recognize Christians and judge them, so that we have nothing more of it than the mere shell. So they come together, and eat and drink, in order that they may commemorate his death. All the power is said to be in this commemoration, the bread and wine are no more than a sign and a color by which one may recognize that we are Christians. Why do they do this? Because they cast to the winds the words: "Eat, this is my body, which is given for you." The words mean nothing to them; they rumble by over their heads. They are supposed to mean nothing more than the proclaiming and preaching of his death. To be sure, one should proclaim his death, and we have also preached it in grander fashion than they ever did. And if they did not have it from us, they would know nothing of it, because the papists have never spoken of it at all. Therefore, the fanatics have no right to teach this to us and make great boasts about it, as if they had invented something new.

Therefore we too are preaching the death of Christ according to the words: "Do this in remembrance of me." However, a distinction has to be made here. When I preach his death, it is in a public sermon in the congregation, in which I am addressing myself to no one individually; whoever grasps it, grasps it. But when I distribute the sacrament, I designate it for the individual who is receiving it; I give him Christ's body and blood that he may have forgiveness of sins, obtained through his death and preached in the congregation. This is something more than the congregational sermon; for although the same thing is present in the sermon as in the sacrament, here there is the advantage that it is directed at definite individuals. In the sermon one does not point out or portray any particular person, but in the sacrament it is given to you and to me in particular, so that the sermon comes to be our own. For when I say: "This is the body, which is given for you, this is the blood, which is poured out for you for the forgiveness of sins," I am there commemorating him; I proclaim and announce his death. Only it is not done publicly in the congregation but is directed at you alone.

Thus Christ has ordained that when we come together each one shall take of the bread and the cup, and afterwards preach of him. Why? For we are to give this to no one except those who are Christians and who have heard Christ preached beforehand. But the preaching or proclamation is intended for everyone in general, even for those who are not yet Christians. The Christians alone are to partake of the sacrament, but at the same time they are to take thought that their number may increase.

Therefore one should shout it out publicly and hold such public commemoration, that even those who do not yet know of it will attend. That they hold such commemoration privately is worthless. It should take place publicly before the congregation, and there should be preaching at the mass at all times. Therefore the words: "Do this in remembrance of me" are as much as to say: "As often as you do this, preach of me," as Paul interprets it in I Cor. 11 [:26], when he calls it "proclaiming the death of Christ." He uses the word, "proclaim," in order to show that it is not to be done privately, only among Christians who know of it beforehand and who stand in need, not of proclamation, but only of admonition. Rather it is to be done publicly before the multitude, for those who do not know of it. Thus both "remembrance" and "proclamation" mean nothing else than the preaching of him publicly, as is done in all sermons.

This, I say, we should always do when we receive the sacrament. Those who go to the sacrament, however, should believe and be assured, not only that they are receiving the true body and blood of Christ in it, but also that it is there given to them and is their own. Why? Not as a work for the sake of money or merit, as the monks and priests hold mass, but for the forgiveness of our sins. Now we surely know what forgiveness of sins means. When he forgives, he forgives everything completely and leaves nothing unforgiven. When I am free of sin, I am also free of death, devil, and hell; I am a son of God, a lord of heaven and earth.

Thus everyone, especially when he is attacked or subjected to persecution, should know how to answer and be able to say: "This is how I understand the words, that in the sacrament his body and blood are given to me for the forgiveness of sins." For this reason every Christian must know these words, letter for letter: "Here my Lord has given me his body and blood in the bread and wine, in order that I should eat and drink. And they are to be my very own, so that I may be certain that my sins are forgiven, that I am to be free of death and hell, have eternal life, and be a child of God and an heir of heaven. Therefore I go to the sacrament to seek these things. I am a poor sinner with death before me, I must go through it; and the devil threatens me with all kinds of trouble and danger. Because I am in sin, a captive of death and the devil, because I feel that I am weak in faith, cold in love, wayward, impatient, envious, with sin clinging to me before and behind; therefore I come hither where I find and hear Christ's word that I shall receive the gift of forgiveness of sins." Once we have the gift, we are then to proclaim it, so that we may bring other persons to it also. See, this is how one should instruct children and simple hearts concerning the sacrament, so that they may know what to seek in it.

This then is what we call the correct use of the sacrament. It is not a matter of mere performance and of rendering obedience to the church, for even a pig might go to the sacrament in this way. It is not to be done for the sake of a good work, but in order that your heart should be strengthened, as the words say: "Which is given for you, which is poured out for you." And even if the words were not there, as when Paul omits them [I Cor. 11:25], you still have the body which died for your sins and the blood which was poured out for them. But when Christ is given to you, forgiveness of sins is also given to you, and all that is procured through the treasure. If you have grasped it with your heart (and it cannot be grasped in any other way) and if you believe, you must say: "No work, no deed, will help me out of my sins, but I have another treasure, the body and blood of my Lord, given to me for the forgiveness of sins. This is the only treasure, the only forgiveness, and there is no other in heaven or on earth."

For this reason Christ has given himself to us completely, and wishes to be and remain with us until the day of judgment [Matt. 28:20]; not merely that he may be present, as the papists have him and carry him about to no avail, nor as the others say, *ut signum*, that is, as a mere sign, which would bring us neither improvement nor benefits. Should Christ institute so great a thing in vain, without any use or profit? No, this is the benefit that you ought to derive: that you strengthen your faith and make your conscience secure, so that afterwards you may also be able to preach. So they say that it is merely a useless commemoration, which can be of no advantage to you or to anyone else. Be on guard! May God continue to preserve us as he has done until now. The devil has nothing to do anywhere except to come and besmirch the place where the gospel has taken root. Therefore we must build firmly on these words and stand fast in them, and thus we will be able to give a proper answer to the heretics. For these words are expressed in clear enough German. In substance they say this: first, that here we obtain forgiveness of sins as a gift, and second, that we afterwards preach and proclaim the same.

Here then you have the distinction as to what the commemoration is, and how one should use the sacrament and derive benefit from it, namely, by simply correcting our shortcomings and failings. We share the common frailties of other people, and each has his own peculiar frailties; because of these we come here to seek strength. This is why this sacrament is called a food for hungry and thirsty souls, who feel their misery and would gladly be rescued from death and all misfortune. The papists have taught: "Beware, do not go thither unless you are pure and have no evil conscience," so that Christ may be certain to have a pure abode. They have so stupified and frightened the poor souls by this that they have fled from the sacrament, and yet have had to receive it under constraint—with such trembling that they would as gladly have entered a fiery furnace.

We are to be pure in the sense that we are sorry for our sins and would gladly be rid of them, and are vexed that we are such miserable people—insofar as we are serious about it and not just pretending. Complete sinlessness, however, no one will ever attain. Even if you should do so, you would not dare to go to the sacrament, for it was instituted specifically for the sake of the weak. So much for the use of the sacrament: it is to strengthen the conscience against all distress and temptation.

Now there remains the part concerning the fruit of the sacrament. Of this I have had much to say at other places. It is nothing other than love. The early fathers too have emphasized this most of all, and for this reason they called the sacrament *communio*, that is, a communion. This is also presented to us here in two ways—first, by way of an example, and second, by way of a symbol or sign which is the bread and wine—so every Christian, no matter how crude he may be, may be able to comprehend here in the sacrament the whole Christian doctrine, what he is to believe and what he is to do through faith. For it is necessary for each one to know that Christ has given his body, flesh, and blood on the cross to be our treasure and to help us to receive forgiveness of sins, that is, that we may be saved, redeemed from death and hell.

That is the first principle of Christian doctrine. It is presented to us in the words, and his body and blood are given to us to be received corporeally as a token and confirmation of this fact. To be sure, he did this only once, carrying it out and achieving it on the cross; but he causes it each day anew to be set before us, distributed and poured out through preaching, and he orders us to remember him always and never forget him.

The second principle is love. It is demonstrated in the first place by the fact that he has left us an example. As he gives himself for us with his body and blood in order to redeem us from all misery, so we too are to give ourselves with might and main for our neighbor. Whoever knows this and lives accordingly is holy, and has not much more to learn, nor will he find anything more in the whole Bible. For these two principles are here inscribed together as on a tablet which is always before our eyes and which we use daily.

Besides the example, there is also in the second place the figure or symbol. The teachers of old have diligently pointed out that he wished to give us his body and blood under the form of things which are of such a nature that they are themselves constituted by the fusing together of many individual things into one; just as a loaf is constituted by many kernels out of which one makes a single lump of dough, so that a loaf is nothing else than many kernels baked into one another. "We who are many" (says Paul in I Cor. 10 [:17]), "are nevertheless all one loaf and one body." Just as each grain loses its form and takes on a common form with the others, so that you cannot see or distinguish one from the other, and all of them are identical, yet separately present; so too should Christendom be one, without sects, that all may be one, of one heart, mind, and will, just as faith, the gospel, and baptism are one [Eph. 4:5]. That is how a Christian acts. He is conscious of nothing else than that the goods which are his are also given to his neighbor. He makes no distinction, but helps everyone with body and life, goods and honor, as much as he can. A similar picture is portrayed in the wine. Here many grapes are pressed together, and thereby each grape loses its form and a juice emerges. All the grapes are present in the wine, but there is nothing by which we could distinguish one from another; they have all flowed together and become one juice and one drink.

Thus Christ has beautifully portrayed and smoothly carved, as it were, the whole Christian way, so that, unless it is to be delineated at greater length, one needs no further books to perceive and grasp it clearly. Here we have a lesson, the study of which is sufficient to occupy us all our lives. You need not concern yourself with anything that others do not know, as our new sects are doing when they constantly invent new things. Here you have the whole thing. You can study it as long as you wish, but your flesh and blood will always be with you so that you will never be perfect in faith, love, and patience. Thus this sacrament is a taskmaster by which we order our lives and learn as long as we live. What good is it to try to know some special thing better than anybody else, if you do not know that which matters most of all? Whoever knows this, knows all that he ought to know. Without this, everything else that one might be able to know is nothing. I Cor. 13 [:2]: "And if I have prophetic powers and understand all mysteries and all knowledge, etc., but have not love, I am nothing."

The devil leads people by the nose, so that they pay no heed to the most important thing, but want to go beyond it and bring forth something special. Thus they lose the highest and only treasure. See—this is presented in the simplest of words, so that the simple souls can easily understand how to use the sacrament. They can know also the fruits by which they may see whether they have used it rightly. Let everyone follow this, and he will see wherein he is lacking; and let the others make up fables and prattle as they wish.

PART III

Concerning Confession

In addition we must also preach concerning confession [*beicht*], again in order to instruct the plain people. For it is a well-known fact that up to the present we have allowed ourselves to be tortured and humiliated with confession [*beichten*]. We have been troubled so much with it that there has been no more burdensome command since the world began. First, I hold that the word *beichten* comes from the little word *jahen*, from which is formed *bejychtet*, *bejehet*, that is, *bekennet* [confess]. From there we have reduced it to one syllable and call it *beichte*, that is, a confession.[12] Just as certain saints were called in Latin *Confessores*, in German *Beichtiger*, for *Bejychter*, that is, *bekenner* [confessors].

There are, however, as I have said before, three kinds of confession. One, before God: for it is necessary above all that I acknowledge before God that I am a sinner, as the gospel concludes in Rom. 3 [:23], and John 3 [:3]: "Unless one is born anew, he cannot see the kingdom of God." Whoever owns that he is born of woman must do God the honor of saying: I am nothing but a sinner, as David sings in Ps. 51 [:5]: "Behold, I was brought forth, or originated, in iniquity, and in sin did my mother conceive me." As if he were to say: I must indeed be a sinner, it was born in me;

[12] Luther's etymology is essentially correct. *Beichte* is derived from the Middle High German *biht*, a contraction of the Old High German *bijiht*, *bigiht* (meaning "declaration before the court"), which is the verbal noun for the Middle High German *bejëhen*, Old High German *bi-jëhan* (meaning "confess"). Though *jëhan* alone usually meant "say" or "declare" it also occasionally meant "admit" or "confess." Friedrich Kluge, *Etymologisches Wörterbuch der deutschen Sprache* (Berlin, 1957), *Beichte*.

as soon as I was formed in the womb, I was a sinner. For the flesh and blood of which I was made, were sin. As the saying has it: "Where hair and hide are bad, no good pelt will come of it."[13] Thus the clay, out of which we are made,[14] is not good. That which father and mother contribute is itself already sin.

Whoever refuses to confess this or will not admit that he is a sinner, but still claims to have a free will so that there may yet be some good in him, blasphemes God and gives him the lie, and must be eternally damned, as is proper. For he wants to be in the right and not suffer God's judgment. Therefore the prophet says again [Ps. 51:4]: "Against thee, thee only, have I sinned, and done that which is evil in thy sight, so that thou art justified in thy sentence and blameless in thy judgment." As if he would say again to God: I will not wrangle with you, but will let your Word be right and will confess that I am wrong and that you are right. But those who accuse you want to have the light of reason and something through which they will receive grace; surely you will remain blameless rather than they.

Now we must continue to make this confession as long as we live, always saying: "Lord, before thee I am a knave in the skin."[15] A distinction must be made, however; for even a knave and un-Christian person can say this, but he is certainly lying. No one but a true Christian says it from his heart, as Ps. 32 [:5-6] says: "I said, 'I will confess my transgressions to the Lord'; then thou didst forgive the guilt of my sin. Therefore let every one who is godly offer prayer to thee at an opportune time." All the godly, as many as there are of them, have this virtue in them, that they confess their sins to God and therefore pray. Hence none but those who are Christians and godly make such a confession. Now it is a marvelous thing that he who is righteous before God and has the Holy Spirit says that he is a sinner. It is right, however; he confesses what he has been and still is. He has the Holy Spirit, but he is still a sinner because of the flesh. For this reason all the godly cry out against the flesh. The devil, too, is not far off; he keeps stirring up the

[13] Cf. *Sprichwörter-Lexikon, op. cit.*, II, col. 441, *Haut*, Nos. 99 and 100.

[14] Cf. *Ibid.*, IV, col. 1155, *Thon*, No. 9: "He is made of the same clay."

[15] Rörer's sermon copy says instead: "As long as I am in this flesh, I am a sinner before thee."

flesh to cause it to sin. For this reason this is a great and lofty confession.

The others also say that they are sinners, but when other people say it of them they will not hear of it. But if one says this to the godly, or if God punishes them for their sins, they say: "Yes, it is right." Those hypocrites can indeed humble themselves, but they cease doing so whenever they wish. They do not want to be accused, but honored, by other people. It is the same with the priests and monks. They too say that they are sinners, but they will not hear it said by us. This is why God does not care about such confession. Genuine confession, now, is commanded and necessary and obligatory upon everybody. But no one makes it except the Christians.

The second kind of confession is that which one makes not to God but to one's neighbor. Of this Christ speaks in Matt. 5 [:23-25] and 6 [:14-15]. James also writes of it in his Epistle [Jas. 5:16]: "Confess your sins to one another," that is, conduct yourselves in such a way that each humbles himself before the other and confesses his guilt, if he has offended someone.

But there are many kinds of offense, both general and particular. In the general kind, I fear, we are all included; the Lord's Prayer puts us all there together [Matt. 6:12]. This kind consists in the fact that we do not help our neighbor as we are obligated to help him, namely, with words, preaching, advice, consolation, and with money, goods, honor, body, and life. This requirement is so rigorous that no one is so holy but that he is involved in guilt. Therefore we must all say to one another: "I am obligated to you; you are obligated to me." But especially the man to whom God has given much owes much in return [Luke 12:48]. I too owe him more than perhaps twenty or a hundred people. God will demand this from me, too. There is no other way, and he will reckon it down to the last farthing, how I have invested it and what profit I have gained from it. This obligation affects all in common and applies to no one in a particular way. I am under obligation to everyone; in return everyone owes consolation and assistance to me when I am in need and require help. We are not zealous enough, however, in seeking out the people who need us and offering them our service. It seems too much for us.

Now when we look at the account to see how much we owe we must quiver and quake and have no other recourse than to say: "I am in debt to others, but there are those who are in debt to me; I shall remit to them, one and all, whatever they owe me, and then O Lord, I pray thee, forgive me also." With that I draw a line through the reckoning and cancel it out. If we did not have this expedient we should be badly off. Therefore the Lord's Prayer remains valid, and it is necessary that we forgive our debtors, if our own debts are to be forgiven [Matt. 6:12-15], as Christ teaches in the Gospel (Matt. 18 [:21-35]).[16] This is one kind of confession, the kind which one must make openly before men, acknowledging one's guilt. I am not righteous before God; neither am I righteous before the world, when measured by the common kind of guilt. Each one has a claim on every other one, and no one satisfies that claim; therefore each must pray the other to forgive him.

Now no one but a Christian makes this confession. For un-Christian people do not permit this to be reckoned as sin. They cite the canon law which says: "To each man belongs his own";[17] and they believe that the goods which they possess they have for their own sakes. Therefore they use all sorts of goods only for their own honor and pleasure, as Solomon says in Proverbs: "The gain of the wicked leads to sin" [Prov. 10:16], "but the righteous is generous" [Ps. 37:21]. The wicked man uses his goods, his shrewdness, his skill, and honor in order to gain pleasure and profit from them. All this is sin, and sin of such a kind that he still believes that it is not sin, but right. God has created us in order that we should be our neighbor's steward, but in this we all fall short. We do have this advantage, however, that we recognize the fact and are sorry for it, and strive to do more and more every day, fearing God and doing as much as we can and as much as the Adam in us

[16] Both sermon copies follow the language of Matthew more closely, mentioning debts of 100, and of 1000 or 10,000 talents. *WA* 19, 517.

[17] The shorter sermon copy here quotes in Latin the Roman civil law: ***unicuique tribuendum suum ius. Institutionum Justiniani,*** lib. i, tit. I: ***de Iustitia et Iure:*** "Justice is the constant and perpetual wish to render every one his due." "The maxims of law are these: to . . . give every one his due." ***The Institutes of Justinian,*** trans. Thomas Collett Sandars (London, 1922), pp. 5-6. Cf. ***A New Pandect of the Roman Civil Law*** by John Ayliffe; folio (London, 1734), lib. i, tit. I, 2. Cf. also ***Cicero's Three Books of Offices*** (***De officiis,*** I, 5), trans. Cyrus R. Edmonds (London, 1856), p. 11.

permits. What we fail to do above and beyond this, God cancels by drawing a line through it, as we have said before; we cannot hope to pay it, for it is too much. Therefore we say: "Forgive me, I will forgive in return."

Besides this general kind of guilt there is also a special kind. Of this Christ speaks in Matt. 5 [:22-24]. If a particular person is offended, deceived, injured, reviled or slandered, one should confess this too and admit that he has done wrong and ask forgiveness of his neighbor. O how it hurts, to break the Adam thus and to humble one's self toward a poor human being whom one despises, and to admit that he is right and grant to him the highest honor and to one's self the greatest shame. This was formerly a custom in monasteries, which the monks were forced to observe, but it was absurd.[18]

A godless person will not humiliate himself so deeply as to shame himself. He does not see that to humble himself would be a great honor to him before God and before devout people. Christians can guard against this kind of guilt to some extent, both for themselves and for others, by covering it up and punishing it where one hears of it or sees it in others. But from the general kind of guilt no one can escape.

However, we are not speaking here of those two kinds of confession, for they go on constantly throughout the year, and not merely when one wishes to go to the sacrament. We are speaking here of the private confession; and this, I maintain, has developed from the public confession. This took place in this way, that Christians put together into one the two kinds of confession we have described above. Thus everyone confessed publicly, before God and men, before he went to the sacrament. Where Christians were few in number, each individual said the confession separately to the other. From this they reached a point where they tried to classify and enumerate the sins. It would be better if they remained unenumerated, for you will never reckon up how much you have left undone of that which you ought to have done.

[18] Both sermon copies specify that this applied to the younger monks. The shorter calls it "a good custom," and adds: "they went to all the rest and begged forgiveness if they had offended them; but at least they would go to those whom they had never offended."

Concerning this last confession let me say this: if those other two kinds of confession take place in public, one is not obliged to make this last kind. God is well aware of your sins. If you only confess them before him, and then before your neighbor, your sins are forgiven. Yet for the sake of those who would like to make use of it, private confession is by no means to be rejected. The reason is this: there is much that is beneficial and precious in it. First of all, the absolution, in which your neighbor[19] absolves you in God's stead, is just as if God himself were speaking, and that should indeed be comforting to us. If I knew that God were in a certain place and would absolve me I would not go to some other place, but would receive absolution in that place as often as I could. Such absolution he has put into the mouth of man,[20] hence it is most comforting, especially to burdened consciences, to receive it there.

Second, private confession serves a good purpose for the simple, childlike people. For since the common herd is indolent, continually hearing sermons and learning nothing, there is no one in the homes either to urge anyone to do it. So, even if private confession did not serve any other purpose, it is at least useful because it gives opportunity to instruct the people and hear what they believe, teach them to pray, etc., otherwise they go along like cattle. For this reason I have said[21] that one ought to give the sacrament to no one unless he is able to explain what he is receiving and why he goes to the sacrament. This can be done most conveniently in confession.

Third, there is comfort in the fact that if anyone has an evil conscience, or some other desire or need, and would like advice, he may ask for advice here. Therefore we cannot despise private confession. For God's Word is present, which comforts us and strengthens us in faith, and in addition instructs us and teaches us what we lack, and also gives us advice in time of need. For this reason no one makes this confession properly either except devout Christians, because they must be the sort of people who feel that they really want advice and consolation. The difficulty with the matter, however, is that the people have not paid attention to the

---

[19] The shorter sermon copy has the word "priest."

[20] The Rörer sermon copy has "in the mouth of the priest."

[21] Cf. *Receiving Both Kinds in the Sacrament* (1522), in this volume, pp. 231-267.

absolution, but to their own works, to how well and correctly they have made their confession. Moreover, they have attempted to enumerate their sins, and this cannot be done, because the number of them would be too great and it would be too great a task to hear them. Therefore the best way would be to make short work of it: "Dear brother, I come and want to lament my sins, that I am a sinner before God and man; I am especially concerned with this or that," etc. (whether you wish to say this or not, is up to you). Afterwards, conclude: "Therefore I pray, give me good comfort and strengthen my soul," etc. Thus it would require no effort and no toil. Moreover, it is a precious work, which none but a devout Christian does.

From all this you see that it is the devil's own doing when the pope commands private confession for everyone on pain of disobedience and mortal sin, and when he consigns to the devil those who do not practice it. For indeed this is not a matter which is in our power to take or give, but it is a gift which has come down from heaven. Because God has not commanded it, no man can command it. Even if I were to drive all men to it, how many of them would there be who would confess willingly and not merely out of compulsion? Not one in twenty thousand. With the rest one accomplishes no more than a mockery of God and dreadful blasphemy. For the priest there pronounces a judgment in God's stead that is wrong and will not be carried out. The man confesses unwillingly and hears the absolution unwillingly, and does not believe in it either. The fault does not lie with the priest, but with the one who confesses when he is insincere and does not truly wish the absolution from his heart. God has no desire that one should take his Word in vain [Exod. 20:7]. If you do not want to confess, then let it be, even all three kinds of confession. Confession is only for the devout people, and if you are not devout it is better to let it be, for then it is not righteous but damnable. So we have until now gone to confession only to serve the pope, not to serve our souls. This is rightly called obedience to the pope or to the church. He has had profit and honor from it. The rest, however, have had damnation of their souls.

Thus you have a brief and clear course of teaching concerning the two things, the sacrament and the confession. It should all be done willingly and freely. If you come of your own accord and recount your sins, if you seek consolation and strength, then it is beneficial and salutary. Children and simple people ought to be urged to do this. It should be taught, but with kind words and not with coercion. For, as has been said, it is especially useful also for that purpose, and should therefore be done. Amen.

INDEXES

INDEX OF NAMES AND SUBJECTS

INDEX TO SCRIPTURE PASSAGES